ANALYTICITY

Analyticity, or the 'analytic–synthetic' distinction, is one of the most important and controversial problems in contemporary philosophy. It is also essential to understanding many developments in logic, philosophy of language, epistemology and metaphysics. In this outstanding introduction to analyticity, Cory Juhl and Eric Loomis cover the following key topics:

- The origins of analyticity in the philosophy of Hume and Kant
- Carnap's arguments concerning analyticity in the early twentieth century
- Quine's famous objections to analyticity in his classic 'Two Dogmas of Empiricism' essay
- The relationship between analyticity and central issues in metaphysics, such as ontology
- The relationship between analyticity and epistemology
- Analyticity in the context of the current debates in philosophy, including mathematics and ontology.

Throughout the book the authors show how many philosophical controversies hinge on the problem of analyticity. Additional features include chapter summaries, annotated further reading and a glossary of technical terms, making the book ideal for those coming to the problem for the first time.

Cory Juhl is an Associate Professor at the University of Texas at Austin. His papers have appeared in Philosophy of Science, Synthese, Analysis, Philosophical Studies, The Monist, The Journal of Philosophical Logic, and the book Reading Putnam (Blackwell, 1994).

Eric Loomis is an Associate Professor at the University of South Alabama. His papers have appeared in Synthese, Theoria, Logical Analysis and History of Philosophy, and Pacific Philosophical Quarterly.

New Problems of Philosophy Series
Series editor: José Luis Bermúdez

The *New Problems of Philosophy* series provides accessible and engaging surveys of the most important problems in contemporary philosophy. Each book examines either a topic or theme that has emerged on the philosophical landscape in recent years, or a longstanding problem refreshed in light of recent work in philosophy and related disciplines. Clearly explaining the nature of the problem at hand and assessing attempts to answer it, books in the series are excellent starting-points for undergraduate and graduate students wishing to study a single topic in depth. They will also be essential reading for professional philosophers. Additional features include chapter summaries, further reading and a glossary of technical terms.

Also available:

Fiction and Fictionalism
Mark Sainsbury

Forthcoming:

Physicalism
Daniel Stoljar

Embodied Cognition
Lawrence Shapiro

Noncognitivism in Ethics
Mark Schroeder

Game Theory
Don Ross and Tadeusz Zawidzki

Perceptual Consciousness
Adam Pautz

Semantic Externalism
Jesper Kallestrup

Moral Epistemology
Aaron Zimmerman

Consequentialism
Julia Driver

Folk Psychology
Ian Ravenscroft

Self Knowledge
Brie Gertler

ANALYTICITY

Cory Juhl and Eric Loomis

Routledge
Taylor & Francis Group

LONDON AND NEW YORK

This edition published 2010 by Routledge
2 Park Square, Milton Park, Abingdon, Oxon OX14 4RN
Simultaneously published in the USA and Canada by Routledge
270 Madison Ave, New York, NY 10016

Routledge is an imprint of the Taylor & Francis Group, an informa business

Typeset in Joanna and Scala Sans by The Running Head Limited, Cambridge,
www.therunninghead.com
Printed and bound in Great Britain by TJ International Ltd, Padstow, Cornwall

British Library Cataloguing in Publication Data
A catalogue record for this book is available from the British Library

Library of Congress Cataloging in Publication Data
Juhl, Cory.
Analyticity / by Cory Juhl and Eric Loomis.
p. cm. — (New problems of philosophy)
Includes bibliographical references and index.
1. Analysis (Philosophy I. Loomis, Eric. II. Title.
B808.5.J84 2009
146'.4—dc22
          2009006638

ISBN10: 0–415–77332–6 (hbk)
ISBN10: 0–415–77333–4 (pbk)
ISBN10: 0–203–87257–6 (ebk)

ISBN 13: 978–0–415–77332–4 (hbk)
ISBN 13: 978–0–415–77333–1 (pbk)
ISBN 13: 978–0–203–87257–4 (ebk)

CONTENTS

PREFACE

This work is an introduction to the problem of analyticity, or the analytic–synthetic distinction. Analyticity is a notion that has been central to the development of analytic philosophy, and yet to our knowledge, there is no introductory level text on the topic. In fact, we know of only one other book-length treatment of analyticity, and it appeared only very recently. We intend this book to be accessible to undergraduate philosophy students who have some prior exposure to philosophy, perhaps through a metaphysics or epistemology course, and who want to explore this important topic in more detail. However, we also include material that should be of interest to graduate students and professional philosophers, for many of the arguments that we present throughout the book are relevant to contemporary philosophical pursuits.

In current philosophical usage, a sentence or statement is analytic if it is true solely in virtue of meaning. Behind this simple formulation lies a long and complex history, one that involves both the definition of the term itself, and also the role of analyticity within philosophical theories. As we will show, much of the contemporary philosophical landscape has been shaped by this history.

Yet analyticity has been largely neglected for the past few decades. Why? One reason may be that a common contemporary attitude toward analyticity stems from the belief that Willard V. Quine, along with others such as Gilbert Harman, conclusively showed that there is no such thing as analytic truth, or that if there is such a thing, it is of no philosophical relevance. For such philosophers, analyticity loses its relevance when one gives up on the idea of any 'first philosophy,' that is, of philosophy as a mode of inquiry that is fundamentally distinct from, and in some interesting sense prior to, that of the natural sciences, with its own distinctive methods, sources of knowledge, and objects of study. Indeed, for Quine and his followers the rejection of analyticity just is a part of the rejection of first philosophy, for as we shall see, analyticity was supposed by many of its early advocates to help to explain how philosophical knowledge was distinct from the empirical knowledge obtained by natural science.

There is another prominent line of contemporary thought that has led to a decline of interest in analyticity. According to this line of thinking, the notions of meaning and synonymy needed to define analyticity are legitimate ones, and philosophers have reasonable theories of them. Yet on this view the philosophical relevance of analyticity is nonetheless uncertain, not so much for the reasons put forward by Quine and his defenders, but for reasons given by Saul Kripke, Hilary Putnam, and others. Kripke in particular has argued that apriority and necessity come apart, and that both of these are distinct from, and not illuminated by, analyticity. These arguments, which we explore in the book, have been widely accepted, and they undercut the philosophical interest of the account of analytic truth commonly attributed to logical empiricism. To the extent that any notion of analyticity is necessarily tied to the philosophical project of logical empiricism, one might naturally think that the arguments undercut the significance of analyticity in general. We think that it is a mistake to tie analyticity this closely to logical empiricism, however, for reasons that we will develop more fully in the book.

In spite of its relative neglect, we suspect that for many philosophers, it remains unclear whether or not there is some philosophically interesting notion akin to analyticity that can be salvaged. Some philosophers may think that there must be some such notion, but they do not know how to give an account of it. They may find at least some of Quine's objections persuasive, and fail to see how to answer them. They might also find the overall dialectic surrounding the debate over analyticity to be difficult to follow. For it is a dialectic with many strands, some of which have to do with the supposed unintelligibility of the notion, the existence or nonexistence of meanings or synonymy relations, as well as with behaviorism, physicalism, and worries concerning the possible circularity of accounts of analyticity. Yet further strands have to do with holism and verificationism concerning meaning. Moreover, so many of the most prominent philosophers of the last fifty years have expressed views concerning analyticity that it can seem

impossible to obtain a perspicuous or synoptic picture of the overall philosophical landscape.

To anticipate our discussion, we think that Quine's arguments fail to
show that there is no philosophically interesting notion of analyticity. We
think that one can argue for this even without appealing to meanings or
synonymy. This claim may surprise many readers, since the most common
objections to the analytic–synthetic distinction tend to begin with broadly
Quinean arguments against synonymy. In our view, Kripke's argument
impugns only accounts of analyticity that see necessity, apriority, and analyticity as intimately related or even analytically coextensive. We give reasons,
deriving from Quine and many others, for casting doubt on logical empiricist accounts of analyticity, and we agree that logical empiricism faces severe
difficulties at best. Nevertheless, we think that neither Quine's arguments,
nor the errors of some logical empiricists, nor the post-Kripkean developments undermine the significance of a family of notions akin to analyticity.
Instead, we think that there is a notion akin to analyticity that can be used
to illuminate some current philosophical controversies. At the same time,
we find Quine's objections to analyticity to be worth taking seriously, in
contrast to those who think that it has been established that there are meanings, and truths in virtue of meanings.

In addition to being among the very few book-length treatments of analyticity, this book has two further distinctive features. First, we provide a
more detailed and nuanced historical and philosophical reconstruction of
the debates over analyticity than is found in shorter discussions. We look
at the emergence of the notion in the early modern period, and explore its
increasingly central role up through the logical empiricism of the Vienna
Circle. Then, we look in considerable detail at the debate over the analytic–
synthetic distinction as it developed between Rudolf Carnap and Quine.
Most discussions of analyticity, we think, tend to view the dispute from a
somewhat Quinean position, or accept various Quinean characterizations
of the issues. We develop the debate against the background of a careful
reconstruction of Carnap and Quine's broader philosophical projects, and
in doing so reveal Carnap's position to be stronger than is commonly recognized, at least in the context of his debate with Quine over analyticity.
Much of our discussion of analyticity is devoted to exploring the broader
philosophical positions motivated by the acceptance or rejection of analyticity. Carnap and Quine continue to hold center stage here, the former with
his conception of philosophy as a process of linguistic engineering called
'explication,' the latter with his competing conception of philosophy as an

endeavor continuous with natural science. But a variety of contemporary philosophers find themselves linked, directly or indirectly, with the dispute surrounding analyticity as well. We look at how the dispute connects with the views of many recent and contemporary philosophers, including Jody Azzouni, Marc Balaguer, Laurence BonJour, David Chalmers, Noam Chomsky, Mark Colyvan, H. Paul Grice, Frank Jackson, Saul Kripke, Gillian Russell, Stephen Schiffer, Richard Schuldenfrei, and Peter Strawson among others.

The second distinctive feature of our book is the presentation and development of a positive view concerning analyticity, along with some applications of that view to stipulative definitions, controversies in the philosophy of mathematics, and some recent meta-ontological disputes. Many philosophical works pertaining to analyticity distance themselves from Quine, or show why this or that Quinean argument fails. Yet they tend to stop there without presenting a positive proposal for how to properly characterize analyticity. This has usually led to a stalemate, as objectors to Quine accuse his arguments of being implausible, circular, or resting on outdated empirical assumptions, rather than presenting constructive demonstrations of the viability of an analytic–synthetic distinction. In the absence of a positive view, it can remain unclear whether some alternative elaboration of a Quinean argument could, in a plausible and non-question-begging way, show that there is no analytic–synthetic distinction. Our positive view provides a vantage point from which one can more clearly discern some places where Quinean arguments fail, and also permits the exploration of possible applications of the notion to current controversies, such as the possibility of a non-empiricist approach to mathematical epistemology.

Our text is loosely ordered chronologically, with chapters 1–3 concerned primarily with the emergence of analyticity as a philosophical notion and the ensuing Quine–Carnap debate over its existence and role. Thus in chapter 1 we provide some historical background to the disputes concerning analyticity, with particular emphasis on the views of Immanuel Kant, Gottlob Frege, and the Vienna Circle. In chapter 2 we elaborate some of the central themes of Carnap's early views concerning analyticity, and then recount how Carnap's views change during his transition from his earlier 'syntactic' picture to a 'semantic' picture. We then introduce the core ideas of Quine's philosophy. Against this background, we turn in chapter 3 to a discussion of Quine's primary objections to analyticity. We also consider some Carnapian responses, as well as other important responses to Quine, and we develop the ensuing dialectic. In chapters 4 and 5 we discuss some connections between disputes concerning analyticity and questions concerning ontology (chapter 4) and epistemology (chapter 5), and connect those disputes to philosophical projects of recent decades. Finally, in chapter 6 we sketch our positive proposals, outline some possible applications, and conclude with some general observations concerning the large-scale picture of what is at stake in the disputes concerning analyticity. We hope that readers are persuaded, as we are, that further reconsideration of the disputes concerning analyticity is in order, and that appeal to some notion akin to analyticity remains a live and potentially fruitful option for a variety of philosophical controversies ranging from the epistemology of mathematical objects and other abstracta, to meta-ontological disputes, to very general controversies concerning the nature of philosophy.

ACKNOWLEDGMENTS

We thank our colleagues, both faculty and graduate students, at the University of Texas at Austin (Cory Juhl), and the University of South Alabama (Eric Loomis). We have both been fortunate to have a highly congenial environment for doing philosophy. In particular, David Sosa, Dan Bonevac, Josh Dever, Kevin Meeker, Ted Poston, and Sahotra Sarkar have been capable and engaging participants in many helpful discussions on analyticity and related topics. Al Martinich, Todd Stewart, and Jack Justus read various versions of papers related to work in this book, and provided insightful comments. The anonymous reviewers of early proposals and drafts of the text were also helpful.

Eric Loomis received funding support for work on this project through a University of South Alabama Arts and Sciences Summer Research Award. Some of Cory Juhl's work was done while on leave provided by a generous Dean's Fellowship from the College of Liberal Arts at the University of Texas at Austin.

Finally, we are grateful to our wives Lynn and Karen for their love and support.

1

CONCEPTIONS OF ANALYTIC TRUTH

1.1 Introduction

In this chapter we survey the emergence of the analytic–synthetic distinction. The notion of analytic truth has played an important role in many central philosophical projects of the late modern and contemporary period, including the work of Immanuel Kant, Bernard Bolzano, Gottlob Frege, the Vienna Circle, and Rudolf Carnap. Philosophers have taken analytic truths as paradigms of necessary truths, of truths knowable a priori, or of truths knowable with absolute certainty. As a result, philosophers skeptical of the existence of such properties as necessary truth or a priori knowledge have frequently bolstered their skepticism with an attack on analyticity.

Our purpose in this chapter is to develop the history of the notion of analyticity and the correlative distinction between analytic and synthetic statements, with an emphasis on showing how the notion shaped individual philosophers' conceptions of what philosophy is, and on how those conceptions informed subsequent developments of the notion. Our investigation of the philosophical controversy surrounding analytic truth begins with the work of Scottish philosopher David Hume.

1.2 Hume's Fork

David Hume (1711–76) formulated an important prototype of the analytic–synthetic distinction. Many of the ideas that guided the main figures in this book, Rudolf Carnap and Willard V. Quine, received their earliest articulation in the work of Hume. Hume found much of the philosophical tradition of metaphysical speculation that preceded him to be 'not only painful and fatiguing' but also 'the inevitable source of uncertainty and error' (1988, 11). This complaint would be echoed by Carnap and Quine over two centuries later. Like them, Hume saw the reason for this perceived failure of metaphysics in the fact that metaphysics was not conducted as a science, for it had substituted abstract speculation for close analysis of 'the operations of the mind' (13). Hume saw philosophy's proper role as that of knowing 'the different operations of the mind, to separate them from each other, to class them under their proper heads' (13). To do this, Hume adopted an empiricist theory of knowledge, dividing all the 'perceptions of the mind' into the more lively 'impressions,' as 'when we hear, or see, or feel, or love, or hate, or desire, or will,' and the less lively 'ideas' formed as copies from the impressions (18–19). All thinking, and all ideas, originated in their corresponding impressions, Hume argued. Attempts by abstract thought to go beyond impressions, as prior metaphysics had done, involved going beyond the very things that gave our thoughts content. The antidote to such metaphysics was, Hume argued, to introduce a 'greater clearness and precision into philosophical reasonings' by analyzing the definitions of disputed or obscure concepts in terms of their component impressions:

> Complex ideas may, perhaps, be well known by definition, which is nothing but an enumeration of those parts or simple ideas, that compose them. But when we have pushed up definitions to the most simple ideas, and find still some ambiguity and obscurity; what recourse are we then possessed of? . . . Produce the impressions or original sentiments, from which the ideas are copied. These impressions are all strong and sensible. They admit not of ambiguity. (1988, 62)

Hume used this method to investigate a variety of traditional metaphysical concepts, most famously including the ideas of causation, cases of seemingly necessary connections among ideas, and freedom of the will (cf. 1988 40–55, 60–79, 80–103). The verdict of Hume's investigation into these concepts was invariably a 'skeptical' one. He could not find a corresponding impression for them that was strong and sensible, and so argued that our belief that these concepts corresponded to something real (an impression) rested instead on the 'custom or habit of the mind' (43). Insofar as traditional metaphysics rested on the claim that these concepts did correspond to some real object, it was mistaken.

Nonetheless, Hume granted a distinction that would anticipate the later analytic–synthetic distinction. The distinction, known as 'Hume's Fork,' divided all objects of human reasoning into 'relations of ideas' and 'matters of fact':

> Of the first kind are the sciences of Geometry, Algebra, and Arithmetic; and in short, every affirmation which is either intuitively or demonstratively certain . . . *That three times five is equal to the half of thirty*, expresses a relation between these numbers. Propositions of this kind are discoverable by the mere operation of thought, without dependence on what is anywhere existent in the universe.
>
> Matters of fact, which are the second objects of human reason, are not ascertained in the same manner; nor is our evidence of their truth, however great, of a like nature with the foregoing. The contrary of every matter of fact is still possible; because it can never imply a contradiction, and is conceived by the mind with the same facility and distinctness, as if ever so conformable to reality. *That the sun will not rise to-morrow* is no less intelligible a proposition, and implies no more a contradiction, than the affirmation, *that it will rise*. (1988, 25–6)

As Hume used the terms, our reasoning concerning relations of ideas and matters of fact must involve judgments or statements, for they concern things that are knowable, affirmable, or deniable, and have implications. Relations of ideas are knowable through intuition or demonstration, independent of what exists, and the denial of the consequences of demonstrably certain reasoning implies a contradiction and cannot be distinctly conceived (26). Matters of fact are knowable only through evidence such as 'the present testimony of our senses, or the records of our memory,' or from causal inferences drawn from these things (26). Their denials are 'intelligible' and (or because) they imply no contradiction.[1]

Hume's real interest lay with 'matters of fact,' and he apparently believed that if metaphysical concepts like causation and necessary connection were to have any content, it would be because they concerned matters of fact. Relations of ideas received no further attention from Hume. Yet their introduction by him raises a variety of interesting questions, most prominently why he found it necessary to acknowledge them. Was Hume granting that some knowledge could be had a priori, contrary to what is suggested by his theory that all ideas originate in impressions? If so, could metaphysics take root here, in this realm of relations independent of matters of fact?

Although Hume did not further develop the distinction, we can nonetheless surmise that his likely answer to these questions would have been negative. Certainly the fact that he thought that his empirical approach to the analysis of philosophical concepts would fix the foundation of morals, reasoning, and criticism 'beyond controversy' (6) strongly indicates that he regarded further inquiry into the relations of ideas to be of limited philosophical interest. Our next philosopher, Immanuel Kant, would see things very differently.

1.3.1 Kant and the Analytic–Synthetic Distinction

The contemporary distinction between analytic and synthetic judgments traces its roots most directly to Kant (1724–1804). It was Kant who first articulated the notion in something close to its current usage. Kant introduced the notion as a part of his larger philosophical theory, one aimed, in part, at rebutting Hume's 'skeptical' conclusions. His response to Hume was to argue that Hume had tried to find in the realm of our experience the conditions which make that experience possible (Kant 1965, sections A760/B788). But this, Kant thought, was mistaken, for we should not expect to find the conditions which make experience possible in that very experience. Rather, we should search outside of experience in the realm of a priori knowledge in order to find the conditions of experience (cf. 1965, B1–9). Kant believed that philosophy could discover substantive, informative truths that were nevertheless knowable a priori, what he called 'synthetic a priori' knowledge.

What led Kant to believe in the synthetic a priori? Kant thought that the modality of a judgment, that is, its being contingent or necessary, was tied in an important way to the manner in which that judgment was known.[2] More specifically, he thought that all necessary judgments were in principle knowable a priori, and conversely, that all judgments knowable a priori were necessary (A7/B12, A595/B623). To see why he linked a priori knowledge and necessary truth, consider the judgment that 7 + 5 = 12. This judgment is true, and more importantly it is true in a way that seems to place it beyond falsification by any experience. We can motivate this idea with a simple thought experiment. Suppose that we wish to 'test' the truth of the judgment that 7 + 5 = 12 by applying it to empirical objects. Perhaps we start with drops of a colored liquid. Using a dropper, we drop seven drops of the liquid into a beaker, followed by five more drops, and count the result, whereupon we find only one big 'drop' – not twelve. Why haven't we just empirically 'refuted' the judgment that $7 + 5 = 12$? Most of us likely feel certain that we haven't, but what explains our certainty here?

Kant had a sophisticated, although somewhat obscure, answer to this question. His answer rested on two important moves. First, he regarded every judgment that seemed to be immune to any empirical refutation as knowable independently of experience. The a priori knowability of immune judgments was, Kant reasoned, the most plausible account of how such judgments were known. Second, Kant accounted for the seeming immunity of some statements to empirical evidence in terms of their distinctive modal status as necessary truths. Let's look at these two moves in turn.

Kant thought that the immunity of some judgments, like $7 + 5 = 12$, to any experimental refutation (or, in the case of some false judgments like $7 + 6 = 12$, to any experimental confirmation), was evidence of their being knowable a priori, as well as for their necessity. But how is it that we can know something a priori? Kant's answer varied with the type of judgment at issue. In some cases, Kant thought that our a priori knowledge came from a special, non-sensory intuition. An intuition, in Kant's terms, can be thought of as a kind of direct acquaintance to the mind of something. Kant believed that space and time were intuitions, but not sensory intuitions, in part because he believed that space and time are a *precondition* of sensory experience. Arithmetical judgments, Kant argued, are themselves only possible in time. A number series, for instance, is only possible as the successive iteration of an operation in time. Arithmetical judgments thus derived from our a priori intuition of time, for Kant. Similarly, Kant thought that geometrical judgments, such as that the sum of the internal angles of a triangle is 180°, derive from a priori intuitions of space. He also believed that geometrical judgments are immune to empirical refutation. While a priori intuitions of space and time were thought by Kant to be the source of much of our a priori knowledge, he believed that there were other sources as well. One such source was a priori concepts, concepts which 'spring, pure and unmixed, out of the understanding' (A67/B92). Another source of a priori knowledge is our knowledge of rules through which empirical experience becomes possible (A177/B218f.).

Kant's second move was to tie the a priori knowability of certain judgments with their having a distinctive modal status, that is, with their being necessary truths or necessary falsehoods. Kant believed that a judgment is knowable a priori if, and only if, it is necessary (cf. A7/B12, A595/B623). Again, consideration of the $7 + 5 = 12$ example above might offer some support for this idea. For one explanation of why this judgment cannot be falsified by empirical observations is that it cannot possibly be falsified at all, that it is a necessary truth.

The Kantian picture raises another question. What is it that makes a statement necessary, and how is the truth of necessary judgments knowable a priori? This is where Kant introduced a distinction between two different types of judgments, analytic judgments and synthetic judgments. The explanation of what makes a statement necessary, as well as knowable a priori, differs for the two types of judgment.

Kant's various attempts to draw the distinction between analytic and synthetic were at times unclear, and some have charged that they are equivocal (a charge that is also leveled against subsequent attempts to draw the distinction, as we will see). We will begin with Kant's most famous characterization of the distinction, the 'containment characterization,' which occurs at the start of his *Critique of Pure Reason*:

> In all judgments in which the relation of a subject to the predicate is thought . . . this relation is possible in two different ways. Either the predicate B belongs to the subject A as something that is (covertly) contained in this concept A; or B lies entirely outside the concept A, although it does indeed stand in connection with it. In the first case I call the judgment analytic, in the second synthetic. (Kant 1965, B11)

Kant's own example of an analytic judgment is 'All bodies are extended.' Here Kant conceived of extension as the 'predicate' of the subject 'body.' In this judgment, Kant said, 'I do not require to go beyond the concept which I connect with "body" in order to find extension bound up with it' (ibid.). By contrast, Kant thought that 'when I say, "All bodies are heavy", the predicate is something quite distinct from anything that I think in the mere concept of body in general, and the addition of such a predicate therefore yields a synthetic judgment' (ibid.).

Two features of this way of drawing the analytic–synthetic distinction are worth remarking upon. The first is that the containment criterion applies only to statements that have a subject–predicate form. But what are we to make of judgments that don't, or don't obviously, have such a form, such as disjunctive statements like 'It's raining or it's snowing,' conditional statements like 'If it's raining, then it's wet outside,' or existential statements like 'Unicorns exist' (Kant famously argued that existence is not a predicate)? Is Kant's analytic–synthetic distinction meant to include these as well? In his later writings, Kant recognized twelve primitive judgment-types, including statements similar to these, without claiming that they are all judgments 'in which the relation of a subject to a predicate is thought.' This raises the possibility that for Kant, not all judgments can be classified as analytic or synthetic. Recent commentators have argued that this was indeed a consequence that Kant accepted (cf. DeJong 1995; Proops 2005). We will not go further into this issue here.

A second feature of the containment criterion concerns the problematic idea that a predicate concept might be '(covertly) contained in' the subject concept. In what sense is the concept of *extension* contained in the concept of *body*? Clearly, it is not in the same sense in which the predicate 'black' is explicitly contained in the subject 'black horse' in the judgment 'A black horse is black.' The containment in Kant's example is 'covert.' But what does 'covert' mean here?

One possibility is that we cannot think the subject concept *at all* without thinking of certain predicates, and those predicates are the ones that are analytically contained in it. On this reading, when one thinks the concept of *body*, one must think of *extension* (and any other analytically contained predicate in that concept). This interpretation of Kant's position, however, is unduly strong, for Kant distinguished between 'thinking the manifold in a concept' and being conscious of it; in an analytic judgment 'I need only become conscious of the manifold I always think in the [subject concept] in order to encounter [the predicate] in it' (1965, A7/B11). Thus, I may not be conscious of the concept of *extension* every time I am conscious of the concept *body*, even though the latter contains a 'manifold' of concepts that includes extension. An alternative interpretation of Kant here would be to understand 'thinking a concept' in dispositional terms. Then, to think the concept of body might be merely to say that I am disposed to act in certain ways, for instance, that I am disposed to assent when asked: Are all bodies extended? One doesn't have to explicitly think of the concept of extension on such occasions, but only has to be disposed to act (or think) in the appropriate way under the right circumstances.

In any case, there are at least two distinguishable 'containment' metaphors at work. Logical containment need not have any connection to psychological states, introspectible states in particular. As we shall see, this unclarity about the containment metaphor would attract the attention of subsequent commentators on Kant.

It can appear that Kant had a second 'criterion' of analyticity, one which invoked the Principle of (Non-)Contradiction. However, there is an argument to be made that this second criterion is not independent of the containment criterion. Here is what Kant wrote about it:

> If the judgment is analytic, whether it be negative or affirmative, its truth must always be cognized sufficiently in accordance with the principle of contradiction

And,

> If the judgment is analytic, whether it be negative or affirmative, its truth must always be able to be cognized sufficiently in accordance with the principle of contradiction. (B190–1)

Imagine again a simple judgment like 'A black horse is black.' It seems that we can cognize the truth of this judgment in accordance with the principle of contradiction, simply because the denial of this judgment (A black horse is *not* black) seems to affirm a contradiction, saying of a horse that it both does and does not have a certain property. By contrast, in a synthetic judgment like 'The horse Strider is black,' no contradiction emerges from its negation. Of course in the first judgment the predicate is *overtly* contained in the subject. It's less clear why 'A body is not extended' also affirms a contradiction, unless of course we assume, as we know Kant did, that the concept *body* already contains the concept of extension. But assuming this is relying on the containment criterion again. As such, it's likely that the contradiction criterion of analyticity is not independent of the containment criterion.[3]

1.3.2 Synthetic A Priori Propositions

Let us return to the above question of what, according to Kant, accounts for the necessary truth or necessary falsehood of some statements. In the case of necessary truths or falsehoods that are analytic, Kant now had a ready answer: their necessity derives from the simple fact that the predicate is contained in the subject. To deny this is to violate the Law of (Non-) Contradiction, itself a seemingly inviolable necessary truth.

Yet, as we noted in passing above, Kant did not think that every necessary truth is analytic. The judgment that $7 + 5 = 12$ is his most famous example of a synthetic necessary truth:

> We might, indeed, at first suppose that the proposition $7 + 5 = 12$ is a merely analytic proposition, that follows by the principle of contradiction from the sum of 7 and 5. But if we look more closely we find that the concept of the sum of 7 and 5 contains nothing save the union of the two

> numbers into one, and in this no thought is being taken as to what that single number may be which combines both . . . Arithmetical propositions are therefore always synthetic. This is still more evident if we take larger numbers. For it is then obvious that, however we might turn and twist our concepts, we could never, by the mere analysis of them, and without the aid of intuition, discover what is the sum. (B15–16)

The notion of *intuition* that appears in this last remark holds the key to Kant's account of the necessary but synthetic propositions of mathematics and geometry. Such propositions are necessarily true, and known a priori, in virtue of what Kant called a 'construction in intuition' (A720/B748). Kant's idea, in the case of mathematics and geometry, was that we have certain 'pure' a priori intuitions of space and time. 'Intuitions' in Kant's sense were a kind of immediate relation of the mind with an object of knowledge. This relation is 'immediate' in the sense that it is a direct relation with the object of knowledge unmediated by signs, marks, or concepts (cf. A19/B33, A25/B40). The intuitions of space and time are not sensory, Kant believed, but instead constitute part of the basis for our sensory experience. His idea here was, roughly, that space and time are not *discovered* in experience but rather *presupposed by* experience. Kant presented several arguments in support of this claim, one of which was that space must be presupposed before we can say that our sensations refer to something 'outside' of us (cf. B38f.).

Our intuitions of space and time were thus a priori conditions of possible sensory experience, Kant thought, and furthermore the conditions that made possible the synthetic a priori truths of geometry and mathematics:

> Geometry is a science which determines the properties of space synthetically, and yet a priori. What, then, must be our representation of space, in order that such knowledge of it may be possible? It must in its origin be intuition; for from a mere concept no propositions can be obtained which go beyond the concept – as happens in geometry. Further, this intuition must be a priori . . . For geometrical propositions are one and all apodeictic, that is, are bound up with the consciousness of their necessity. (B41)

Kant appeared to be saying that we are able to 'obtain propositions' about geometry, such as the axioms and theorems of a geometrical system like Euclid's, because of our a priori intuition of space. And since this intuition of space was, as we have noted, a condition of the possibility of experience, geometrical propositions are necessary, and we are conscious of this. In other words, the same pure intuition of space that makes experience possible makes the propositions of geometry true; these propositions are thus necessary in the sense that they derive from one of the conditions (the intuition of space) which makes our experience possible. Yet at the same time, these judgments are synthetic since they are 'constructed' by us in accord with our intuition through what Kant (rather vaguely) called 'a necessity inherent in the concepts themselves' (B16–17).

Kant made similar remarks about number:

> The pure *schema* of magnitude, as a concept of the understanding, is *number*, a representation which comprises the successive addition of homogeneous units. Number is therefore simply the unity of the synthesis of the manifold of a homogeneous intuition in general, a unity due to my generating time itself in the apprehension of intuition. (A142–3, B182)

So number, Kant thought, is somehow connected with our intuition of time. We form numbers by synthesizing the same homogeneous units together in a process that unfolds in time.[4] Mathematical propositions, like geometrical ones, must also derive their status as necessary and a priori from the role that the a priori intuition of time plays in making our experience possible (A719–20/B747–8).

Kant thought that there were still further kinds of synthetic a priori truths, which were formed not by construction in intuition but by a 'synthesis' that proceeds a priori according to certain concepts (cf. A719/B747). Some a priori concepts are constructible in intuition, such as the concept of number, and some are not. In this latter class belong what Kant called the 'categories' or 'pure concepts of the understanding.' These are concepts such as unity, plurality, existence, causation, and possibility (A80/B106). Kant's idea was that such concepts expressed constraints or rules on possible thoughts (A87/B120f.). So for example, the concept of causation is an a priori one that determines what kind of judgments about causes are possible. It does so by constraining the thoughts and judgments that we can form about causes by, for example, requiring that every event has a cause (cf. B233f.). This judgment is synthetic, a priori, and necessary in virtue of the fact that it derives from a concept (causation) which determines how we are to think about certain things, such as causal sequences (B163–4).

Kant left a rich legacy. His distinction between analytic and synthetic judgments informed a vision of the nature of philosophy which inspired philosophers for more than a century after Kant's death. Kant's interest in the conditions which make our experience possible led him to focus on the synthetic a priori truths as keys to our understanding of why our experience is the way it is. And he thought that philosophy had a distinctive task in exploring our knowledge of such truths, and revealing how the conditions which make experience possible impose limits on what thought, and especially traditional metaphysics, can meaningfully achieve.

At the same time, Kant's philosophy, with its appeal to a priori intuitions and categories of the understanding, was far removed from the comparatively simple empiricism of Hume. And the complexity of Kant's work concealed ambiguity and vagueness at certain crucial points, and left many open questions. What is it, for instance, to 'construct' a number using our intuition of time? How does our a priori intuition of space lead us to find certain geometrical propositions 'apodeictically certain and necessary'? And which propositions have this status? What exactly is the 'necessity inherent in concepts' that makes certain synthetic judgments necessarily true? Can the 'containment' metaphor be specified in a way that clearly distinguishes it from this other necessity 'inherent in the concepts'? And in the case of analytic judgments, how are we to know which predicate concepts are contained in the subject concept, given that this isn't always transparent?

1.4 Bolzano and Analyticity

The lack of transparency in Kant's notion of an analytic truth was quickly remarked upon. An early critic of Kant's method of drawing the distinction was Bernard Bolzano (1741–1848), who in 1837 wrote:

> Kant asserts that in analytic judgments the predicate is contained (in a hidden manner) in the subject . . . These are, in part, only figurative modes of speech which do not analyze the concept to be explicated, in part expressions which permit of too many interpretations. (Bolzano 1973, 201)

For his part, Bolzano suggested a broader conception of analyticity. His conception is important because it anticipated a later notion of analyticity in terms of a proposition's remaining true under different interpretations of certain of its components. Bolzano wrote of Kant's explanation of 'analytic' that it was:

> fit only for one kind of analytical propositions, namely those of the form 'A which is B is B'. But should there really be no others? Should we not count among analytic judgments 'A which is B is A' and 'Everything is either B

> or not *B*'? Generally, it seems to me that none of these explications suf-
> ficiently emphasizes what makes these propositions important. I believe
> that this importance lies in the fact that their truth or falsity does not
> depend upon the concepts of which they are composed, but that it remains
> the same irrespective of the changes to which some of their concepts are
> subjected. (ibid.)

Bolzano's own proposal for defining 'analytic' was to treat analytic propositions as those in which there was some 'referring idea' which 'could be
arbitrarily changed without altering the truth or falsity of the proposition'
(Bolzano 1973, 198). Propositions which do not contain any ideas which
can be changed without altering their truth or falsity Bolzano labeled 'synthetic.' Thus,

> For example, I call the following propositions analytic: 'A depraved man
> does not deserve respect' and 'A man may be depraved and still enjoy con-
> tinued happiness'. The reason for this is that both contain a certain idea,
> namely 'man', which can be exchanged for any idea whatever, for instance
> 'angel', 'being', etc., yet the former remains always true, the latter always
> false, provided only that they continue to have reference. (ibid.)

The proposition 'God is omniscient,' on the other hand, is synthetic by Bolzano's criterion, since we 'could not point out a single idea which could be
arbitrarily changed' without making the proposition false.

There is a difficulty here. Consider again Bolzano's second example of
an analytic proposition, call it (D): A man may be depraved and still enjoy
continued happiness. Must it always be false that a man may be depraved
yet still happy? And even if it *is* false for a man, must it be false for an angel?
How about a devil, or a stone? It certainly doesn't seem that the proposition
'A devil may be depraved and still enjoy continued happiness' *must* be false;
indeed it might well be true.

Bolzano offered a partial attempt to respond to this kind of objection
by suggesting a distinction between 'logically analytic' propositions such
as '*A* is *A*' or 'Every object is either B or not-B,' and propositions that are
analytic in a 'broader sense' such as the one about depravity (ibid., 199).
Of the first kind, he wrote that in order to appraise them as analytic 'no
other than logical knowledge is necessary, since the concepts which form
the invariable part of these propositions all belong to logic' (ibid., 198). The
latter, on the other hand, require a 'wholly different kind of knowledge'

since 'concepts alien to logic intrude.' We might think of the concept man as a 'concept alien to logic.' Understanding it is not something we get from logic alone, for it requires experience to know what a man is. Furthermore, having this understanding might lead us to recognize a restriction on what kinds of things we might meaningfully substitute for it in a given proposition, allowing us to meaningfully substitute some concepts for 'man' in (D), but not others. Bolzano himself suggested as much by saying that there might be a restriction on the variation possible for some concepts in certain propositions (ibid., 196). But he did not develop this idea, apart from suggesting that the restriction might be 'stipulated.'

Bolzano nonetheless offered an important extension of the notion of analyticity beyond Kant, particularly with his suggestion that analytic statements ought to include those that are logically true, such as his examples of the law of identity (A is A), or the principle of the excluded middle (every object is either B or not-B). These ideas would find a sympathetic response in the writings of Gottlob Frege.

1.5 Analyticity in Frege

Like Bolzano, Gottlob Frege (1848–1925) rejected Kant's conception of analyticity as being too vague. And like Bolzano, Frege saw a connection between the notion of analyticity and the statements of logic. But Frege went beyond both Kant and Bolzano by developing a significant extension of formal logic. Classical Aristotelian logic, which Kant had employed, tended to place all propositions, including propositions with quantifiers, or expressions of generality like 'all,' 'some,' or 'none,' into subject–copula–predicate form. General propositions like

P: All pious men are happy

were analyzed into the subject 'pious men,' the copula 'are,' and the predicate 'happy.' This general proposition in turn would be slotted into one of the four categorical propositions, such as 'All F are G.' Yet Aristotle's method of argument analysis posed problems when dealing with statements not obviously of such a form, such as mathematical equations, statements involving relations with multiple terms (such as 'x gives y to z'), or statements involving several quantifiers like the statement 'Everyone knows someone.'

Frege re-conceived the logical treatment of statements involving quantifiers with his quantificational predicate logic. Frege's insight began with the recognition that general propositions like P could be analyzed, not in subject–copula–predicate terms, but rather as a conditional of the form: If something is a pious man then it is happy. Consider the statements 'Schmidt is a pious man' and 'Schmidt is happy.' Frege saw in them an analogy with mathematical functions by removing the subject term ('Schmidt') and replacing it with a variable, resulting in the 'function' expressions 'x is a pious man' and 'x is happy.' This move connected the copula 'is' with the predicate expression 'is a pious man' in a way similar to the way in which the copula in '2^2 is 4' is connected with the function expression $x^2 = y$. In both cases, there is no need to see the copula as an extra element, rather it is incorporated into the function. Indeed, to be a function is simply to return a unique, definite value (y) for a given argument (x) as input. Frege had thus replaced the subject–copula–predicate model of the proposition with the function–argument model. In more contemporary notation, Frege saw in a statement such as P the following general propositional form:

PF: If x is a pious man, then x is happy.

Here 'x' is a variable indicating the position occupied by a name within the propositional functions 'x is a pious man,' and 'x is happy.'[5]

We can see PF itself as denoting a concept, one that is true of some object if that object is not a pious man or else is happy. Frege realized that P says of this concept that it is true of everything. That is, if P is true, then it is true of every object that it is not a pious man or else it is happy. The quantifier 'all' in the context of P says of the concept expressed by PF that it is true of all things. It is, Frege thought, a 'second-level' concept that applies to the first-level concept PF if and only if P is true. In more modern terms, the quantifier 'all' has as its scope the concept denoted by PF.

Frege used these logical ideas to approach the problem of the foundations of mathematics. He wished to avoid Kant's conclusion that the foundations of mathematics rested on an intuition of time, a conclusion which Frege found objectionable in that it would seemingly require an infinite number of such intuitions in order to comprehend the infinite number series. Rather, Frege hoped to show that arithmetical propositions were not synthetic a priori, but rather analytic (1974, 99). However, Frege understood analyticity differently from Kant. Within the sphere of mathematics, Frege regarded analytic truths as those which have a proof resting solely upon 'general logical laws and on definitions' (1974, 4). More generally,

> If it is impossible to give the proof without making use of truths which are not of a general logical nature, but belong to the sphere of some special science, then the proposition is a synthetic one. (1964, 2)

What of the general laws of logic themselves? Frege assigned them a special status as 'guiding principles for thought in the attainment of truth,' but added that we must distinguish two senses of 'law':

> In one sense a law asserts what is; in the other it prescribes what ought to be. Only in the latter sense can the laws of logic be called 'laws of thought': so far as they stipulate the way in which one ought to think . . . [They] are the most general laws, which prescribe universally the way in which one ought to think if one is to think at all. (1964, 12)

One plausible way of interpreting this passage is to see Frege as saying that the laws of logic are *constitutive* of thinking. If we are to think at all, we must follow them. They are also universal, applying to every proposition in the most general way.

Frege hoped to prove how mathematics could be derived from these basic laws of logic. His 'fundamental insight' was the recognition that statements about numbers could be analyzed using his new logical methods (1964, 5). Number statements, Frege saw, could be treated in a manner akin to quantified statements: in both cases, we say of a concept that some number of objects 'falls under' or 'satisfies' that concept. Thus:

> If I say 'the King's carriage is drawn by four horses', then I assign the number four to the concept 'horse that draws the King's carriage'. (1974, 59)

The number statement is thus the assignment of a number to a concept. It says of the concept that four things satisfy it.[6] Frege's logic is, as we have seen, designed to accommodate quantification over the things that satisfy concepts. Hence the extension of his new logic to cover number statements was easy for him. For example, the statement that there are exactly two Martian moons would, in modern logical notation, be expressed as follows (where 'Mx' means that 'x is a Martian moon'):

$$(\exists x)(\exists y)[x \neq y \land Mx \land My \land (z)(Mz \rightarrow (z = x \lor z = y))]$$

which says that there exists something x and something y, both of these things are Martian moons, and anything else that is a Martian moon is identical to x or to y. Now, this statement expresses something about the concept 'Martian moon,' namely that there are two individuals which satisfy it. But what about 'pure' statements of number, such as mathematical equations, which are not about specific things like moons?

Frege's analysis of such statements derived from his analysis of statements involving concepts like 'is a Martian moon.' Frege realized that part of what M expresses is that exactly two things fall under a certain concept. Other statements might express the same fact about other concepts, such as the statement that there are two poles of the Earth $((\exists x)(\exists y)(x \neq y \wedge Px \wedge Py \wedge (z)$ $(Pz \rightarrow (z = x \vee z = y)))$, where 'Px' means '$x$ is a pole of the Earth'). Here the concepts M and P both satisfy the same condition, namely, that there exist two things that fall under them. If these two quantified statements are true, then we can pair any object falling under M with exactly one object falling under P. Likewise for any other concept C which has exactly two things falling under it. The 'equinumerosity' of all such concepts serves as the basis for the definition of the number 'two,' that is, the number two just is the class of all concepts under which two objects fall (Frege 1974, 79–80).

Frege combined his definitions of number with the basic laws of logic to derive the basic theorems of arithmetic. This project became known as *logicism*. Insofar as Frege could show us how arithmetic derived from basic laws of logic plus definitions, he could show against Kant that arithmetic contains only analytic truths. The synthetic a priori, and corresponding Kantian a priori intuitions of time, are unnecessary for arithmetic.[7]

1.6 Russell's Paradox and the Theory of Descriptions

There was, however, a serious flaw in Frege's logicist program. As it turned out, one of the basic laws (Law V of Frege's 1964) was found by the philosopher Bertrand Russell (1872–1970) to lead to a contradiction known as 'Russell's Paradox.' Russell's paradox asks us to consider a set C containing exactly those sets that are not members of themselves. Russell noticed that Frege's basic axioms entail the existence of C. Yet consider the question whether the set C is a member of itself or not. If C is *not* a member of itself, then since it is the set of all and only things that are not members of themselves, it *is* a member of itself. Conversely, if it *is* a member of itself, then it must *not* be a member of itself. So either a yes or no answer to the question yields a contradiction. Russell's Paradox undermined Frege's logicism. It also undermined Frege's idea that the apparently obvious truth of the basic laws could serve as an indicator of their analyticity. After all, an 'obvious truth' that turns out to yield a contradiction is not true.

The discovery of Russell's paradox ultimately led Frege to abandon logicism. Russell, however, remained convinced that a modified form of Frege's logicism was viable. The modification Russell proposed was his 'Theory of Types' (cf. Russell and Whitehead 1997, 161ff.). This modification would allow subsequent philosophers, most notably members of the Vienna Circle, to hold on to a version of logicism and, in particular, to continue to regard mathematical knowledge to be expressed by analytic statements, not by synthetic a priori ones. However, the later forms of logicism all include some theory akin to set theory, and many philosophers question whether set theory should be counted as a part of logic. The fact that set theory entails existence claims (the existence of an empty set, for example) leads many to reject the assimilation of set theory to logic. For that reason the contemporary inheritors of the logicist program have tended not to call themselves 'logicists.'

Another contribution of Russell's played an important role for later notions of analyticity. In 'On Denoting,' Russell advanced a powerful theory that made use of Frege's new logical methods to analyze both definite descriptions (such as 'the horse that won the last Kentucky Derby') and indefinite descriptions (such as 'a man'). Russell argued that indefinite descriptions such as 'a man' do not denote an entity (Russell 1956, 42–3). Rather, such expressions denote within the context of a proposition like 'All men are mortal' by combining with the other propositional components to express the proposition: '"If x is human, x is mortal" is always true' (43). For definite descriptions, Russell proposed an analysis whereby the proposition in which the definite description occurred would be replaced by a sentence asserting that the predicate used was uniquely satisfied by whatever object had that property denoted by the predicate. As Russell put it:

> Thus 'The father of Charles II was executed' becomes: 'It is not always false of x that x begat Charles II and that x was executed and that "if y begat Charles II, y is identical with x" is always true of y.' (1956, 44)[8]

Russell conjoined his new theory of descriptions with an epistemological thesis according to which one can understand a proposition only if one is immediately acquainted with every constituent of it (56). As he saw, the theory of descriptions neatly complemented this thesis; one need not be immediately acquainted with the subject of a description in order to understand a proposition involving it. Thus for example, one might know that the last Roman governor of Germania lost three Roman legions, despite not being acquainted with that governor. By the theory of descriptions, the proposition known when one knows this fact about the governor does not contain him as an element. Rather, one is acquainted with the constituents of the propositional functions (*x is a governor*, *x lost three Roman legions*, etc.) that comprise the original proposition. Thus,

> In every proposition that we can apprehend (i.e. not only those whose truth or falsehood we can judge of, but in all that we can think about), all the constituents are really entities with which we have immediate acquaintance. (56)

The conjunction of the principle of acquaintance with the theory of descriptions gave Russell the means to show how we might 'construct' an entity logically, by means of the theory of descriptions, out of elements with which we are acquainted. Inferred entities can be avoided, except insofar as they can be analyzed into the objects of immediate acquaintance. Indeed, not only can irreducibly inferred entities be avoided, Russell's 'supreme maxim of scientific theorizing' would claim that they ought to be: 'Wherever possible, logical constructions are to be substituted for inferred entities' (Russell 1932a, 155).

In 'On Denoting,' Russell gave only a sketch of what the objects of acquaintance in such an analysis are (1956, 55–6). In later essays he gave a more detailed characterization of these objects, variously identifying them with the 'particulars acquired in sensation' or sense-data, with certain universals, and with logical forms and constants (cf. Russell 1932, 1956a). Russell regarded it as at least possible, if perhaps unlikely, that the application of the supreme maxim could yield an account of physics which would exhibit matter wholly in terms of sense-data (1932a, 179). Rudolf Carnap would develop these ideas in great detail.

1.7 The Vienna Circle

Frege had shown how it could be, in principle, possible to analyze mathematics without appeal to Kantian intuitions, and Russell had shown how to modify Frege's methods to avoid Russell's Paradox. But could Frege's basic idea be taken further? Could the methods of logical analysis that Frege had inaugurated with his predicate logic and his analysis of numbers be applied to include other domains of knowledge? And could extensions of Frege's methods, such as Russell's theory of definite descriptions, be further extended to an analysis of experience in general, including our experience of the world of physical objects? If so, the result could, in principle, form the basis for a powerful rejection of the need for the Kantian synthetic a priori, and provide a new, expanded role for analytic truth.

The Vienna Circle was a group of scientists, mathematicians, and philosophers who met in Vienna from 1928 to 1936. Their intention was to combine the methods of logical analysis discovered by Frege, Russell, and other philosophically minded mathematicians and philosophers with a positivist and empiricist outlook that stemmed from physicists such as Ernst Mach, Henri Poincaré, and David Hume. Their efforts marked a major reorientation of philosophy away from the broadly speculative tradition of metaphysics and toward a new tradition more closely connected with and informed by empirical science, and by physics in particular.

One of the most important influences on the Vienna Circle came from the early work of Ludwig Wittgenstein (1889–1951). A student of both Russell and Frege, Wittgenstein was invited to some of the Vienna Circle meetings by the Circle's founder, Moritz Schlick (1882–1936). What intrigued Schlick and other Circle members was Wittgenstein's *Tractatus*, a book that synthesized and extended many of the logical ideas of Frege and Russell into a single, unified picture of the relation between language and the world. Of particular importance for our purposes was the *Tractatus*' analysis of logical truths, such as instances of the Law of Non-Contradiction. Unlike Frege, Wittgenstein did not treat logical truths as universal laws that apply to every statement. Indeed, he did not treat logical truths as *statements* or *propositions* at all. Rather, he saw such truths as 'tautologies' which, while they might *show* the 'logical scaffolding of the world' (Wittgenstein 1986, section 6.124), do not themselves *say* anything.

Behind this striking claim lay Wittgenstein's 'picture theory' of the proposition (see Wittgenstein 1986, 2.1–3.84). A genuine proposition is a picture, in that like a picture it depicts how things are or (if the picture is 'false') how things could be but aren't (4.6). A true picture/proposition corresponds with the way things are, while a false one does not. But whether true or false, a picture/proposition must depict the way things might *possibly be* or *possibly not be*. It must depict a possible state of affairs (4.01–4.05). A picture/proposition cannot depict something that cannot possibly be the case, for there is nothing to depict in such an instance. Conversely, Wittgenstein thought, a picture/proposition cannot depict something that must be the case, i.e., that cannot possibly not be. Any attempted 'picture' of such a state of affairs would not possibly be false (5.61). But then what would it tell us about the way the world actually is? Nothing. Since it could not fail to be true, it would be compatible with every possible circumstance, and so would not tell us how the world in fact is (4.063). Wittgenstein developed this theory in detail, but for our purposes what is important is that according to it an expression of necessary truth or necessary falsity is not a genuine proposition. Rather, such statements would (upon a proper analysis) be revealed to be tautologies (if true) or contradictions (if false) (6.1). Wittgenstein extended this idea to the propositions of arithmetic as well, suggesting that they too are technically 'pseudo-propositions' that express no thoughts, although for different reasons from logical truths (6.2–6.21).

Wittgenstein's picture theory of the proposition, and his analysis of the propositions of logic and all other necessary propositions as tautologies, captured the interest of the early members of the Vienna Circle. They saw in his ideas the possibility of a new approach to the issues raised by the Kantian synthetic a priori. If the statements of logic and mathematics are treated as pseudo-propositions which say nothing, then the question of how we know what those propositions say is immediately defused. No Kantian appeals to intuition of space and time are required, nor is it necessary to say with Frege that the laws of logic state maximally general truths about the world.

While heavily influenced by him, the Vienna Circle's own theory differed from Wittgenstein's. For the latter, the fact that certain expressions are tautologies showed 'the formal – logical – properties of language, of the world' (6.12). That is, the fact that language, and the world it pictured, possesses certain 'formal' features was thought by Wittgenstein to be shown (although not said) in the fact that certain expressions are tautologies. But the Vienna Circle was dissatisfied with this conception. Wittgenstein's talk of 'showing formal properties of the world' smacked of the metaphysics they, as empiricists, were concerned to avoid. Rather, Circle members (Moritz Schlick and Rudolf Carnap in particular) proposed treating the truths of logic as expressions of the *conventions* governing a given language (cf. Schlick 1985, 71). Their role was thus not one of saying anything about the way things are – on this point they agreed with Wittgenstein – but rather that of spelling out the relations of implication among statements. And to the extent that mathematics could be reduced to logic following Frege and Russell, a similar account could be given of mathematical truths as well – they too express implication relations between statements.

There thus emerged a new conception of analytic truths as expressions of the conventions governing language. Some of the core ideas behind this conception were outlined in Schlick's *General Theory of Knowledge* (Schlick 1985). There, Schlick adopted discoveries in axiomatic theory made by the mathematician David Hilbert. Hilbert had shown how the intuitive, ordinary meanings of terms like 'point' and 'line' in axiomatic Euclidean geometry played no essential role within 'pure' or mathematical geometry. That is, Hilbert thought that such a theory 'is merely a framework or schema of concepts together with their necessary relations to one another, and that the basic elements can be construed as one pleases' (Hilbert 1971, 13). Stripped of reference to objects like points and lines, Hilbert used the resulting 'pure' geometry to prove a number of significant results. Schlick saw in Hilbert's methods the possibility of implicitly *defining* certain concepts within the context of a formal (axiomatic) system:

> A system of truths created with the aid of implicit definitions does not at any point rest on the ground of reality. On the contrary, it floats freely, so to speak, and like the solar system bears within itself the guarantee of its own stability. (Schlick 1985, 37)

A system of truths is in part 'created' through stipulation, Schlick thought. Here Schlick was referring not to empirical or synthetic truths, but to formal, a priori ones. We could guarantee the stability of such a system if we could find a consistency proof for the axioms (ibid., 357). Such a stipulated, provably consistent system would 'float freely.' There would be no need for an 'explicit' definition of the primitive terms that connected them with the empirical world. A priori knowledge was thus conceived by Schlick to consist of stipulations of symbol systems that implicitly defined a set of concepts.

In principle, the above ideas enabled the Vienna Circle to account for several characteristics of analytic propositions. First, Wittgenstein's idea that tautologies were empty of empirical content was to be explained without his corresponding 'metaphysics': as stipulated conventions governing the use of expressions in a language, analytic truths were tautologous principles of language use, not descriptions or reports of observations. Second, the apriority of analytic truths was accounted for by their being conventions of language which as stipulations were knowable a priori, or at least knowable without appeal to experiences other than those required for understanding the language. Third, the seeming *necessity* of analytic truths such as the laws of logic was accommodated by their being akin to rules or axioms for the use of a particular language. As such, their adoption would be necessary at least insofar as they were preconditions of speaking that language. Finally, the *scope* of analytic truth could be greatly expanded by treating them as conventional stipulations. For not only would the laws of logic and mathematics be analytic, some propositions of science, such as those defining law-governed expressions such as 'force' or 'simultaneity,' would be as well.

Analytic truth thus carried a heavy explanatory burden for the Vienna Circle.[9] But in principle, all but one of the classes of synthetic a priori propositions originally indicated by Kant now appeared to be explainable as analytic truths. Only the propositions of metaphysics remained unaccounted for, and those propositions were, following Wittgenstein, discounted as empty of cognitive significance.

This last step required an extra argument, and the Vienna Circle supplied it with their famous verifiability criterion of significance. This criterion required of synthetic statements that they be empirically verifiable in order to be significant. The justification for this criterion came about through a linkage of verifiability with meaning, such that the meaning of a synthetic sentence was identified with its method of verification (for a canonical articulation of this view, see Carnap 1959). The exact formulation of the verifiability criterion was to be heavily debated within the Circle, but central to all formulations was the idea that the classical statements of metaphysics would fail to satisfy it.

1.8 Carnap and Logical Empiricism

The most detailed attempt to fill out the above picture was Rudolf Carnap's 1928 book *The Logical Structure of the World* (1967: hereafter 'Aufbau'). Like Russell, Carnap (1891–1970) was very much concerned with the epistemology of the sciences, and like Schlick, he was concerned to establish the objectivity of scientific knowledge using the resources of the new logic of *Principia Mathematica*. Carnap shared Russell's conception of philosophy as a scientifically informed investigation of the logical forms of the statements of science.[10] Yet, apart from an early use of the notion of spatial intuition in his dissertation on space, Carnap was uncomfortable with Russell's appeals to special, non-empirical intuitions.[11] For Russell, non-empirical intuition explained our having justified belief in cases in which non-observational knowledge proved inadequate, such as our knowledge of universals, forms of propositions, inference, and axioms of mathematics and logic.[12] By contrast, Carnap thought that the introduction of special, non-empirical intuitions was tantamount to a retreat into metaphysics, and thereby a flight from scientific philosophy (cf. Carnap 1959, 76–7).

Carnap's alternative explanation was to show that epistemology is a purely logical science. He expressed this idea, and his dissatisfaction with traditional epistemology, quite explicitly in a text written shortly after the *Aufbau*, his 'Pseudoproblems in Philosophy':

> For those who are not satisfied with the expressions 'given', 'reducible', 'fundamental', or those who want to eschew using these concepts in their philosophy, the aim of epistemology has not been formulated at all. In the following investigations we propose to give a precise formulation of this aim. It will turn out that we can formulate the purpose of epistemological analysis without having to use these expressions of traditional philosophy. We only have to go back to the concept of implication (as it is expressed in if – then sentences). This is a fundamental concept of logic which cannot be criticized or avoided by anyone: it is indispensable in any philosophy, nay, in any branch of science. (1967, 306)

The strategy, in other words, was to show that a proper account of logic in general, and implication in particular, was both necessary *and sufficient* to explain our knowledge of logic, mathematics, and much of the objectivity of science.

In the *Aufbau*, Carnap attempted to show how the seemingly epistemological notions of 'reduction,' 'construction,' or 'constitution' could be replaced by logical or structural notions that would be precisely defined. He aimed to provide:

> the establishment of an epistemic-logical system of objects or concepts. The word 'object' is here always used in its widest sense, namely, for anything about which a statement can be made. (1967, 5)

This broad objective was to be achieved by means of a 'constitutional system' that would begin with certain basic concepts and then use them to construct higher-level concepts. This construction, Carnap thought, would proceed in a stepwise fashion by means of explicit definitions and derivations from them (6–7). Borrowing Russell's notion of a definite description, Carnap hoped to provide 'purely structural definite descriptions' that would illustrate a system for the characterization of the objects of human knowledge, without having to indicate any single object by intuition or acquaintance (24–8). Carnap thought that 'structural' objects could be 'reduced' to others by means of Russell's technique of definite descriptions. In other words, Carnap thought that 'an object is said to be "reducible" to others, if all statements about it can be translated into statements which speak only about these other objects' (60). So for example, fractions can be reduced to natural numbers in this sense, for a given statement about fractions can be transformed into a statement about natural numbers (61). Concepts, Carnap said, could also be 'constructed' by means of 'rules of translation.' The idea here is that a reducible concept could be transformed into a coextensive propositional function in which it no longer occurred. The simplest case of such a construction would be a translation which replaced a propositional function in which a occurs with one in which only b and c occur (61).

Carnap was thus proposing a very general theory of objects and concepts. But it was not intended by him to be simply an exercise in pure abstract thinking. It was, we have noted, supposed to show how epistemology, with its appeal to intuitions, the synthetic a priori, and so on, was replaceable by the logic of science in this new, formally precise form. Yet to do this it had to connect Carnap's very abstract constructions with experience. He had to show, for example, that his 'structural definite descriptions' of objects could describe possible objects of experience. Carnap thus needed bases for his reductions that nonetheless avoided any appeal to special intuited principles or entities. The required bases were of two types: one logical, the other non-logical and capable of linking constructed concepts to experience.

The logical basis of Carnap's constructions was found easily enough in the ideas outlined by Schlick. 'Logic,' Carnap declared, 'consists solely of conventions concerning the use of symbols, and of tautologies on the basis of these conventions' (ibid., 178).

What was the non-logical basis for Carnap's reductions? Obviously, he did not wish to appeal to a notion of 'the given,' since that would land him back in the position of adopting Russell's objects of acquaintance. What he actually accepted, however, is not clear and is a point of debate, for there are at least two rival interpretations of the Aufbau, and they offer different answers to this question. We will first describe a 'traditional' interpretation of the Aufbau that dates back at least to Quine (cf. Quine 1953, 39ff., 1969a, 74f.), and which played a role in the Quine–Carnap debate.

According to this traditional interpretation, Carnap was engaged in a strict empiricist project concerned with establishing the 'language of sensation' as epistemologically privileged and prior to any other. His reductions were thus aimed at translating the language of science into this sensation language. At bottom, the language of physics would be reduced to the assignment of sensory qualities like colors to ordered-quadruples of real numbers serving as the coordinates of space-time points (cf. Quine 1953, 39). On this Quinean interpretation, Carnap's dissatisfaction with traditional epistemology was motivated by a commitment to radical empiricism. The bases of his constructions, the things that they started from, were units of experience, such as sensory qualities.[13] Carnap himself appeared at times to endorse this interpretation of the *Aufbau*, writing for instance that his *Aufbau*-period use of the method of the analysis of complexes into components of the visual field

> was probably influenced by Mach and phenomenalist philosophers. But it seemed to me that I was the first who took the doctrine of these philosophers seriously. I was not content with their customary general statements like 'A material body is a complex of visual, tactile, and other sensations', but tried actually to construct these complexes. (Carnap 1963, 16)

As noted, however, there is a rival school of *Aufbau* interpretation that has emerged in recent years, and which downplays this empiricist component of Carnap's work, and sees in it instead a greater neo-Kantian influence.[14] On this rival interpretation, Carnap was not attempting to provide any epistemologically privileged basis for his construction project (such as sense-data), but was rather attempting to provide a rational reconstruction that would show how objective knowledge is possible, despite the fact that our knowledge has what appears to be a subjective origin in individual experience.[15] Carnap, on this interpretation, did not wish to defend idealism, but was rather attempting to replace traditional epistemology – empiricism and idealism included – with his constitution project.[16] The real question to be answered, on this interpretation, was the question: 'how, given the distinct streams of experience had by different subjects, can there be even one statement of science which is objective?' (Carnap 1967, 107).

We will not adjudicate between these rival interpretations of the *Aufbau*. For our purposes, it is enough that Carnap at times granted something like the traditional interpretation, as the above quotation indicates, and we will assume this interpretation in much of our subsequent discussion of the *Aufbau*.

Carnap's *Aufbau* was both inspiring and controversial. It is a difficult work which, as we have seen, generated interpretive disputes that continue to this day. As with much of the work of the Vienna Circle, it was not a work likely to reach a wide audience on its own. For better or worse, many of the ideas of the *Aufbau* and the Vienna Circle received a much more accessible expression in the writings of A. J. Ayer, and in particular in his widely read *Language, Truth and Logic* (1946). We shall return to the Vienna Circle's and Ayer's account of analyticity in chapter 5.

1.9 Chapter Summary

In this chapter we have reviewed the origin of the analytic–synthetic distinction in the western philosophical tradition. We have observed several different but related conceptions of analytic and synthetic truths, and have noted how those conceptions shaped how philosophy was viewed by those who held them. Here are the main points of the chapter.

We first saw how David Hume recognized that certain statements, such as that three times five is equal to fifteen, expressed 'relations of ideas' that are 'discoverable by the mere operation of thought, without dependence on what is anywhere existent in the universe,' while other statements, which he labeled 'matters of fact,' rely for their truth upon our sensory experience.

Hume's interest lay with statements expressing matters of fact. His successor Immanuel Kant, however, saw a new role for philosophy in the possibility that certain relations could be discoverable a priori by the 'mere operation of thought.' Kant drew two overlapping distinctions to develop this idea. One distinction was between 'analytic' statements (or judgments) and synthetic ones. For Kant, analytic statements are those in which the concept of the predicate is somehow contained in the concept of the subject. Synthetic statements are those in which the concept of the predicate is not contained in the subject. Because they only express something already 'contained' in the subject, analytic judgments do not expand our knowledge, Kant thought, while synthetic judgments do. The second distinction that interested Kant was that between statements that are knowable a priori and those that are knowable a posteriori. Kant thought that at least some a priori statements expand our knowledge, such as the theorems of mathematics and geometry and some statements of metaphysics. Since they expand our knowledge, these statements could not be analytic. Hence, Kant reasoned, there must exist *synthetic* a priori statements. But how is our knowledge of such statements possible? Answering this question required an appeal to special intuitions and categories of the mind. The exploration of these intuitions and categories, and the ways in which they shape and limit what is conceivable, is the proper role of philosophy, on Kant's view.

Both Bernard Bolzano and Gottlob Frege found Kant's explanation of analyticity in terms of containment to be vague, and wished to account for our knowledge of a priori truths in a way that was not so reliant on Kant's appeal to special intuitions or mental faculties. Frege saw the possibility of doing so in terms of his new predicate logic which seemed to allow for an account of some mathematical knowledge in purely logical terms by showing how to logically derive them from logical truths. This theory, known as logicism, removed the need for Kant's appeal to intuitions, at least in the case of arithmetic. Frege accordingly defined analytic truths as those statements which are general laws of logic or are derivable from those laws alone. Although the original version of Frege's logicism was flawed, it was later modified by Bertrand Russell. Russell further found a way to extend Frege's method of logical analysis to give a theory of our knowledge according to which our understanding of statements describing items with which we are not acquainted could in principle be explained as logically constructed out of our knowledge of those things with which we are acquainted.

The Vienna Circle was a group of scientists and philosophers who combined the logical methods of Frege and Russell with an empiricist attitude toward knowledge. The two Vienna Circle members that we discussed, Moritz Schlick and Rudolf Carnap, wanted to completely overcome Kant's idea that there exists a special domain of philosophical inquiry, the domain of synthetic a priori statements and the conditions that make them possible. Frege and Russell had shown how to do this for arithmetic, but not for statements of geometry, logic, or metaphysics. Vienna Circle members saw in Ludwig Wittgenstein's picture theory of the proposition a new role for analytic truths. Analytic truths could be treated as 'tautologies,' statements which do not say anything about the world, but which instead express logical properties among concepts or among statements. These tautologies were to be understood as conventional stipulations that governed the use of a given language by telling us what its words mean, or what statements could be inferred from what others. Knowledge of the truths of mathematics, geometry, metaphysics, and other supposedly synthetic a priori truths were instead seen as expressions of the analytic 'tautologies' that governed our use of language. This allowed Vienna Circle members to explain our knowledge of such truths without appealing to intuitions or other 'mysterious' faculties of knowing. The true statements of mathematics and geometry are indeed necessary and they are knowable a priori, but only because they express conventions of language. They say nothing about the world itself; to know facts about the world, we must turn to experience. Thus, the Vienna Circle supplied a theory of analytic truth which they believed to be compatible with empiricism.

We concluded chapter 1 with a look at Carnap's attempt to develop the Vienna Circle's ideas. Carnap tried to show how a proper account of logic, and in particular of the relation of implication among statements, could be sufficient to explain our knowledge of logic and mathematics, and could further account for the objectivity of scientific knowledge. Carnap proposed a 'constitutional system' which he believed could show how our knowledge of the world could be reduced to our sensory knowledge. Such a reduction, if successful, would give an account of our knowledge of the world that required no appeal to Kant's notions of intuitions or other special faculties of knowledge besides sensation.

Throughout chapter 1, we attempted to highlight how individual philosophers' explanations of analytic and synthetic statements informed their view of the scope and nature of philosophy itself. Kant's belief that synthetic a priori statements exist led him to conclude that philosophy has a special job and a special domain of inquiry – that of finding and explaining the conditions which make our knowledge of such statements possible. Frege and the Vienna Circle members that we discussed all took issue with Kant to varying degrees. While Frege granted that there might be some kinds of synthetic a priori knowledge (of geometry, for instance), he thought that his logic could remove the need for it in the case of mathematics and logic. The Vienna Circle went still further, attempting to remove the need for the synthetic a priori altogether. In doing so, they, like Hume, hoped to eliminate metaphysics and any appeal to non-empirical knowledge. To do this, they needed an account of a priori and necessary truths which made such truths acceptable from an empiricist standpoint, and their theory of analyticity provided this account.

1.10 Further Reading

Georges Dicker's book *Hume's Epistemology and Metaphysics* (1998) is a fine introduction to Hume which includes a discussion of Hume's Fork. *The Cambridge Companion to Kant*, edited by Paul Guyer (1992), contains several nice introductory essays on Kant, including discussions of the role of intuition in

Kant and the status of scientific knowledge according to Kant's philosophy. Peter Hylton's *Russell, Idealism and the Emergence of Analytic Philosophy* (1990) is an outstanding introduction both to Russell's philosophy and to much of the early history of analytic philosophy. A. J. Ayer edited a volume entitled *Logical Positivism* (1959) which remains one of the best collections of many of the important essays by and about the Vienna Circle. A more contemporary collection of papers on the Circle is edited by Michael Friedman and titled *Reconsidering Logical Positivism* (1999). This collection includes papers discussing analytic truth, Carnap's *Aufbau*, and other important contributions of the Vienna Circle. A more detailed discussion of the *Aufbau* is Alan Richardson's *Carnap's Construction of the World: The Aufbau and the Emergence of Logical Empiricism* (1998). Richardson provides a sophisticated defense of the 'alternative' interpretation of the *Aufbau* that we mentioned in section 1.8. One of the better introductions to Wittgenstein's picture theory of the proposition is Thomas Ricketts' 'Pictures, Logic, and the Limits of Sense in Wittgenstein's *Tractatus*' (1996a). Two other noteworthy collections of papers on the early analytic tradition are *Early Analytic Philosophy: Frege, Russell, Wittgenstein* edited by William Tait (1997), and *The Legacy of the Vienna Circle: Modern Reappraisals* edited by Sahotra Sarkar (1996).

2

CARNAP AND QUINE

2.1 Introduction and Overview

In chapter 1, we surveyed the emergence of the analytic–synthetic distinction. Our discussion there concluded by observing how the Vienna Circle used the notion of analyticity to give an account of a priori knowledge and the truths of logic and mathematics that was allegedly free of the allegedly dubious metaphysical commitments of Kant, Frege, Russell, and Wittgenstein. Our discussion in this chapter begins with a series of problems with that account that quickly emerged. In particular, we focus on difficulties with Carnap's *Aufbau* account. We then turn to Carnap's attempts to resolve the difficulties with his *Aufbau* account after the dissolution of the Vienna Circle. Carnap wanted to preserve many of the guiding insights of the Circle. Generally speaking, Carnap provided two different ways of developing his philosophy in the face of the objections raised against the *Aufbau*. One was presented in his book *The Logical Syntax of Language*, and the second was given in his later work and inspired by the semantical theories of Alfred Tarski and others.

As Carnap's philosophy developed, his account of analyticity underwent several significant changes. He proposed numerous definitions and 'adequacy conditions' for analytic truths, and we will look at many of his more important proposals in this chapter. There is a unity behind all of Carnap's various formulations, however. It is the idea that analytic truth is a *language-relative* notion. Analytic statements are true and immune to revision, but only relative to a given language system. In fact, analytic truths largely define what makes something into a 'language' in Carnap's specialized sense. This proposed language-relativity of analytic truth was a radical step with important consequences, as we shall see.

Carnap's philosophy is interesting in its own right, and it had an important influence on the emergence of contemporary analytic philosophy. It is not, however, easy to understand. The reason for this is that Carnap made heavy use of technical methods in logic and set theory to develop his position. In this chapter, we have attempted to include some discussion of Carnap's technical methods. There are two reasons for doing so. One is that Carnap was one of the very first philosophers to incorporate into philosophy many of the central logical discoveries of the twentieth century, such as Gödel's Incompleteness Theorems, the distinction between meta-languages and object-languages, and Tarski's 'semantical' methods in logic. These discoveries still play an important role in much contemporary analytic philosophy. If one wishes to understand how the analytic tradition has developed in the direction that it has, part of that understanding requires seeing how these discoveries have been used and incorporated into the debate over analyticity. A second reason for our looking at Carnap's technical methods in some detail is that these methods had a significant influence on Carnap's student and friend, Willard V. Quine. In the latter sections of this chapter, we explore how Quine adopted many of Carnap's guiding ideas, and then developed them in a radically new direction. Ultimately, Quine's discoveries would lead him to a thoroughgoing critique of the notion of analyticity and the analytic–synthetic distinction. This critique, and the philosophy that emerged from the rejection of the analytic–synthetic distinction, will be the topic of chapters 3–5.

2.2.1 Demise of the *Aufbau*

Engaging in a philosophical argument in which important concepts have vague, shifting, or even inconsistent definitions can be a frustrating experience. After long and perhaps heated argument, the disputants may discover that they haven't gone anywhere; their dispute stemmed from a misunderstanding – perhaps it was 'merely verbal.'

Carnap was no stranger to this experience. In his 'Intellectual Autobiography,' he described how it motivated his entire approach to philosophy:

> most of the controversies in traditional metaphysics appeared to me sterile and useless. When I compared this kind of argumentation with investigations

and discussions in empirical science or in the logical analysis of language, I was often struck by the vagueness of the concepts used and by the inconclusive nature of the arguments. I was depressed by disputations in which the opponents talked at cross purposes; there seemed hardly any chance of mutual understanding, let alone agreement, because there was not even a common criterion for deciding the controversy. (1963b, 44–5)

Carnap wanted to introduce greater clarity and precision into philosophical debate, and thereby avoid inconclusive disputations. But how should we do so, precisely?

In chapter 1, we considered Carnap's project in the *Aufbau*, and noted how he attempted to provide a construction system which would allow us to derive, step-by-step, all concepts from certain fundamental concepts, and do so in a way that could be shared by all observers. A central tenet of Carnap's program in the *Aufbau* was his assumption of a single, unique logic. Like Frege, Russell, and Wittgenstein, Carnap in his early writings assumed a *universalist* conception of logic, one derived from Russell and Whitehead's *Principia Mathematica* (1997). According to this conception, a single logic underlies all of our reasoning, whether it be about science, mathematics, or philosophy.

Carnap's belief in a single underlying logic was shattered in 1930 by one of his own students, Kurt Gödel (1906–78). In that year, at a conference in Königsberg that Carnap attended, Gödel made the announcement of the first of his famous incompleteness theorems. In chapter 1, we noted how philosophers such as Frege and Russell had attempted to derive arithmetic from basic 'logical' laws and axioms, plus some definitions. Gödel proved that in any consistent formal system that is sufficiently strong to express ordinary arithmetic, there will be a sentence, known as a Gödel sentence, that is true in standard arithmetic, but not provable in the system itself.[1] Given any such formal system S, there is some sentence G of that system that is true, but such that neither G nor its negation is provable in S. Furthermore, adding G to S (as a new axiom), to get a new system S' will not get around the incompleteness result.[2] For while G will, trivially, now be provable in S', by Gödel's proof there will be *another* sentence G' that will be true but unprovable in S'. Thus, no consistent formal system sufficiently strong to express ordinary arithmetic will ever be complete in the sense of allowing the derivation of every true arithmetical formula. This was Gödel's discovery, and Carnap was among the first to learn of it.

The significance of Gödel's result for Carnap's philosophy was immense.

By proving that no consistent formal system could allow the derivation of every true arithmetical formula, Gödel's result undermined Carnap's belief in a universal logic, for it made clear that at least some formulas of any consistent formal system of sufficient strength to express standard arithmetic would fall 'outside' what was derivable (provable or disprovable) in any given system of logic. Furthermore, Gödel's result seemed to raise serious doubts about the extent to which truths of arithmetic could be regarded as analytic in the way that Frege and the Vienna Circle had hoped. For if, given any consistent axiomatic system of number theory, true arithmetical statements could always be found that could not be derived within that system, it seems as if mathematics is not exhausted by any such system.

Carnap was quick to realize that Gödel's incompleteness theorem would require significant modification to the philosophy of the *Aufbau*. And there was a second factor that led Carnap to realize that the *Aufbau* project could not work as originally conceived. Originally, Carnap believed that the detailed execution of the *Aufbau*'s constructional system would have to incorporate some results of *empirical* psychology in order to identify the basic elements of the constitution, and thereby connect the logical constructions of the *Aufbau* with the facts of human experience (1967, 190).[3] But there was a problem here. Carnap was on the one hand claiming in the *Aufbau* to construct a system of concepts that would show how the objectivity of science could rest on a basis such as 'autopsychological' subjective experience, while at the same time appealing to the results of empirical psychology to construct that very system. This raised the risk of vicious circularity at the heart of the *Aufbau*. Carnap was both proposing to demonstrate how objective empirical science was possible, and appealing to the discoveries of such science in that very demonstration. Years later, Quine expressed the problem with the *Aufbau*'s constructions here as follows:

> But why all this creative reconstruction, all this make-believe? The stimulation of his sensory receptors is all the evidence anybody has had to go on, ultimately, in arriving at his picture of the world. Why not just see how this construction really proceeds? Why not settle for psychology? Such a surrender of the epistemological burden to psychology is a move that was disallowed in earlier times as circular reasoning. If the epistemologist's goal is validation of the grounds of empirical science, he defeats his purpose by using psychology or other empirical science in the validation. (Quine 1969a, 75–6)[4]

Although Quine wrote this comment in 1968, concerns about the relationship between empirical psychology and the *Aufbau* project had been raised against Carnap in the late 1920s by the Vienna Circle, in particular by Otto Neurath (1983).[5] We consider this issue further in chapters 3 and 5.

2.2.2 Philosophy as Logical Syntax

In response to these challenges posed by Gödel and Neurath, Carnap advanced a major revision to the philosophical program of the *Aufbau* in the early 1930s. The revision would be less 'entangled with psychological questions' (Carnap 1937, 278), while at the same time providing a response to Gödel's incompleteness theorems. The new philosophy, presented in Carnap's 1934 book *The Logical Syntax of Language* (hereafter 'Syntax') would set the tone for the remainder of his philosophical career.

The most radical change in Carnap's philosophy came in the opening chapter of the *Syntax*. We noted above that in his earlier work, Carnap had assumed a single, universal logic. With *Syntax*, this changed. Carnap had now adopted his famous 'Principle of Tolerance':

> *In logic, there are no morals.* Everyone is at liberty to build up his own logic, i.e., his own form of language, as he wishes. All that is required of him is that, if he wishes to discuss it, he must state his methods clearly, and give syntactical rules instead of philosophical arguments. (1937, 52)

This was a radical move. If there are no 'morals' in logic, then the question whether there is a single correct logic is a moot one. There are no 'facts of the matter' about logic about which we might disagree or that we can appeal to in order to settle disagreements.

But what could it mean to 'build up' one's own logic? And how could philosophers disagree about logic in the first place? In fact, there are disputes about logic, and by the 1930s Carnap was aware of them.

One such dispute, which Carnap hoped to help resolve, was between intuitionists and other philosophers of mathematics, such as logicists or formalists. *Intuitionism* is a school of philosophy founded by the mathematician L. E. J. Brouwer. Brouwer was impressed by Kant's treatment of mathematical knowledge as a product of the mind through our intuition of time. As a product of the mind, mathematical truth is not determined by any mind-independent realm of mathematical objects or facts. As such, Brouwer thought, a mathematical proposition only becomes true when the mind has experienced its truth by constructing it. This metaphysical claim had an important consequence for logic. For it led Brouwer to reject the Principle of the Excluded Middle, which states that for any proposition p, either p or its negation is true (i.e., $p \lor \sim p$). Brouwer thought that open mathematical problems, such as Goldbach's Conjecture that every even number greater than 2 is the sum of two primes, could not have a truth value until they were proven. Since Goldbach's Conjecture is neither true nor false until a proof is constructed, the Principle of the Excluded Middle is false for it and many similar open statements. So this Principle ought to be rejected in logic, and intuitionists set themselves the task of using logic and mathematics without it.

Opposing intuitionism were two competing views of mathematics and logic: the logicism of Frege and Russell (which Carnap had initially adopted), and formalism as it derived from the work of David Hilbert. Both positions accepted 'classical logic,' including the Principle of the Excluded Middle. Yet each position had its own philosophical motivations. In the case of Frege's logicism, much of this motivation stemmed, as we saw in chapter 1, from an attempt to dispense with the Kantian synthetic a priori in mathematics.[6] In the case of Hilbert's formalism, the motivation came from epistemological worries about the possibility that mathematics might ultimately rest on an inconsistency (similar to what Russell had discovered in Frege's work). Such worries had led Hilbert to propose treating basic arithmetic as the bare manipulation of signs, that is, of 'extralogical concrete objects that are intuitively present as immediate experience prior to all thought' (Hilbert 1927, 464).

What impressed, or perhaps depressed, Carnap in all of this was the fact that 'there can be endless fruitless discussion as to which of them is right and what numbers actually are' (1937, 300). So Carnap put forward a proposal: let each side in the debate construct their preferred system of language (to include mathematics, and logic, as needed), but do so in a way that requires them to state their methods clearly. In this process of clarification, however, there could be no appeal to alleged intuitions or other evidence that had proven so contentious in the past. Rather, what is to count as evidence within a system would itself need to be spelled out clearly in the formulation of the languages. That is, the proposed languages should each specify under what conditions one is justified in using a particular sign (such as a logical sign like 'or,' or an observational predicate like 'red'), and how to make inferences among them.

Carnap was thus proposing to use the logical innovations of Frege, Russell, Hilbert, and others to build formal languages – languages consisting of precisely defined rules for forming sentences and making inferences between them – to clarify the philosophical dispute between the intuitionists, logicists, and formalists. He thought that such languages would allow us to replace seemingly interminable philosophical disputes with the clear specification of proposed languages, each of which could be assessed to see whether it achieved whatever 'pragmatic' goals (discussed in section 2.4 below) the language's inventor had in mind:

> The aim of logical syntax is to provide a system of concepts, a language, by the help of which the results of logical analysis will be exactly formulable. *Philosophy is to be replaced by the logic of science* – that is to say, by the logical analysis of the concepts and sentences of the sciences. (1937, xiii)

This conception of philosophy brought about a complete re-orientation of the goal of philosophical inquiry. Carnap would not claim to seek truth, conceived of as a language-transcendent goal, or to provide 'foundations' for science in subjective experience or shared, inter-subjective structures. Instead, he contented himself with a more modest, language-relative conception of truth. To call a statement true, or even well-justified, would on his new view be to say that it satisfies the conditions of assertion, or justification, in language L, ideally, a precisely specified one.

2.2.3 Logical and Descriptive Languages

We have yet to explain, however, how this was to work as a response to the problems encountered by the *Aufbau*. By itself, the principle of tolerance provides an answer to neither of the problems we have noted, viz.:

1 the incompleteness of any formal system for arithmetic that Gödel discovered,
2 the problem of linking a formal reconstruction of language to experience that led to Quine's and Neurath's criticisms of the *Aufbau*.

As it turns out, the solution to both of these problems involved re-conceiving the notion of analyticity.

We will start with the problem of Gödel incompleteness. We have noted that by Gödel's result, as long as we remain within a given consistent system of axioms and rules that is sufficiently strong to prove truths of basic arithmetic (an example of this would be the Peano Axioms for arithmetic), that system will be incomplete, in the sense that there will be sentences that are true but not provable or disprovable in the system. In the *Syntax*, Carnap found a way to seemingly circumvent this result

We have remarked that in the *Aufbau*, Carnap restricted himself to the universalist logic inherited from Russell and Whitehead's *Principia Mathematica*. As such, Carnap did not distinguish between the statements made *about* a logical system, and those made *in* it. Every logical statement was a part of 'the' system of logic. In the early 1930s, however, Carnap was actively engaged in conversations both with Gödel and with the Polish logician Alfred Tarski (1901–83). As Carnap would later report, they, along with the works of Hilbert, allowed him to see the possibility of a 'meta-theoretical' alternative to Russell's conception of logic (cf. Carnap 1963b, 52). He began to see, in other words, that he could draw a distinction between a statement expressed *by* a formula, and a statement *about* a formula. For example, a rule of the form (ML_R) 'An expression of Language II is *descriptive* iff φ' (where φ is some set of conditions expressed in English, say), need not itself be a statement of the object-language under consideration ('Language II,' in this example). Nonetheless, a statement like ML_R has a distinctive status. It is a meta-language *rule* that stipulates what counts as a descriptive expression in a distinct object-language. It uses the resources of the meta-language (English, in the example of ML_R) to specify conditions that apply to the object-language. This distinction, with which modern students of logic are familiar, allowed Carnap a greater precision and expressive power in formulating his languages, as he saw:

> I emphasized the distinction between that language which is the object of the investigation, which I called the 'object language', and the language in which the theory of the object language . . ., is formulated, which I called the 'metalanguage' . . . Whereas Hilbert intended his metamathematics only for the special purpose of proving the consistency of a mathematical system formulated in the object language, I aimed [in the *Logical Syntax*] at the construction of a general theory of linguistic forms. (Carnap 1963b, 54)

The distinction between meta-language (ML) and object-language (OL) was used by Carnap to respond to Gödel's incompleteness theorem in the following way. Gödel's result shows us that we will never have a complete set of axioms for basic number theory, given certain constraints. So suppose that we regard some language system that includes some incomplete set of axioms as our OL, and then proceed to use the resources of the ML that we employed to formulate the object-language in order to confer on the object-language whatever properties we need to complete it. For example, if 'G' turns out to be the name of some true-but-unprovable Gödel sentence in the system of the OL, we can use the resources of the ML, strengthening it if necessary by adding new axioms, in order to 'prove' G. To be sure, Gödel's theorem ensures that there will be also some new statement G' in the ML that is true-but-unprovable in it (assuming, once more, that the ML conforms to the same constraints). But if we needed to we could appeal to yet a further meta-language – a meta-meta-language – and formulate in the meta-meta-language whatever conditions are required to make more 'complete' the ML. And so on, ad infinitum.[7,8]

In the Syntax, Carnap used basically this method in constructing his second example language system, 'Language II.' But the method involved a big concession, namely, that *'everything mathematical can be formalized, but mathematics cannot be exhausted by one system; it requires an infinite series of ever richer languages'* (1937, 222). No single language system L, in other words, can ever ensure that we can derive every mathematical truth within L. But we can still formulate any given object-language in terms of a finite set of rules, and permitting only finitely long derivations. So while Gödel's result guarantees that any given object-language system will remain formally incomplete, it is still possible for Carnap's proposed methods to be applied to allow formalists, intuitionists, logicists, or other disputants in the philosophy of mathematics to choose their preferred language and logic, without Gödel's incompleteness results leading us to despair of ever capturing what is essential to mathematics in a formally precise way. We must simply admit that we cannot fully capture all of mathematics in a single language or even a recursively enumerable sequence of 'languages.'

As Carnap understood the notion of a 'language' in the Syntax, languages were partially constituted by the logical rules or 'L-rules' which specify which statements were consequences of which other statements. As such, when he spoke of a 'system' or a 'language,' he did not distinguish the deductive rules and axioms from all of the other parts of the language, such as its semantical rules, in the way that is common to much contemporary logic. Today, logicians typically distinguish between the 'semantically true' statements of a language, that is, the statements which are true according to the semantical rules for the language, and the statements which are 'syntactically' derivable from the axioms of a given deductive system in that language. In more contemporary terms, what Gödel proved would be expressed by saying that certain statements of mathematics are 'true but unprovable' in the sense that there will always be some statements that are true according to the semantics of a given language, but not derivable by any given recursively deductive system; they aren't 'syntactically' true in the sense of being derivable from the system. Hence, contemporary logicians and philosophers would be unlikely to speak of mathematics not being 'exhausted by one system' as Carnap did. But from Carnap's perspective in the *Syntax*, there was no clear distinction between what was 'semantically true' and what was 'syntactically derivable,' so for him it made sense to speak in this way. As Carnap would later acknowledge, his 'syntactical' methods already employed what would later be included as part of semantics (Carnap 1942, 247).[9]

The appeal in the *Syntax* to the resources of an ML in order to characterize properties of an OL was to prove highly important both for Carnap's subsequent work and in the debate between him and Quine. It allowed him to give a second, broad definition of *logical-* or 'L-truth,' which Carnap treated as synonymous with 'analytic' (1937, 182). Intuitively, what Carnap wanted to capture was the Vienna Circle's idea that 'an analytic sentence is absolutely true whatever the empirical facts may be. Hence, it does not state anything about facts' while '*synthetic sentences are the genuine statements about reality*' (41). Consonant with the ideas of the Vienna Circle, Carnap wanted to include mathematical truths among these analytic truths. He gave three definitions of 'analytic' in the *Syntax*: one for Language I, one for Language II, and a third, general definition (cf. 39, 110, 182, respectively). To capture the idea of being true 'whatever the empirical facts may be,' all of Carnap's definitions of analytic truth would have the feature of not requiring any further special assumptions to be true. In other words, they would be consequences of the *empty set* of premises.

To get the result that analytic truths are consequences of the empty set of premises, Carnap had to evaluate some statements as analytic in Language II in a way that makes essential reference to the meta-language of II (1937, 113; cf. also 219).[10] This was a direct consequence of Gödel's incompleteness result. Because of it, an object-language mathematical truth T, say, might only be specifiable as analytic if 'T is valid' is a logical truth in the meta-language of T. As such, Carnap had to distinguish the notion of something's being *demonstrable* in an OL from the notion of something's being *determinate* in that OL. Something is demonstrable in an OL just if we can derive it from the basic axioms and rules of that OL (99f.). Since Gödel's theorem prevents us from saying that everything is demonstrable in the OL by such means, however, the notion of being 'true in virtue of the rules of the language,' which mathematical statements supposedly are, requires something stronger than demonstrability. It requires determinacy. Determinate statements are those which are either demonstrable, or require proof 'with the resources of a syntax formulated in a language richer than II' (133). Simply put, Carnap's idea was that all determinate statements are analytic.[11]

With a notion of analyticity in hand, Carnap had what he wanted, namely, 'an exact understanding what is usually designated as "logically valid" or "true on logical grounds"' (41). In other words, Carnap could give a formal characterization of the difference between those statements which hold true solely in virtue of the rules of a language system, and those which hold true in virtue of a reality that is independent of that logical system. Reports of that independent reality would be given by synthetic sentences (41). But Carnap thought that the analytic statements could now be said to include all of the arithmetical sentences in the OL, given the assumption of an infinite hierarchy of meta-languages for that OL.

2.2.4 Physical Languages

The languages that Carnap was proposing to construct to replace philosophical debates began as fairly 'stripped-down' systems of inference, similar to the system of predicate logic that one studies in an introductory logic class, but supplemented with axioms for getting basic arithmetic and an inference relation (a 'consequence relation') that is strong enough to yield determinacy. In the context of the dispute between formalists, intuitionists, and logicists that we mentioned above, this might be enough to allow the disputants to frame their disagreement in a more precise way that would let it be resolved. They might begin to see, for example, that their dispute was 'merely verbal,' that it involved unclarity or imprecision in the use of language which a more precisely specified language could remove. At least Carnap hoped so. But what of broader philosophical disputes that might involve the language of empirical science? For instance, the history of science is filled with seemingly 'metaphysical' disputes, such as the dispute over whether space is a substance, or whether unobservable entities such as gravitational fields or the ether exist. More generally, one might wonder whether realism about the external world must be accepted in order to do empirical science (cf. Carnap 1963b, 46). Carnap wanted to bring these kinds of philosophical disputes within the purview of his precisely specified languages as well. But to do so, the languages would have to be expanded. They would have to include 'descriptive' expressions, such as 'red' or 'mass.'

Carnap recognized the possibility of incorporating into a language special 'physical-' or 'P-rules' that would govern sentences containing descriptive expressions. While his example languages I and II were limited to only logical transformation rules, he saw that:

> We may, however, construct a language with *extra-logical rules of transformation*. The first thing which suggests itself is to include amongst the primitive sentences the so-called laws of nature, i.e. universal sentences of physics. (1937, 180)

Carnap's idea here was to axiomatize a given body of accepted empirical theory such as, say, the kinetic-molecular theory of gases, within a language. Given the principle of tolerance, there could be no objection to doing this, he thought, since it is a matter only of convention how many such P-rules we include. Corresponding to the L-rules that generate L-valid sentences, a language with P-rules would have P-valid statements: statements that are consequences of the P-rules.[12] For example, the statement:

> (S) 'In this vessel b of volume 5000 cc there are 2 grams of hydrogen under such and such a pressure'

might have as a P-consequence the statement:

> (C) 'In b there are 2 grams of hydrogen at such and such a temperature,'

given certain P-rules (such as ideal gas laws) governing the relation of temperature and pressure (185). In conjunction with empirical premises, P-rules could thus have observable, empirical consequences, and these consequences could, as Carnap saw, be tested (317).

The introduction of P-rules greatly expanded the scope of Carnap's proposed languages. He thought that such languages could, in principle, be used to resolve seemingly philosophical disputes (cf. 1937, 178). The P-rules also led Carnap to three important theses that would prove significant for the later debate over analyticity.

The first thesis concerned the following possibility. Suppose a statement like C is derived from a system including P-rules, and C makes an empirical claim that may or may not be true or verified. What happens if C is observed to be false? Carnap considered just such a possibility, writing that:

If a sentence which is an L-consequence of certain P-primitive sentences [P-rules] contradicts a sentence which has been stated as a protocol-sentence [observation report], then some change must be made in the system. For instance, the P-rules can be altered in such a way that those particular primitive sentences are no longer valid; or the protocol-sentence can be taken as being non-valid; or again the L-rules which have been used in the deduction can also be changed. There are no established rules for the kind of change which must be made. (1937, 317)

Consider for example a gas law example similar to Carnap's. We have a law-statement P, which we might suppose is an example P-rule, and a series of observation-reports O_1-O_5:

P: At a constant temperature, the pressure of a gas is inversely proportional to its volume.
O_1: The initial volume of a gas is measured to be 5000 cc.
O_2: The initial pressure is measured at 1 atmosphere.
O_3: The pressure is increased and measured at 2 atmospheres.
O_4: The temperature is measured and found to be constant.
O_5: All of the equipment used in verifying observations O_1-O_4 has been tested and observed to work properly.

From these premises, we use an inference rule, an L-rule, to infer the following experimental hypothesis H:

/∴ H: The volume will be observed to decrease to 2500 cc.

The prediction H is a consequence of the premises. Yet suppose that when we check this prediction experimentally, we find that H is false (e.g., that the volume is only 2300 cc). What should we conclude? In such a case, we know only that at least one premise is false. We don't know which one(s), for the available evidence underdetermines what we should infer next. From Carnap's 'tolerant' perspective, we seem to have a choice of options. We might reject the P-rule, thereby 'saving' the truth of the observation statements. But alternatively, we might 'save' the P-rule and insist on rejecting one or more of the O-statements. After all it is always *possible* that we made a mistaken observation somewhere. Finally, we might even save all of the premises by rejecting the logic, that is, part or all of the system of L-rules that allows us to infer the conclusion from the premises. Consistently with his principle of tolerance, Carnap did not see any convention-independent fact of the matter about what we should do. Independent of whatever conventional choices we make, nothing can compel us to accept or reject a particular rule. As Carnap put it:

> There is in the strict sense no refutation (falsification) of an hypothesis; for even when it proves to be L-incompatible with certain protocol-sentences, there always exists the possibility of maintaining the hypothesis and renouncing acknowledgement of the protocol-sentences. Still less is there in the strict sense a complete confirmation (verification) of an hypothesis. (1937, 317)

We have seen how any given hypothesis could be accepted in the face of seeming counterevidence. Here Carnap also drew the converse point, namely, that even if the observational evidence E seemed to support a hypothesis, as in a case in which E were in fact observed, the hypothesis could still be rejected. His reasoning here was simple: no empirical results could ever *entail* that a given hypothesis is true or false. They could at most provide increasingly strong inductive reasons for or against it (318).

These considerations led Carnap to two further important theses. One was the realization (which he attributed to Pierre Duhem and Henri Poincaré) that empirical claims are never tested in isolation, but only within systems of hypotheses:

> It is, in general, impossible to test even a singular hypothetical sentence. In the case of a single sentence of this kind, there are in general no suitable L-consequences of the form of protocol-sentences; hence for the deduction of sentences having the form of protocol-sentences the remaining hypotheses must also be used. Thus *the test applies, at bottom, not to a single hypothesis but to the whole system of physics as a system of hypotheses* (Duhem, Poincaré). (1937, 318, Carnap's emphasis)

A simplified version of this point can be seen in the above example. The conclusion H simply doesn't follow from any proper subset of the premises P–O_5. We need all of these to get H. Moreover, both P and each of the observation statements rely on other statements of physical theory. For instance, the notions of *gas, pressure,* and *atmosphere* are theory-laden; their contents are determined by other statements, including other P-rules. Likewise, the instrumentation used in the experiment was constructed according to further statements of physical theory. If we wanted to, we could make these statements explicit in the above argument by, for example, adding premises that explain just what pressure is. Suppose that we did so. Then any of these statements too could, in principle, be rejected if our prediction-statement H is falsified. In this sense, they are all 'hypotheses' and, as Carnap saw, are 'tested' when we test H, even if only indirectly.

The last thesis that Carnap drew was a consequence of the above. If we assume that any part of a language with P-rules can be modified in the face of seemingly disconfirming observations, and that empirical tests apply only to an entire system of physical theory, then is there any statement in a language with P-rules which *cannot* be revised (or removed) in the face of the evidence? Carnap thought not, and as a result, he believed that the various types of statements in a physical language – L-rules and their consequences, P-rules and their consequences, and observation statements – differed only in the *degree* to which we hold them:

> No rule of the physical language is definitive; all rules are laid down with the reservation that they may be altered as soon as it seems expedient to do so. This applies not only to the P-rules but also to the L-rules, including those of mathematics. In this respect there are only differences in degree; certain rules are more difficult to renounce than others. (318)

To find this claim coming from *Carnap's* typewriter may be surprising to many philosophers, not least since it is a view commonly associated with *Quine's* work some twenty years later. But it really should not surprise us, for it is likely that Carnap believed it to be compatible with, if not a consequence of, the principle of tolerance. If we are all 'at liberty to build up our own logic,' how could we be compelled to accept any particular statement as true? Since nothing compels us, we should count both the rule-statements of a language and the observation statements made in it as alike open to revision due to empirical or methodological considerations (320).

To summarize then, the three theses that Carnap's consideration of physical languages led to were the following:

1   No statement of a physical language is ever strictly confirmed or refuted; any statement can be preserved, and any statement can be discarded, given suitable changes in the language.
2   No hypothesis is ever tested in isolation; rather, empirical tests apply to whole systems of hypotheses.

3   Differences between statements such as L-rules, P-rules, and observation reports are differences only in the degree to which they are held true. Any statement can be modified or rejected to accommodate empirical results or methodological considerations.

We shall return to these three theses in subsequent chapters, for they will constitute important premises in Quine's arguments *against* Carnap's notion of analyticity. In a nutshell, the problem which these theses pose for analyticity is that they raise the question of whether there is an *epistemological* difference between analytic and synthetic truths. Carnap needed there to be an epistemological difference in kind in order to separate the analytic statements, which are rules for possible languages and the determinate consequences of such rules, from the synthetic ones, whose truth or falsity depends on 'extra-linguistic' matters of fact. Analytic and synthetic statements are supposed to be introduced and justified in very different ways. But these theses concerning physical languages seem to undermine this difference, and replace it with a difference only in the *degree* to which different statements are held true. As we shall see in the next chapter, Quine would make more or less this very point against the notion of analyticity as Carnap conceived of it. In the meantime, however, we need to spell out more clearly what that notion was in light of the introduction of P-rules

2.2.5 Analyticity in *Syntax*

Let us review first the notion of analyticity as it applied to languages without P-rules (which, as we noted above, may nonetheless include descriptive expressions). In the *Syntax*, Carnap claimed that if we consider the fact that:

> all the connections between logico-mathematical terms are independent of extra-linguistic factors, such as, for instance, empirical observations, and that they must be solely and completely determined by the transformation rules of the language, we find the formally expressible distinguishing peculiarity of logical symbols and expressions to consist in the fact that each sentence constructed solely from them is determinate. (1937, 177)

We have seen that Gödel's incompleteness results required that Carnap distinguish between what is *demonstrable* in a given object-language (i.e., what we can derive from the basic axioms and rules of that OL), and what is *determinate* in that language (i.e., fully characterizable only in terms of what is a consequence in a richer meta-language). More specifically, a sentence is determinate if and only if it is either a consequence of the empty set of premises (L-valid), or has every sentence as a consequence (L-contra-valid) (174). Here 'consequence' was understood by Carnap in the 'strong' sense such that statement S is a consequence of S' if "'S'→ S" is true' is derivable in the ML (172–3). As we saw, the stronger or more permissive notion of consequence (and the determinate sentences that it generates) allowed Carnap to characterize analyticity, or L-truth, in terms of the idea of 'truth in virtue of the rules of the language,' despite Gödel's results. Carnap puts this idea of truth in virtue of rules to philosophical work, as we will explain below. But first let us consider how Carnap extended the notion of analyticity to languages which contain P-rules.

In the *Syntax*, Carnap supposed that we are given a physical language with both L- and P-rules. He wanted to make sure that the consequences of these two sets of rules would be distinguishable, and the notion of analyticity would deliver, he hoped, the required distinction. Why did he wish to keep the two sets of rules separate? The answer appears in the last quotation above. Logic, Carnap thought, has the 'distinguishing peculiarity' that it is determinate independently of 'extra-linguistic factors,' a notion formally captured by the idea of a determinate sentence's being a consequence of the empty set of sentences (or having all sentences as consequences). It seemed to Carnap that there is some relevant difference between those statements that might directly eventuate in a testable hypothesis – P-rules – and those that would (normally) not do so – the L-rules.

Thus, besides the definition of analytic truth in languages without P-rules (like Languages I and II), Carnap also wanted to give a general account of analytic- or L-truth. But he had to give us a general way of classifying these truths, for the L- and P-rules both generate certain valid statements, statements true in virtue of the rules alone, and certain contra-valid ones. For example, in a language that includes among the L-rules the laws of 'classical' logic, the statement '~(p & ~p)' would be L-valid and its negation L-contra-valid. If that same language included axiomatic molecular-kinetic gas theory, for example, it would include P-validities and contra-validities like, for instance, the P-valid statement 'The volume of a gas increases proportionately to its temperature' (this statement's negation would be an example of a P-contra-validity).

In giving his general characterization of 'analytic' Carnap did not assume that we are given the distinction between the L- and P-valid and contra-valid statements beforehand. Rather, he supposed only that we are given a language, and that we could figure out the set of all determinate state-ments in it, using the notion of strong consequence as necessary to avoid limitations stemming from Gödel incompleteness (1937, 177–8). This set would include all the L- and P-validities and contra-validities, but not neces-sarily distinguished as such. Next, Carnap proposed distinguishing logical from descriptive vocabulary in a language. He assumed that certain signs in any language are 'primitive,' in the sense that they are uncompounded. The signs '&' and 'temperature,' for example, could be primitives in our imagined language. The primitive logical vocabulary would be the largest set of all those signs such that every statement constructed solely from them is determinate. For example, finding that 'p & $\sim p$' is determinate (since it's contra-valid), would make $\{p, \&, \sim\}$ a candidate subset of the set of logical vocabulary.[13] Any primitive vocabulary that does not meet this requirement is *descriptive* in Carnap's technical sense.

With this distinction between logical and descriptive vocabulary in hand, Carnap could give his general definition of 'analytic.' An *analytic* statement is one which is valid, that is, is a consequence of the empty set of premises in its language, and which either contains only logical vocabulary, or is such that every sentence obtainable from it by substituting descriptive signs for other descriptive signs is determinate.[14] Contra-valid sentences are contra-dictory, and indeterminate ones are synthetic.[15]

Here is an overview of these ideas. Carnap was considering languages that include descriptive vocabulary and contain special P-rules that govern that vocabulary. He believed that he could preserve the distinction between analytic statements and the other statements in such a language, including the P-rules. The distinction still requires appealing to the notion of logical truth in a meta-language in order to define determinacy in a given object-language. Nonetheless, given such an appeal, Carnap seemed to have found a general method of finding[16] the analytic sentences of a language, at least for any language that allows us to figure out which sentences are determi-nate in it. In this sense, 'analytic' receives a language-general specification. Carnap thus presented us with what he had hoped for, an 'exact under-standing' of the vague, pre-theoretical notion of 'logically valid' or 'true on logical grounds.'

In the *Syntax*, Carnap soon put this notion of analyticity to use. Briefly, Carnap called sentences such as 'Five is not a thing, but a *number*' or 'Time is continuous,' 'pseudo-object sentences,' because they are 'formulated as though they refer (either partially or exclusively) to objects, while in reality they refer to syntactic forms, and specifically to forms of the designations of those objects with which they appear to deal' (1937, 285). He proposed replacing them with 'quasi-syntactic sentences' like: '"Five" is not a thing-word, but a number-word' and 'The real-number expressions are used as time co-ordinates.' These are sentences which replace apparent talk of properties of language-independent things with talk of syntactical properties of the *expressions* used to designate things (233f.).

The details of this replacement process are many.[17] But we can note that it relied on general definitions of notions like 'logical vocabulary,' 'descriptive vocabulary,' and 'analytic.' In particular, the identification of quasi-syntactic sentences required a general definition of 'analytic,' since quasi-syntactical sentences were identified by means of L-properties that yield analytic truths.[18]

Carnap's efforts in his *Syntax* phase were directed at deflating philosophically problematic notions like *fact*, *property*, and *reference*. These were the sorts of notions which he thought tended to lead to fruitless philosophical squabbles. Carnap knew that for most sentences, the question of their truth or falsity could not be settled simply by appeal to the language. Indeed, precisely this fact led him to claim that for languages with descriptive (as opposed to purely logical or mathematical) terms, 'truth and falsehood are not proper syntactical properties' (216). In languages dealing only with logical and mathematical expressions, we could identify the notions of truth and falsity with analyticity (L-validity) and L-contra-validity, given the resources of the infinite hierarchy of meta-languages noted above. But in languages that contain descriptive terms like 'red' or 'pressure,' there will be sentences that are 'indeterminate' in the sense that their truth cannot be determined by appeal to rules of language. Their truth or falsity will be a function of the empirical facts. Truth and falsity in general, as a result, fell outside the scope of syntax as Carnap conceived it. Unlike languages such as I and II, Carnap did not try to give a complete specification of truth for languages that included descriptive predicates, even through an appeal to the meta-language. Nonetheless, *Syntax* provided a general way of separating the descriptive vocabulary of a language from the logical and mathematical vocabulary. By carving up a given language into its logical and descriptive vocabulary, Carnap thought we could then see exactly which sentences of a given descriptive language could be replaced with syntactic ones (all the philosophical sentences, for example), and which could not (like scientists' observation reports).

2.3 Carnap's Move to Semantics

We have observed that in the *Syntax*, Carnap had assumed that only logical truth, interpreted as provability, and not the truth of synthetic statements, could be given the kind of precise philosophical analysis that Carnap sought. In the mid-1930s, however, Alfred Tarski persuaded Carnap to abandon this limitation:

> When Tarski told me for the first time that he had constructed a definition of truth, I assumed that he had in mind a syntactical definition of logical truth or provability. I was surprised when he said that he meant truth in the customary sense, including contingent factual truth. Since I was thinking only in terms of a syntactical metalanguage, I wondered how it was possible to state the truth-condition for a simple sentence like 'this table is black'. Tarski replied: 'This is simple; the sentence 'this table is black' is true if and only if this table is black'. (Carnap 1963b, 60)

Tarski's 'Semantic Conception of Truth' (Tarski 1944) attempted to provide a rigorous definition of *true sentence*. His definition aimed to 'catch hold of the actual meaning of an old notion,' but to do so in a way which made the notion precise (341). To do so, he introduced two conditions on a satisfactory definition: *formal correctness* and *material adequacy*.

The intuitive idea behind formal correctness is that a definition not be circular. The simplest way to do this is to ensure that, given some concept C that we wish to define, and some defining characteristic ψ, we observe the constraint that ψ not contain the concept C.[19]

Roughly speaking, a definition would be 'materially adequate' if it would select all and only those things which the meaning of the 'old notion' would. In the case of truth, the material adequacy condition required that we find some condition φ such that, for a given sentence S in the object-language L that we are studying, the following equivalence holds (344):

S is true if and only if φ

By itself, a material adequacy condition did not constitute a definition of truth, Tarski explained (ibid.). For unlike a definition, it was not a sentence at all, but a sentence-schema. And even if we substituted the schema in with particular instances, for instance filling in 'S' with a particular sentence and 'φ' with some condition co-extensive with the truth of that property, it would still not be a definition, but only a particular instance of the adequacy condition. Instead of being itself a definition, the adequacy condition places a condition on any proposed definition of 'truth,' one which states that any adequate definition of truth for a language should entail the above biconditionals (for appropriate substitution instances of 'S' and 'φ').

Tarski's application of the idea of material adequacy to a definition of 'true' was both clever and disarmingly simple: make φ the meta-language translation of whatever sentence was expressed by the object-language sentence S. Thus emerged Tarski's famous 'Convention T': a definition of truth in L (an object-language) is materially adequate if it yields, in the meta-language of L, all biconditionals of the form:

'S' is true if and only if p.

Here 'p' would be a sentence of the meta-language which would *translate* whatever was expressed by object-language sentence S, and 'S' would be the name of that object-language sentence in the meta-language (1944, 344). So for example, if we assume: (i) that 'This table is black' is a sentence of object-language L; (ii) that we can 'name' this sentence in the meta-language by putting it in quotation marks; and (iii) that the meta-language contains a translation of this sentence (e.g., with the English sentence 'This table is black'), then we can apply Convention T to produce a meta-language sentence which gives the truth-condition of the object-language sentence 'This table is black':

(B) 'This table is black' is true if and only if this table is black.

It is important to note that the object-language sentence named on the left-hand side of this biconditional is not the same as the meta-language translation of it on the right.[20] Tarski introduced this constraint because he believed that the liar paradox forced us to be careful to keep the object- and meta-languages distinct. The liar paradox is the paradox generated by statements like 'This sentence is false.' This statement, if false, truly reports its falsity, and so is true. And if it is true, then the statement truly reports that it is false, and so it is false. Either way, we have an apparent contradiction. To avoid such contradictions in the object-language brought about by his definition of 'true,' Tarski thought that the object-language should be restricted in such a way that it does not contain its own truth-predicate. This predicate would appear only in the 'essentially richer' meta-language, which formulates materially adequate truth-conditions such as B (351). The object-language thus could not state that its own sentences are true or false. Only a meta-language could predicate truth or falsity of the OL sentences. By including the restriction that truth only be predicable of a sentence from within a richer meta-language, Tarski removed the threat of paradox.[21] Tarski thus used Convention T to show how to provide a semantic definition of truth for formal languages in which 'true' was defined in an essentially richer meta-language in a way that was both formally correct and materially adequate (1944, 353; this latter point required a detailed proof).

How did Tarski's Convention T influence Carnap? In the *Syntax* Carnap did not try to define truth and falsity for a language. He thought that any attempt to do so would generate a liar paradox (Carnap 1937, 214). Indeed, he denied that truth and falsehood are proper syntactic categories (215). While Carnap knew of the importance of Tarski's results, while writing the *Syntax* he did not think that Tarski's Convention T would allow him to give a specification of a language in terms of a notion of truth for that language. However, after his discussion with Tarski, he realized that he could use Convention T to impose a material adequacy condition on a definition of truth for a language. Further, he saw a way to specify a language in terms of a notion of truth that satisfied the adequacy condition, that is, to specify a language by, in part, specifying which sentences in it are true.

Tarski's Convention T also led Carnap to think that his earlier worries that reference (and related notions like designation) were unacceptably 'metaphysical' could now be put aside. For, just as Convention T allowed a specification of an adequacy condition on truth without defining 'true,' likewise an adequacy condition on *designation* could be given for a language without entering into 'metaphysical' worries about the nature of designation and reference. The idea was, again, to use the meta-language. In *Introduction to Semantics*, his first major work after his conversion to Tarski's semantical methods, Carnap put it thus:

> Let us suppose for the moment that we understand a given object language S, say German or [model language] S_3, in such a way that we are able to translate its expressions and sentences into the metalanguage *M* used, say English (including some variables and symbols) . . . Then we will lay down a definition of adequacy for the concept of designation, which is not itself a definition for a term 'Des$_S$' (or 'to designate in S'), but a standard with which to compare proposed definitions. In a similar way, we had before a definition of adequacy for truth, and later we shall have one for L-truth. (Carnap 1942, 53)[22]

The idea here is fairly simple. Carnap provided an analog of Tarski's 'material adequacy' condition for truth that is appropriate for the notion of designation. A definition of *designates* satisfying the adequacy condition could be introduced through meta-language rule formulations such as:

's' is a symbolic translation of 'Walter Scott'

or:

'Bx' − 'x is a biped' (Carnap 1956, 4).

Here the meta-language of English is used to formulate the rules of object-language expressions such as 's' or 'Bx.' Likewise, Carnap began to provide 'truth-rules' for a language, by first setting out some basic truth-conditions for simple sentences like:

The sentence 'Bs' is true if and only if Scott is a biped.

And then adding to these 'rules of truth' for different connectives, such as 'or' ('V'):

Rule of truth for 'V'. A sentence S_i V S_j is true in S_1 if and only if at least one of the two components is true. (Carnap 1956, 5)

And so on for other logical signs; each is specified by means of a meta-language translation of the sentences defined.[23] Carnap extended this approach to the notion of analytic- or L-truth, as we will see below.

The adoption of Tarski's semantical methods, Convention T and its extension to designation, thus allowed Carnap to use the notions of *truth* and *designation* in a way that deflated them of worrisome paradoxical (for 'true') or metaphysical (for 'designates') consequences. Instead of having to bypass these notions, Carnap could use them in the specification of the kinds of formal languages that he was interested in. In particular, he could claim to *explicate* these and other philosophically troublesome notions, that is, provide exact replacements for them without defining them (we discuss explication below). Thus, one motivation for writing the *Syntax*, namely, the clarification of philosophical disputes through the logical analysis of language, remained intact in the new semantic context.

However, the move to Tarski's semantical methods also carried a price for Carnap, for he had to abandon the definition of 'analytic' that he had given us in *Syntax*. This definition had relied, as we saw, on Carnap's general method of separating logical and descriptive vocabulary, and *that* method relied in turn on using the meta-language to distinguish the determinate statements from the others. In the *Syntax*, Carnap did not have any general notion of truth, because of his worries about the liar paradox. He had only notions of L-truth for particular languages. With the transition to semantics, truth and falsehood conditions were now used to specify languages. That is, the specification of a language includes truth-rules which consist of meta-language biconditionals of the form '"S" is true if and only if p.' But now the meta-language gives the truth-conditions of even 'indeterminate' object-language sentences like 'This table is black.' There was no longer a distinction corresponding to the L-determinate/indeterminate distinction in the *Syntax*. And without this distinction, Carnap no longer had a general method of dividing logical vocabulary from descriptive vocabulary, for the *Syntax* method relied on a difference between those sentences which were determinate based on the L- and P-rules, and those which were not.

Carnap recognized this, and in *Introduction to Semantics* admitted that he had to abandon his earlier definition of 'analytic' (cf. 1942, 59). What could he give in its place? Surprisingly, the adoption of Tarski's semantical methods meant that Carnap now faced a new problem in defining analytic truth ('L-truth'). The reason was that for given a sentence S_i in S, a characterization of L-truth

> cannot be taken as a definition of 'L-true in S'. If we expand the phrase 'the truth of S_i follows from the semantical rules of S', we see that it does not belong to the metalanguage M, in which the definition of 'L-true in S' has to be formulated, but to the metametalanguage MM, i.e., the language in which the rules for M are formulated. (1942, 83)

Giving a definition of L-truth in the meta-language M is not possible because the notion of 'following from' (in the above-quoted phrase, for example) is not one defined in M, the meta-language in which we state the rules for S. Rather, 'following from' in M is defined only in *its* meta-language MM. Hence, when we spell the above notion of L-truth out:

> the full formulation of the above phrase is like this: 'The sentence (in M) "S_i is true in S" is an L-implicate in M of the rules of S'. Now, the rules of S are nothing else than a definition of 'true in S'; and if a definition is

incorporated in a system (here in *M*), any sentence which is an L-implicate of it is L-true in that system. Therefore we may reformulate the above phrase in this way: 'the sentence "S_i is true in *S*" is L-true in *M*'. This phrase, however, speaks about *M* and hence belongs to *MM* but not to *M*. Therefore, it cannot be taken as a definiens for 'S_i is L-true in *S*'. It rather expresses a requirement which must be fulfilled for all sentences of *S* if the definition of 'L-true in *S*' is . . . to be accepted as adequate. (83–4)

Saying 'the sentence "S_i is true in *S*" is L-true in M' required, Carnap realized, talk about (not just within) the meta-language M itself. So it could only be uttered in M if M were rich enough to refer to itself. But this was not the kind of reference that Carnap wanted to endorse. While he was happy to employ 'deflationary,' non-metaphysical, notions of reference by requiring only that their definition meet a minimal adequacy condition, he did not want to use them in presenting his own position. For to do so was to risk being asked for a philosophical account of them, which Carnap most certainly wanted to avoid giving. He wanted to stick to 'proposing' various formal languages instead of giving philosophical accounts. So 'the sentence "S_i is true in *S*" is L-true in M' had to be regarded as a sentence in the meta-meta-language MM. Carnap saw that he could give no account of L-truth that didn't assume L-truth in a corresponding meta-language, and so would have to restrict himself to giving an adequacy condition.[24]

The significance of Carnap's shift to the semantic approach is two-fold. First, Carnap could only identify the analytic truths of a language on a case-by-case basis, by either enumerating them, or by enumerating the particular rules of that language which had the analytic sentences as consequences (cf. 1942, 247–8). This fact, in turn, would form the basis for another of Quine's complaints about analyticity, as we shall see in chapter 3. And second, since Carnap appealed to analyticity in some meta-meta-language MM in order to define analyticity for the object-language L, his approach seemed viciously circular. Quine also noticed this problem. These two issues (the 'case-by-case,' non-language-general form of the definition of analyticity, and the circularity problem) are worth noting and separating. In fact, some of the difficulties that Carnap had in making sense of Quine's contrasting positions may be related to this distinction. The reason that the 'case-by-case' objection might have seemed puzzling to Carnap is that a similar objection could have been raised to Carnap's earlier *Syntax* approach, since those notions require appeal to stipulated 'consequence' relations in artificially constructed languages, rather than explain what consequence relations are across arbitrary languages. Yet Quine seems to accept much of the *Syntax* approach. If vicious circularity is the concern, on the other hand, then the semantic approach is more obviously problematic than the *Syntax* approach, since the latter does not appeal to the same notion in a meta-language in order to specify analytic truths in the object-language.

2.4 Explications

Rather than provide us with a general system of syntax, Carnap's post-1937 writings placed an ever-greater emphasis on the idea of giving *explications* of disputed concepts by means of formally precise languages. In *The Logical Foundations of Probability*, he gave a nice summary of this idea:

> *explication* consists in transforming a given more or less inexact concept into an exact one or, rather, in replacing the first by the second. We call the given concept (or the term used for it) the **explicandum**, and the exact concept proposed to take the place of the first (or the term proposed for it) the **explicatum**. The explicandum may belong to everyday language or to a previous stage in the development of scientific language. The explicatum must be given by explicit rules for its use, for example, by a definition which incorporates it into a well-constructed system of scientific either logicomathematical or empirical concepts. (Carnap 1950, 3; a similar description appears in Carnap 1956, 7–9)

Carnap distinguished explications from both the *definition* and the *analysis* of a concept (1950, 7). Unlike the latter two notions, an explication is compatible with the possibility that there be some change of meaning of the explicandum in the explication. In addition, Carnap regarded it as possible and sometimes even desirable to have several distinct explications of the same concept. Unlike analyses or definitions, explications may be aimed at *replacing* their explicanda, at least for scientific or philosophical purposes.

Carnap gave an example of an explication with the case of the replacement of the ordinary concept fish by the scientific concept *piscis* (Carnap 1950, 5–6). The ordinary concept fish is vague and broad. In the past, it might have included, for instance, tadpoles, seals, whales ('Walfische' in German) and possibly other aquatic animals that are not cold-blooded or that do not have gills throughout life. The concept *piscis*, on the other hand, was stipulated to denote just those aquatic animals having the characteristics of being cold-blooded and having gills throughout life. This stipulation was introduced, Carnap noted, because it was more fruitful, within zoology, to classify these animals together. Within a systematic zoology, *piscis* would function as the explicatum of *fish*, the explicandum.

Yet at the same time, the concept *piscis* is at least similar to the concept *fish*. And indeed, similarity is the first of four constraints that Carnap placed on explications:

i   The explicatum should be *similar* to the explicandum.
ii   The explicatum should be given an *exact* specification within a rule-governed system of scientific concepts.
iii The explicatum should be a *fruitful* concept, and in particular allow for the formulation of many universal statements.
iv   The explicatum should be as *simple* as possible. (7–8)

These are broadly 'pragmatic' goals. They don't concern the truth of statements that contain such concepts. Rather, they concern the instrumental benefits of adopting one concept over another. As before, Carnap's goals in philosophy remained modest. At the same time, the vagueness and ambiguity of many philosophical concepts that upset Carnap remained open to clarification through explications. Carnap's semantical methods appeared to offer him even more powerful ways of addressing a wider range of disputed concepts. In particular, semantical explications could allow for definitions of notions like *truth, meaning,* and *designation,* by giving minimal adequacy conditions for such definitions, without any commitment to spurious 'metaphysical' theses.

In Carnap's hands, the full working-out of the explication project continued in a 'formal' fashion similar to the kind of philosophy Carnap had done in the *Syntax,* but with the deletion of general syntax and the addition of semantical methods that we have observed (cf. Carnap 1942, 246ff.). The principle of tolerance, for example, was maintained, with the new proviso that the adequacy conditions on semantical concepts like truth and designation must be met (247). Philosophical activity, for Carnap, was replaced by *language engineering.* The philosopher would identify an area of inquiry in which there was some confusion over, say, whether the truth of a given sentence is purely 'linguistic,' or is answerable by empirical means. Or she would note some vagueness or ambiguity in a disputed concept. Instead of arguing, the philosopher would propose explicating the disputed statements or concepts in a precise language system that she engineered. Such a system might, for example, include accepted statements of physical theory as axioms (for a simple example, see

Carnap 1938, 199f.). Following the principle of tolerance, it would in many cases be a conventional matter whether or not someone accepted the philosopher's proposals. Whether or not they accepted some proposal would, Carnap believed, be decided by broadly pragmatic benefits such as the added fruitfulness, exactness, and simplicity that a good explication could provide, but several comparably fruitful or theoretically attractive options might remain.

Carnap spent much of his later career providing examples of this method of explication by way of linguistic engineering. Most of his examples derived from problematic concepts in the philosophy of science, such as verification, inductive inference, and probability. In *Logical Foundations of Probability*, Carnap treated these concepts as explicanda, and explicated them by way of precise concepts such as confirmation, logical probability, and degree of confirmation. Other examples of explication came more directly from traditional philosophy. Thus in *Meaning and Necessity*, Carnap would use his semantical methods to explicate philosophical ideas such as Frege's distinction between the sense (or 'mode of presentation') and the reference (or denotation) of an expression (cf. Carnap 1956, 35f.). Another set of troublesome notions to receive explication would be those of 'L-concepts' such as logical truth, implication, and our main focus, analyticity.

2.5 Analyticity in a Semantic Setting

In section 2.3, we saw that Carnap's use of Tarski's semantical methods led him to abandon his *Syntax* method for defining 'analytic.' But the notion of analyticity remained central to his explication project, for Carnap still intended to distinguish between those analytic statements which formulate the rules for a language or expressed consequences of those rules, and those synthetic statements whose truth rested upon 'extra-linguistic' matters of fact. The task of explication relied on this distinction, for only by means of it could we clearly separate the 'genuine' questions about reality from the questions about the language (questions which might, mistakenly, appear to be philosophically profound, as we discuss below). So Carnap had to find a new way of characterizing this central distinction. He approached the issue by emphasizing an idea that had first appeared in the *Syntax*, that analytic truths, and the rules of formation and transformation that produce them, are already present in ordinary, natural languages, if only in a vague and unclear way (cf. 1937, 2). This idea allowed Carnap's attitude toward analyticity to resemble his attitude toward other philosophical notions, in the sense that he came to regard analyticity as *itself* a candidate for explication.

As we have noted, explications start with an explicandum, a 'given' concept for which a more precise surrogate would prove pragmatically beneficial. In his later work, Carnap laid more emphasis on the belief that there is an ordinary, informal notion of analyticity waiting to be explicated. He expressed this belief most directly in 'Meaning and Synonymy in Natural Languages' (1956b). There, Carnap considered statements of a natural language like English or German, such as 'A unicorn is a thing similar to a horse, but having only one horn in the middle of the forehead' (1956b, 238). He imagined asking a 'man on the street' whether such sentences are true, and seeing what his response was. Carnap's goal here was to illustrate that there is a pre-philosophical explicandum for 'analytic.' In other words, there is a pre-systematic notion of analyticity in natural languages, and 'if an empirical criterion for analyticity with respect to natural languages were given, then this concept could serve as an explicandum for a reconstruction of a purely semantical concept of A-truth [analytic truth]' (919; cf. also 1956, 8).[25]

In semantics, Carnap thus believed himself to be explicating the notion of analyticity itself. He took it to be a *datum* that there exists in natural languages a genuine (if vague) distinction between those statements that are true in all possible situations, and those which are only true in some situations, and which therefore must be discovered to be true or false. As he had done with concepts such as *probability* (cf. 1950, 23f.), Carnap proposed more than one method of explicating analyticity.

His best-known method used the idea of 'state-descriptions' (1950, 70f.; 1956, 4–15). A state-description is a set of sentences which contains either every atomic sentence of a language, or the negation of that sentence. The idea is that a state-description,

> gives a complete description of a possible state of the universe of individuals with respect to all properties and relations expressed by the predicates of the system. Thus the state-descriptions represent Leibniz' possible worlds or Wittgenstein's possible states of affairs. (1956, 9)

State-descriptions are thus complete descriptions of possibilities; of possible ways the world could be. Carnap used his notion of a state-description to give a definition of L-truth that would satisfy the following adequacy condition:

> *Convention.* A sentence S_i is **L-true** in a semantical system S if and only if S_i is true in S in such a way that its truth can be established on the basis of

the semantical rules of the system S alone, without any reference to (extra-linguistic) facts. (10)

We have seen above that Carnap, like Tarski, distinguished between an adequacy condition and a definition. This 'convention' gives us a condition that any definition of L-truth must meet, but is not itself a definition of L-truth. Nonetheless, Carnap thought that state-descriptions could allow us to define L-truth, and thus analyticity, for a given language S_1:

2-2. *Definition.* A sentence S_i is **L-true** (in S_1) $=_{Df}$ S_i holds in every state-description (in S_1). (ibid.)

We should consider carefully what this definition provides. First, the definition does satisfy the adequacy condition just mentioned. If sentence S_i holds in every state-description in the language S_1, then it holds in whatever state-description describes the way the world is in fact, and so is true without reference to any extra-linguistic facts (about what state-description fits the actual world). Conversely, if there were some state-description D in which S_i were false, then whether S_i were true of the way the world is in fact would depend on 'the facts of the universe' as Carnap puts it (11). But if that were the case, it would not be possible to regard S_i's truth on the basis of semantical rules alone, since one would need to know whether the state-description in which it is false is not actual. So if S_i is true in virtue of the rules of the system S_1, without reference to extra-linguistic facts, then it is true in every state-description. Carnap's definition 2-2 of L-truth thus satisfies his adequacy condition.

The definition also goes beyond the earlier adequacy condition for L-truth that Carnap provided in *Introduction to Semantics*. That condition, as we observed above, failed to constitute a satisfactory definition, since it characterized the sentence 'S_i is true in language S_1' in terms of 'S_i''s being L-true in a meta-meta-language M. This used the notion of L-truth to define the notion of L-truth, as Carnap saw. But definition 2-2 of L-truth does not appear to do this; it specifies L-truth in terms of a seemingly distinct definiens, that of 'holding in every state-description in S_1.'

However, there is an important limitation to observe here. A state-description, Carnap thought, contains every atomic sentence of a language or its negation (1956, 9). So it is a 'complete' description of a possible state of the universe in a given language. This completeness requires that any two atomic sentences be logically independent of each other, in the sense that no class of atomic sentences can logically entail the truth or falsity of another atomic sentence. The reason for this is the following: suppose some atomic sentence i implied another atomic sentence j. Then, 'any state-description containing both i and ~j would be self-contradictory since it would assert both j and ~j' (Carnap 1950, 73). The requirement of the logical independence of atomic sentences must thus be invoked to prevent contradiction. But it imposes a significant constraint on what languages that use definition 2-2 to explicate 'analytic' must be like. For example, such seemingly simple sentences of English as: 'Point p is red at time t' could *not* count as atomic sentences. For this sentence entails the falsity of numerous other sentences like 'Point p is blue at time t.' Hence, simple predicates like 'red' and 'blue,' as well as 'warm,' 'above,' and many others could well be excluded from atomic sentences in Carnap's proposed explication languages. Indeed, it is hard to know what descriptive predicates *could* appear in atomic sentences while meeting Carnap's independence requirement. This limitation would form the basis for an important criticism of definition 2-2, as we shall see (cf. section 3.4).[26]

2.6 Eliminating Metaphysics: Carnap's Final Try

In chapter 1, we observed how Carnap hoped in the *Aufbau* to eliminate metaphysics through the careful application of a meaning criterion for statements. In this chapter, we have seen him explore a different tack using the resources of the *Syntax*, by which 'pseudo-object statements' (including metaphysics) would be replaced with 'quasi-syntactical statements,' sentences which replace apparent talk of properties of language-independent things with syntactical properties of the expressions used to designate them. Yet this tack too had to be abandoned with the move to semantics. We have already seen one of the reasons for this: the replacement procedure required a non-circular account of 'analytic' that semantical methods do not seem to permit.[27] And Carnap could no longer refuse to countenance concepts like *designation, meaning, reference,* or *truth* either, for these now played a crucial role in his new semantic methods. Yet despite these changes, Carnap continued to maintain that metaphysical utterances are void of 'cognitive content.' Why? And what distinguishes a meaningful statement of science from a metaphysical pseudo-statement?

Carnap's most extended discussion of these issues after his move to semantics appeared in his paper 'Empiricism, Semantics, and Ontology' (1956a). Carnap there considered the question of what sort of abstract entities, like propositions, classes, numbers, relations, and so on, empiricists might feel they are committed to (205–6). Empiricists, he said, are uncomfortable with any such 'abstracta,' and in the case of mathematical objects, might comfort themselves with the thought that they can treat mathematics as an uninterpreted formal system (a bit like Language II of *Syntax*, perhaps). But what of the abstract entities used in physics, for example? Empiricists cannot treat all of the language of physics as an uninterpreted formal system, for it refers to entities like forces, space-time-points, relations, and the like. Similar problems arise for semantics, which seems to deal with abstracta like properties and propositions. How should the sober-minded empiricist deal with these?

Carnap's proposal began with his explication project. 'New' entities, such as abstract objects required by modern physics, should first be placed in a new linguistic framework:

> If someone wishes to speak in his language about a new kind of entities, he has to introduce a system of new ways of speaking, subject to new rules; we shall call this procedure the construction of a linguistic *framework* for the new entities in question. (ibid., 206)

Given such a framework, which presumably would be something like an explication language, we can distinguish two kinds of 'questions of existence':

> First, questions of the existence of certain entities of the new kind *within the framework*; we call them *internal questions*; and second, questions concerning the existence or reality *of the system of entities as a whole*, called *external questions*. (ibid.)

Internal questions are formulated with the help of the rules of the linguistic framework. They are answered either by 'purely logical methods,' such as seeing what statements are consequences of the framework rules, or by empirical methods (e.g., using criteria that the framework specifies for applying descriptive expressions).

For example, consider the question of whether there are prime numbers greater than a hundred. One natural response is 'Of course there are. In fact, it follows from the fundamental principles of arithmetic that there are infinitely many such prime numbers.' The respondent might then proceed to give one example of such a prime number, and show via calculations that it is indeed prime. Thus the question would be answerable by 'purely logical methods' since the answer could be determined by looking at the rules governing concepts like 'number,' and drawing consequences from them by calculation.[28]

External questions, on the other hand, are more problematic. These are the kinds of questions that philosophers might be tempted to ask. They are questions like 'Are there numbers?' or 'Are there *really* numbers?' If we were to respond with, 'Of course, didn't you just note that there are prime numbers greater than a hundred?' we would seem to be missing the point of the question. For the philosopher might be taken to be asking whether anything, such as an abstract entity, corresponds to the language used in talking about numbers. Are there really entities like the number 100, or are they merely products of our ways of talking, akin to Santa Claus or Sherlock Holmes?

Carnap considered such external questions to be confused. For him, asking whether there are really numbers is tantamount to asking whether the linguistic framework that governs number talk is 'true' or 'correct.' But such questions are not theoretical questions. To answer such questions we would need some framework, some rules to guide us and to tell us what might count as an answer. For example, we need some rules of *evidence and justification* specifying what is to count as evidence in answering them. We need rules for determining what *kind* of question is being asked; whether it is empirical, logical, or something else. And we need *rules of inference* telling us what we can infer from the evidence we acquire. All such rules are provided by a linguistic framework, and would be expressed as the analytic truths, and consequences of such truths, within that framework. But the philosophical questions in the last paragraph are not intended to be questions *in* a framework (in which case they'd have clear answers), but rather questions *about* a framework. Yet as such, we are left without any clear explanation of what such questions mean or how we are to answer them. Therefore, Carnap proposed,

> Our judgment must be that [philosophers] have not succeeded in giving to the external question and to the possible answers any cognitive content. Unless and until they supply a clear cognitive interpretation, we are justified in our suspicion that their question is a pseudo-question, that is, one disguised in the form of a theoretical question while in fact it is non-theoretical. (1956a, 209)

Carnap thought that if and when the philosopher did provide a 'clear cognitive interpretation' to his questions, they would do so by way of a specification of rules for interpreting the question. That is to say, they would provide a linguistic framework within which the question could be posed. But in doing so, their question would become an *internal* one. It would cease, in other words, to be a question about frameworks, and become instead a question within a framework. But then it would become answerable! It would either be a 'purely logical question' and so answerable by scrutinizing the rules of the framework, or it would be an empirical question, and the framework would tell philosophers (or scientists) what to look for to answer it. Carnap thus neatly inverted what he thought was the expected order of justification (an inversion that betrays a hint of Kant's 'Copernican revolution'). Philosophy does not proceed by first establishing that such-and-such entities are real, and then constructing a language to describe them. Rather, it proceeds by formulating a clear linguistic framework and *then* using it to state that such-and-such entities are real (214).

All of this is a return to the anti-metaphysical ideas voiced in the *Aufbau* and the *Syntax*. What differs is that Carnap can no longer claim to show that 'external questions' are devoid of cognitive content by showing them to be replaceable by, for instance, 'quasi-syntactical' sentences. We have seen the reasons for this above. Instead of replacing philosophical sentences, Carnap now simply made it a condition on a meaningful theoretical question that it be embedded within a framework that provides the conditions for its being asked and answered. Questions about frameworks are then contentless, except in one respect. They might concern 'the practical question of whether or not to accept those linguistic forms.' (218). However, Carnap was careful to block any hint that such 'practical' questions might lead back to metaphysics (in a pejorative sense):

> This acceptance is not in need of a theoretical justification (except with respect to expediency and fruitfulness), because it does not imply a belief or assertion. (ibid.)

One doesn't *assert*, in other words, that such-and-such a linguistic framework is right or true, but only that it's *expedient* or *fruitful* to adopt it. Pragmatic benefits such as these continue to be relevant, just as for the explication project more generally.[29]

We have thus returned to the opening ideas of this chapter. Carnap's long trip through the logical developments of the early twentieth century, Gödel's incompleteness theorems, the rise of alternative systems of arithmetic and logic, the development of meta-theory, and Tarski's semantical methods, did not shake Carnap's fundamental belief that philosophy is best done through the removal of vagueness by way of a wholesale re-engineering of language. As we shall now see, Quine would, in his way, agree with many of Carnap's goals, but turn Carnap's methods in dramatic new directions.

2.7 W. V. Quine: Explication is Elimination

Willard V. Quine (1908–2000) was a student and friend of Carnap's. Quine visited Europe in 1932, met several members of the Vienna Circle, and then followed Carnap to Prague. There, Quine read Carnap's *Logical Syntax of Language* 'as it issued from Ina Carnap's typewriter' (Quine 1986, 12). Quine's early papers reveal him to have been strongly influenced by Carnap. Upon returning to Harvard in 1934, Quine gave a series of lectures articulating and expanding upon the viewpoint of *Logical Syntax*, and worked to secure a visiting fellowship at Harvard for Carnap. Yet as time passed, Quine found himself unable to accept Carnap's reliance on the analytic–synthetic distinction, and in the early 1940s he distanced himself from Carnap's work.[30]

What led to this break with Carnap? The answer must be teased out carefully, for as we shall indicate, Quine shared much of Carnap's philosophical worldview. In particular, he adopted Carnap's idea of the explication of disputed concepts, giving it his own unique emphasis:

> [In] every case of explication: *explication is elimination*. We have, to begin with, an expression that is somehow troublesome. It behaves partly like a term but not enough so, or it is vague in ways that bother us, or it puts kinks in a theory or encourages one or another confusion. But also it serves certain purposes that are not to be abandoned. Then we find a way of accomplishing those same purposes through other channels, using other and less troublesome forms of expression. The old perplexities are resolved. (Quine 1960, 260; see also Quine 1963, 401; 1966, 149)

This idea of explication as elimination worked in the service of Quine's conception of philosophy, and in particular of his proposal to:

> Ponder our talk of physical phenomena as a physical phenomenon, and our scientific imaginings as activities within the world that we imagine. (Quine 1960, 5)

This striking remark reveals a subtle but important difference between Quine and Carnap. For Quine, philosophers begin their investigation from the standpoint of our being embedded in the physical world (that is, the world as it is studied by physical science) *as* physical entities. For Carnap, on the other hand, we don't begin with the assumption of physicalism. Although Carnap expressed a preference for languages employed within the empirical sciences, he saw the philosopher's task as that of clarification. Explication for Carnap serves *this* purpose, while for Quine explication is the elimination of those expressions that preclude an understanding of ourselves as physical phenomena:

> I am a physical object sitting in a physical world. Some of the forces of this physical world impinge on my surface. Light rays strike my retinas; molecules bombard my eardrums and fingertips. I strike back, emanating concentric air waves. These waves take the form of a torrent of discourse about tables, people, molecules, light rays, retinas, air waves, prime numbers, infinite classes, joy and sorrow, good and evil . . . All I am or ever hope to be is due to irritations of my surface, together with such latent tendencies to response as may have been present in my original germ plasm. And all the lore of the ages is due to irritation of the surfaces of a succession of persons, together, again, with the internal conditions of the several individuals. (Quine 1966, 228)

This radical conception of human experience was reflected in Quine's vision of philosophical analysis. That analysis would focus on what is observable about language:

> For instruments of philosophical and scientific clarification and analysis I have looked rather in the foreground, finding sentences . . . and dispositions to assent. Sentences are observable, and dispositions to assent are fairly accessible through observable symptoms . . . I begin with occasion sentences, indeed with observation sentences in my special sense; I thus filter out the complexities, complex almost to the point of white noise, that come of the subjects' concurrent preoccupations and past experience. (Quine 1981, 184–5)

Here too, there is an important difference between the method of philosophy that Quine is suggesting, and that proposed by Carnap. Both refused to engage in traditional ontological and metaphysical debates. Yet Carnap's refusal to do so was motivated by the idea that in the logical analysis of the concepts and sentences of the sciences, questions of justification can play no role.[31] This point emerged out of Carnap's belief that the correctness of a particular inference or alleged confirmation instance could be assessed only relative to the specification of the rules governing inference and confirmation. Antecedent to such a specification, the notion of correctness in cases of inference or confirmation could not be formulated with any precision, and arguably could not be formulated at all. Thus, within Carnap's developed position there was no possibility of appealing to an empirical theory prior to the project of constructing linguistic frameworks for science.[32] But for Quine, we begin with the empirical theory of physics and the language used to express it: light rays, molecules, concentric air waves, utterances, dispositions to assent. Why? Because, Quine asserted:

> Truth is immanent, and there is no higher. We must speak from within a theory, albeit any of various. (1981, 21–2)

Truth is 'immanent' for Quine as 'that which makes sense in naturalism' (Quine 1994, 501). It is immanent in the sense that we must begin our inquiries from a certain position, from within a given theory:

> Neurath has likened science to a boat which, if we are to rebuild it, we must rebuild plank by plank while staying afloat in it. The philosopher and the scientist are in the same boat. If we improve our understanding of ordinary talk of physical things, it will not be by reducing that talk to a more familiar idiom; there is none. It will be by clarifying the connections, causal or otherwise, between ordinary talk of physical things and various further matters ... Our questioning of objects can coherently begin only in relation to a system of theory which is itself predicated on our interim acceptances of objects. (1960, 3–4)

In section 2.2.1, we noted how both Quine and Neurath accused Carnap of using the results of empirical science in his Aufbau project of giving an epistemology for the foundations of science. Carnap thus seemed to have adopted a double standard toward the results of science. This accusation (from Neurath) initiated the long series of revisions to Carnap's philosophy that we have traced. Carnap's efforts throughout these revisions were to avoid assuming the results of empirical science in his work. Yet here, we see Quine use Neurath's analogy to flip Carnap's approach on its head. Instead of avoiding the results of empirical science in doing philosophical work, we should *embrace* those results as embodying a part of our best theory of the world. From Quine's perspective, the double standard that Quine and Neurath had found in the *Aufbau* is avoided not by a retreat away from empirical science and into the formal philosophical methods of Carnapian explication, but by an open embrace of the results that empirical science provides.

We will return in subsequent chapters to the question whether where we begin is best thought of as a prior 'system of theory,' as opposed to a language or linguistic practice or conceptual system that we already understand. There is an important difference, we shall argue, between accepting a theory and understanding a practice or a concept. However, back to the Quinean picture. Given Quine's belief that we must begin from within a system of theory, which theory should we choose? Quine's general answer was: the best we have available, and the best we have available is that provided to us by natural science:

> As naturalistic philosophers we begin our reasoning within the inherited world theory as a going concern. We tentatively believe all of it, but believe also that some unidentified portions are wrong. We try to improve, clarify, and understand the system from within. We are the busy sailors adrift on Neurath's boat. (Quine, quoted in Orenstein 2002, 178)

> Have we now so far lowered our sights as to settle for a relativistic doctrine of truth – rating the statements of each theory as true for that theory, and brooking no higher criticism? Not so. The saving consideration is that we continue to take seriously our own particular aggregate science, our own particular world-theory or loose total fabric of quasi-theories, whatever it may be. (Quine 1960, 24)

Carnap and Quine thus had very different starting points, and accordingly, very different conceptions of how language should be approached. For Carnap, language is a tool to be refined for the clarification of philosophical puzzles and as an aid to science. For Quine it is first and foremost a physical occurrence. This is not to say it is *only* that, for Quine granted that the parts of language that constitute sentences are a certain kind of abstract object – a universal.

> A sentence is not an event of utterance, but a universal: a repeatable sound pattern, or repeatedly approximable norm (1960, 191)

However, in an application of his method of explication, Quine showed how sentences as universals can be analyzed in terms of sets; more specifically, in terms of ordered pairs – the 'paradigm of explication' (1960, 258):

> A sentence is . . . a linguistic form that may be uttered often, once, or never; and its existence is not compromised by failure of utterance. But we must not accept this answer without considering more precisely what these linguistic forms are. If a sentence were taken as the class of its utterances, then all unuttered sentences would reduce to one, viz., the null class; they might as well not exist so far as propositions are concerned, for all distinction lapses among them . . . But there is another way of taking sentences and other linguistic forms that leaves their existence and distinctness uncompromised by failure of utterance. We can take each linguistic form as the *sequence*, in a mathematical sense, of its successive characters or phonemes. A sequence $a_1, a_2, \ldots, a_n$ can be explained as the class of the n pairs $< a_1, 1>, < a_2, 2>, \ldots, < a_n, n>$. We can still take each component character a_i as a class of utterance events, there being here no risk of non-utterance. (1960, 194–5)

In other words, a sentence is a sequence of ordered pairs, which are themselves sets of sets, and the elements of these sets are the sets of utterances of the characters or phonemes that constitute the sentence. Now, these sets of characters or phonemes are composed of concrete objects as elements: particular inscriptions or sounds. Quine could thus speak of unuttered sentences by treating them as sequences of ordered pairs, the elements of which are composed of utterances that are concrete, observable phenomena. Sentences are thus sets of concrete, observable phenomena – thus did Quine propose treating language as a physical phenomenon.

But what of the sets with which sentences are identified? Quine freely granted that they are not concrete, observable phenomena. They are rather abstract entities. So how do they integrate with Quine's treatment of language as a physical phenomenon? Quine's answer is disarming in its straightforward simplicity: sets are admissible elements of our description of the physical world because they are an indispensable part of our best theory of that world:

> Looking at actual science as a going concern, we can fix in a general way on the domain of objects. Physical objects, to begin with – denizens of space-time – clearly belong . . .

But we do need *abstract* objects, if we are to accommodate science as currently constituted. Certain things we want to say in science compel us to admit into the range of values of the variables of quantification not only physical objects but also classes and relations of them; also numbers, functions, and other objects of pure mathematics. For mathematics . . . is best looked upon as an integral part of science, on a par with physics, economics, etc. . . .

Researches in the foundations of mathematics have made it clear that all of mathematics in the above sense can be got down to logic and set theory, and that the objects needed for mathematics in this sense can be got down to a single category, that of *classes* (1966, 229).

Quine here ingeniously combined Frege and Russell's logicism within his own naturalistic perspective: sets (classes) are legitimate theoretical posits because they provide, using Frege and Russell's methods, the best explication of mathematics. And mathematics is an integral part of our 'inherited world theory' of physical science. So while sets are not concrete objects, they are naturalistically acceptable objects. And sentences, construed as sets of physical objects or events, are thus naturalistically acceptable objects too. They are physical phenomena, and should be examined as such.

2.8 Behaviorists Ex Officio

Quine's naturalism led him to take a behavioristic view of many standard philosophical notions such as propositions, meanings, and synonymy:

When a naturalistic philosopher addresses himself to the philosophy of mind, he is apt to talk of language. Meanings are, first and foremost, meanings of language. Language is a social art which we all acquire on the evidence solely of other people's overt behavior under publicly recognizable circumstances. Meanings, therefore, those very models of mental entities, end up as grist for the behaviorist's mill. (Quine 1969, 26)

Quine did not deny that sentences have meanings. Rather, he insisted that sentence meanings be regarded not as further abstract entities, but be strictly connected with overt behavior and the use of sentences:

Both ['Two Dogmas of Empiricism' and] 'The problem of meaning in linguistics' reflected a dim view of the notion of meaning. A discouraging

response from somewhat the fringes of philosophy has been that my problem comes from taking words as bare strings of phonemes rather than
seeing that they are strings with meaning . . . They fail to see that a bare
and identical string of phonemes can *have* a meaning, or several in one or
several languages, through its use by sundry people or peoples. (1980, viii)

So Quine did not insist that there is nothing to language beyond a string
of phonemes, for he acknowledged that those phonemes have a use, and
thereby a meaning. But when Quine spoke of 'use' here, he meant 'use' as
explicated through behavior or dispositions to behave:

[E]ven those who have not embraced behaviorism as a philosophy are
obliged to adhere to behavioristic method within certain scientific pursuits;
and language theory is such a pursuit. A scientist of language is, insofar, a
behaviorist *ex officio*. Whatever the best eventual theory regarding the inner
mechanism of language may turn out to be, it is bound to conform to the
behavioral character of language learning; the dependence of verbal behavior on observation of verbal behavior . . . Thus, though a linguist may still
esteem mental entities philosophically, they are pointless or pernicious in
language theory. (Quine 1970a, 4–5)

It is worth considering what Quine meant by 'verbal behavior.' Quine
clearly did not mean to include 'mental entities,' such as private thoughts
or intentions, which might accompany an utterance, or a response to an
utterance. Such things are not 'overt behavior under publicly recognizable
circumstances.' But what kinds of things would count as such 'overt behavior'? A paradigm case of such a verbal behavior might be an utterance such
as 'rabbit' or 'it is raining,' and accompanying behaviors, such as assent and
dissent behavior. From Quine's naturalistic standpoint, the philosopher or
linguist ought to approach such utterances in a 'causal vein' by trying to
establish by observation and experiment what types of stimulations prompt
behavior such as assent and dissent to given utterances (cf. Quine 1960,
30f.). Quine proposed treating the analysis of language from the standpoint
of translation; more specifically, of *radical* translation: the translation of the
language of a 'hitherto untouched people' with whom we share no historical or cultural connections whatsoever (ibid., 28). This approach to the
analysis of language led Quine to one of his most radical – and controversial – theses, that of the indeterminacy of translation. We will consider
this thesis, and its relationship to analyticity, in chapter 4. The point to be

noticed here is how far Quine was willing to go in regarding the examination of language as an empirical enterprise.

Quine's extensional, and also empirical (behaviorist in particular) approach to meaning spilled over to the notion of synonymy. Two expressions are synonymous, we might think, if they have the same meaning. But then we are stuck with meanings – what are they? Quine was particularly concerned to avoid the hypostasis of meanings as abstract entities, or at least as entities that could not be either accounted for or eliminated through explication in empirical terms.

> It is argued that if we can speak of a sentence as meaningful, or as having meaning, then there must be a meaning that it has, and this meaning will be identical with or distinct from the meaning another sentence has. This is urged without any evident attempt to define synonymy in terms of meaningfulness, nor any notice of the fact that we could as well justify the hypostasis of sakes and unicorns on the basis of the idioms 'for the sake of' and 'is hunting unicorns.' (1960, 206–7)

Rather than hypostasizing meanings, Quine saw in radical translation the possibility of giving an attempted characterization of synonymy from his empirical perspective. Translation is the attempt to capture relations of synonymy between sentences of two languages. By considering this attempt from the standpoint of radical translation, Quine hoped to illustrate what it is to regard synonymy as part of a physical phenomenon:

> We observe a speaker of Kabala, say – to adopt Pike's myth – and we look for correlations or so-called causal connections between the noises he makes and the other things that are observed to be happening. As in any empirical search for correlations or so-called causal connections, we guess at the relevance of one or another feature and then try by further observation, or even experiment, to confirm or refute our hypothesis. (Quine 1953, 60)

Radical translation forces us, Quine thought, to treat meaning and synonymy in an austere way that coheres with our best current theory of the world, that of physical science. It forces us to account for linguistic phenomena such as meaning and synonymy in terms solely of physical and behavioral facts. Quine's aim in introducing the notion of radical interpretation is best regarded, we think, as methodological. He was not attempting to claim that all linguistic communication is a procedure of radical translation, and in fact distinguished radical translation from translation between 'kindred languages,' which takes place against the background of a shared culture (1960, 28). Moreover, he acknowledged that as a general rule we 'translate' our own language 'homophonically' by replacing each string of phonemes with itself (1969, 46). The point of radical translation is rather to illustrate what it is to regard language as a physical phenomenon.

In contrast with meaning, Quine viewed reference as relatively unproblematic, since it is, he thought, an extensional notion, not an intensional one. While reference is relative to a particular background language (Quine 1969, 49), and indeed on one level 'inscrutable' (a point we develop in chapter 4), once we 'acquiesce in our mother tongue,' Quine thought, we can 'take its words at face value' (ibid., 48). Indeed we must acquiesce in our mother tongue, for if we don't at some point take a background language as given, reference determination could never begin. For instance, to say that 'An F is a G' only makes sense 'relative to the uncritical acceptance of "G"' (ibid., 53).

Quine also regarded truth as an unproblematic notion. His reason was simple; he saw in Tarski's Convention T a clear explication of the notion of truth:

> There is surely no impugning the disquotation account; no disputing that 'Snow is white' is true if and only if snow is white. Moreover, it is a full account; it explicates clearly the truth or falsity of every clear sentence. (Quine 1990, 93)

This account presupposed, as Quine saw, that the 'disquoted sentence' on the right-hand side of the biconditional is intelligible (cf. Quine 1994, 498). The intelligibility of a sentence comes from the theory of which it is a part (Quine 1960, 24). This is an idea we will develop further below. The important point here is that from Quine's perspective, Tarski had explicated truth in a way that rendered it unproblematic.

Besides the intelligibility of the disquoted sentence, there is another feature of Tarski's account of truth that Quine did not explicitly remark upon but which will be important to our later discussion. Consider again Tarski's Convention T:

'S' is true if and only if p.

Here, Tarski requires that 'p' is a sentence of the meta-language that (correctly) *translates* whatever was expressed by the object-language sentence 'S.' This requirement of correct translation is crucial for Tarski. If we do not grant that p correctly translates S, or do not grant something similar such as that (to use terms unacceptable to Quine), 'S' *means the same as* 'p', or that 'S' *express the same proposition as* 'p', then some replacement for Tarski's adequacy condition must be found. Quine's view was that the expression including the quotation marks on the left side must be a *name of* the sentence on the right. Whether the associated theory of truth is satisfactory, however, is at best controversial.[33]

2.9 Analyticity in the Crosshairs

On the surface, Quine and Carnap can appear to be articulating compatible, and even complementary, philosophical viewpoints. Both philosophers agreed that philosophy relies, at least in part, upon the project of explication. Both accepted scientific explanation as a model for philosophical work, and rejected traditional philosophical claims to *substantive* a priori knowledge such as Kant had proposed, in favor of empiricism. Both regarded classical metaphysics with deep suspicion, and saw philosophy's role as subservient to physical science as far as explaining the world is concerned.

Yet beneath these surface similarities lay deeply different conceptions of philosophy, a difference which would erupt into one of the most famous disputes of twentieth-century philosophy. From Quine's radically naturalistic perspective, there was no fundamental difference between the pursuit of philosophy and the pursuit of natural science. This is not to say that Quine thought that philosophy and science are the same, for he allowed that philosophical theories may be more *general* than scientific ones (cf. Quine 1966, 210; we return to this issue in chapter 4). But this difference between philosophy and natural science is one of degree of generality, not a difference in *kind*. For Quine, philosophy has no separate domain of inquiry. There is nothing like, say, Kant's idea that philosophy alone investigates the conditions which make synthetic a priori knowledge possible. Nor is there any correlate in Quine to Frege's, Russell's, or the early Wittgenstein's idea that philosophy could investigate the a priori conditions which make thought or language possible.

And finally, Quine came to question the epistemology of science that the Vienna Circle and Carnap had extracted from this tradition. Was the epistemology of science that was developed in Carnap's *Aufbau* itself a part of scientific inquiry? As we saw at the start of this chapter, Carnap's answer to such a question appeared unclear to Quine. On the one hand, Carnap seemed to share with his philosophical predecessors a desire to provide philosophical 'foundations' for science by, for instance, showing us how empirical science can be objective despite its origin in subjective experience. But in doing so, Carnap appeared to use the results of empirical science in using psychological theories to describe the subjective starting point. Quine found this to be confused – if Carnap was interested in psychology, then why not just do that?

Suppose we do stick to the methodology of natural science. Does actual scientific practice require a notion of analytic truth? Does this notion play a role in any scientific theory? Carnap did not claim that it did. So why introduce the notion? Carnap, as we have seen, had an answer to this question: we introduce a notion of analytic truth in order to separate questions about language from questions about the world. The notion of analytic truth thus plays a role in task of philosophy, which is the clarification of linguistic practice, particularly so for the language of science. But notice what this does on Carnap's conception, it introduces a distinctively *philosophical* distinction – the analytic–synthetic distinction – and a distinctively *philosophical* task – the clarification of the languages of science by means of their precise specification. In other words, the notion of analytic truth in Carnap's hands makes philosophy *discontinuous* with natural science, or at the very least, it seemed to do so to Quine.

For reasons that we will elaborate in the next chapter, Quine famously rejected the analytic–synthetic distinction. In the context of the tradition that preceded him, this contributed to Quine's rejection of the very idea that there is a distinctive topic of philosophical inquiry. Philosophy as Quine conceived it has no special status, no special title, and certainly no special authority that it does not share with natural science. By rejecting the analytic–synthetic distinction in all of its main forms, Quine was ultimately rejecting the very idea that there is something unique and distinctive about philosophical inquiry. As we shall see in subsequent chapters, the impact of this rejection on both Quine's philosophy and the development of analytic philosophy would be considerable.

2.10 Chapter Summary

In this chapter, we considered in some detail the views of two of the most important figures of twentieth-century philosophy, Rudolf Carnap and Willard V. Quine. We presented Carnap's philosophical development as a response to difficulties facing the Vienna Circle's account of analytic truth and of scientific knowledge, particularly as this was presented in Carnap's *Aufbau*. We then presented Quine's philosophical development as a radical reaction to Carnap's later philosophy. We noted how the development of each philosopher's position went hand-in-hand with changing conceptions of, and attitudes toward, analyticity.

We began this chapter by considering two philosophical challenges to the Vienna Circle's conception of philosophy, particularly as it had been developed in Carnap's *Aufbau*. One challenge came from Kurt Gödel's discovery of the incompleteness of axiom systems for arithmetic. The second challenge came from the fact that Carnap's *Aufbau* used the results of empirical science to try to show how the objectivity of empirical science is possible. These challenges led to a profound modification of Carnap's later philosophy, which we divided into two stages, the 'syntax' period as defined by his book *The Logical Syntax of Language*, and the second, later 'semantic' period.

In his *Syntax* period, Carnap introduced his 'Principle of Tolerance,' according to which there are no 'morals' in logic. Rather, we can freely construct logical systems and 'languages' consisting of inference rules, axiom systems, and whatever else we please without concern for whether such languages are 'true' or 'correct.' Carnap thought that traditional philosophy could be replaced by the construction and study of such languages, with our goal being that of resolving traditional philosophical disputes by building and agreeing upon formal language systems that embody our preferences through our choice of linguistic rules. These rules and their consequences, Carnap thought, are the analytic truths of the language. They are statements which are true solely in virtue of the linguistic system itself. Carnap thus replaced his earlier efforts to 'reduce' scientific knowledge to subjective experience with the construction of formally precise languages, and thereby avoided the objections of Neurath and others to the *Aufbau*. And as we saw, Carnap responded to Gödel's incompleteness results for a given language by allowing the use of a richer meta-language.

Carnap's move to semantical methods was motivated by his discussions with Alfred Tarski. Tarski helped Carnap to see that he could extend his plan to replace philosophy with precise artificial languages so that Carnap's languages could include precise replacements for philosophically troublesome concepts like reference and truth, and thereby could give a richer account of the truth of synthetic statements as well. The key to doing so was Tarski's 'Convention T,' which Carnap adopted. However, this required Carnap to abandon his earlier account of analytic truth. Instead, he proposed various ways of 'explicating' analyticity using particular artificial languages. Explication is the process of replacing an inexact or vague concept by an exact and precise one, ideally within the context of an artificial, precise language. Carnap's semantic period philosophy identified the explication of philosophically troublesome concepts with precise surrogate concepts as the task of philosophical inquiry. Carnap believed that traditional philosophy could be replaced by the project of explicating philosophically disputed concepts such as 'true,' 'number,' 'reality,' 'designates,' and even 'analytic' itself. In chapter 2, we noted two such attempted explications of 'analytic,' and saw how philosophy would, on Carnap's view, become a kind of linguistic engineering. Properly executed, an explication would show us how what looked like meaningful philosophical statements were in fact the result of confusing 'internal' questions about what is true within a particular language (such as the analytic truths of that language) with 'external' questions about the system of language as a whole. In fact, Carnap argued, only internal questions are genuine, but internal questions do not require philosophers to answer them.

Willard Quine was influenced by Carnap's ideas. We saw that Quine endorsed the general idea of explication, and that he shared Carnap's desire to use formal methods such as Convention T to clarify philosophical disputes. However, Quine modified Carnap's explication idea in a dramatic way. For Quine, explication is elimination; it is the elimination of concepts that prevent us from understanding the world and its contents as physical phenomena. Quine rejected Carnap's 'tolerant' attitude and instead took as his starting point the perspective of natural science, and particularly of physics. Quine held that natural science gives us our best theory of the world, and hence our best starting point for describing it. This starting point also applied to language, which Quine proposed treating as a physical phenomenon fundamentally consisting of strings of marks or series of phonemes. While Quine granted that some abstract objects, such as classes, could be justified by the role they play in theory, his aim was to use logical methods to produce a theory of the world as consistent as possible with our best physical theories.

This aim led Quine to take a behavioristic attitude toward language by approaching it from the standpoint of 'radical translation.' From this standpoint, we regard language in the same way that a linguist would when encountering the language of a hitherto unknown people. We can then resist the temptation to regard language as something other than a physical phenomenon, and so can resist the temptation to 'hypostatize,' or treat as entities, linguistic phenomena such as meanings or synonymies. Quine would thus take a dim view of the notion of analyticity insofar as it was to be explained in such terms. Quine did, however, still allow that notions such as truth could be legitimate, provided that they can be clearly explicated using methods like Tarski's Convention T.

We concluded the chapter by noting that there are many similarities between Quine's and Carnap's works, but that these similarities conceal deep differences in approach. Both accepted the idea of explication, rejected traditional philosophy, and saw the clarification of the scope and language of science as central to philosophy. However, Quine's naturalistic conception of philosophy would leave him at odds with Carnap, for it would require Quine to abandon the notion of analytic truth on which Carnap's artificial languages are based. The resulting dispute forms the topic of our next chapter.

2.11 Further Reading

In this chapter, we noted how two important advances in logical methods, namely Gödel's Incompleteness Theorems and Tarski's semantical methods, informed the philosophy of Carnap and Quine. Both Torkel Franzen's *Gödel's Theorem: An Incomplete Guide to its Use and Abuse* (2005), and *Gödel's Proof* by Ernest Nagel and James Newman (2001) provide helpful introductions to this important result. Alfred Tarski's 'The Semantic Conception of Truth' (1944) is a fairly accessible introduction to one of his most seminal papers. Carnap's 'Empiricism, Semantics, and Ontology' (1956a) is probably the most accessible of Carnap's later papers, and sketches his overall conception of philosophy. Some noteworthy recent scholarship on Carnap's later writings includes A. W. Carus' 'Carnap, Syntax, and Truth' (1999) and Thomas Ricketts' 'Carnap: From Logical Syntax to Semantics' (1996). Both of these papers discuss the development of Carnap's philosophy and its motivation. Arthur Pap's *Semantics and Necessary Truth: An Inquiry into the Foundations of Analytic Philosophy* (1958) remains one of the most detailed discussions of Carnap's philosophy. Pap was critical of Carnap's methods, but for reasons different from those developed by Quine. There are many fine books on Quine. Two more introductory level books are Alex Orenstein's *W. V. Quine* (2002) and Christopher Hookway's *Quine: Language, Experience and Reality* (1988). Orenstein provides a clear and largely sympathetic account of Quine's philosophy, while Hookway's text is somewhat more critical of Quine. Peter Hylton's *Quine* (2007) is a recent and more detailed analysis of Quine's work. Roger

Gibson's (ed.) *The Cambridge Companion to Quine* (2004) is a collection of papers discussing various elements of Quine's view, including his attitude toward science and toward analyticity. Finally, Gary Ebbs' *Rule-Following and Realism* (1997), chapters 4 and 5, gives a very interesting and penetrating analysis of the debate between Carnap and Quine concerning analyticity.

3

ANALYTICITY AND ITS DISCONTENTS

3.1 Introduction and Overview

Quine rejected the analytic–synthetic distinction in nearly all of its traditional forms. We concluded the last chapter with the observation that this rejection was an important element in his vision of naturalized philosophy, and consequently of his re-conception of the business of philosophy. Yet Quine's discontent with the analytic–synthetic distinction took many years to reach its full expression. By Quine's own telling, the seeds of his 'apostasy' appeared in his 1936 paper 'Truth by Convention,' and the arguments of that paper formed the basis of one of Quine's later criticisms of analyticity (Quine 1986, 16). By 1951, after discussions with Carnap, Alonzo Church, Nelson Goodman, Alfred Tarski, and Morton White (Quine 1953a, xii), Quine composed his most direct attack on the notion of analyticity with 'Two Dogmas of Empiricism.' The impact of this 'apostasy' is both widely recognized and yet difficult to explain. Why did so much appear to hang on this one distinction? Why did the dispute over the distinction exercise so many analytic philosophers for so long?

In chapter 2, we attempted to lay the groundwork for a full answer to this question. We focused on Carnap's views in some detail, and noted how his shift from the earlier *Syntax* model of languages to a 'semantic view' put him in a much more precarious position from which to defend the analytic–synthetic distinction. In this chapter we further elaborate how the picture that Carnap provided in his 'semantic' phase appealed to something like an analytic–synthetic distinction in a meta-meta-language in order to distinguish analytic and synthetic statements within a precisely formulated object-language. This appeal to essentially the same notion of analyticity in another language to explain the notion in an object-language naturally led to questions of whether a non-circular, illuminating, or language-general notion of analyticity could be provided. As we shall see in this chapter, Quine argued that neither Carnap nor anyone else had provided a non-circular and general account of analyticity, and that furthermore there were reasons to think that the notion was ultimately unintelligible. Moreover, Quine claimed, actual scientific practice requires no appeal to analytic statements. Other philosophers such as Gilbert Harman would later develop Quine's claim that analyticity did not explain anything, and for this reason even if some coherent account of analyticity could be provided, its introduction would be scientifically and philosophically pointless.

In this chapter, we will survey many of the central arguments of 'Two Dogmas' and Quine's related criticisms of analyticity (most notably those found in Quine 1960, 1963, and 1966a). We will not try to provide a detailed analysis of all of the arguments, but will focus on those that have proven most influential and enduring. Quine's arguments against Carnap's account of the analytic–synthetic distinction must count among these. For Carnap's characterization of the distinction has been counted by many – Quine included – as the most explicit and clearest of any (cf. Quine 1963, 385). So if Carnap's characterization failed, Quine held a rhetorical advantage in the disputes concerning analyticity.

Indeed, if successful, Quine's rejection of analyticity and the corresponding analytic–synthetic distinction would undercut any claim to a distinctively philosophical task or field of inquiry such as Kant, Frege, the Vienna Circle, and Carnap had envisioned. As we have surveyed in the previous chapters, the analytic–synthetic distinction enabled Kant to carve out a distinctive task for philosophy as the analysis of the grounds of synthetic a priori truth. It allowed Frege to distinguish those statements of a 'general logical nature' from all others. It gave the Vienna Circle an account of logical truth and a priori knowledge consistent with their empiricism. And the distinction was central to Carnap's explication project at every stage, supporting as it did Carnap's distinction between language-internal statements and external 'pseudo-statements.'

Hence, Quine's attack on analyticity challenged important portions of the western philosophical tradition. In the cases we have looked at, the

analytic–synthetic distinction was an important element in delimiting the
role of philosophy as something distinct from natural science. So what would
philosophy be without it? Quine was ready with an answer: philosophy
could no longer lay claim to a distinct area or kind of inquiry, and instead
would become 'continuous with' natural science. In other words, to the
extent it succeeds, Quine's rejection of analyticity supports the *naturalism* in
philosophy that he advocated.

Quine never abandoned his broadly naturalistic perspective. He would,
however, later qualify his rejection of analyticity, explicating, in 1960, a
highly attenuated notion of 'stimulus analytic,' and even acknowledging,
in 1973, a notion of analyticity closely akin to that commonly advanced by
other philosophers (Quine 1973, 79; also 1986a, 93–5). But Quine continued to deny that the forms of the notion of analyticity that he found acceptable carried any philosophical significance (cf. 1966, 113, 119–21; 1986a, 95;
Hahn and Schilpp 1986, 138, 236).

There are many strands to the resultant debate, and the dialectic can
become difficult to track. In section 3.2 we will isolate three different questions about analyticity that are not always clearly distinguished, and in section 3.3 we will present Quine's arguments in outline. In section 3.4, we
will consider Quine's claim in 'Two Dogmas' that the notion of analyticity is
not intelligible. Quine pressed this line of argument against Carnap's account
of analyticity in particular, and in section 3.5 we will develop a response to
Quine that was suggested by Carnap. Section 3.6 will examine another line
of response to Quine from philosophers such as Grice and Strawson, as well
as other figures who defended Quine from within a broader, non-Carnapian
dialectical framework. Especially prominent among the defenders of Quine
is Harman, whose writings present a distinctive generalized Quinean strategy for undermining any proposed analytic–synthetic distinction, and
we will consider some of his responses to Grice and Strawson on Quine's
behalf. Then, we will turn in section 3.7 to a second line of attack on analyticity that Quine developed from within his holistic conception of statement
confirmation. We consider some replies to this line of objection in section
3.8. In section 3.9 we look at an argument against analyticity that rested
on Quine's rejection of truth by convention, as this notion was arguably
employed by the Vienna Circle. Finally, we close the chapter with a discussion, in section 3.10, of the changes in Quine's attitude toward analyticity,
and suggest how his later view of analyticity might affect our assessment of
his debate with Carnap. For the most part, we defer consideration of our
own preferred responses to the Quinean arguments against analyticity until

chapter 6, but we nevertheless sketch some of the main arguments set forth by both defenders of and skeptics about analyticity.

3.2 Questioning Analyticity

We have seen (section 2.7) that for Quine, language is best regarded as a physical phenomenon. Sentences are understood as sequences of sets (ordered pairs) which consist of sets of physical events or inscriptions (uttered or inscribed letters or phonemes) paired with numbers. Philosophical analysis of language begins with observable utterances or dispositions, which provide the criteria for the identification and individuation of linguistic phenomena. The notion of *radical translation* provides a methodological or heuristic device to help us to look at language in this naturalistic way. Applied to linguistic features such as meaning and synonymy, this method restricts us to observable physical and behavioral facts. When he turned his attention to properties of sentences, such as analyticity, Quine expected to find the same criteria for them.

> We find it argued that the standard of clarity that I demand for synonymy and analyticity is unreasonably high; yet I ask for no more, after all, than a rough characterization in terms of verbal behavior (1960, 207)

As we shall see below, by requesting that 'analytic' be characterized in terms of publicly observable verbal behavior, Quine raised a serious challenge to the *intelligibility* of the notion as Carnap and other Vienna Circle members had employed it. From Quine's perspective, if philosophers could provide no observable basis for the distinction between analytic and synthetic statements, such as characterizing it in terms of verbal behavior, then the distinction should, by those philosophers' own standards, be abandoned as a metaphysical 'article of faith.'

Before turning to the details of Quine's arguments, three different questions should be distinguished, we think, when discussing analyticity. One is whether there is a coherent concept that plays some central role or roles associated with 'analytic' truths. The answer to this question will, of course, depend upon what criteria of coherence one adopts for a concept, as well as what is emphasized as a central role of analyticity.

Assuming that some coherent notion of analyticity can be found, a second question is whether there are, as a matter of fact, analytic statements, i.e., whether the concept applies to any statements, or has a nonempty extension. The concept *analytic* could be thought to be like the concepts *phlogiston* or *witch*; the fact that these concepts in fact have empty extensions has no bearing whatever on the question of whether these are coherent notions. We discuss this further in chapter 6.

Third, one might question whether distinguishing some statements as 'analytic' is in some interesting sense pragmatically useful. Of course, this question too requires further elaboration. For instance, what is pragmatically useful for an ordinary language user might be very different from what is useful for someone conducting a scientific inquiry or philosophical investigation.

These three questions are often insufficiently carefully distinguished, leading commentators to argue for one answer to one question and think that the arguments apply to one or another of the other two. That there is no intelligible or coherent analytic–synthetic distinction is supposed to follow from the fact that features that do not play pragmatically useful roles within predictive scientific theories do not exist. Such features are supposed to be analogous to phlogiston and witches, and other categories that have been empirically discovered not to exist.

Whatever the ultimate merit of such arguments, they can certainly seem, on their face, to be illicit conflations of distinct issues. If we consider 'phlogiston,' for example, the fact that there is no phlogiston has no bearing whatever on the question whether there is a coherent notion of phlogiston, and similarly for 'witch.' Furthermore, suppose that we stipulate that a 'frenchelor' is a French bachelor. The fact that there might be no pragmatically useful role for the term 'frenchelor,' used in accord with that stipulation, would seem, prima facie, to have absolutely no bearing on either whether there is a coherent notion of frenchelorhood, nor whether there are instances of frenchelorhood. These might seem to be obvious and trivial points, but they are frequently denied by advocates of the Quinean position on the concept of analyticity.[1]

3.3 Quine's 'Two Dogmas of Empiricism'

Many readers will be familiar with Quine's 'Two Dogmas of Empiricism' (1953). The paper is widely taken to be the source of the main arguments against analyticity, and therefore deserves careful attention. We will summarize those arguments that we take to be the most influential and important within 'Two Dogmas' (TD), leaving aside some that seem to us to be of less importance (such as the one asking about the notion 'word').

The argument of TD is divisible into two parts. The first part contains a variety of arguments against the intelligibility of the notion of analyticity. The dubiousness associated with analyticity is taken to attach also to other closely related notions such as that of synonymy, necessity, and essentially all 'intensional' notions. Many of the objections take the form of 'circularity' objections to various proposed accounts of analyticity. The second part of TD argues against the 'second dogma,' which Quine calls 'reductionism.' Reductionism, on Quine's stipulated use, is the doctrine according to which individual statements are associated with their own distinctive classes of observational statements that would count either for or against that individual statement. Against reductionism, Quine developed the doctrine of 'confirmational holism,' according to which language as a whole (the language of science) 'confronts experience as a corporate body,' rather than confronting experience sentence-by-sentence.[2] Toward the end of this second part Quine introduced his famous 'web of belief' metaphor, according to which the collection of sentences that we are disposed to assent to at any time is analogous to a spider's web. A spider's web attaches to its surroundings in such a way that severing a particular attachment might not distinctively affect any particular node within the interior of the web, but nevertheless will affect various tensions between nodes. Similarly, Quine thought, our beliefs are connected to the entirety of experience in such a way that no particular observation (and its associated 'observation sentence'), whether newly assented to or newly dissented from, need affect other more 'theoretical' beliefs that we have. Instead, we adjust our overall belief structures to conform as well as possible to our experiences.

If we abandon the two 'dogmas,' Quine claimed, we blur the distinction between physics and speculative metaphysics, and further render philosophy 'continuous' with the natural sciences. We also 'shift towards pragmatism.' Whether this is a shift in a positive, philosophically helpful or illuminating direction is controversial, although many have followed Quine in making it.

3.4 Objections to the Intelligibility of 'Analytic'

The main argument of the first part of 'Two Dogmas' centers on Quine's concern that analyticity has no coherent or intelligible explanation, and that the corresponding analytic–synthetic distinction is empty. Quine later described 'Two Dogmas' as arguing that analyticity is 'a pseudo-concept which philosophy would be better off without' (1966, 169). We noted above that for Quine, a coherent explanation of 'analytic' must be at least a rough characterization in terms of verbal behavior (1960, 207). Quine had reasons for insisting on such a characterization, including his belief that it best fits with our most developed theory of the world, and his belief that any linguistic feature must be made sense of solely in terms of the evidence concerning people's overt behavior under publicly recognizable circumstances. Nonetheless, Quine knew better than to assume that all other philosophers would share these beliefs. Kant and Frege, for example, would have rejected Quine's wholesale commitment to naturalism and empiricism. Quine could not hope to persuade others to vote against the analytic–synthetic distinction if he simply assumed his naturalistic perspective. Hence the argumentative burden assumed by much of 'Two Dogmas' and related papers was to show that 'analytic' has no philosophically illuminating characterization even from those other philosophers' own standpoints. He began with a rejection of Kant's use of the Principle of Non-Contradiction to characterize 'analytic.'

Appeal to 'self-contradiction' is viciously circular in characterizing 'analytic'

Recall from chapter 1 that one of Kant's criteria of analyticity was the Principle of Non-Contradiction. Kant believed that 'If the judgment is analytic, whether it be negative or affirmative, its truth must always be able to be cognized sufficiently in accordance with the principle of contradiction' (Kant 1965, B190–1). Kant's idea was that analytic claims are those whose denials lead to self-contradiction. But Quine found the notion of 'non-contradiction,' in the broad sense needed to clarify analyticity, to be in need of clarification itself, and described the notions as 'two sides of a single dubious coin.' (Quine 1953, 20) Although Quine didn't develop this objection further in 'Two Dogmas,' it exposes a feature of analyticity that Bolzano had earlier identified. We saw in chapter 1 that Bolzano recognized a distinction between 'logically analytic' propositions such as 'A is A' or 'Every object is either B or not-B,' and propositions that are analytic in a 'broader sense' such as 'A depraved man does not deserve respect.' Of the first kind, Bolzano wrote that, in order to appraise them as analytic, nothing other than logical knowledge is necessary, but that the latter sentence requires a 'wholly different kind of knowledge' since 'concepts alien to logic intrude' (Bolzano 1973, 198). But what are these 'concepts alien to logic'? Bolzano had little to offer by way of explanation. But Quine was right to suggest that more is needed. Consider Kant's example of an analytic truth such as 'A body is extended.' As we saw in chapter 1, the negation of this statement is not by itself a contra-diction, unless we further assume, as Kant did, that the concept extension is somehow 'contained' in the concept of 'body.' But this assumption is not a logical one, at least in any standard sense. It is an 'extra-logical' one.

Quine repeatedly applied this type of 'guilt by association' argument in TD. He rejected the coherence, clarity, or usefulness of the explicandum, analyticity, by rejecting the coherence or clarity of concepts used in the explicans, which in Kant's case is the notion of 'non-contradiction.' Quine did not take these concepts to show how analyticity might be successfully elucidated, but instead cast suspicion on those purportedly elucidating con-cepts themselves. This sort of guilt by association is a rhetorically powerful but potentially risky strategy. It is powerful because it let Quine grant to his opponents their proposed characterizations of analyticity while denying these characterizations any significance. But it is also risky, for two reasons.

One problem with the 'guilt by association' strategy is that in Quine's hands, the attack on the cogency of 'analytic' is part of an argument *against* the idea of 'first philosophy,' or against philosophy as an enterprise apart from natural science. So if Quine's objections to analyticity rest on natural-istic assumptions that are not shared by his opponents, then they might be seen as begging the question against a defender of analyticity who does not accept those assumptions. This is not to say that Quine could not assume that explanations of concepts proffered from within his naturalistic position must be given in naturalistic terms. Certainly they can be and, as we shall see, Quine eventually offers a very austere definition of 'analytic' that he found acceptable in even his behaviorist terms. But Quine cannot, without begging the question against his opponents, insist that explanations of con-cepts from within *their* philosophical positions be given in *his* naturalistic and behavioristic terms.[3]

There is another potential problem with the guilt by association strategy. If this strategy of rejecting 'analytic' by rejecting the concepts used to expli-cate it is pushed too far, it is unclear whether *any* notion whatsoever could be given an account that would not fall prey to similar 'objections.' It is one thing to reject as unhelpful an explanation of a notion in terms of a syn-onymous one. For instance, if someone has absolutely no notion of a pig, it might be unhelpful to explain to them that a pig is a swine. But if one also rejects any explanation of a notion in terms of non-synonymous concepts, then it is unclear that any explanation can take place at all. For it is hard to imagine explaining any notion without making at least some reference to other concepts in the explanation.[4]

There are no meanings, and 'means the same as' or 'synonymous' is in as much need of elucidation as 'analytic'

Perhaps the most common contemporary characterization of an analytic sentence is that it is 'true in virtue of meaning' – a characterization popularized by Ayer and sometimes attributed to the Vienna Circle (cf. Ayer 1946, 78; we develop this characterization in chapter 5). Meaning and synonymy, in this sense, are things that Quine found suspect since they involve, as we noted in chapter 2, the 'hypostasis' of either abstract or mental entities and are not explicable in empirical, behavioral terms.

> For the theory of meaning a conspicuous question is the nature of its objects: what sorts of things are meanings? A felt need for meant entities may derive from an earlier failure to appreciate that meaning and reference are distinct. Once a theory of meaning is sharply separated from a theory of reference, it is a short step to recognizing as the primary business of the theory of meaning simply the synonymy of linguistic forms and the analyticity of statements; meanings themselves, as obscure intermediary entities, may well be abandoned. (1953, 22)

Quine's argument here might best be regarded as appealing to parsimony considerations. What are philosophers trying to account for by appeal to meanings? If the answer is that meanings give an account of synonymy and analyticity then, given that these latter are characterized in terms of meanings, the answer takes us nowhere. Why not then jettison analyticity and synonymy altogether, or at least insofar as these are explained in terms of 'obscure intermediary entities' such as meanings?

As we saw in chapter 2 (section 2.8), 'extensional' notions like truth and reference were acceptable to Quine. However, he argued that they are not sufficient for analyticity. Sameness of extension, in particular, is not sufficient, because the predicates 'creature with a heart' and 'creature with a kidney' might have turned out to have the same extensions, but they clearly do not have the same meanings. In particular, it is not *analytic* that a creature with a heart is a creature with a kidney (1953, 21).

If meanings cannot be appealed to in order to explicate analyticity, then what of synonymy? If synonymy can be appealed to, then we can characterize analytic truths as those that reduce to logical truths via substitution of synonyms for synonyms. For example, consider 'Bachelors are unmarried.' If 'bachelor' is synonymous with 'unmarried man,' then we can transform

'Bachelors are unmarried,' by substituting synonyms for synonyms, turning the sentence into 'Unmarried men are unmarried,' a logical truth. But
this appears circular in a way akin to Kant's appeal to the Principle of Non-
Contradiction. For we can equally well define 'synonymy' in terms of analyticity by saying that two terms are synonymous just in case a statement of
their equivalence is analytic (30–1; cf. also Quine 1963, 402f.). Such characterizations of 'analytic,' Quine caustically remarked, have 'the form, figura-
tively speaking, of a closed circle in space' (1953, 31). Quine acknowledged
that we might build up a language in such a way that many pairs of predicates would agree in their extension, and in this sense be inter-substitutable
salva veritate, that is, in a way that preserves the truth value of the sentence
before and after the substitution. But even in such a case, Quine thought,
there is

> no assurance of cognitive synonymy of the desired type . . . There is no
> assurance here that the extensional agreement of 'bachelor' and 'unmar-
> ried man' rests on meaning rather than merely accidental matters of fact,
> as does the extensional agreement of 'creature with a heart' and 'creature
> with a kidney'. (31)

Logical truth can be nontrivially and extensionally characterized, unlike
analytic truth.

Quine did not argue that logical truth is unacceptable. Logical truth is
not problematic if we presuppose a notion of 'logical vocabulary.' Given
a logical vocabulary, one can define the extension of 'logical truth' as
consisting of sentences that remain true under all uniform substitutions
of non-logical terms for non-logical terms. In the case of 'No unmarried
man is married,' if we take 'un' to be a logical term, or among the logical
vocabulary, then one can see how the example is supposed to work; the
sentence 'remains true under any and all reinterpretations of "man" and
"married"' (ibid., 22). So Quine allowed for what Bolzano called 'logically
analytic' statements (see section 1.3, above). But Quine rejected analyticity
in the broader sense that Bolzano and many other philosophers accepted,
insofar as they use 'concepts alien to logic' (as Bolzano put it) such as synonymy or meaning, as we saw in Kant's use of the logical principle of non-
contradiction.

Appeal to 'definition' fails, since lexical definitions presuppose meaning/synonymy

So far, we have seen Quine reject explicating 'analytic' by appeals to meaning, synonymy, or to other 'dubious' explanans such as the Principle of Non-Contradiction in the broad sense that Kant required. But what about explicating 'analytic' by appealing to definitions? It is part of the definition of 'bachelor,' one might think, that it is true that no bachelor is married, and when we define 'bachelor' in this way, the two expressions 'bachelor' and 'unmarried man' become synonymous. But Quine would have none of this. The lexicographer is an empirical scientist reporting on patterns of usage (Quine 1953, 24). Here again we get a sense of Quine's desire to rely solely on evidence of other people's overt behavior under publicly recognizable circumstances and, on Quine's view, the good lexicographer does just this. But at best, the lexicographer will describe what speakers count as 'definitions' or as 'analytic,' rather than explaining what analyticity is (ibid., 24–6; see also Quine 1966, 111–12).

Quine did grant that there is one sort of synonymy that is at least relatively intelligible. It is:

> the explicitly conventional introduction of novel notations for purposes of sheer abbreviation. Here the definiendum becomes synonymous with the definiens simply because it has been created expressly for the purpose of being synonymous with the definiens. Here we have a really transparent case of synonymy created by definition; would that all species of synonymy were as intelligible. For the rest, definition rests on synonymy rather than explaining it. (ibid., 26)

Similarly, within mathematics and mathematical logic, one can employ 'definitions' of sorts for correlating statements within one domain with statements of another domain. For example, one might introduce definitions of numbers in such a way that a statement within set theory concerning the set containing the empty set (i.e., $\{\{\}\}$) is 'equivalent' to a statement within number theory concerning the number 1, arbitrarily correlating or 'defining' the number 1 as that particular set. Quine thought that

> These rules of translation are the so-called definitions which appear in formalized systems. They are best viewed not as adjuncts to one language but as correlations between two languages, the one part of the other. (ibid.)

In the end, Quine thought that such rules either presuppose pre-existing synonymies, or else they are mere abbreviations. Thus such phenomena do not provide us with a way of making synonymy or analyticity intelligible. We look further at Quine's account of definition below (section 3.9).

> Interchangeability salva veritate *is insufficient, whereas appeal to 'necessity' is illicitly circular, since it appeals to a suspect notion interdefinable with 'analytic.'*

One of the most famous of Quine's attacks on analyticity is a kind of generalization of the circularity charge we saw above. Quine argued that every attempt to explicate this notion must do so with reference to notions such as 'cognitive synonymy' or 'necessity,' yet these notions are in turn definable using 'analytic.' For instance, consider the sentence:

(i) All and only bachelors are unmarried men.

Given a definition of 'bachelor' that includes 'unmarried man,' (i) appears to be analytic by Frege's criterion: it can be derived from a logical law (such as the Law of Identity) plus the definition. That it is analytic thus can be tested by taking the evident truth:

(ii) Necessarily, all and only bachelors are bachelors

and noting that it can be converted *salva veritate* (that is, without changing the truth value) to the sentence:

(iii) Necessarily, all and only bachelors are unmarried men.

To do this, we need only to be given an antecedently meaningful conception of 'necessarily.' Yet, Quine claimed, we regard (iii) as true only insofar as we accept (i) as analytic. But then we have defined 'analyticity' in a way that

> supposes we are working with a language rich enough to contain the adverb 'necessarily', this adverb being so construed as to yield truth when and only when applied to an analytic statement. (1953, 30)

But this leaves the attempted characterization of (i) as analytic in terms of an appeal to necessity with an air of 'hocus pocus,' Quine claimed, for it assumes that we already have a grasp on 'analytic' – the very thing we are trying to characterize. This is an example of Quine's 'guilt by association' strategy. Any plausible definition of analyticity is taken to cast doubt on the concepts used in the definition, rather than to clarify analyticity.

> Carnap's appeal to formal languages is confused, since either the term 'analytic' appears in the specification, or some other equally unintelligible technical term such as 'semantical rule' is introduced without adequate explanation.

To this point, we have seen how Quine rejected as circular any general characterization of 'analytic' in terms of the notions of *necessity* or *synonymy*. However, another line of attack in TD was much more specific, and focused on Carnap's attempt to explicate analyticity for formally precise languages. The next two of Quine's objections thus concern the specific details of Carnap's developed position (during his 'semantic' period) on analyticity which we discussed in chapter 2. In the subsequent section (3.5) we consider responses to Quine, either from Carnap or on his behalf. Readers interested only in the more general issues raised by Quine might thus skip to section 3.6. However, before doing so remember that Quine himself considered Carnap's account of analyticity to be the most explicit and clearest available (cf. Quine 1963, 385). To the extent that Quine's attack on that account was successful, it would constitute a serious blow to any hopes of making a viable case for analyticity.

In chapter 2 we saw that in his semantic period, Carnap had proposed possible explications of 'analytic' by proposing two adequacy conditions, and then a definition that conformed to them (cf. section 2.5 above). The adequacy condition for L-truth (analyticity) Carnap provided in *Introduction to Semantics*. This condition, we'll call it 'AC1,' stated that for a given sentence S_i in a language S:

> AC1: S_i is analytic (L-true) in S iff the sentence 'S_i is true in S' was L-true in M. (Carnap 1942, 61)

AC1 failed to permit a satisfactory definition, since it characterized the sentence 'S_i is true in language S' in terms of 'S_i's being L-true in meta-language M. Since it used the notion of L-truth to define the notion of L-truth, it was at best unclear how a definition conforming to it would not appear viciously circular.

Carnap's better-known explication of 'analytic' used the idea of 'state-descriptions' which are complete descriptions of possible ways the world could be. In section 2.6, we saw how Carnap used state-descriptions to give a definition of L-truth that would satisfy the following broader adequacy condition, which we abbreviate as 'AC2':

> AC2: *Convention.* A sentence S_i is **L-true** in a semantical system S if and only if S_i is true in S in such a way that its truth can be established on the basis of the semantical rules of the system S alone, without any reference to (extra-linguistic) facts. (Carnap 1956, 10)

Recall that this 'convention' gives us a condition that any definition of L-truth must meet, but is also not itself such a definition.

Quine acknowledged that these strategies for characterizing analyticity avoided the trivial circularity present in defining 'analytic' via terms like 'synonymous.' But he found them unsatisfactory nonetheless, and described the entire attempt to separate analytic statements from synthetic ones by appeal to semantical rules as a 'confusion' (1953, 32). Quine quickly identified what was a major weak-spot of Carnap's account:

> The notion of analyticity about which we are worrying is a purported relation between statements and languages; a statement S is said to be *analytic for* a language L, and the problem is to make sense of this relation generally, that is, for variable 'S' and 'L'. (ibid., 33)

As we saw in section 2.2.5, prior to his move to semantical methods, Carnap arguably[5] had just such a language-general definition of 'analytic,' which was the *Syntax* definition of an analytic statement as one which is valid, and which either contains only logical vocabulary, or is such that every sentence obtainable from it by substituting descriptive signs for other descriptive signs is determinate (Carnap 1937, 181–2). But the move to semantical rules required the abandonment of this definition. What then of the semantic-period adequacy conditions and definition that we have just reviewed? Quine rejected them:

> Let us suppose, to begin with, an artificial language L_o whose semantical rules have the form explicitly of a specification, by recursion or otherwise, of all the analytic statements of L_o. The rules tell us that such and such statements, and only those, are the analytic statements of L_o. Now here the difficulty is simply that the rules contain the word 'analytic', which we do not understand! (Quine 1953, 33)

We should not be thrown here by the fact that Carnap used 'L-true' instead of 'analytic' in AC1, AC2 above, for as Quine well knew, 'L-true' was the explicatum for 'analytic.' So what is Quine's complaint? Look again at AC1; it *uses* the notion of L-truth in M, the meta-language for S, to explicate the notion of L-true in S. But Quine didn't understand L-true! For instance, he didn't know 'whether the statement "Everything green is extended" is analytic' (ibid., 32). AC1 tells him that this sentence is analytic in a language if it is analytic in the meta-language. But Quine professed not to know what *that* means either. Quine's problem was that of 'making sense of the idiom "[sentence] S is analytic for [language] L", with variable "S" and "L"' (ibid., 33). But AC1 seems viciously circular; it assumes a prior grasp of 'analytic in M' in order to make sense of analytic for L.

What then of AC2? It does not use the notion of L-true/analytic in a meta-language to explicate analytic. Rather, it says that a sentence of a language is L-true 'if and only if S_i is true in S in such a way that its truth can be established on the basis of the semantical rules of the system S alone, without any reference to (extra-linguistic) facts.' Quine acknowledged that such a rule does not presuppose the 'un-understood word "analytic"' and he granted that there was no difficulty with its use of the word 'true' (ibid., 34). Still,

> there is really no progress. Instead of appealing to an unexplained word 'analytic', we are now appealing to an unexplained phrase 'semantical rule'. Not every true statement which says that the statements of some class are true can count as a semantical rule – otherwise *all* truths would be 'analytic' in the sense of being true according to semantical rules. Semantical rules are distinguishable, apparently, only by the fact of appearing on a page under the heading 'Semantical Rules'; and this heading itself is meaningless. (ibid.)

The key idea here is given in Quine's second sentence. Take any nonempty set of true sentences, which we may form at random. Call that set T. Now there is a statement that says that all the sentences of T are true, namely, the statement 'All the sentences of T are true.' Is this statement supposed to be a semantical rule? If it is, then any true statement could be said to be true according to semantical rules, since the members of T are arbitrarily chosen true sentences. What Carnap wanted is that the truth of analytic sentences be established on the basis of the semantical rules of the system alone. But unless Carnap further constrains the notion of a 'semantical rule,' this condition can be trivially satisfied for any true sentence, in which case Carnap's explication of 'analytic' in terms of semantical rules appears to be trivial.

On the other hand, Carnap cannot explain 'semantical rule' by appeal to analyticity, on pain of circularity. Thus Carnap is in a tenuous position.

> *Carnapian appeal to 'semantical rules' is unhelpful, and appeal to 'state-descriptions' does not help to assimilate analytic truth into logical truth*

Carnap, as we have seen (section 2.5), thought that state-descriptions could go beyond the adequacy conditions above, and further allow us to define L-truth, and thus analyticity, for a language S_1, by means of the following definition D:

> *D: Definition.* A sentence S_i is **L-true** (in S_1) $=_{Df}$ S_i holds in every state-description (in S_1). (Carnap 1956, 10)

D arguably satisfies Carnap's adequacy condition AC2, and it has the further advantage that it characterizes L-truth in terms of a seemingly distinct definiens, that of 'holding in every state-description in S_1.' But there was an important limitation to this definition that we noted above (section 2.5), namely, the need to make the atomic sentences used in giving state-descriptions *logically independent*. We noted that this requirement imposes a significant constraint on what languages that use D to explicate 'analytic' could be like. For example, such seemingly simple sentences of English as 'Point p is red at time t' could *not* count as atomic sentences, and this put potentially serious constraints on what kinds of descriptive predicates could appear in state-descriptions.

In Quine's hands, this limitation proved devastating:

> In recent years Carnap has tended to explain analyticity by appeal to what he calls state-descriptions . . . But note that this version of analyticity serves its purpose only if the atomic statements of the language are, unlike 'John is a bachelor' and 'John is married', mutually independent. Otherwise there would be a state-description which assigned truth to 'John is a bachelor' and to 'John is married', and consequently 'No bachelors are married' would turn out synthetic rather than analytic under the proposed criterion. (23)

If 'No bachelors are married' fails to be analytic on the state-description account, then Carnap has given at best a very weak explication of analyticity, one which limits the class of analytic statements to those logical truths for which, to borrow Bolzano's phrase again, no 'concepts alien to logic' intrude. And yet 'No bachelors are married' does indeed fail to come out as analytic by D, and for just the reason that Quine indicates. 'John is a bachelor' and 'John is married' are not logically incompatible unless we assume that it is analytically true that no bachelor is married. But if we assume this, then we are again assuming that 'the analytic statements of the artificial language are in effect recognized as such from the analyticity of their specified translations in ordinary language,' which means that appeal is made to a notion that Quine finds unintelligible.

In sum, Carnap's proposed adequacy conditions for analyticity are too weak to give Quine what he wanted, namely, a non-circular way of making sense of the idiom 'S is analytic for L,' and a language-general account, with variable 'S' and 'L.' And definitions like D are too weak to capture the intended scope of analyticity. Moreover, any proposed ways of strengthening such definitions seem to smuggle-in a prior understanding of the notion of analyticity in the meta-language, which for Carnap is, as we shall see presently, the ordinary, shared background language. In the end, Quine found the whole attempt to be so much 'bootstrap tugging':

> It might conceivably be protested that an artificial language L (unlike a natural one) is a language in the ordinary sense *plus* a set of explicit semantical rules – the whole constituting, let us say, an ordered pair; and that the semantical rules of L are then specifiable simply as the second component of the pair L. But, by the same token and more simply, we might construe an artificial language L outright as an ordered pair whose second component is the class of its analytic statements; and then the analytic statements of L become specifiable simply as the statements in the second component of L. Or better still, we might just stop tugging at our bootstraps altogether. (1953, 36)

In less technical terms, the motivation behind Quine's objections to Carnap can perhaps be indicated with the following analogy. Suppose that there is a community of 'reddists' who, after seeing how some Bibles put the words of Jesus in red to contrast them from the remainder, decide to write some statements in red. These statements they take to be special in some as-yet-unspecified way. The rule when speaking the reddist language is that one must reproduce red passages in red ink, and one must speak them with a particular distinctive lilt. Red statements are supposed to play important roles within science and philosophy, according to reddists.

Now, imagine that a skeptic comes along and wonders why some statements are written in red. He claims that he does not understand the distinction, in the sense that he does not understand what motivates the distinction and why the supposedly 'red' statements are special or interesting in any way. The most prominent reddist, Scarnap, grants that in ordinary reddist discourse the distinction is indeed vague and indeterminate. But Scarnap notes that he can define artificial reddist languages, and in such languages there are well-defined rules stating which sentences are to be written in red. The skeptic might object, and justifiably so, that nothing has been done toward motivating the reddist distinction in the first place. And it does not help if the reddist appeals to a red/nonred distinction in a meta-language to explain the distinction in the object-language.

This analogy does not perfectly parallel the Quine–Carnap debate over analyticity. However, it is intended to motivate a worry that skeptics about analyticity may have when confronted with attempts at purely formal explications of the notion. Such explications seem beside the main point, even while they may answer concerns as to indeterminacy of the extension of 'analytic.' Indeterminacy or imprecision is one potential worry, but the much deeper and more significant worry is one of the motivation for using the notion of analyticity. What is its explanation and significance? It is unclear whether Carnap grasped this aspect of Quine's objections to the notion of analyticity, but this may have been partly a result of Carnap's very different conception of the role that appeal to analyticity is supposed to play in explication. We return to something like the 'reddist' objection in chapter 6, where we hope to provide an account of why it is philosophically helpful and illuminating to note a distinction akin to the analytic–synthetic distinction, even if analyticity is not an empirical or explanatory notion in the sense that some logical empiricists took it to be.

3.5 Quine's Coherence Arguments: Carnap's Reply

We saw in section 2.9 that Quine and Carnap each had importantly different attitudes toward explication, and toward philosophy generally. We noted that for Quine, our starting point in philosophy is the language of empirical science, and the theories in which that language is embedded. Language, for Quine, is first and foremost a physical phenomenon, whereas Carnap does not begin with the assumption that language is a physical phenomenon, and in fact would not have regarded characterization of language as a physical phenomenon as a starting point for philosophy. Rather, using the language of physical science would, for Carnap, be the expression of one's adoption of a particular language. Describing language in physical terms would be a 'language internal' affair.

Quine's attack on the coherence of the notion of analyticity poses a potentially grave challenge to Carnap's entire philosophical project. We saw in the last chapter that this project – the explication of disputed concepts in formally precise languages – critically relies upon the distinction between analytic and synthetic sentences. Quine was unable to find any clear, observable distinction between such statements. Insofar as Quine was correct, Carnap seems to be in a very bad position. However, recent scholarship has challenged a number of elements of Quine's interpretation of Carnap.[6] We wish here to focus on just one of them, which is whether Carnap needed to provide the empirical, publicly observable criteria for the notion of analyticity used in his explications that Quine demanded (cf. Quine 1960, 207; quoted above).

On the surface, Carnap appeared to try to answer Quine's demand for 'a rough characterization in terms of verbal behavior.' For as we noted in chapter 2 (section 2.5), Carnap seemed to suggest that there is an empirical test for whether a given sentence of a language is regarded by speakers of that language as analytically true. Carnap proposed asking a 'man on the street' whether sentences such as 'A unicorn is a thing similar to a horse, but having only one horn in the middle of the forehead' are true, in an effort to determine the meaning of a word or phrase (1956b, 238), further remarking that 'It seemed rather plausible to me from the beginning that there should be an empirical criterion for the concept of the meaning of a word or a phrase' (1963c, 919–20). This applied to the notion of analyticity as well, with Carnap proposing to test the truth of statements such as 'The sentence S_1 is analytic in language L for person X' by asking X how he would respond to certain questions involving his attitude toward some counterfactual statements involving S_1, and seeing how he replies (Carnap 1963c, 920).[7] Thus, the existence of analytic statements in a language appeared to be put forward by Carnap as empirical conjectures that answer to Quine's request that the notion of analyticity be given some empirical content (cf. also Carnap 1956b, 240).

However, this appearance is misleading. For Carnap's empirical tests were not intended to legitimize 'analytic' by giving it empirical content, but instead were aimed at providing what Carnap called a 'pragmatic,' pre-explication counterpart to the 'semantical' notion of analyticity given in formal explication. Such tests were intended by Carnap to help those such as

Quine to attain a pre-theoretical understanding of 'analytic' akin to Quine's understanding of 'true.' Thus Carnap wrote that

> In the case of truth [Quine] recognizes a sufficiently clear explicandum; i.e., before an explication had been given, the use of this concept had been sufficiently clear, at least for practical purposes. On the other hand, Quine sees no sufficiently clear, pre-systematic concept of analyticity which could be taken as explicandum. If an empirical criterion for analyticity with respect to natural languages were given, then this concept could serve as an explicandum for a reconstruction of a purely semantical concept of [analytic] truth. (Carnap 1963c, 919)

Quine had accepted that the ordinary, pre-theoretical concept of truth can be explicated satisfactorily, but refused to recognize Carnap's explication of the concept of analyticity. Why? Carnap charitably assumed that Quine simply didn't understand what the explicandum of analyticity is. Hence, he provided the 'pre-systematic' test for the attribution of the predicate 'analytic' in a natural language in order to help people like Quine understand what he was trying to explicate. But he didn't regard his explications of 'analytic' as providing this concept with empirical content in the way that an explication of, say, 'iron' might provide this concept with empirically observable conditions for its ascription. Unlike 'iron,' 'analytic' was not intended to be an empirical predicate when explicated in a formally precise language. Explication is a matter of conceptual clarification, Carnap thought, so as a result, when we explicate a concept like 'analytic':

> It follows that, if a solution for a problem of explication is proposed, we cannot decide in an exact way whether it is right or wrong. Strictly speaking, the question whether the solution is right or wrong makes no good sense because there is no clear-cut answer. (Carnap 1950: 4)

Carnapian explications are intended to provide precision and exactitude, so an explication of an already exact concept is pointless. This is not the same goal that Quine had for explications. For Quine, to explicate a concept is to eliminate it and accomplish whatever purposes it served through other channels. But Carnap's perspective was different. He explicitly rejected the idea that any empirical content could even be given to the explicated notion of analyticity, for from his perspective, 'The analytic–synthetic distinction can be drawn always and only with respect to a language system, i.e., a language organized according to explicitly formulated rules' (Carnap 1952, 432). Carnap's goal in giving an explication was to provide greater precision to a vague or unclear concept. From his perspective, the stipulated distinction between analytic and synthetic sentences satisfied that goal. Carnap seemed to think that this is all that one can do, namely, to give a system with precise rules that replaces a system with vague or indeterminate rules. And from his point of view, his earlier account of analyticity in the *Syntax* phase was equally stipulated, and equally precise. Carnap did not consider there to be more to understanding a formally explicated concept, beyond knowing precise rules for its applicability.

Carnap thus believed that his explication project was consistent with appealing to antecedent, but inexact, concepts, including the concepts to be explicated. Furthermore, he believed that such an appeal would invoke the meta-language used to formulate the explication (object-)language, as was implicit in his use of the meta-language in books like *Syntax*, and explicit in a reply to a thesis of E. W. Beth:

> Beth's thesis says that it is essential for the purpose of my theory that the English words of my metalanguage *ML* are sometimes used with a fixed interpretation. I emphatically agree; I would even say that this is the case not only sometimes but practically always. (Carnap 1963a, 930)

Carnap regarded this point as rather trivial; that people use the same language is a condition of giving an explication in the first place, he thought (ibid., 929). So Carnap held that the meta-language used to formulate the object-language in which we might explicate concepts both carried a 'fixed interpretation' and typically included the concepts to be explicated.

In chapter 4 (section 4.6), we will look more closely at Carnap's explication project. Here, however, let us note the relevance of these points to Quine's objection to the use of semantical rules to clarify 'analytic.' Quine's objection, that Carnap's attempt to characterize 'analytic in L' in terms of 'analytic in meta-L' presupposes a prior understanding of 'analytic,' is a point that Carnap would have freely granted. Indeed, what seemed to puzzle Carnap was Quine's repeated insistence that analyticity in natural language was an unclear concept, for Carnap here *agreed* with Quine. Quine's confusion over 'analytic' was exactly what Carnap was attempting to remove with an explication of the notion! (cf. Carnap 1963c, 919). Indeed, from Carnap's perspective Quine's acceptance and endorsement of Tarski's Convention T as an immensely beneficial philosophical explication of truth was further puzzling:

It seemed to me puzzling why for semantical concepts like analyticity or synonymy the definition of a corresponding empirical, pragmatical concept is required, while for other semantical concepts like truth, . . . a requirement of this kind is not made. (ibid., 918)

Given the fact that Quine had accepted Tarski's explication of the latter notion, he ought to have accepted Carnap's explication of the former as well. Carnap could not understand why Quine seemed to require that 'analytic' be explicated as an 'empirical, pragmatical concept' (in Quine's behaviorist sense) but did not make the same requirement for 'true.'

Where does this leave the Quine–Carnap debate? Quine had asked for something, a characterization of analyticity in terms of verbal behavior, that Carnap had refused to provide. Carnap was perfectly willing to provide a 'pre-systematic' test for the explicandum 'analytic' in natural languages, one that gave a 'pragmatical' characterization of the notion in terms of verbal behavior, in order to help Quine see what he is explicating in a language with explicitly formulated rules. But it made no sense from Carnap's perspective to give him more. Quine had accepted Tarski's explication of 'true' in a formally precise way. So why didn't he accept Carnap's explication of 'analytic'?

Yet from Quine's perspective, none of Carnap's attempted explications were helpful. Carnap labeled certain sentences 'analytically true,' but what does this mean? Either the analytic–synthetic distinction corresponds to some publicly observable distinction in the use of language, or it does not. If it does, then why didn't Carnap provide Quine what he is asking for, namely, a behavioral criterion for 'analytic'? And if it does not, then what does it mean to adopt a Carnapian linguistic proposal at all?

A distinction might bring some clarity to this apparent stalemate. We can distinguish two senses in which a concept might be said to have empirical content. In one sense, a concept c might have empirical content, call it 'empirical content$_1$,' if there are at least some sentences such that c's appearance in those sentences has the result that the sentences imply, or make more probable, the truth of certain 'observation sentences' or sentences about the observable world that the sentences would not imply without c. We might say, for instance, that 'blue' is a concept with empirical content$_1$ in this sense, since there is at least one sentence, like 'My tablecloth is blue' which implies certain sentences about the observable world, such as 'My tablecloth reflects light at a wavelength between 440 and 490 nm.' But in another sense, a concept might have empirical content ('empirical content$_2$') if there are publicly observable behaviors which typify a speaker's adoption of that concept, behavioral criteria for saying of someone that they possess the concept. In this sense, 'blue' would have empirical content$_2$ if a competent speaker in possession of the concept exhibited, say, assent behavior when presented with a blue object accompanied by the utterance 'blue.'[8]

It is fairly clear that that when Carnap explicated 'analytic' in formally precise languages, he did not intend it to have empirical content$_1$, for he did not think that sentences which report that a given sentence is analytic would imply, or make more probable, sentences about the empirical world. What about empirical content$_2$? Carnap granted, we have seen, that the *pre-systematic* use of 'analytic' can be given empirical content in this second sense, as with the behavioral tests that he proposes for the acceptance of a sentence like the one about unicorns. But what about the systematic, explicated sense of 'analytic'? What are the behavioral tests for its adoption? If treating a sentence of a formal language as analytic makes no difference in our behavior, then what is the difference between treating it as analytic and *not* doing so?[9] Here was a likely further source of Quine's concern. It is not enough to appeal to the meta-linguistic or pre-systematic usage, especially if Quine professes not to understand these.

This observation does not by itself break the stalemate, although it may help clarify what was at issue for Quine, that the explicated notion of 'analytic' be given empirical content$_2$. We shall suggest below that a later concession by Quine arguably broke the stalemate between him and Carnap. Before turning to this issue, however, there is another, broader line of response to Quine's coherence objection to analyticity that is worth noting.

3.6 Other Responses to the Coherence Objection: Grice and Strawson on Quine

In the last section, we looked in detail at how a defender of Carnap could begin to reply to Quine's objections to Carnap's explication of 'analytic.' But what of Quine's more general objections to the coherence of analyticity that we saw above? An early and important response to Quine's more general coherence objections, and in particular to the 'circle of terms' objection, was given by H. Paul Grice and Peter F. Strawson in their paper 'In Defense of a Dogma' (Grice and Strawson 1956). We will summarize their main arguments here. In addition, we will give responses that some Quineans made or might be expected to make to Grice and Strawson's arguments. As with our overview of 'Two Dogmas,' we will summarize the main replies in italics, and then provide further elaboration and discussion.

There is a strong presumption in favor of the existence of an analytic–synthetic distinction, since people are able to agree to an open-ended class of examples, and there is a 'long and not wholly disreputable' philosophical tradition surrounding the distinction and related ones.

Grice and Strawson's main argument in 'In Defense of a Dogma' was for the conclusion that there is a strong presumption in favor of the existence of some distinction or other that could be called the 'analytic–synthetic' distinction. Furthermore, they argued, Quine's arguments to the effect that the distinction has not been sufficiently clearly elucidated are insufficient to overcome this strong presumption in favor of the distinction. The reason for this presumption is that many philosophers *agree* on a wide range of cases, and these cases are of an open-ended sort. The 'open-endedness' of the class of cases is crucial to avoid the Quinean response that philosophers' agreement is only a result of corruption with respect to some finite class of cases on which most of us are trained:

> [Quine] declares . . . not merely that the distinction is useless or inadequately clarified, but also that it is altogether illusory, that the belief in its existence is a philosophical mistake . . . Evidently such a position of extreme skepticism about a distinction is not in general justified merely by criticisms, however just in themselves, of philosophical attempts to clarify it. (1956, 142)

A similar point, Grice and Strawson noted, can be made of closely related terms and oppositions, such as 'a priori/empirical' and 'necessary/contingent'; all are elements of a 'philosophical tradition which is long and not wholly disreputable.'

Gilbert Harman, in his essay 'Quine on Meaning and Existence I' (Harman 1967), gave a response to this argument on Quine's behalf. Harman thought that so-called 'paradigm case' arguments, like Grice and Strawson were appealing to, are all bad.[10] One example Harman presses is the notion of a *witch*. He notes that there were paradigm cases of witches, and a lengthy tradition of attributing witchhood to people. Further, it is plausible to think that there would be widespread agreement on an open-ended class of cases. Yet we now know that there are no witches. By the same reasoning, one cannot support the existence of instances of analyticity by appeal to such phenomena as agreement on open-ended classes of cases.

On behalf of Grice and Strawson, one might note a distinction between the question of whether the notion of analyticity is *incoherent*, and the question whether it is *uninstantiated*, that is, whether there are any instances of the notion. It is far less clear that the notion of witch is incoherent or unintelligible, even if we now think that there are no witches. In fact, part of the explanation of our rational certainty that there are no witches derives from our grasp of the concept *witch*.

Harman anticipated this type of objection in his defense of Quine. The worry that Harman considered is that on one hand Quine seems to be arguing that the analytic–synthetic distinction is incoherent or unintelligible, and on the other Quine seems to be arguing that there are no analytic truths, that the extension of 'analytic' is empty in fact. This might seem to be an unintelligible combination of claims. Granting that 'analytic' has a definite extension seems to admit that it's at least intelligible, as the witch example illustrates.

Nevertheless, Harman argued that the two claims are intelligible and compatible. On Harman's reconstruction, the central point is that there is no intelligible notion of analyticity such that the extension turns out to be nonempty. According to this reconstruction, there may be notions of 'analytic' that are in principle intelligible or coherent, but when we observe actual linguistic practice, we find that there are no instances. For example, if analytic statements are defined so that they are immune to revision on the basis of empirical data, Quine has shown that there are no such immune statements, according to Harman. We discuss this argument below.

It is 'absurd and senseless' to say that there is no analytic–synthetic distinction.

Grice and Strawson further argued against Quine that 'there is no need to appeal only to tradition; for there is also present practice.' Philosophers, they wrote,

> do to a very considerable extent agree in the applications they make of [concepts like analytic]. They apply the term 'analytic' to more or less the same cases, and hesitate over more or less the same cases. This agreement extends not only to cases which they have been taught so to characterize, but to new cases. In short, 'analytic' and 'synthetic' have a more or less established philosophical use; and this seems to suggest that it is absurd, even senseless, to say that there is no such distinction. (Grice and Strawson 1956, 142)

This fact, Grice and Strawson argued, undercuts Quine's insistence that there is no distinction at all. Rather,

> Quine's thesis might be better represented not as the thesis that there
> is no difference at all marked by the use of these expressions, but as the
> thesis that the nature of, and reasons for, the difference or differences are
> totally misunderstood by those who use the expressions, that the stories
> they tell themselves about the difference are full of illusion. (ibid., 143)

From this perspective, Grice and Strawson can be seen as adopting a position similar to Carnap's. Like Carnap, they were baffled by Quine's claim not to understand the notion of analyticity at all, and suggest that his objections to the notion are better understood as objections to the notion's lack of clarity. They further note that Quine is committed not only to the nonexistence of an analytic–synthetic distinction, but also to the nonexistence of distinctions such as 'means the same as' versus 'does not mean the same as.' But is this really plausible? They argued that it isn't: the fact that synonymy is an ordinary rather than a philosophical or technical distinction makes the strategy of showing that this latter distinction is based on a theoretical mistake enormously *less* plausible (ibid., 145). We frequently talk of synonymy, but

> Is all such talk meaningless? Is all talk of correct translation . . . meaning-
> less? It is hard to believe that it is. But if we do successfully make the effort
> to believe it, we have still harder renunciations before us. (146)

These 'renunciations' include renouncing questions as to what anything means, and finally renouncing the notion of sense. Grice and Strawson found this extremely paradoxical, and an example of a 'philosopher's paradox.' What generates a philosopher's paradox is that instead of attending to ordinary uses of terms, philosophers apply an inappropriate standard and reject a phenomenon (such as meaning or sense) as illusory when it fails to meet that philosophical standard.

> *The circularity worries raised by Quine do not show that analyticity is a particularly prob-*
> *lematic notion, because most other concepts exhibit the same phenomenon, being explicable*
> *only using other expressions conceptually related to or 'interdefinable with' them.*

What is this inappropriate standard? Grice and Strawson challenged the criterion for explanation that certain of Quine's objections seemed to assume. We saw above that Quine regarded efforts to explain analyticity with reference to notions such as 'cognitive synonymy' or 'necessity,' to be circular, since these notions are in turn definable using 'analytic.' For instance, we can equally well define 'synonymy' in terms of analyticity by saying that two terms are synonymous just in case a statement of their equivalence is analytic. But Grice and Strawson objected that Quine had here assumed an unnecessarily strong requirement on the explanation of an expression:

> Quine requires of a satisfactory explanation of an expression that it should take the form of a pretty strict definition but should not make use of any member of a group of inter-definable terms to which the expression belongs. We may well begin to feel that a satisfactory explanation is hard to come by ... It is perhaps dubious whether *any* such explanations can *ever* be given. (Grice and Strawson 1956, 148)

Grice and Strawson's point here is important. If Quine was demanding that a definition of a term *not* be given with reference to other, interdefinable terms, then his demand is much too strong. After all, a definiens *ought* to exhibit some important conceptual relationship to its definiendum; a definition which did not have this feature would simply fail. Yet if Quine's demands on definition are weakened to allow for the use of conceptually related, and thereby frequently interdefinable, terms, then it's unclear why a Frege-style definition of 'analytic,' for example, cannot satisfy it.

A response from the Quinean perspective is possible here however. The Quinean could reply that 'analytic' is a technical term, and thus circularity worries have a special force with respect to it (See, e.g., Harman 1967, 135f.). Grice and Strawson expressed an awareness of an objection of this kind (1956, 150f.). They responded that even if this objection 'has some force,' it does not demonstrate that the philosophical notion should meet Quine's impossibly high standards in order to show that a genuine distinction has been marked out. They gave as an example two imagined exchanges. In one, person X claims that his neighbor's three-year-old child understands Russell's theory of types. In the other, person Y claims that his neighbor's three-year-old child is an adult. There is a difference between the two cases, Grice and Strawson argued, because the first involves a 'natural' impossibility, whereas the second potentially involves a 'logical' impossibility. In the first, natural impossibility case, one might simply disbelieve the claim that a three-year-old understands the theory of types, for three-year-olds simply aren't capable, as a matter of contingent biological fact, of comprehending such things. But we might readily imagine further evidence showing that as a further matter of fact, some three-year-old indeed understands the theory as well as the typical professional philosopher. We would be very surprised, but we might think that X's statement had been literally true after all. In contrast, Grice and Strawson thought that upon further examination, we might come to think that Y is simply confused, or misunderstands the notion 'adult':

> At this stage . . . we shall be inclined to say that we just don't understand what Y is saying, and to suspect that he just does not know the meaning of some of the words he is using. For unless he is prepared to admit that he is using words in a figurative or unusual sense, we shall say, not that we don't believe him, but that his words have *no* sense. (1956, 151)

Once again, however, there is a further line of reply available to the defender of Quine here. Couldn't empirical phenomena force a revision of our 'theory of childhood'? Suppose we have come up with a new theory of human development, for example, and that according to this novel (and empirically successful) theory, some three-year-olds who would not be taken to be 'special' by ordinary standards, count as 'adults' within the theory. In such a case, the term 'adult' would be the 'correct translation' (or at least 'best translation') within the 'folk-theory' of ordinary human behavior, of which our ordinary term 'adult' is a part. So in this imagined case, the false presumption that all three-year-olds are not adults is the result of our being in the grip of a bad empirical theory. In fact, it turns out that some three-year-olds are. It could be, for example, that various social relations are typical and crucial for counting as an 'adult,' and that these are correlated with, say, characteristic hormone levels.

This kind of case needs, we think, to be carefully distinguished from a further case, in which person Y insists, 'No, I don't have any special theory, I just insist that this kid is an adult. You guys can't prove otherwise.' What then? Such a question is worth considering, we think, since Quineans will insist that in the 'new theory' case the 'correct translation' of 'adult' into our current language is the 'homophonic' one which translates 'adult' as 'adult,' and this might be difficult for Quine's opponents to deny, given a clever enough spelling-out of the imagined 'new theory' case. But what should be said if no such new theory is present, and Y simply insists that some three-year-olds are adults? Intuitively, it seems that Y means something different by 'adult' than we do.

Even in this case, Quineans have developed a kind of response. They appeal to the notion of a good or a best translation (see Harman 1967, 143f.). They grant that in some cases we should translate the word 'adult' in the mouth of someone else by 'child' in our mouths, or by some other theoretically definable notion. In the case just alluded to, in which no new theory is appealed to, Quineans might respond that the best sense to make of the situation is that the person Y is employing a different language from ours, in the sense that Y systematically assents to different expressions than ordinary English speakers would under similar empirical circumstances. However, this notion of 'different language' does not require any appeal to meanings in the 'philosophical' sense, they will insist. We simply have two distinct 'webs of belief' (a notion we develop presently), and the term 'adult' plays a role within our web that is distinct from the role (the causal/logical entailment role) played by 'adult' in Y's web.

We mention this further elaboration in order to illuminate how Quineans might take themselves to be able to handle even the most intransigent cases put forth by their opponents. Where possible, some version of the 'novel theory' response is given. Where that is impossible because it is ruled out in the specification of the thought experiment, Quineans can move to the response that the best translation is not homophonic. The availability of this combination of responses helps to bring out why it is so difficult to provide a definitive objection to the Quinean. As long as the Quinean can appeal to the notion of a good or best translation, and ways in which translations can be better or worse, they have at their disposal what appears to be a foolproof 'surrogate' for notions like 'having the same meaning.' They can thereby make sense, they will argue, of situations which we would intuitively characterize as involving different meanings, by appeal to the fact that the 'best translation' of the respective expressions is non-homophonic.

Nevertheless, we shall argue in chapter 6 that Quine's appeal to principles of good translation provides a wedge for reintroducing a distinction akin to the analytic–synthetic distinction. Roughly speaking, our argument will be that once Quineans are forced to appeal to principles of good translation, we can consider whether, say, a stipulated definition or a mathematical statement is ever best translated as an empirical statement. We deny that such translation should plausibly count as a best or even a good one.

How satisfying such an appeal to 'goodness of translations' is as a response to Grice and Strawson's examples can be further questioned. They might claim to be bewildered at what the fuss was about. Is the Quinean arguing that there is no such thing as sameness of meaning, but there is such a thing as similarity of meaning? Or that 'has the same meaning' is vague in many cases?

Quineans are liable to insist that there is an important issue that is brought out by their shift from 'sameness of meaning' to 'degrees of goodness of translation.' The appeal to goodness of translation provides no temptation to posit entities, 'meanings,' shared by intertranslated terms or expressions. All that is needed is that there be principles of better or worse translation, ways of correlating words for some purpose – where that purpose is not, of course, mapping synonymous expressions, or any other assumption of synonymy as taken to explain goodness of translation. However, suppose that Grice and Strawson ask where principles for ascertaining goodness of translation come from. Are they empirically determined? If so, from what data are they determined? What would distinguish principles for evaluating translations from judgments as to what terms mean the same thing? We will return to this important matter in the final chapter (section 6.6).

> Quine's acceptance of abbreviative stipulations does not cohere with the rest of his argument.

A related line of objection from Grice and Strawson concerns Quine's remarks about explicit stipulative definitions for the purposes of abbreviation. We noted above that Quine considers only certain 'extreme' cases of stipulative definitions to be intelligible, namely those in which 'the definiendum becomes synonymous with the definiens simply because it has been expressly created for the purpose of being synonymous with the definiens' (Quine 1953, 26, quoted in full above). Grice and Strawson found this puzzling. They presented the following analogy: imagine someone who grants that they understand what it is for two things to fit each other when the two things are made to fit each other, but who denies understanding of what it is for two things to fit each other in any other case (1956, 153). To say that this person understands what fitting together is scarcely seems intelligible, just as it scarcely seems intelligible that one might understand one of Quine's 'extreme' cases of stipulative definition but not any other definition. Moreover, just what is this relation of synonymy in the 'extreme' case, on Quine's view, and why is just this relation or a close relative intelligible? Grice and Strawson suggested that we should indeed take Quine at face value and reject his conclusions concerning the unintelligibility of synonymy, remarking that 'Synonymy by explicit convention would be unintelligible if the notion of synonymy were not presupposed' (1956, 153).

Grice and Strawson had a further, important line of objection to Quine's attack on analyticity. However, it concerns another line of Quine's argument that we have yet to introduce, namely, Quine's use of the second 'dogma' of empiricism to undercut the idea that there is a useful analytic–synthetic distinction in fact. We will consider this Quinean objection, and Grice and Strawson's response to it, below.

3.7 A Second Dogma of Empiricism

Quine introduced another, broader line of argument in 'Two Dogmas.' The argument concerned the second of the two alleged 'dogmas' of empiricism, namely 'reductionism.' In its more radical form, reductionism is the view that 'Every meaningful statement is held to be translatable into a statement (true or false) about immediate experience' (Quine 1953, 38). Quine gave as an example of this view Hume's Theory of Ideas, according to which every idea must originate in a sense impression. Quine thought that this basic view had been subsequently modified by Frege, Russell, and others to treat not individual ideas or their corresponding terms, but entire sentences as the units of significance. Radical reductionism, Quine wrote, 'conceived now with statements as units, set itself the task of specifying a sense-datum language and showing how to translate the rest of significant discourse, statement by statement, into it. Carnap embarked on this project in the *Aufbau*' (39). Thus on Quine's stipulated use, radical reductionism is the doctrine according to which individual statements are associated with their own distinctive 'evidence profiles,' classes of observational statements that would count either for or against that individual statement.

Quine found radical reductionism objectionable, and we noted one of his objections to it at the start of chapter 2. There we saw that Quine considered Carnap's *Aufbau*-constructions to be 'make-believe' (Quine 1969a, 75–6). In opposition to what Quine perceived to be the failures of reductive empiricism in the work of Carnap, Quine introduced his own doctrine of 'confirmational holism,' according to which language as a whole (the language of science) 'confronts experience as a corporate body,' rather than confronting experience sentence-by-sentence:

> The totality of our so-called knowledge or beliefs, from the most casual matters of geography and history to the profoundest laws of atomic physics or even of pure mathematics and logic, is a man-made fabric which impinges on experience only along the edges. Or, to change the figure, total science is like a field of force whose boundary conditions are experience. (1953, 42)

Quine's holistic metaphor of our knowledge as consisting of a man-made fabric, or field, or as he said later, web of belief, has an interesting similarity to the holism that we saw Carnap develop in chapter 2 (section 2.2.4). Remember that Carnap remarked in the *Logical Syntax* that 'It is, in general, impossible to test even a singular hypothetical sentence . . . *the test applies, at bottom, not to a single hypothesis but to the whole system of physics as a system of hypotheses* (Duhem, Poincaré)' (Carnap 1937, 317). As we saw, Carnap went further and argued that the various types of statements in a physical language – L-rules and their consequences, P-rules and their consequences, and observation statements – differed only in the *degree* to which we hold them, saying that 'No rule of the physical language is definitive; all rules are laid down with the reservation that they may be altered as soon as it seems expedient to do so' (ibid., 318). We concluded from our discussion of Carnap that he held: First, that no statement of a physical language is ever strictly confirmed or refuted; any statement can be preserved, and any statement can be discarded, given suitable changes in the language. Second, that no hypothesis is ever tested in isolation; rather, empirical tests apply to whole systems of hypotheses. And third, that differences between statements such as L-rules, P-rules, and observation reports are differences only in the degree to which they are held true.

Quine adopted these theses, minus the talk of 'L-rules' and 'P-rules,' of course. His holism allowed for all of the three Carnapian conclusions (cf. Quine 1953, 43, 44; 1990, 14–15, 100). Yet ironically, Quine thought that these conclusions constituted an argument *against* the existence of analytic statements, not on the grounds that analyticity is unintelligible, but on the grounds that they are uninstantiated in fact.

Quine placed special emphasis on the *fallibilist* consequences of the holism he found in Carnap and earlier philosophers like Duhem. In chapter 2 section 2.2.4, we gave an example of an empirical hypothesis H about gas behavior deduced from a statement of physical theory P plus supporting observational statements O and mathematics. We noted that, in the event that the observation predicted by H failed to obtain, we could conclude that at least one of the premise-statements (P, O, or even one of the mathematical statements) must be false, but that the bare non-confirmation of H did not tell us which was to be counted as false. All the statements are 'fallible' in the sense that the truth of any one of them can, in principle, be undermined by further evidence. This fallibilism seems to rule out the possibility that any of the statements used in the deduction of H has a special role. In particular, no statement can be said to have empirical content in isolation, and no statement can be said to lack empirical content in virtue of being immune to revision or abandonment in the face of 'recalcitrant experience.' Quine used these ideas to develop his 'field of force' metaphor:

> If this view is right, it is misleading to talk of the empirical content of an individual statement – especially if it is a statement at all remote from the experiential periphery of the field. Furthermore, it becomes folly to seek a boundary between synthetic statements, which hold contingently on experience, and analytic statements, which hold come what may. Any statement can be held true come what may, if we make drastic enough adjustments elsewhere in the system. Even a statement very close to the periphery can be held true in the face of recalcitrant experience by pleading hallucination or by amending certain statements of the kind called logical laws. Conversely, by the same token, no statement is immune to revision. (1953, 43)

The dogma of reductionism must deny these conclusions, Quine thought, since it regards individual ideas (Hume) or statements (Frege, Russell, Carnap) as admitting of confirmation or 'infirmation' (disconfirmation) 'in isolation from its fellows' (ibid., 41). The dogma that holds to the existence of an analytic–synthetic distinction must deny them as well, since it holds that analytic statements are distinguished from all others in virtue of being 'held true come what may.' Quine saw these two dogmas as stemming from a common root:

> The two dogmas are, indeed, at root identical. We lately reflected that in general the truth of statements does obviously depend both upon language and upon extralinguistic fact; and we noted that this obvious circumstance carries in its train, not logically but all too naturally, a feeling that the truth of a statement is somehow analyzable into a linguistic component and a factual component. (ibid.)

In other words, if any statement can be revised in the face of empirical experience, then there is no purely 'linguistic component' of the truth of a statement that is immune to revision. Hence, there are no statements whose truth is solely a consequence of that alleged purely linguistic component, in other words, no analytic statements in fact (see also Quine 1960, 66–72; 1963, 406; 1991, 269).

Quine nonetheless allowed for a notion of 'nearness to the periphery of the web' of our beliefs (1953, 43). Some sentences are more likely to be jettisoned or added to our 'web' on the basis of some small number of experiences, whereas others remain relatively 'entrenched,' very difficult (or very unlikely; we will consider below the question of whether this is a pragmatic difference or a probabilistic one) to revise on the basis of 'recalcitrant experiences':

> Certain statements, though *about* physical objects and not sense experience, seem peculiarly germane to sense experience – and in a selective way: some statements to some experiences, others to others. Such statements, especially germane to particular experiences, I picture as near the periphery. But in this relation of 'germaneness' I envisage nothing more than a loose association reflecting the relative likelihood, in practice, of our choosing one statement rather than another for revision in the event of recalcitrant experience. (ibid.)

This distinction is often invoked by Quine and his defenders who try to explain the apparent 'immunity to revision' shared by mathematical claims. Quineans could insist that this apparent immunity is only a 'pragmatic' phenomenon, that the difficulty in giving up such statements as 'two plus two is four' results in our being *unlikely* or *unwilling* to give them up. It does not show that such statements are in principle unrevisable, and as we have seen above, Quine considered it possible that even the logical laws could be 'amended' if doing so allowed us to preserve the truth of other statements that we, for whatever reason, wished to maintain. Thus, the alleged impossibility of revising or abandoning the laws of logic – laws which Frege regarded as constitutive of what we call 'reasoning' – at most expresses psychological or pragmatic limitations, for Quine. These limitations stemmed from what Quine called the 'maxim of minimum mutilation,' according to which our overall web of belief ought to be disturbed as little as possible. Thus, when we attempt to accommodate a false observation statement implied by a set of statements S:

> We exempt some members of S from this threat [of being rescinded] on determining that the fateful implication still holds without their help. Any purely logical truth is thus exempted, since it adds nothing to what S would logically imply anyway; and sundry irrelevant sentences in S will be exempted as well. Of the remaining members of S, we rescind one that seems most suspect, or least crucial to our overall theory. We heed a maxim of minimum mutilation. If the remaining members of S still

conspire to imply the false categorical, we try rescinding another and restore the first . . .

If asked why he spares mathematics, the scientist will perhaps say that its laws are necessarily true; but I think we have here an explanation, rather, of mathematical necessity itself. It resides in our unstated policy of shielding mathematics by exercising our freedom to reject other beliefs instead. (1990, 14–15)

Quine at times, especially in his last writings, seemed to go even further, and suggested that the statements of logic and mathematics possess no empirical content whatsoever, saying that 'whole infinite class of . . . mathematical truths lacks empirical content' on the grounds that mathematical statements exhibit a 'paucity of primitive predicates, with consequent emphasis on logical construction' (1998, 53–5). Yet even from this perspective, the difference between mathematics and statements with empirical content still could be seen as a matter of degree (of primitive predicates).

Quine's holism had two aspects. It was a semantic holism, in that it held that the meaning of a sentence was determined by the evidence that would count for or against it (see 1969a, 78–9). And it was also a holism of confirmation, one which maintained that the 'unit of empirical significance is the whole of science' (1953, 43). Given his denial of any substantive distinction between the analytic and synthetic, it was natural for Quine to see these two aspects as going hand-in-hand. What a sentence means is derived from the theory of which it is a part, and that theory gives meaning to sentences by, in part, specifying the conditions under which they are verified. There isn't a further source of meaning which might deliver 'truth in virtue of meaning.'

There was an important later qualification that Quine made to his holism, however. In 'Two Dogmas,' the holism advocated was a 'global' one:

The unit of empirical significance is the whole of science . . . Any statement can be held true come what may, if we make drastic enough adjustments . . . Conversely . . . No statement is immune to revision. (1953, 43)

This claim, which as we have seen was anticipated by Carnap, is prima facie implausible. In fact, Quine himself admitted that this global holism was 'needlessly strong' and retracted it in favor of a more modest holism, one which preserved the idea that statements have 'varying degrees of proximity to observation,' while granting that their significance might derive from smaller clusters of related statements (cf. Quine 1991). But Quine did not think that such a qualification affected the force of this objection to analyticity.[11]

3.8 Responses to the Existence Objections to Analyticity

In the final part of 'In Defense of a Dogma,' Grice and Strawson addressed Quine's 'positive' view of statements and their relations to evidence. They considered both the claims that:

(i) No statements are immune to revision; and
(ii) Statements do not admit confirmation or disconfirmation individually (the verificationist form of meaning holism).

One response that they provided to Quine's holistic verificationism was to suggest that, even if holism is true, a cogent account of 'means the same as' can nonetheless be given, and analyticity is thus preserved if construed in terms of synonymy. The adjustment is this: two statements mean the same thing if, no matter what other 'background' statements are accepted, the same evidence counts, to the same degree, for or against both statements relative to the background. Nothing that Quine says in 'Two Dogmas' shows that this adjusted notion of verificationist 'means the same as' is problematic.

Grice and Strawson simply granted claim (i), while nevertheless insisting on a distinction between changing concepts or ceasing to employ concepts on the one hand, and merely giving up a statement as false (while retaining concepts and not changing them). This is similar to what many, including Carnap, have said in response to this 'no-immunity' view of Quine's. Almost anyone would grant that any particular sentence might stop being employed by some group of language users. But this has no bearing, Grice and Strawson insisted, on whether the sentences as used at some time are such that their denials require us to change our meaning assignments to expressions (Grice and Strawson 1956; cf. also Glock 2003, 86f.).

This response to Quine is such an obvious one that it may seem at first to be devastating. So it is worth presenting what we think is a standard Quinean response to this objection. The response is this: there is no intelligible distinction between giving up or changing concepts and giving up or changing theories. Hence, there is no intelligible distinction between changes of meaning in a language and changes of theory. All that the

Quinean must grant is that sometimes speakers no longer assent to some sentence to which they previously assented. Those who claim that what occurred in such a case is a *change of language*, or a *change of concepts*, as opposed to a *change of theory*, presuppose the very analytic–synthetic distinction (or something similar, such as synonymy) that this argument is supposed to be defending!

There is, however, an equally obvious rejoinder to Quine here. It is that denying the theory-change/language-change distinction already pre-supposes that there is no analytic–synthetic distinction (or some similar distinction equal to the task), and so cannot yield a successful argument against that distinction. So we seem left with a standoff.

Here is one way Quineans might attempt to break the standoff to their advantage. Recall the notion of a good translation that Quine used, which we invoked in the context of how a Quinean might best translate the claim that a three-year-old is an adult. Quine, or his defenders, might grant that there is an intuitive difference between cases in which we are inclined to say that a change in meaning has occurred, and cases in which there is a change of theory. But all that they need to appeal to in order to make sense of such intuitions is to observe that in some cases in which dispositions to assent to sentences are different we are inclined, on the basis of 'principles of charity' and other principles of good translation, to translate theoretical terms homophonically. When we do so, we describe such cases as theory changes. But in other cases, we are inclined to translate theoretical terms non-homophonically, and in such cases we will naturally describe what occurred as a 'change of meaning' of the theoretical term. When we com-pare the theories of Newton and Einstein, for example, we find that differ-ent basic theoretical principles are taken to govern 'mass.' Is the change a change in the meanings of 'mass' and other terms, or merely a change in theory? Following their thesis of meaning holism, Quineans will insist that there is no fact of the matter, and that there is a continuum of cases separat-ing any given sort of case, so that the difference is always merely a matter of degree and not a matter of fundamental principle.

Grice and Strawson were aware of such examples. They pointed out that the fact that a distinction is vague, or that there are examples in which it seems indeterminate which of a pair of distinguished concepts applies, does not show that there is no distinction (1956, 145). There may be clear cases of each element of a contrasting pair of concepts, and this is enough to show that some distinction is being captured by the concepts, even if one cannot apply them determinately in all possible cases.

A Quinean might retort that to the extent that we are primarily concerned with statements and concepts within empirical theories, the indeterminate cases are practically ubiquitous, so that there is simply no interesting role for the analytic–synthetic distinction within science. Even if one could imagine a situation in which there is no question whether a statement is 'analytic' or 'immune from empirical disconfirmation,' there are no such situations within the realm of primary concern to Quineans and Carnapians, namely empirical science. Thus even if one might salvage some distinction that applies to some cases, there is no notion that applies in interesting ways within the scientific enterprise, contrary to what Carnap and many others had thought.

Is the claim that there is no interesting application of the distinction within science plausible? This will depend to some extent on one's attitude toward mathematics. Quineans' treatment of mathematics has proven controversial, and we shall return to it in our final chapter (section 6.8).

One point worth emphasizing in this debate is that the Quinean, when giving some far-out scenario under which he says that we would stop assenting to some sentence *s* (where *s* might be 'Bachelors are unmarried men,' for instance), must even by his own lights be limited to considering cases in which a translator would or should translate *s* homophonically between the two languages/theories. As we have noted, Quineans arguably introduce a surrogate for 'means the same,' when they appeal to their notion of a 'good' or 'best' translation scheme. A sentence 'retains its meaning' across changes, on this Quinean picture, just in case the sentence would or should be translated homophonically across the change in language. But given this 'surrogate' for synonymy, it seems as if Quineans can now make sense of what Carnap, Grice and Strawson, and a host of others are worried about when considering the possibility of 'giving up' a statement on the basis of empirical evidence. It is not enough for the Quinean to show that we could give up our practice of asserting sentence *s*, for some purportedly analytic *s*. Rather, in order to address the worries of his opponents, the Quinean must show that the sentence can be given up while retaining its meaning across the change in language, that is, he must show that the sentence is such that it should be translated homophonically across the change. It may be that some sentences might plausibly stop being asserted, but homophonic translatability imposes a further constraint, and narrows the range of sentences which meet it. Whether any of the usual examples (bachelorhood in the face of new marriage laws, etc.) meet this constraint is likely to remain controversial.

Quine's holism, and the rejection of the philosophical significance of the analytic–synthetic distinction which he took it to support, has been subject to a variety of other objections. One such objection (cf. BonJour 1998; Wright 1980) begins by pointing out that Quine's web-of-belief-type metaphors require that there exist connections among the elements (beliefs or sentences) that constitute the web. At the very least, these connections relate the elements by allowing inferences to the effect that one set of statements confirms or disconfirms another statement or set of statements. Quine granted, for instance, that 'a theory is tested by deducing an observational categorical from it and testing the categorical' (1998, 44). At the same time, both Quine's semantic holism and his confirmational holism seem to require that no statements, even the statements of logic which allow for the deduction of observation categoricals from other statements, have any special conceptual or constitutive role in the web. But, the objection goes, inferential connections, and the statements of logic (and perhaps also mathematics) that express them, *do* seem to have a special place in the web of belief. For if we regard the 'test' of an observation categorical as possibly falsifying the very inferential rules in terms of which that categorical was deduced, then it becomes unclear how the web of belief can continue to be affected by experience. This is because those rules must be used in order to make the changes that 'recalcitrant' experience imposes on the belief system in the first place, by initially allowing us to infer what experience may be like according to those beliefs. But this in turn seems to assign the inferential rules a special role after all, one which makes them seemingly immune to the kind of empirical testing that they make possible.

The force of this objection against the Quinean position is debatable. It seems to raise a kind of coherence question for Quine, given that he allows the possibility of falsifying the very rules in terms of which the falsification of hypotheses becomes possible. But remember that Quine need not claim that there is no difference at all between the sentences which express the rules of inference and all others. He need claim only that there is no *conceptual* or *epistemological* difference, no difference that cannot be accommodated in terms of the degree with which we hold a sentence to be true. Quine granted that the laws of logic were learned when we learn a language, and that logical laws, like mathematics, were 'furthest from observation' (1986b, 100). But for him, this is only to say that

> Mathematics and logic are supported by observation only in the indirect
> way that those aspects of natural science are supported by observation;

> namely, as participating in an organized whole which, way up at its empiri-
> cal edges, squares with observation. (ibid.)

This last point, however, can be used to motivate another objection to the consequences that Quine drew from holism, this one suggested by Putnam (1975). As we have just seen, Quine accounts for the apparent non-revisability of seemingly analytic or necessary statements, like the logical rules of inference, by proposing that such statements play a particularly central role in our web of belief. We are very reluctant to abandon them because the 'maxim of minimum mutilation' causes us to tend to avoid the drastic revision of beliefs that their rejection would require. But Putnam points out that Quine's account here appears mistaken for many standard examples of analytic statements. Putnam asked us to consider that, 'In the case of "All bachelors are unmarried," we have the highest degree of linguistic convention and the minimum degree of systematic import' (39). This fact poses a simple but potentially serious problem for the Quinean. On the one hand it seems like 'All bachelors are unmarried' has a very high degree of 'isolation' from empirical counterexamples. But as Putnam notes, it has only minimal 'systematic import' – unlike, say, a law of logic, rejection of this sentence would not seem to require making massive adjustments to our system of beliefs. And even if one were somehow to deny this, patently trivial examples can easily be constructed in support of Putnam's observation, such as our stipulation above that 'A frenchelor is a French bachelor.' Once adopted, this statement seems to be fairly isolated from empirical disconfirmation, even if we grant that Quine's fallibilism applies to it in principle. But the maxim of minimum mutilation fails to explain this feature, for it seems perverse to suggest that abandoning this trivial stipulation would significantly 'mutilate' our system of beliefs. Quine's attempt to account for allegedly analytic or necessary statements in terms of their distance from observation and role in our broader theory thus seems unable to accommodate the apparent evidence-immunity of statements such as these.

Putnam suggested that one call 'analytic' those terms that have only a single criterion for their application (1975, 54f.). Such a definition, he thought, would allow us to include as analytic and 'true by stipulation' statements like 'All bachelors are unmarried,' while nonetheless excluding much more problematic statements of physical theory such as the statement, (M) 'An object's momentum is its rest mass times its velocity.' This latter statement, Putnam argued, ought not to be counted as analytic, and for broadly Quinean reasons. For instance, within the context of Newtonian physics, it might also be true that momentum is conserved in a perfectly elastic collision. But as Putnam pointed out, within the physics of Special Relativity, the constraint that momentum be conserved requires that it *not* be exactly equal to rest mass times velocity. This in turn seems to require that we abandon the claim that M is analytic. Our earlier belief that M is analytic turned out to be fallible — as fallible as Newtonian physics itself proved to be (cf. Putnam 1988, 8–11; Quine 1966a). So Putnam's 'one-criterion' notion of analyticity would exclude many 'classically' analytic statements such as M, while nonetheless granting that the notion of analyticity has instances.[12]

3.9 Analyticity by Convention

One last important attack on 'analytic' can be derived from Quine's 1936 paper 'Truth by Convention' (1966a). There, Quine raised a challenge for the notion that logical laws might be analytic in virtue of being conventional stipulations, a view espoused by some members of the Vienna Circle including Carnap. At the time 'Truth by Convention' was written, Quine had not yet seriously challenged the notion of analyticity, but the opening lines of that paper suggest an emerging dissatisfaction:

> Developments of the past few decades have led to a widespread conviction that logic and mathematics are purely analytic or conventional. It is less the purpose of the present inquiry to question the validity of this contrast than to question its sense (1966a, 70; see also Quine 1963)

Quine's core argument attacked the conventionality of logical truth by attempting to show that any conventionally true logical law must presuppose logic for its application. To see why, consider a candidate logical convention MP (modus ponens) of the form:

> MP: 'Let all results of putting a statement for "p" and a statement for "q" in the expression 'If if p, then q and p, then q' be true.'

In order to apply this convention to particular statements A and B, it seems that one must reason as follows: MP and if MP, then (A and if A, then B imply B); therefore, A and if A, then B imply B. But this requires that one *use* modus ponens in applying the very convention that stipulates the soundness of this inference. The conclusion Quine drew in such cases was that 'if logic is to proceed *mediately* from conventions, logic is needed for inferring logic from the conventions' (Quine 1966a, 97). But if conventions of logic are mediated by the very logic they are supposed to establish, then there is no establishment of logic by convention.

Quine's objection presents a regress problem for any account of analytic truth that attempts to account for such truth in terms of the conventionality of laws of logic, such as, perhaps, those given by Schlick (1985) and Ayer (1946). The challenge it poses may nonetheless be answerable if, for example, the conventionalist holds that the formulation of the convention in language comes after that convention is realized in behavior. Quine himself considered this response:

> It may be held that the verbal formulation of conventions is no more a prerequisite of the adoption of the conventions than the writing of a grammar is a prerequisite of speech; that explicit exposition of conventions is merely one of many important uses of a completed language. So conceived, the conventions no longer involve us in a vicious regress. (1966a, 98)

Quine's remark here seems to grant the conventionalist a line of response; conventions originate in language use prior to their being explicitly formulated in a 'completed language.' However, this remark is also consonant with Quine's rather dim view of the notion of definition that we discussed in section 3.4. We saw that Quine considered the 'the explicitly conventional introduction of novel notations for purposes of sheer abbreviation' to be acceptable, but that this kind of 'discursive' definition simply 'sets forth a pre-existing relation of interchangeability or coextensiveness between notations in already familiar usage' (Quine 1966, 112). By contrast, Quine considered 'legislative definition' to be what 'introduces a notation hitherto unused . . . or used only at variance, so that a convention is wanted to settle the ambiguity.' (ibid.)

Quine did not give examples of this difference, but we might plausibly suppose that defining *chess* by conventionally settling that it is the game played in *this* way (where we indicate some set of rules, or some particular chess games, etc.) is an example of legislative definition, while 'defining' chess by saying that it is the game known in German as 'Schacht' would be an example of discursive definition. This example would accord with what Quine says next about the two cases:

> It is only legislative definition, and not discursive definition or discursive postulation, that makes a conventional contribution to the truth of

sentences. Legislative postulation, finally, affords truth by convention unalloyed. (1966, 112)

It is not up to us, assuming that we wish to conform to pre-existing and familiar usage, to decide whether 'chess' and 'Schacht' are expressions for the same game. Yet the legislative postulation that 'chess' refers to this game did conventionally 'make it true' that chess is the game played in such-and-such a way. Quine, however, went on to claim that this distinction comes to nothing:

> Definitions so used can be either legislative or discursive in their inception. But this distinction is in practice left unindicated, and wisely; for it is a distinction only between particular acts of definition, and not germane to the definition as an enduring channel of intertranslation.
>
> The distinction between the legislative and the discursive refers thus to the act, and not to its enduring consequence, in the case of postulation as in the case of definition. This is because we are taking the notion of truth by convention fairly literally and simple mindedly, for lack of an intelligible alternative. So conceived, conventionality is a passing trait, significant at the moving front of science, but useless in classifying the sentences behind the lines. (1966, 112)

Since Quine saw no 'enduring consequence' of a legislative definition, he thought that the distinction is useless for characterizing anything more than the act of definition. This picture is reinforced by Quine's describing both forms of definition as 'postulates.'

Some further scrutiny of Quine's claims is advisable here, however. Consider first Quine's assimilation of both kinds of definition under the category of 'postulates.' That we can so categorize them may seem to work to Quine's advantage, but we observe a distinction in ordinary usage among types of postulates. We say quite naturally that one can *postulate* a rule by, for instance, stipulating that r is to be a rule governing some activity *A*. Alternatively, we can also *postulate* a hypothesis: for instance, someone might postulate the existence of the Higgs Boson. Here we have not 'stipulated a truth' in even a weak sense; we must find out empirically whether this entity exists.

Now it is open to Quine to insist that this feature of ordinary usage amounts to no meaningful distinction in practice, 'behind the lines' of initial usage. But is this correct? Is there really no lasting difference between *stipulating* that such-and-such is to hold, and *hypothesizing* that such-and-such does hold? We think not. Consider a sentence such as the following:

B. The bishop in chess moves along the diagonals.

This sentence obviously presupposes certain facts and practices in order to be understood, such as what a game is, what a piece in a game is, what it is to move something diagonally, and other things. Within this framework, B might plausibly be said to have a canonical reading according to which it:

(i)   formulates a rule of chess.

But this sentence could also be used in other ways, for instance:

(ii) to express an inductive generalization regarding the movements of some object called the 'bishop in chess,'
(iii) to formulate an empirical hypothesis about a particular activity, or even,
(iv) to express an indirect command to someone.

That B has these different usages is something that continues to be relevant to its application even *after* its inception. For instance, someone who didn't grasp the difference between (i) and (iii) would not be in a position to correct a player who moved the bishop along the rank and file. For if B is treated merely as a hypothesis, in the second sense of 'postulate' just noted, then a move of the bishop along the rank and file is not *incorrect*, but rather simply a falsification of the hypothesis itself. Yet in actual practice, someone who moves the bishop along the rank and file in the course of a chess game has made an error. They have not simply falsified a hypothesis, or refuted an empirical generalization of the type expressed by use (ii).

   From Quine's perspective, the distinction between following a rule and merely engaging in some regular pattern of behavior comes to very little. Of course ignoring this distinction is itself a loss only if there are independent reasons for making it. But there are, for there is an intelligible distinction between a mere behavioral regularity and following a rule. Waves lapping upon the shore at an even interval, a clock ticking every second, and any number of similar regularities are not rightly characterized as instances of rule-following, even though they will always *conform* to some specifiable rule. A typical clock, for instance, conforms with the rule expressed by the imperative 'Tick every second.' But it hardly seems right to say it *follows* this rule. Quine might, of course, reject the claim that there is any distinction to be made between conforming to a rule and actually following it. But in that case, he seems saddled with the implausible conclusion that nothing is an actual instance of rule-following or, alternatively and equally implausibly, that every regularity is an instance of rule-following. Yet on the other hand, if Quine can acknowledge that this distinction can be captured behavioristically, then he has no basis for resisting it.

In chapter 6, we shall propose a positive account of analyticity which allows that certain kinds of explicit stipulations are a species of analytic truth. We shall further extend our positive account to include mathematical truths as a kind of 'mathematical stipulation.' Our account will expand on the idea that there may be rules which connect a sentence with how it is to be used, and that, contra Quine, these rules can have the 'enduring consequence' of guiding the use of the sentence long after it is first introduced. There, in section 6.6, we shall argue in more detail that, contrary to Quine, there is a substantive distinction between stipulating that something is true, and postulating its truth in Quine's sense.

3.10 Quine's Developed Attitude toward Analyticity

Quine's philosophy evolved after writing 'Two Dogmas.' One early evolution was Quine's characterization of 'stimulus-analytic' sentences in *Word and Object* (1960). A stimulus-analytic sentence is one which a subject would assent to after every relevant stimulation, a definition Quine extended to a community of language speakers by saying that a 'socially stimulus analytic' sentence is stimulus analytic for almost everybody (1960, 55, 66). Since assent is a behavioral or dispositional trait, stimulus analyticity is a notion Quine regarded as suitably behavioristically based, and it constitutes his explication of the idea that analytic statements are those 'held true come what may' (ibid., 66). However, the notion is too weak, Quine argued, to be more than a 'behaviorist ersatz' of the philosophical notion of analyticity, for even in the social sense, stimulus analyticity would 'apply as well to "There have been black dogs" as to "2 + 2 = 4" and "No bachelor is married"' (ibid.).

However, Quine's subsequent treatment of analyticity allowed for a still stronger notion. We close this chapter by noting it, and observing how it could be construed as strengthening Carnap's position in his debate with Quine over analyticity.

In *The Roots of Reference*, Quine proposed a broader account of analyticity in terms of 'the learning process.' He continued to object that 'analytic' had been given 'no empirical meaning.' But he allowed that 'We learn to understand and use and create declarative sentences only by learning conditions for the truth of such sentences,' and that it would thus

> seem reasonable, invoking the controversial notion of analyticity, to say that by this account the sentence 'A dog is an animal' is analytic; for to learn even to understand it is to learn that it is true. (1973, 78–9)

Quine further granted that this characterization might succeed in 'drawing a rough line between sentences like "No bachelor is married" or "We are our cousins' cousins", which are ordinarily said to be analytic, and sentences that are not' (ibid., 80), adding that analytic sentences in the present sense are 'a subclass of [stimulus-analytic] sentences, and a somewhat nearer approximation to the analytic sentences uncritically so-called' (ibid.). Quine repeated this account in a later work, *Pursuit of Truth* (1990, 55–6).

Quine continued to insist, however, that the notion of analyticity was objectionable. One line of objection derived from the 'indeterminacy of translation' thesis which could, at least indirectly, be invoked against analyticity. We consider this line of objection in the next chapter (sections 4.3–4.4). Another line objected to analyticity insofar as it lacked explanatory value:

> The importance of analyticity for epistemology lapses, be it noted, in the light of holism. Carnap invoked analyticity to explain how mathematics could make sense despite its lack of empirical content; but holism depicts mathematics, when applied, as already participating in the empirical content of testable sets of sentences. (Quine 1990, 55; cf. Quine 1986c, 207)

Quine's objections thus increasingly focused on the claim that analyticity lacks explanatory value. This represented a shift away from the objection that there is no coherent notion of analyticity, in favor of a different objection that analyticity is *unimportant* for epistemological purposes. For with Quine's concession that there is a coherent notion of analyticity that is narrower than that of stimulus analyticity, and which can be explicated in terms of our learning of the meanings of words, his intelligibility arguments against analyticity lost much of their force. In particular, Quine's apparent concession offered Carnap the possibility of characterizing analyticity in a way that Quine himself would grant is at least coherent, even if 'unimportant,' and left the door open to a defender of Carnap to reply that the notion of analyticity as invoked in his explication project is at least one that can be coherently introduced. A defender of Carnap could point out that it then is, or properly ought to be, a pragmatic, even empirical matter of whether a philosophical explication that employs the notion of analyticity is better than one that does not.[13] Once Quine had provided behavioral criteria for a 'somewhat nearer approximation to the analytic sentences uncritically so-called,' Carnap could simply point out that by Quine's own lights the question of which type of philosophical explication project, Quine's or Carnap's, best satisfies our pragmatic ends ought to be a pragmatic question to be decided by testing and observation, not one to be answered a priori by Quine.

3.11 Chapter Summary

Chapter 3 explored a variety of objections to the notion of analyticity and the analytic–synthetic distinction by Quine and Gilbert Harman, and also considered some responses to those objections. We began the chapter by reflecting on how the debate over analyticity was relevant to philosophical projects prior to Quine. We saw how a rejection of analyticity could undermine the idea that there exists a particular task for philosophy, such as the investigation of the conditions for a priori knowledge, or of the foundations of science, or the clarification of the language of science. As such, we noted that the debate over analyticity is central to the debate over whether philosophy is continuous with natural science, as Quine and Harman have argued, or is instead something distinct from the empirical sciences, as Kant, Frege, the Vienna Circle, and Carnap all believed.

We next considered in some detail the arguments of Quine's revolutionary paper 'Two Dogmas of Empiricism.' The two empiricist 'dogmas' that Quine identified were the belief in the existence of an intelligible analytic–synthetic distinction, and the belief in 'reductionism,' which Quine regarded as the belief that meaningful statements are individually associated with 'extra-linguistic' evidence, such as sensory experience that can confirm or disconfirm them. As we observed later in the chapter (section 3.7), Quine believed that these two dogmas were 'at root identical.' We divided Quine's arguments against analyticity into several categories: those that claim that 'analytic' is unintelligible, those that claim that analyticity is intelligible but there are no instances in fact, and those that claim it is intelligible but explanatorily useless.

In section 3.4 we saw how the claim that 'analytic' is unintelligible was supported by a variety of sub-arguments, such as Quine's contention that all attempts to explicate analyticity are viciously circular, that they involve appeal to equally problematic notions like synonymy or meaning, or that Carnap's attempts to explicate 'analytic' by means of formal languages or semantical rules are confused and unhelpful. However, we also saw, in section 3.5, how Carnap replied to some of Quine's objections to his explication of 'analytic.' In particular, we noted that Carnap saw Quine's objections to rest on a double standard, since what Quine had rejected about Carnap's explication of 'analytic' seemed similar to what he had accepted in Tarski's explication of 'true' using Convention T. In section 3.6, we looked at H. P. Grice and P. F. Strawson's important defense of the coherence of the notion of analyticity against Quine, and suggested some ways in which the Quinean might reply. Among other things, Grice and Strawson rejected Quine's assertion that common definitions of 'analytic' are viciously circular, and accused Quine of adopting an impossibly high standard of acceptability for concepts and their definitions.

In section 3.7, we introduced the second 'dogma' of empiricism, reductionism. Reductionism should be replaced, Quine argued, by 'confirmational holism,' according to which language as a whole (the language of science) 'confronts experience as a corporate body,' rather than confronting experience sentence-by-sentence. As we noted, this idea was actually presaged not only by Pierre Duhem, but by Carnap himself. Connected with this holism, Quine adopted a fallibilist attitude toward all the statements used in a given theory. In principle, any belief could be abandoned in the face of 'recalcitrant' experiences, given sufficiently many other changes in the 'web of belief' in which that belief was embedded. Likewise, any belief could be 'protected,' or 'held true come what may' given suitable changes to other beliefs. This led to a further argument against analyticity, this time on the grounds that there are no analytic truths in fact. At best, calling a statement 'analytic' reflects an unusually strong disposition to hold that statement to be true. In section 3.8, we considered a line of response to this holism argument from Grice and Strawson, one which would still allow a notion of sameness of meaning by defining this notion in terms of sameness of degree of relevance for arbitrary empirical evidence. We then considered how a Quinean might respond to this proposal by denying a distinction between changing a language and changing a theory, and we explored a number of ways in which the dialectic here has been developed, including the Quineans' appeal to principles of good translation as a surrogate for appeals to meaning.

In section 3.9 we turned to another argument of Quine's relevant to the analyticity debate, namely his denial of any meaningful sense in which the laws of logic might be said to be analytic in virtue of being true by convention. Quine argued that attempts to render logic true by convention presuppose logic in order to apply the logical conventions they are supposed to establish. Quine allowed that there might exist 'legislative' definitions that might be conventionally true, but he denied that their status as conventional truths had any enduring consequences for the use of such sentences beyond the initial act of definition. Contra Quine, we argued that there are, in fact, substantive and enduring differences between some statements that are stipulated to be true and those that are not, a point that will be relevant to our discussion in chapter 6.

We concluded the chapter with a brief look at how Quine later modified some of his earlier objections to analyticity. In later writings, Quine allowed that there could be a notion of 'stimulus analyticity,' but denied that it was strong enough to do the work philosophers such as Carnap required of analyticity. Still later, Quine granted that some notion of analyticity akin to the traditional one of 'truth in virtue of meaning' is coherent, but denied that it possessed any explanatory value. We observed that, if nothing else, this constituted an important concession to Carnap.

3.12 Further Reading

Quine's 'Two Dogmas of Empiricism' (1953) is both accessible and a classic of twentieth-century philosophy. Grice and Strawson's 'In Defense of a Dogma' (1956) is perhaps less well-known, but remains a fine example of an early response to Quine, as does Carnap's 'Quine on Logical Truth' (1963c). Richard Creath's essay 'Every Dogma Has its Day' (1991) gives a nice historically oriented overview of the importance of 'Two Dogmas'. For those interested in the details of the Quine–Carnap debate over analyticity, Creath has edited a volume entitled *Dear Carnap, Dear Van: The Quine–Carnap Correspondence and Related Work* (Carnap and Quine 1990) which consists of much of their correspondence and a few unpublished papers of Quine and Carnap. As we saw in this chapter, Gilbert Harman is among Quine's staunchest defenders. His papers 'Quine on Meaning and Existence I' (1967) and 'Quine on Meaning and Existence II' (1967a) present a forceful defense of Quine on analyticity and related topics. Harman has more recently returned to his defense of Quine with 'Analyticity Regained?' (1996) which is in part a response to another defense of a notion of analyticity from Paul

Boghossian entitled 'Analyticity Reconsidered' (1996). In addition to Quine, another early attack on analyticity came in Morton White's 'The Analytic and the Synthetic: An Untenable Dualism' (1951). More recently, H. J. Glock has critically examined many of Quine's major arguments and their impact in his excellent book *Quine and Davidson on Thought, Language and Reality* (2003).

4

ANALYTICITY AND ONTOLOGY

4.1 Introduction and Overview

In chapter 3 we presented an overview of what we take to be the main arguments given by Quine against the notion of analyticity, along with some responses. In the next two chapters, we investigate some connections between the issue of analyticity and broader questions of ontology and epistemology. Our investigation is not intended to be exhaustive, and the division between these issues is somewhat artificial, for in these discussions ontological and epistemological considerations rarely admit any neat partition. Nonetheless, certain disputes, such as those concerning the existence of mathematical objects and truths, of logical objects and laws, of universals, of propositions, meanings, and other 'intensional' entities, classically form a part of ontology, broadly conceived.

We have already seen how analyticity is intimately connected to ontological disputes. Kant, for instance, saw in the supposed vacuity of analytic statements a partial reason in favor of the existence of more substantive necessary truths as expressed by synthetic a priori statements. The Vienna Circle saw in that vacuity a possible explanation of alleged necessary truths. Carnap saw in analytic statements a way of eliminating ontological concerns altogether, to the extent these concerns are 'metaphysical.' In section 4.2, we are going to consider Quine's conception of ontology in more detail with a look at his idea of how language could be regimented to reveal or remove ontological commitments. In section 4.3 we will look at a related notion of Quine's, that of the radical indeterminacy of translation, and note its connection with analyticity and ontological issues in section 4.4. Section 4.5 will look at some responses to Quine's view of ontology. In sections 4.6–4.7 we will turn to our other primary protagonist, Carnap, and look more closely at his 'Empiricism, Semantics, and Ontology' (1956a), which we introduced in chapter 2. Sections 4.8–4.10 discuss a few connections between the analyticity debate and contemporary ontological disputes, including disputes concerning the notion 'existence' itself, and disputes concerning whether propositions or mathematical abstracta exist and which, if any, mereological sums exist. Finally, in section 4.11 we consider a contemporary picture broadly similar to Carnap's *Aufbau* project, which has been labeled the 'Canberra project.'

4.2 Quine's Naturalized Ontology

As we have seen in chapter 2, Quine adopted a naturalistic conception of philosophy, one which sees science and philosophy as forming a continuum of inquiry and theory. Quine refused to acknowledge a fundamental distinction between the scientific (mathematical) question whether there are numbers with a certain property, and the philosophical question whether there are numbers, or between the scientific (linguistic) question of whether two expressions are stimulus synonymous, and the philosophical question of whether 'synonymy' denotes an abstract or mental entity. Philosophical questions differ from scientific ones at most in their generality (cf. Quine 1966, 210). Like science, philosophy ought to begin with our best theory, physical science, which itself is an extension of the commonsense lore which we can do no better than to accept. Hence, Quine wrote:

> Let us therefore accept physical reality, whether in the manner of unspoiled men in the street or with one or another degree of scientific sophistication . . . Then, pursuing in detail our thus accepted theory of physical reality, we draw conclusions concerning, in particular, our own physical selves, and even concerning ourselves as lorebearers. (1966, 217)

Quine thus assumed our physical account of the world as a starting point for inquiry. As we shall see, this assumed starting point also carried ontological consequences for Quine. Nonetheless, he did not regard this assumption as one wholly unguided by further considerations, for he recognized broadly pragmatic criteria that ought to influence our acceptance of one theory over another, including (doxastic) conservatism (minimiz-ing belief changes), simplicity, generality, explanatory power, and refut-ability (cf. Quine 1966, 233f.; Quine and Ullian 1978, 64–82). These criteria can guide our formation of hypotheses and our acceptance of the theories of which they are a part. But they offer us no certainty or even anything remotely like it. Recall Quine's endorsement of Neurath's ship metaphor from chapter 2; like the sailors at sea, we have no anchorage, no a priori certainties from which to begin. We begin with the best we have, our sim-plest, most conservative, most general and explanatory theory.

Quine's attitude toward our current-best theory was fallibilist. A theory could, at any time, be replaced by something that better fulfilled Quine's pragmatic criteria. Our acceptance of the entities hypothesized by our cur-rent theory, whether they be macroscopic, everyday objects like tables and sheep, microscopic ones like chromosomes, or sub-microscopic objects like electrons, is entirely provisional. The entities are *posits*, even if some of the macroscopic ones, like tables and sheep, are likely to survive future changes of theory (cf. 1966, 210–11). These posits are a part of our web of belief, of our conceptual apparatus:

> Our talk of external things, our very notion of things, is just a conceptual apparatus that helps us to foresee and control the triggering of our sen-sory receptors in the light of previous triggering of our sensory receptors. (1981, 1)

However, Quine was not here proposing a 'fictionalist' view of the posits of theory according to which such posits are mere fictions introduced for instrumental purposes since, as we have seen above, he believed that we must 'acquiesce' in our current theory and accept it simply as true (1960, 3–4; 1981, 21). He insisted that 'to call a posit a posit is not to patronize it,' for posits are real from the standpoint of the theory that posits them (1960, 22). If a theory posits objects in an external world, we accept them in a scientific vein as real, for the 'notion of reality independent of language is carried over by the scientist from his earliest impressions' (1966, 220). Thus we do commit to the existence of certain entities (external things) when we accept a theory as true, and Quine took what he considered to be a realistic attitude toward them.[1] We are realists about such entities only because, and insofar as, they are required in order to best make sense of the 'flux of our experience' (cf. 1953a, 16–18).

While philosophical inquiry is distinct from scientific inquiry only in generality, Quine believed that philosophers did have a particular task, distinct from the conduct of empirical experiment and observation. This task stemmed from the fact that a good theory is not just a matter of collecting evidence but of *systematizing* that evidence: 'Theoretical terms should be subject to observable criteria, the more the better, and should lend themselves to systematic laws, the simpler the better' (1981, 31). Science requires language, and that language may be made more or less systematic. In its less systematic, ordinary form, language is subject to ambiguity and variation, for example the variation brought about by indexical or 'indicator' words like 'I,' 'this,' and 'now' (1966, 222–4). Our language and theory is further prone to the reification or hypostatization of certain of its posits, such as the hypostasis of *sakes* or *unicorns* deriving from idiomatic expressions that we saw Quine discuss in chapter 2. From the ambiguity, variation, and hypostasis of pre-systematic language, a distinct job emerges for the philosopher, for:

> the scientist can enhance objectivity and diminish the interference of language, by his very choice of language. And we, concerned to distill the essence of scientific discourse, can profitably purify the language of science beyond what might reasonably be urged upon the practicing scientist. (ibid., 222)

What Quine was proposing here sounds rather Carnapian – recall Carnap's idea that the philosopher-scientist 'introduce a system of new ways of speaking, subject to new rules' for the purposes of explication (Carnap 1956a, 206). But in Quine's hands there was a crucial difference, for Quine saw the further systematization of language as a *systematization of existing scientific theory*, complete with its ontological commitments, rather than as a *proposal* about which of many possible languages to adopt. The difference here is subtle but crucial. Quine, as we have seen, was willing to accept whatever entities or categories our best current theory requires, unless and until a better theory becomes available. Carnap, on the other hand, was dismissive of the very idea that we can speak of ontology in any kind of general way. There is for him no genuine question or issue of our trying to find the language-transcendent truth (cf. section 2.2.2). Any attempt to do so was, he thought, a confusion of internal questions with external ones. Extending Neurath's ship metaphor, we could perhaps say that Carnap saw us not so much trapped on a ship at sea, but rather as customers in a shipyard, or even as ship-designers, free to choose whatever proposed ship best served our needs.

Quine's 'purification' of the language of science involved the regimentation of that language into the 'canonical notation' of first-order logic. His guiding idea was that a language purged of ambiguity and 'indicator words' such as 'here,' 'there,' and 'now,' would provide 'a kind of objectivity, to begin with, appropriate to the aims of science: truth becomes invariant with respect to speaker and occasion' (Quine 1966, 223). Furthermore, Quine thought that the regimentation of the language of science would offer a *conceptual* clarification of its ontology as well:

> Each elimination of obscure constructions or notions that we manage to achieve, by paraphrase into more lucid elements, is a clarification of the conceptual scheme of science . . . Here the objective is called philosophical, because of the breadth of the framework concerned; but the motivation is the same [as that of science]. The quest of a simplest, clearest overall pattern of canonical notation is not to be distinguished from a quest of ultimate categories, a limning of the most general traits of reality. (1960, 161)

Quine's project of regimenting the language of science into a canonical notation would expose to us what ontological categories and entities that language was committed to. Here again, there is an important difference with Carnap. Carnap would not have spoken of a *language* as committed to any entities at all. For him, the question of whether something exists is a language-internal question. Existence attributions are not a matter of language, but of the theory formulated within a given language. Yet Quine blurred any such distinction, speaking, as above, of a canonical notation as indistinguishable from the quest of ultimate categories of reality. Why?

The answer, as the reader may have already guessed, returns us to the analyticity debate. As we saw in chapter 3, Quine refused to countenance any language/theory distinction, because he took such a distinction to rely upon the existence of statements whose truth is 'vacuously confirmed, *ipso facto*, come what may; and such a statement is analytic' (Quine 1953, 41). This derived from Quine's semantic and confirmational holism that we discussed in chapter 3. Quine relentlessly extended the Duhemian holism that Carnap had endorsed, pushing it into a semantic form of holism that rejected any significant distinction between 'truths of language' and matters of fact. Hence for Quine, the ontological commitments of theory are the ontological commitments of language. While Quine did advocate a kind of ontological relativity, which we discuss below, it had nothing to do with Carnap's Principle of Tolerance-inspired advocacy of a moral-free choice of logic and

language. Carnapian tolerance of alternative linguistic forms is not an interesting possibility, Quine thought. By starting with our accepted theory of
physical reality, we are starting with its ultimate categories of reality. Carnap,
by contrast, saw our choice of linguistic forms as precisely the interesting
one. For him, the suggestion that we should not, or could not, propose new
linguistic forms would be as absurd as the suggestion that we could not
design a better boat. While our design may or may not be better than what
we have, it is certainly possible to make a new proposal. To be sure, like
Carnap Quine endorsed the regimentation of language, and granted that
doing so can clarify what our current theory's ontological categories are and,
through the process of explication as elimination, show which are essential
and which might be inessential. But in regimenting languages, we cannot
adopt a neutral attitude toward them. As a consequence, there is no correlate in Quine to Carnap's idea that our ontological commitments might be
relative to our choice of language. For we aren't in a position to choose in
the way Carnap had supposed – we are stuck aboard the ship we find ourselves on.[2] We will here briefly sketch how Quine imagined regimentation
could increase the objectivity of scientific language and expose its ontological commitments.[3]

As noted, Quine wanted to first render sentence-truth invariant with
respect to speaker and occasion. He thus began by replacing sentences containing indicator words with 'observation categoricals,' which are general
statements of the form 'Whenever this, that' (1990, 10; cf. also 1966, 223–
4). Such a statement is compounded from observation statements, but:

> The 'Whenever' is not intended to reify times and quantify over them. What
> is intended is an irreducible generality prior to any objective reference. It
> is a generality to the effect that the circumstances described in the one
> observation sentence are invariably accompanied by those described in the
> other. (ibid.)

For instance, 'When a willow grows at the water's edge, it leans over the
water' is an observation categorical, and it allows testing and refutation by
observation. It may itself be implied by other statements of theory, including hypotheses such as: 'A willow root nourishes mainly its own side of the
tree,' which when conjoined with other bits of theory, implies the observation categorical (11).

To make clear how theory might imply an observation categorical, we
must make the inferential relations among the statements of the theory

clear. Quine proposed that we do this by further regimenting language into first-order logic. First-order logic is a complete system of inference, with a well-defined syntax that imposes no particular ontological commitments of its own, apart from a commitment to the existence of at least one object. Quine thus found it the best language for the regimentation of logic. Furthermore, first-order logic is strong enough, Quine thought, to eliminate ontological commitments that are eliminable (recall from chapter 2 that, according to Quine, explication is elimination). For instance, singular terms such as proper names and indexicals *seem* on their face to commit one to the existence of the objects to which they refer. 'Pegasus,' for instance, seems to refer to a winged horse, and talk of Pegasus seems to commit us to the existence of this horse (1953a, 3). But, Quine noted, we can use the machinery of first-order logic to remove this appearance by using Russell's Theory of Descriptions. To do this Quine needed to convert 'Pegasus' into a description, which he did by appealing to the:

> *Ex hypothesi* unanalyzable, irreducible attribute of *being Pegasus*, adopting, for its expression, the verb 'is-Pegasus', or 'pegasizes'. The noun 'Pegasus' itself could then be treated as a derivative, and identified after all with a description: 'the thing that is-Pegasus', 'the thing that pegasizes'. (ibid., 8)

Quine did not deny that this identification was artificial. It was enough for him that it be possible, and that if we adopt it, we can replace statements involving nouns like 'Pegasus' into Russellian definite descriptions expressible in first-order logic. In general:

> Chief among the omitted frills is the *name*. This again is a mere convenience and strictly redundant, for the following reason. Think of '*a*' as a name, and think of '*Fa*' as any sentence containing it. But clearly '*Fa*' is equivalent to '$\exists x (a = x . Fx)$' . . . we can as well render '$a =$' always as a simple predicate 'A', thus abandoning the name '*a*'. (Quine 1986b, 25)

Thus, 'Pegasus exists' could be replaced with '$\exists x(Px)$,' where 'Px' says that 'x pegasizes.' On Quine's objectual interpretation of the variable x, this formula says that there is at least one element in the domain of quantification which satisfies the predicate 'P,' in other words, there is at least one thing that pegasizes.

If we imagine applying this kind of regimentation to all of the statements of a theory, we would, Quine thought, be able to easily identify the ontological commitments of that theory.[4] Those commitments would be 'the objects that some of the predicates of the theory have to be true of, in order for the theory to be true' (1969, 95; cf. 1953a, 15–16). That is, the entities required by the values of the variables needed in order to make the statements of the theory true give us the 'ultimate categories' that we are committed to when we have adopted the theory. The regimented language of the theory thus provides us with both a clarification of the inferential relations required to infer observation categoricals (through the inferential rules of first-order logic) and a presentation of the ontological commitments of that theory once 'frills' such as names are regimented into the language using Russellian descriptions. These are revealed as the values of the bound variables of the theory's true statements, which gives us Quine's famous criterion of ontological commitment: 'To be is to be the value of a bound variable' (1953a, 15).

Quine thought that regimentation into first-order logic would help reveal our ontological commitments in another way, for it helped, through the use of the identity sign and the device of quantifiers and variables, to expose the fact that talk of objects as existing presupposes *identity conditions* for them. Quine thought that the positing of objects was intelligible only given identity conditions for them (1969, 23). More generally, he argued that one could not fully master talk of enduring bodies and their properties without having criteria for their identity and individuation at different times. Thus, for example, talking of unspecified dogs

> scarcely makes sense until we are in a position to say such things as that in general if *any* dog undergoes such and such then in due course that *same* dog will behave thus and so. This sort of general talk about long-term causation becomes possible only with the advent of quantification or its equivalent, the relative clause in plural predication. (1981, 7–8)

As such, 'there is no entity without identity' (ibid., 102). To speak of a physical object, or a property, requires having a principle of individuation for that thing.

Quine concluded that the criterion of identity, when conjoined with the criterion of ontological commitment, revealed our current ontological commitments to consist of three broad categories: universals, classes, and physical objects. Universals Quine regarded as indispensible insofar as they are implied by the predicate letters of first-order formulas that are taken as translations of true statements of theory:

Universals are irreducibly presupposed. The universals posited by binding the predicate letters have never been explained away in terms of any mere conventional notation of abbreviation. (1953, 122)

We saw in section 2.7 that Quine regarded classes, which are distinctive in being *abstracta*, as indispensable to any explication of mathematics (cf. 1953, 122; 1960, 262f.). And physical objects are presupposed by the working scientist, as we noted above. Intensional objects, such as propositions, meanings, synonymies, and so on, failed the criterion of identity, Quine argued (cf. 1960, 203). Quine saw meanings in particular as failing to have identity criteria (1960, 206–7, quoted in chapter 2).

Quine's criteria of ontological commitment and identity, and the ontology which these criteria led him to accept, provoked a heated philosophical debate. Objections to his position included the claims that his identity criterion is perfectly compatible with admitting intensional entities like meanings (Strawson 1997), that his attempt to eliminate indicator words like indexicals would reduce scientific explanatory power (Perry 1979), that his criterion of ontological commitment fails to capture our ordinary existential commitments (Azzouni 2004; Dummett 1981; Glock 2003; we consider Azzouni's objections in section 4.9), and that Quine's treatment of nouns in terms of predicates conflated important differences in their respective functions (Geach 1951). There is little question, we think, that if taken as a translation of language as it is ordinarily used, Quine's proposed regimentations would severely constrain both science and ordinary language. However, we think it is important to note that Quine did not intend to use them in this way. For recall Quine's above-quoted comment that his regimentations would 'purify the language of science beyond what might reasonably be urged upon the practicing scientist.' He was well aware that his proposals were 'idealized schematisms' that would be of little pragmatic value to scientific work. Of course, this observation does not by itself exempt these proposals from all of the many criticisms that have been leveled against them. But it does buffer Quine from some of the most obvious objections. He does not need to insist that, for instance, the noun 'Pegasus' is a derivative of the attribute 'pegasizes,' but only that it can be *treated* as such, which is just what he said (1953a, 8, quoted above).[5]

4.3 The Indeterminacy of Translation

One of Quine's most famous and controversial conjectures was his thesis of the (radical) *indeterminacy of translation*. This thesis, if accepted, has important consequences for analyticity and also for Quine's ontology. The thesis has been intensively discussed over several decades.[6] The intensity of the debate has waned in recent years, signaling an apparent reduction of interest in Quine's indeterminacy of translation thesis. Nonetheless, it plays an important role in Quine's thinking, and deserves consideration. Our purpose here will be limited to a consideration of whether or not it can offer an independent argument for Quine's rejection of analyticity and his endorsement of naturalism, 'independent' in the sense that it would not presuppose the very naturalism and absence of a meaningful analytic–synthetic distinction that it is sometimes taken to establish. We shall argue that it does not.

Quine's thesis of the indeterminacy of translation is introduced in detail in *Word and Object* (Quine 1960, 26–61). As we have observed, Quine found it helpful to regard linguistic utterances in a 'causal vein' by trying to establish by observation and experiment what types of stimulations prompt behavior such as assent and dissent to given utterances, which led him to the standpoint of *radical* translation: the translation of the language of a 'hitherto untouched people' or 'natives' with whom we share no historical or cultural connections whatsoever (ibid., 28). Radical translation limits itself, at least initially, to the 'forces that [the linguist] sees impinging on the native's surfaces and the observable behavior, vocal and otherwise, of the native.' The linguist is focused upon a native's disposition to assent to sentences, asking only for a verdict of 'true' or 'false':

> The linguist tentatively associates a native's utterance with the observed concurrent situation, hoping that it might be simply an observation sentence linked to that situation. To check this he takes the initiative, when the situation recurs, and volunteers the sentence himself for the native's assent or dissent. (1990, 39)

An observation sentence is one which reports some observable feature of the environment on a given occasion (1960, 42). Quine further assumed a maxim of charity to the effect that 'assertions startlingly false on the face of them are likely to turn on hidden differences of language' (1960, 59; 1969, 46). From such a limited basis, the observed situation of utterance and a maxim of charity, Quine sought to understand how much of a native language could be made sense of from the standpoint of radical translation.

Quine's answer to this question was, unsurprisingly, that we are very limited in what we can make sense of from such a standpoint. He granted that we could make sense of:

1 observation sentences;
2 the truth-functional operators of the native's language;
3 the notion 'stimulus analyticity' that we introduced in chapter 3, and;
4 the notion of 'stimulus synonymy,' or the idea that two expressions exhibit the same stimulus meaning, as with 'bachelor' and 'unmarried man' (cf. 1960, 38, 46–7, 55–7, 68).

Correlations of native utterances with English utterances constitute the linguist's 'analytical hypotheses,' and these hypotheses ought to conform, at least loosely, with (1)–(4). In general, Quine rejected the idea that we can expect more than such a correlation from the standpoint of radical translation. In particular, Quine used the notion of radical translation to introduce the thesis of the indeterminacy of translation:

> Manuals for translating one language into another can be set up in divergent ways, all compatible with the totality of speech dispositions, yet incompatible with each other. (27)

Quine's central idea was that there can be two or more 'rival' translation manuals of a language. The manuals translate observation sentences into the linguist's home language by 'correlating sentences compatibly with the behavior of all concerned' (1990, 48).[7] These correlations may each be fully compatible with observed speech behavior, including speech dispositions, but not equivalent with each other in the sense of not being 'interchangeable in English contexts' (ibid.). Thus in Quine's most famous example, an occasion sentence such as 'Gavagai' might be uttered in the presence of a rabbit, and translated by the English sentence '[Lo, a] rabbit.' But there might nonetheless exist 'persistent discrepancies' on every occasion of utterance. For instance, there might be a 'local rabbit-fly, unknown to the linguist' which leads native speakers to utter 'Gavagai.' Now a rival translation manual might translate 'Gavagai' with the English sentence '[Lo, a] rabbit fly.' Quine granted that the linguist might be able, through further tests, to separate rabbit expressions from rabbit-fly expressions (39). But given the limited nature of the data the radical translator has to work with, Quine thought it obvious that there would always be other, alternative, and incompatible translations of an utterance of 'Gavagai,' such as 'undetached rabbit part' or 'rabbit stage' which would still be compatible with observed native behavior, remarking that 'One has only to reflect on the nature of possible data and methods to appreciate the indeterminacy' (72; cf. also 47).

One of the confusions that infected Quine's earlier versions of the indeterminacy of translation thesis was the fact that it implicitly contained two
separable claims: one concerning the translation of complete sentences, the
other concerning the translation of proper parts of sentences. Quine later
acknowledged that these two distinct claims needed to be separated into:
(i) a claim of the indeterminacy of reference and (ii) a claim of sentence-
level or 'holophrastic' indeterminacy (Quine 1970, 182; cf. Orenstein 2002).
Indeterminacy of reference, which Quine also called 'inscrutability of reference,' begins with the fact that there is a kind of 'gap' between the ascription of meaning to an entire sentence and the ascription of meaning to a
sentence-part like a word. Quine regarded the reference of individual parts
of a sentence as a 'mere auxiliary' to the use of the sentence as a whole:

> True sentences, observational and theoretical, are the alpha and the omega
> of the scientific enterprise. They are related by structure, and objects figure
> as mere nodes of that structure. What particular objects there may be is
> indifferent to the truth of observation sentences. (1990, 31)

This claim has a consequence for reference. Even supposing a linguist can
assign a meaning to a given sentence, such as a stimulus meaning, it does
not follow that she can establish what individual terms in that sentence
refer to. After all, 'divergent interpretations' of the terms in a sentence 'can
so offset one another as to sustain an identical translation of the sentence as
a whole' (ibid., 50). The general reason Quine gave for this idea stemmed
from his contention that the criteria for individuating and identifying the
referent of a term *themselves* require a command of the native language:

> Point to a rabbit and you have pointed to a stage of a rabbit, to an inte-
> gral part of a rabbit, to the rabbit fusion, and to where rabbithood is man-
> ifested. Point to an integral part of a rabbit and you have pointed again
> to the remaining four sorts of things; and so on around. Nothing not dis-
> tinguished in stimulus meaning itself is to be distinguished by pointing,
> unless the pointing is accompanied by questions of identity and diversity:
> 'Is this the same gavagai as that?', 'Do we have here one gavagai or two?'.
> Such questioning requires of the linguist a command of the native language
> far beyond anything that we have yet seen how to account for. (1960, 53)

In other words, taken alone, a component part of a native sentence might
alternatively, and incompatibly, be translated as 'same individual as,' 'same

part as,' 'same property as,' and so on, while nonetheless preserving identical stimulus meaning for the entire native sentence holophrastically considered. But if this is granted, then the reference of these component parts is underdetermined by the evidence available to linguists.

Quine presented a second argument for indeterminacy of reference (cf. 1969, 55f; 1981 18–19; 1990, 31–2). His idea here was to consider a mapping of objects (of our ordinary ontology, say) onto objects. In the simplest case, such a mapping might be the identity function, mapping every object onto itself. A more unusual case would map an object onto some proxy, such as its 'cosmic complement,' understood as the set of all (spatiotemporal) things other than that object. Call such a 'proxy function' 'f.' This function would allow us to reinterpret every sentence containing a referring expression x in terms of the cosmic complement of x. The reinterpreted sentence would not be about x but about fx. Predicates that appeared in the sentence would then also be reinterpreted so that they would be true of fx just in case the original predicate was true of x. The result would be that

> We leave all the sentences as they were, letter for letter, merely reinterpreting. The observation sentences remain associated with the same sensory stimulations as before, and the logical interconnections remain intact. Yet the objects of the theory have been supplemented as drastically as you please. (1990, 32)

In addition to indeterminacy of reference, Quine held, as we have seen, 'holophrastic indeterminacy,' the indeterminacy of sentences taken as a whole. It was this type of indeterminacy that Quine thought was represented by his 'Gavagai' example; this latter being a sentence translated by '(Lo, a) rabbit' (1970, 182). Quine thought that this kind of indeterminacy would be apparent upon reflection on 'the nature of possible data and methods' available to the radical translator. However, Quine also appeared to provide a second argument for holophrastic indeterminacy.[8] This argument returned to the 'Quine–Duhem' thesis (cf. section 3.7). Quine seemed to think that it also argued for indeterminacy:

> If the English sentences of a theory have their meaning only together as a body, then we can justify their translation into [a native language] Arunta only together as a body. . . Any translations of the English sentences into Arunta sentences will be as correct as any other, so long as the net empirical implications of the theory as a whole are preserved in translation. But

> it is to be expected that many different ways of translating the component sentences, essentially different individually, would deliver the same empirical implications for the theory as a whole; deviations in the translation of one component sentence could be compensated for in the translation of another component sentence. (1969, 80)

In other words, there is more than one way that the sentences of an entire theory can be translated while preserving identical empirical implications.

4.4 Some Consequences of the Indeterminacy Arguments: Ontological Relativity and Analyticity

The indeterminacy of translation arguments in both forms led Quine to three striking conclusions. One was his provocative, if at times misunderstood, claim that indeterminacy of reference begins 'at home,' and its corollary claim of ontological relativity:

> The inscrutability of reference can be brought even closer to home than the neighbor's case; we can apply it to ourselves. If it is to make sense to say even of oneself that one is referring to rabbits and formulas and not to rabbit stages and Gödel numbers, then it should make sense equally to say it of someone else. After all, as Dewey stressed, there is no private language. (1969, 47; see also 1990, 52)

Quine here seemed to be suggesting that just as the reference of a native's expressions is underdetermined, so in the same way the reference of one's own expressions is underdetermined as well. This suggests that we don't in fact know what we are referring to, even when we speak sincerely and deliberately, for there is no 'fact of the matter' in such cases (1969, 47). As a general rule we 'translate' our own language 'homophonically' by replacing each string of phonemes with itself (ibid., 46), but nothing compels such translation, for there might again be alternative translations which, for example,

> systematically reconstrue our neighbor's apparent references to rabbits as really references to rabbit stages, and his apparent references to formulas as really references to Gödel numbers and vice versa. We can reconcile all this with our neighbor's verbal behavior, by cunningly readjusting our translations of his various connecting predicates so as to compensate for the switch of ontology. (1969, 47)

The ontology imputed to our homophonic neighbor is thus different from our own; we imagine him speaking of rabbit stages and Gödel numbers rather than of rabbits and formulas. The ontology imputed to him is thus relative to our choice of translation, but there is no fact of the matter as to what translation scheme is correct. We must take some background theory with its ontology, ours or some other one, and interpret another speaker as adopting it when we translate his utterances (ibid., 66–7). Of course our translations must maintain compatibility with our neighbor's observed behavior. But assuming they do, we can translate his utterances into one of many alternative ontologies, each incompatible with each other, Quine thought. Ontology is thus relative to how one translates another's utterances.

However, the idea that indeterminacy of reference begins at home carries with it a threat of incoherence, as Quine realized.[9] For if it is true, then reference would, he said, 'seem now to become nonsense not just in radical translation but at home' (1969, 48). This in turn seems to raise a coherence problem for the indeterminacy of translation thesis itself, for when one asks:

> 'Does "rabbit" really refer to "rabbits"?' someone can counter with the question: 'Refer to rabbits in what sense of "rabbits"?' thus launching into a regress. (ibid., 48–9)

Quine endorsed a part of the radical conclusion that emerges here, but only with an important qualification. Recall that Quine thought we must always speak from within an 'inherited theory,' and in the process 'we continue to take seriously our own particular aggregate science, our own particular world-theory or loose total fabric of quasi-theories, whatever it may be.' (1960, 24) This theory or 'background language' – and recall that Quine eschewed any substantive difference between theory and language – is that which we can regress into:

> The background language gives the query [about the reference of 'rabbit'] sense, if only relative sense; sense relative in turn to it, this background language. Querying reference in any more absolute way would be like asking absolute position, or absolute velocity, rather than position or velocity relative to a given frame of reference. (1969, 49)

Quine thus believed that the indeterminacy of reference stopped with the home language in which we 'acquiesce.' As such, we could choose as our 'home language translation manual' the identity function (rather than a proxy function like the cosmic complement function): 'Reference is then explicated in disquotational paradigms analogous to Tarski's truth paradigm; thus "rabbit" denotes rabbits, whatever they are, and "Boston" designates Boston' (1990, 52).

While this response may or may not defuse the potential incoherence raised by Quine's claim that indeterminacy of reference can be applied to ourselves, it adds an interesting twist to the Quine–Carnap debate over analyticity. Recall Quine's 'Two Dogmas' objections to Carnap's invocation of the meta-language in explicating 'analytic,' whether that explication is given through adequacy conditions or through definitions. Quine thought it completely un-illuminating to explicate *analytic* by what were 'in effect rules of translation into ordinary language, in which case the analytic statements of the artificial language are in effect recognized as such from the analyticity of their specified translations in ordinary language' (1953, 36, quoted in full in section 3.4, above). Carnap, as we have seen, thought that such appeals to the meta-language were perfectly legitimate, since the meta-language simply is the shared language of a given community of researchers, and one with a 'fixed interpretation' (cf. Carnap 1963a, 930, quoted above). Yet when Quine, in his discussion of the indeterminacy of reference, asked us to take at 'face value' our background language, it is difficult to see how he could also object to Carnap's use of the background language in explicating 'analytic.' Indeed, given the 'disquotational paradigm' Quine endorsed, what prevented Carnap from asserting that '"analytic" denotes analyticity,' where the reference of 'analyticity' is fixed with reference to the background language of philosophical English? And even if philosophical English is somehow objectionable, surely Carnap could appeal to ordinary English in asserting that '"synonymy" denotes synonymy.' To be sure, the author of 'Two Dogmas' could continue to object that he doesn't know what this is. But, as Grice and Strawson nicely illustrated, if our background language is English, he would seem to be in a minority. A related problem for Quine here is that a natural response to 'explaining' analyticity by noting that 'analyticity' refers to analyticity would be that this at best gives us the referent, but does not explain the meaning of 'analytic.' For reasons that we have canvassed above, however, such an appeal to meanings would not cohere with Quine's views.

A second conclusion of the indeterminacy arguments also connects them with analyticity, this time via holophrastic indeterminacy. If we again regard analyticity as characterized in terms of truth in virtue of meaning, or in terms of statements that remain true on any substitution of synonyms for synonyms, holophrastic indeterminacy of translation poses a potential further problem for the notion. As we have seen (section 2.8), in *Word and Object* Quine claimed that if intensional notions such as 'meaning,' 'synonymy,' and 'proposition' are to make any sense at all, then they must be elucidated in terms of verbal behavior, and in particular in terms of verbal responses to stimuli, since the relation between a speaker's utterances and the stimuli affecting him is all we have to go on in learning and teaching languages. Yet the indeterminacy of translation argument gives us reason to believe that the antecedent of this conditional is false. If, as Quine thought, rival translation manuals which are compatible with the totality of verbal behavior and yet not equivalent with each other are always possible, then a translation's compatibility with verbal behavior does not guarantee that meaning is preserved (at least where 'meaning' is intended as something richer than Quine's 'stimulus meaning').[10] Hence, we can never determine meaning in the intuitive sense. Apart from a small number of cases that *are* settled by verbal dispositions, such as stimulus meaning and stimulus synonymy, questions of meaning and synonymy do not concern objective matters of fact. As a consequence, definitions of 'analytic' that rest on notions of meaning or synonymy themselves have no definite content. Quine was well aware of this consequence, offering among the conclusions of his indeterminacy arguments the claim that, insofar as the notion of analyticity rests on intuitions of synonymy, 'it would be a mistake to look to them for a sweeping epistemological dichotomy between analytic truths as by-products of language and synthetic truths as reports on the world' (1960, 67).[11]

This consequence of the indeterminacy arguments for analyticity goes hand-in-hand with another ontological consequence, beyond that of ontological relativity. Quine regarded the indeterminacy arguments as establishing that there is no fact of the matter as to which of two rival translation manuals is correct and, as such, 'nothing for the lexicographer to be right or wrong about' (1953, 63). As a corollary, meaning, synonymy, propositionhood, and similar intensional entities as traditionally conceived have no ontological standing. They are not to be regarded as elements of the world, and are not required by our best theory of the world. From the perspective of holophrastic indeterminacy, 'we are left with no general concept of the meanings of sentences of less than critical semantic mass,' where critical mass pertains only to 'testable sentences and sets of sentences' such as the observation categorical and logical connectives that Quine countenanced

(1990, 53). Furthermore, propositions are typically characterized in terms of synonymy; sentences express the same proposition if they are synonymous. But limited by the indeterminacy of translation, the only acceptable notion of synonymy remaining – stimulus synonymy – is too weak to grant propositions any status as 'language-transcendent sentence meanings' (ibid.), for:

> If propositions are to serve as objects of the propositional attitudes, then the broad sort of sentence synonymy [stimulus synonymy] would be unsatisfactory as a standard of identity of propositions even if adequately formulated. It would be too broad. For it would reckon all analytic sentences as meaning an identical proposition; yet surely one would not want to regard all analytic sentences as interchangeable in contexts of belief or indirect quotation. (1960, 201–2)

If, in other words, the indeterminacy arguments provide only stimulus synonymy, then 'Two plus two equals four' and 'Bachelors are unmarried' would mean the same proposition, since they elicit assent come what may from English speakers. But it is certainly not the case that 'R believes that two plus two equals four' is interchangeable with 'R believes that bachelors are unmarried.' So propositions fall with synonymy insofar as this is understood in the richer, 'intuitive' sense, and synonymy falls with indeterminacy.

4.5 Responses to Quine's Indeterminacy Arguments

As with so much of Quine's work, the indeterminacy of translation arguments have generated a massive secondary literature. Objections to Quine have included arguments that his constraints on radical translation are unrealistically strong, and depend upon an undefended prior commitment to behaviorism (cf. BonJour 1998; Chomsky 1975; Putnam 1983; Searle 1987), that incompatible translation manuals are unlikely to remain faithful to the assent conditions of all native sentences (Evans 1985); that the notion of a proxy function leads to unacceptable consequences (Mellor 1995); that misunderstandings of the type that Quine's argument (seems to) presuppose tend not to occur (Glock 2003), and that Quine's arguments illicitly slide from behavioral indeterminacy to something stronger (Putnam 1983; Ricketts 1982). We will focus here on just one line of criticism that we find powerful, and which takes its cue from this last-mentioned objection. We will not try to dispute that Quine's conclusions of indeterminacy follow from his premise of radical translation (although that has also been disputed; cf. Glock 2003; Kirk 1986). Rather, we shall argue, following a line of criticism first suggested by Chomsky (1975), that the premises required for the indeterminacy of translation and radical interpretation are so strong as to render Quine's conclusions of only very limited interest.

To see why we think this, recall again the 'yield' of the methods of radical translation that Quine recognized with items (1)–(4) above, viz. that a radical translator can translate: (1) observation sentences; (2) the truth-functional operators of the native's language; (3) 'stimulus analytic' sentences, and; (4) 'stimulus synonymous' sentences (1960, 68). Hilary Putnam observed the following about these four conditions (which he paraphrased slightly into (1')–(4)):

> [Quine's] position, after all, does not differ much, if at all, from saying that (1')–(4) are *Meaning Postulates* for the notion of 'translation', and that they are all the Meaning Postulates that there are for the notion of 'translation'. (1983, 171)

Of course Quine should not be happy with the notion of 'meaning postulates,' having rejected them, as we have seen, in 'Two Dogmas' and elsewhere. But what is it about Quine's account that compels us to accept (1)–(4) as the most that a translation can yield? Is it just a stipulation of what is to count as a translation, or does Quine have compelling reasons for accepting just these results and nothing more?[12]

As we have seen, Quine would likely reply that all of the evidence available to a linguist underdetermines any translation, and that this underdetermination would become apparent upon reflection. But what counts as evidence here? Why not also include, in addition to Quine's behavioral evidence, other kinds of evidence, such as 'facts about human psychology which are universal, i.e. independent of culture' as Putnam proposes (ibid., 170)? Could there not be, for example, psychological generalizations about human language use that go beyond what Quine allows, and that could be appealed to in order to distinguish some rival translation manuals as preferable? As Putnam rightly notes, Quine would say 'no,' because 'he would say there is simply no fact of the matter as to whether the analytical hypotheses that we customarily accept are correct, and the proposed psychological generalization is correct, or whether noncustomary analytical hypotheses are correct, and the proposed psychological generalization is false' (ibid.).

In other words, Quine would likely say that given any psychological generalization that might favor one translation manual over another, there is another manual that is consistent with observed behavior and yet rejects the alleged psychological generalization.

Yet Putnam's remarks bring out the fact that Quine's arguments must make a fairly strong assumption about what kinds of evidence are available to the philosopher-linguist. That is, Quine must reject any appeal to psychological or linguistic entities that do not get expressed in his preferred behavioral terms.

As it happens, Putnam's objection to the indeterminacy of translation dovetails with an earlier objection advanced by the linguist Noam Chomsky (1975). Like Putnam, Chomsky expressed puzzlement about why a linguist must be limited to 'analytical hypotheses' that do not go beyond items (1)–(4). Chomsky didn't deny that a linguist limited to just these would find translation indeterminate. Rather, he questioned:

> why [Quine's statement of them] is important. It is, to be sure, undeniable that if a system of 'analytical hypotheses' goes beyond evidence then it is possible to conceive alternatives compatible with the evidence, just as in the case of Quine's 'genuine hypotheses' about stimulus meaning and truth-functional connectives. Thus, the situation in the case of language, or 'common sense knowledge', is, in this respect, no different from the case of physics. (Chomsky 1975, 63)

That physical theories are *underdetermined* by the evidence available for them is something neither Quine nor Chomsky would deny. Given a theory of physics, such as General Relativity Theory, there is no question that the theory is underdetermined by the available data, in the sense that there are other theories that are also compatible with that same data. Here, Chomsky charged Quine with inflating this trivial point about the underdetermination of a physical theory by the available evidence into the *stronger* indeterminacy of translation thesis. Of course data underdetermines theory, in the case of linguistics as well as of physics. But this is scarcely worth mentioning, Chomsky thought.

There is a second component of Chomsky's objection. Physicists are allowed to posit entities, laws, and the like in the construction of a tentative theory in order to explain some class of phenomena. But Quine does not allow the linguist the same latitude:

> The physicist works within the framework of a tentative theory. The linguist cannot [on Quine's view], nor can the psychologist studying a 'conceptual system' of the 'common sense' variety . . . this is a relatively clear formulation of classical empiricist doctrine. It involves, at every step, certain empirical assumptions which may or may not be true, but for which Quine does not seem to regard evidence as necessary. (63)

From Chomsky's perspective as a practicing linguist, Quine's empiricist constraints are far too strong – indeed, they are dogmatic, and not in accord with actual linguistic practice:

> It is difficult to see why this dogma should be taken more seriously than any other. It receives no support from what is known about language learning, or from human or comparative psychology . . . In general . . . it is in conflict with the not inconsiderable information that is now available. (66)

Chomsky thought that linguists should be allowed the same latitude to propose tentative theories that physicists are, even when such theories postulate intentional and intensional phenomena that Quine would find unacceptable, such as unconscious principles, innate linguistic capacities, a distinction between *langue* and *parole* or between *competence* and *performance* (64–5).

Chomsky had other objections, but these two in particular posed a potentially serious embarrassment for Quine. By Chomsky's lights Quine had exaggerated a humdrum observation about the underdetermination of theories by evidence and, more embarrassingly still, substituted his own armchair philosophy in place of the empirical methods developed by working linguists. Why did Quine refuse to include what linguists such as Chomsky were actually doing as a part of empirical science?

Quine gave a detailed reply to Chomsky (Quine 1975). His response to the two objections we have canvassed is revealing. Quine granted that translational synonymy and physical theory are underdetermined by all possible data, that is,

> the totality of possible observations of nature . . . is compatible with physical theories that are incompatible with each other. Correspondingly the totality of possible observations of verbal behavior, made and unmade, is compatible with systems of analytical hypotheses of translation that are incompatible with one another. (1975, 302–3)[13]

And Quine further granted that physicists and linguists will make predictions based on their existing theory (303). However, he thought, there is also a crucial difference:

> theory in physics is an ultimate parameter. There is no legitimate first philosophy, higher or firmer than physics, to which we can appeal over physicists' heads . . . Though linguistics is of course a part of the theory of nature, the indeterminacy of translation is not just inherited as a special case of the under-determination of our theory of nature. It is parallel but additional. Thus, adopt for now my fully realistic attitude toward electrons and muons and curved space-time, thus falling in with the current theory of the world despite knowing that it is in principle methodologically under-determined. Consider, from this realistic point of view, the totality of truths of nature, known and unknown, observable and unobservable, past and future. The point about indeterminacy of translation is that it withstands even all this truth, the whole truth about nature. This is what I mean by saying that, where indeterminacy of translation applies, there is no real question of right choice; there is no fact of the matter even to within the acknowledged under-determination of a theory of nature. (303)

This striking passage reveals that Quine's indeterminacy of translation arguments presuppose a 'realistic point of view' about physics, one according to which there is no 'fact of the matter' about aspects of language such as what translation is correct. From this perspective, meanings, synonymy, a *langue/parole* distinction, and 'innate properties of the mind' such as Chomsky wants aren't real. But why not? Quine does not appear to have an argument for treating physics as different from or more basic than other sciences, such as linguistics. (In section 4.11 we discuss the more recent 'Canberra project' that faces similar questions concerning how to pick out the basic facts on which everything else must supervene.)

Certainly, if meanings were regarded as real, Quine would have no reason to say that 'indeterminacy of translation withstands even all this truth,' for if Chomsky is granted his linguistic categories, there could perhaps be real answers to questions like: 'Which language is this person speaking?' 'What does "p" mean in the Native language?', 'Is "q" synonymous with "r"?,' etc. These answers would not be *indeterminate* in the way that Quine's indeterminacy argument presupposes; for there would presumably be facts of the matter about what words mean or what words were synonymous with what others, even if the data *underdetermined* a given translation (as Chomsky granted it could). Now, Quine could reply that he rejects these things as real since they aren't acknowledged by science, but as we have seen, Chomsky, a practicing scientist, says they *are* a part of science and that as a result there is no indeterminacy of translation.

For our purposes, the importance of Quine's debate with Chomsky is not so much the question of whose theory of linguistics ought to be adopted, as what it reveals about the assumptions that Quine must make in order to get his indeterminacy of translation arguments, and their consequences for analyticity, to work. Quine adopted a 'fully realistic attitude toward electrons and muons and curved space-time' in which 'indeterminacy of translation is that it withstands even all this truth, the whole truth about nature.' In other words, he adopted a standpoint according to which the entities posited by a linguist such as Chomsky are excluded *ab initio*. Like anyone else, Quine is free to adopt whatever assumptions and posits he wishes. But if those assumptions are required in order to show that other philosophical or linguistic assumptions or posits are unwarranted, then we need further reasons for their adoption, assuming they aren't shared by everyone. Quine's reasons for adopting them are, presumably, that they are part of our 'current theory of the world.' But which theory? Without some further criteria that rule-out empirical theories like Chomsky's, and rule-in all and only the phenomena that Quine is willing to adopt – electrons, muons, and so forth – this question goes unanswered.

We suggest, then, that the indeterminacy of translation arguments and the consequences Quine draws from them presuppose rather than help to support the strong, *physicalist* assumptions that Quine had adopted from the outset. Quine's debate with Chomsky revealed that he had assumed more than naturalism, where this is broadly conceived to include what passes as empirical science. It rather required the stronger claim of physicalism – that all and only the entities, laws, and explanatory devices of physics are to be countenanced. It's not surprising to learn that a position which assumes a realistic attitude toward electrons and muons and curved space-time as the fundamental 'truths of nature' finds little room for meanings, synonymy, propositions, and the like. Nor is it especially interesting.

Our objection here is that Quine's presupposing of physicalism undermines the force of his attempts to argue against mental (intentional) and intensional entities such as meanings and propositions. In other words, we deny the force of the arguments in supporting Quine's conclusion that:

> To accept intentional usage at face value is, we say, to postulate translation relations as somehow objectively valid though indeterminate in principle relative to the totality of speech dispositions. Such postulation promises little gain in scientific insight if there is no better ground for it than that the supposed translation relations are presupposed by the vernacular of semantics and intention. (1960, 221)[14]

Some of Quine's defenders, however, have tried to defend Quine against the charge of circularity in similar circumstances. The defense frequently comes by acknowledging that Quine's argument is circular, but denying that the circularity vitiates his position. The most detailed defense of Quine on this point that we have seen is due to Richard Schuldenfrei, who concedes that while Quine's argument is circular, it is not vitiating, since Quine's account of what counts as evidence must itself be seen as deriving from empirical inquiry, and that account supports Quine's assumption of physical theory in a non-vitiating way (see Schuldenfrei 1972; also Hylton 2007). This defense of Quine introduces elements of Quine's naturalized epistemology. Hence we will return to it, as well as some related responses to the circularity charge, in chapter 5.[15]

4.6 Carnap's 'Empiricism, Semantics, and Ontology'

In section 2.6, we summarized Carnap's (1956a) famous paper 'Empiricism, Semantics and Ontology' (ESO). We noted there how Carnap distinguished 'external' questions from 'internal' ones. The distinction, Carnap wrote, is between the 'question of the existence of certain entities of the new kind *within the framework*; we call them *internal questions*; and second, questions concerning the existence or reality of *the system of entities as a whole*, called *external questions*' (1956a, 206). Internal questions, such as 'Are there prime numbers greater than one hundred?' or 'Are some trees deciduous?' have a possible answer, provided that we have specified the linguistic framework sufficiently to imbue them with meaning. This answer may come from using 'purely logical methods' by looking at the consequences of the rule-system for the language (as in the prime number case), or from finding and testing empirical consequences of the statement when conjoined with other elements of physical theory (as in the tree case). As long as the philosopher or scientist provides a specification of rules and associated methods for answering the question, at least in principle, then she has provided a 'clear cognitive interpretation' to her questions. Philosophers ought to provide a linguistic framework within which the question is both meaningful and answerable.

By contrast, external questions, such as 'Are there *really* numbers?' or 'Do physical objects exist in reality?' are frequently devoid of cognitive content. Independent of a framework, there are no clear standards of evidence or rules of justification that give them a sense (and thereby a possible answer). They have a content only insofar as they concern 'the practical question of whether or not to accept those linguistic forms,' a question that concerns at most the 'expediency and fruitfulness' of adopting those forms (ibid., 218). Philosophers are tempted to ask external questions, but fail to see that what they are asking is not in need of or even capable of a theoretical justification or answer. Carnap wrote:

> Therefore nobody who meant the question "Are there numbers?" in the internal sense would either assert or even seriously consider a negative answer. This makes it plausible to assume that those philosophers . . . do not have in mind the internal question. And, indeed, if we were to ask them: "Do you mean the question as to whether the framework of numbers, *if* we were to accept it, would be found to be empty or not?", they would probably reply: "Not at all; we mean a question *prior* to the acceptance of the new framework." They might try to explain what they mean by saying that it is a question of the ontological status of numbers; the question whether or not numbers have a certain metaphysical characteristic called reality (sic) . . . Unfortunately, these philosophers have so far not given a formulation of their question in terms of the common scientific language . . . Unless they supply a clear cognitive interpretation, we are justified in our suspicion that their question is a pseudo-question, that is, one disguised in the form of a theoretical question while in fact it is non-theoretical. (1956a, 210)

We will argue here that much in ESO actually supports the later Quinean picture. In what follows we raise objections to some of Carnap's proposals in ESO, emphasizing aspects of Carnap's proposals that seem to us unmotivated or unnecessary, and that seem to lead naturally to a Quinean picture, including a rejection of analyticity.

The more philosophically interesting questions surround Carnap's philosophical picture of the 'ontological' questions that have long interested philosophers. Should we agree with Carnap that philosophers are not really interested in (or really asking) the internal question concerning the existence of numbers? There are good reasons for doubting Carnap's proposal.

One might imagine a philosopher's reply to Carnap along something like the following lines: 'Look, Carnap, I want to know whether there are numbers. I want to know whether there really are numbers. I know that most of us in ordinary situations would assent to the statement that there is at least one number greater than two and less than four, and that therefore there is at least one number. But the fact that people say that something is true doesn't mean that it really is true. Furthermore, I don't know what you're talking about in alluding to this "metaphysical characteristic, reality." I don't even know what "reality" is, qua feature. I just want to know whether it's really true that there are numbers. Furthermore, I'm using ordinary English when I ask the question. So appeal to some possible or actual artificial language, and what is true in that language, seems irrelevant to whether the question "are there numbers?," as uttered by an English-speaking philosopher, has an affirmative answer. And whether the "internal" question does have an affirmative answer is very difficult to ascertain. Some philosophers claim that they intuit that there are numbers. Others may intuit that there are not numbers. Are there intuitions, and if so, should we take intuitions to have any bearing on the question? (And by "should" in the last sentence I mean an "internal" should having to do with what counts as justification in our actual language, English in this case.) Others, such as Mill, claim that empirical evidence supports the existence of numbers. Is this correct? Matters are not at all straightforward, in the sense that it is not straightforward to see how to answer the internal question. But among the difficult questions is whether we are justified in either an affirmative answer or a negative answer, according to our actual concept of justification. Part of what is obscure is the question of just what is true concerning our actual concepts, including concepts of justification, that are expressed by terms in our actual language. So, contrary to what you claim, Carnap, the correct answer to the internal question about the existence of numbers is far from trivial or obvious. If anything, it is the answer to the external question that is trivial and obvious. Of course arithmetic is pragmatically useful. I don't care about that. To repeat, I want to know whether there are numbers, really.'

One possible Carnapian response to this line of objections might appeal to a distinction between vague and imprecise natural languages on the one hand and precise, scientifically respectable, although artificially engineered or constructed, languages on the other. Carnap might say that in ordinary English the word 'number' is vague and imprecise ('ordinary' and 'natural' will be taken as interchangeable for present purposes). The rules governing the use of number words in ordinary languages are indeterminate and perhaps even confused in various ways. It is hopeless, Carnap might claim, to try to discover 'the' correct rules that govern number-terms in ordinary languages. What we should instead do is consider various precise (albeit artificial) counterparts that fit fairly well with actual ordinary uses, but whose precision avoids such indeterminacies concerning the rules of natural and ordinary languages. But once we move to the precise and scientifically respectable artificial languages, there is no longer any indeterminacy. Each such language will have rules governing the correct application of the words correlated with the various concepts, and so 'internal' questions, which are to be answered in accord with those rules, will no longer be endlessly controversial. There will remain some controversies, of course, having to do for example with whether the empirical data jointly support this or that hypothesis more than some other hypothesis. But they will not be of the fruitless, endless, 'metaphysical' variety that have entrapped philosophers historically.

We think this response on Carnap's behalf is in accord with his philosophy as we have presented it. But is it effective? Consider a question such as whether there are atoms. This was a controversial question even among scientists for centuries. Part of the dispute, in fact, concerned whether atoms, being 'unobservable,' were 'metaphysical' posits, illegitimate in empirical physics. A Machian such as Ostwald, along with Mach himself, would have considered them 'metaphysical' in a pejorative sense.[16] Suppose that a Carnapian came upon an argument between a Bolzmannian who believed in atoms and a Machian who denies that the empirical data to date supported the existence of atoms. The Carnapian might explain to these scientists how they are confused due to the imprecision of natural language. We can adopt a language according to which the current data supports the existence of atoms, or we can adopt a language according to which the current data fails to support the existence of atoms. We could even adopt a pair of languages in which the existence of atoms was analytic, or their nonexistence was analytic, respectively. So there is no point in disputing the existence of atoms. All that we really need to do to make the internal dispute concerning atoms well-defined is to adopt a language with precise rules. Yet a natural response to such a suggestion would, we think, be incomprehension and perplexity. Surely, the scientists might say, the question whether *there are atoms*, and the related question whether some collection of data supports or undermines the claim that there are atoms, is not to be decided by something like stipulation, by stipulating the rules for some artificial language. We want to know, given what we mean by 'atom' (which is itself partly at issue), and 'justified,' whether atoms exist and whether we are justified in believing that atoms exist on the basis of the empirical data. Noting the fairly obvious fact that one could speak a variety of languages with various rules does nothing toward illuminating the question that we are interested in, namely, whether there are atoms! Eventually, the empirical data convinced most skeptical scientists that atoms exist, and this might be taken to show that the rules of science can provide clear verdicts in at least some important cases. But this fact does not help the Carnapian. As we have reconstructed his position, the Carnapian thinks that there was no particular need to wait for further empirical data to resolve the question. Scientists could have resolved the methodological questions by stipulation, and that should have ended any interesting methodological disputes concerning the question of whether the data justified the claim that atoms exist, as well as whether there are atoms. In some languages, the data at that time justify the assertion of the sentence 'there are atoms,' and in others the data at that time do not justify the assertion. Other languages are such that 'there are atoms' is among the analytic statements, and in these languages there is no interesting internal question, either.

On behalf of the Carnapian, one might respond that in the case of the sentence 'there are atoms,' it is the external question that was of greatest interest. But this does not conform well to the natural construal of what scientists claimed at the time. Many of the skeptics who denied the existence of atoms, or denied the justification for such a 'metaphysical,' evidence-transcending (they might say) assertion, would have granted that there were pragmatic advantages to adopting the sentence 'there are atoms' to empirical prediction and explanation. There was not much of a dispute about the *pragmatic* benefits of the application of a theory that posited atoms. What they disputed was whether there really were atoms, and whether scientists were justified in asserting or believing that there were atoms. It seems to us rather clear that the interesting action in these disputes involved what Carnap would have considered the 'internal' question.

Philosophers concerned with whether there are numbers can point to such cases and explain that the disputes concerning whether there are numbers (asked in the internal sense) are similar. In fact, they are even more perplexing, because it is even less clear what sorts of evidence could support or disconfirm the existence of numbers, and so there are much more difficult questions concerning justification that must be answered. Methodological questions concerning justification themselves seem non-empirical and about as difficult to discern an internal answer to as questions concerning the existence of numbers themselves. Thus nominalists and Platonists, even those who accept Carnap's internal/external distinction in a general sense, might say that it is the difficulty of the questions that leads to the lengthy disputes, rather than confusion about whether the question is an internal or an external question, or whether the rules of some language settle whether some sentence can be asserted by stipulation or fiat.

Thus it seems that scientists in interesting historical cases dispute 'internal' questions even when it is relatively easy to answer the 'external' question, and if so, perhaps philosophers dispute internal questions as well. But this does not by itself show what is wrong, if anything, with Carnap's suggestion that the only two questions that can be asked are the internal and the external question. (We are here focusing on existence or 'ontological' statements, but the distinction can be raised for any sort of statement.) Even if we are correct in claiming that the internal questions are the ones of chief scientific and philosophical interest, Carnap could nevertheless continue to insist that the difficulty in resolving them lies in the indeterminacy and vagueness and imprecision of natural languages. That such disputes are possible is precisely the reason that, for scientific purposes, we should adopt precisely specified languages with well-defined rules for adjudicating all disagreements concerning whether statements in those languages are justified by some experience or some rules of the language.

Carnap's approach to philosophical disputes (whether concerning 'ontology' or other controversies) in ESO is one that we find unsatisfactory for a variety of reasons. First let us consider how helpful an appeal to precise artificial languages is in resolving disputes that concern philosophers, such as the question whether there are numbers. Suppose someone has read some Platonist views on this issue, along with some nominalist arguments against the existence of numbers. Upon reading both, they are not sure whether the things that they took themselves to have learned about in grammar school really exist. Both Platonists and nominalists have nontrivial arguments for and against the existence of numbers and for and against various methodological proposals, such as claims that intuitions justify our beliefs that numbers exist, or that empirical evidence supports or undermines belief in numbers. Carnap in effect suggests that the way to adjudicate this dispute is to consider some precisely defined artificial language containing the sentence 'there are numbers,' and ask whether the rules of that language entail either the sentence itself or entail that the evidence that we have obtained thus far either supports or undermines the existence of numbers. Yet how, precisely, is this supposed to help with the initial perplexity? It is not clear that this helps at all, and arguably it is irrelevant to what interests philosophers.

Consider another related case. A large proportion of readers of this book will have either taught or participated in introductory undergraduate courses in philosophy. Often, in an early session of the course, questions arise concerning whether some actions are morally right, or some political system or law is just. Some bright student will wonder what all of the fuss is about. 'We just need to define our terms precisely,' this student will say. 'Just tell me what you mean by "moral," give me a precise rule for determining whether something is moral, and we can then give you the correct answer as to whether X is moral.' What one might be tempted to explain to the student who raises this is that while such stipulation might 'settle' questions of 'morality' in a sense, the sense in which it does so is trivial. That someone can stipulate that murdering children for fun is 'morally laudable' (i.e., that the sentence 'Murdering children for fun is morally laudable' can be stipulated as true in the language that we will henceforth speak) has little if any bearing on what we wanted to know in the first place, which is whether murdering children for fun is really moral or really immoral or what have you, given our actual concept of morality. Unfortunately, Carnap's proposals in ESO look like a more sophisticated form of the suggestion of the undergraduate student who wants to stipulate meanings for basic concepts of interest to philosophers in an attempt to resolve disagreements.

Even pointing out the intuitive triviality of stipulative 'resolutions' of philosophical controversies does not quite by itself show what is wrong with this approach to philosophical controversies. Carnap might simply retort, 'sure, I realize that philosophers continue to engage in fruitless controversies. My point is that the undergraduate you just described is basically correct, and that there is nothing to dispute intelligibly, beyond what the rules of a precise language say, or whether the adoption of a language with those rules has pragmatic virtues of various sorts.'

We will continue our discussion of Carnap's ESO perspective below. First we will raise some questions that naturally arise in contrasting Carnap's viewpoint with Quine's.

4.7 Some Quinean and Other Responses to 'Empiricism, Semantics, and Ontology'

In important respects, Carnap's approach in ESO was tantalizingly close to Quine's views in TD and thereafter. In this section we recount some key features of Quinean responses, and clarify the various respects in which Carnap and Quine disagree, as well as important matters on which they are in agreement.

Carnap had long held that any sentence whatever can be taken to be analytic (cf. section 2.2.4). While there is a relatively trivial sense in which this is correct in our view, there is another sense, a sense which Carnap would seem to have to accept, in which it is incorrect. In his *Logical Syntax of Language*, as we mentioned in chapter 2, Carnap allows for the possibility that a statement concerning the heat capacity of some substance can be added to a theory as in effect a further stipulation, an analytic claim. The potential problem here is that the act of taking a statement involving some expressions to be analytic is not independent of the meanings of at least some of the expressions contained therein. This is particularly true if we have expressions from a background language which have presupposed or already understood meanings. If we already understand what 'cat' and 'mat' mean, along with other terms in the sentence 'The cat is on the mat,' we cannot simply stipulate 'the cat is on the mat.' (We are proceeding here at a fairly intuitive level. Our preferred account of empirically indefeasible stipulation is given in chapter 6.) The reason is intuitively fairly straightforward. Given what we already meant by 'the cat is on the mat,' that statement expresses an empirically defeasible claim. A stipulation of the sort that should be considered 'analytic,' even by Carnap, is a statement that, whatever other features it is understood to have, is not empirically defeasible, at least not in the sense that answering 'internal' questions concerning whether 'the cat is on the mat' is true requires appeal to empirical data. Being derivable from the rules of the language rather than by appeal to empirical evidence is precisely one of the features that Carnap assumes is characteristic of analytic statements. But one cannot coherently, intelligibly, treat the same sentence, as used on a particular occasion, as both empirically defeasible and as empirically indefeasible. If one tried, the rules given for the language would be contradictory, both permitting and ruling out the possibility of empirical evidence bearing on some statements. As we discuss further in chapter 6, if we allow some statements to be indefeasibly stipulated, there are necessary restrictions on what statements can be stipulated, 'added' to a current linguistic practice, given features already understood to be in place. Any practice should be coherent in the sense of having intelligible rule sets governing it, and the practice of making stipulations is no exception.

Another related problem for Carnap is that the stipulated rules governing the use of an expression are not independent of the meaning of that expression. Thus the syntactic sequence s, in a language in which sentence s is a stipulation, means something different from s as employed within a language in which s is an empirically defeasible descriptive statement. This is a point we have argued for in section 3.9, and return to in chapter 6. The fact that some syntactic string is true-in-L for some artificial L has no bearing on whether s is true in English.

We have raised a worry about Carnap's view that any sentence can be stipulated, and our own objections to it. But Carnap's view is one which naturally leads toward a Quinean picture that discards both the analytic–synthetic distinction and the 'theory change vs. language change' distinction. The reason is this. If absolutely any of our sentences can be labeled 'analytic,' including statements concerning heat capacities or other seemingly empirically defeasible statements, while preserving their meaning at least in the sense of remaining roughly equivalent in correct translation, then it becomes very hard to see the point of distinguishing the analytic from the synthetic sentences, just as Quine argued (cf. sections 2.2.4, 3.7). It can look like there is a distinction without a difference between a 'language' whose rules include the stipulation LEAD = 'The heat capacity of lead is C . . .' on the one hand, and a 'language' otherwise similar but that fails to contain that stipulation, but allows us to assert (as justified or as true) the sentence LEAD on the basis of empirical evidence. Carnap would describe our justification for the adoption of a 'language' with sentence LEAD as stipulated or analytic to be the 'pragmatic' fact that use of such a language has virtues when it comes to making some predictions concerning lead. Whereas if we adopted the 'different language' not stipulating LEAD, Carnap would describe our situation as applying the 'internal' rules for justifying sentences to the actual empirical evidence, and thereby 'internally' establishing that LEAD is true. But one cannot blame Quineans for wondering what the point of these distinctions is. Upon reading ESO, one might naturally begin to doubt the relevance of the distinctions, if all that they do is arbitrarily label some changes 'changes in language' and other changes 'changes in theory,' when the resultant class of sentences accepted as true is the same, and accepted for what appear to be the same reasons.

A related problem with Carnap's presentation in ESO is vagueness about what counts as 'pragmatic reasons' for adopting a new language, as opposed to empirical justifications applied in accord with the rules of the language 'from within.' To the extent that he wants to allow that sentences like LEAD can be stipulated and the corresponding language(s) can be adopted for pragmatic reasons, it is hard to see what other 'pragmatic' basis there is to prefer such an adoption beyond the standard empirical virtues of a theory, such as empirical predictive and explanatory adequacy. But if these are the criteria to be used, then external 'pragmatic' criteria for adopting a language system seem to collapse into internal, 'empirical' criteria for adopting a sentence or theory of a language. But in that case, Carnap seems to be uncomfortably close to Quine on this issue, who denies that there is a distinction between epistemic and pragmatic reasons.[17]

There is a further unclarity in the notion of an 'internal' statement. In some applications of the notion Carnap seems to take 'internal' to mean 'internal to the language' in a narrow sense, such that it means something like 'can be settled or is answerable on the basis of the rules of language alone, without appeal to empirical evidence.' In other applications, though, Carnap seems to allow that empirical questions can also be settled 'internally,' in the broader sense that the rules of language specify the conditions under which the sentence would, in principle, be confirmed or refuted by empirical evidence ('in principle' because Carnap does not require that we can, right now, answer every internal empirical question). In our discussion we are interpreting 'internal' in the broader sense. However, even if we interpret 'internal' in the narrow sense, this does not help Carnap to avoid the problem we raised concerning the incoherence of stipulating already meaningful non-stipulations, or rescue Carnap from the Quineans' worry concerning the distinction between adopting for pragmatic reasons a language with 'semantic rules' or stipulations versus changing one's theory within a language for empirical reasons. We will proceed on the assumption that 'internal' is to be taken in the broad sense, to the extent that we think that similar arguments and objections can be given no matter which sense is adopted.

To anticipate the positive view that we present in chapter 6, we wish to express some differences between the viewpoint that we are inclined to adopt and Carnap's. We do not think that philosophical questions in general are to be addressed by stipulating precise rules for some artificially engineered language. On our positive view, a statement being stipulated, or 'analytic-like,' is a matter of how it is understood, the rules or conventions that determine the sentence's meaning within our language. Thus, unlike both Carnap and Quine, we think that there is an important distinction between sentences understood as expressing stipulations versus sentences understood as expressing more ordinary empirical descriptions. Connected with this, we think that the conventions or understood norms governing our uses of mathematical statements (that they are empirically indefeasible in an interesting sense that we describe, for example) are partly constitutive of their meanings, and are what makes them mathematical statements as opposed to empirical descriptions. This difference is one that should be preserved across correct translations (where we need not presuppose that there is a uniquely correct translation), in our view. We think that by observing some of these differences, we can avoid many of the central objections that Quine and others raise against the analytic–synthetic distinction that the Carnap of ESO seems ill-positioned to respond to.

A further observation concerning Carnap's discussion of philosophical methodology in ESO is that as a matter of fact, the examples that Carnap focuses on are all 'abstracta' (aside from the difficult case of spatiotemporal points), that is, those entities our knowledge of which appears to be non-empirical. The positive position that we develop in chapter 6 is consistent with Carnap's idea that these kinds of entities are special or distinctive in a philosophically interesting way, and that our purported knowledge of some of the statements that refer to such abstracta may be best explained by appeal to a notion akin to analyticity. But unfortunately, from our point of view, Carnap does not emphasize that, or clarify how, these entities are special and different from, say, electrons. Instead, he focuses on the internal/external distinction in general, and does not clearly distinguish empirical reasons for acceptance of a statement from pragmatic virtues of adopting a language whose rules include stipulation of a sentence of the same syntactic form. In our view, Carnap's overgeneralization of the applicability of the analytic–synthetic distinction contributed to a perception that the distinction was philosophically unhelpful and un-illuminating, as Quineans argued.

The considerations just raised against the Carnapian conception of proper philosophical methodology extend to his overall 'explication project.' While there are virtues to that project, it conceals difficulties of the sort just raised against Carnapian methodology. Carnap was concerned to avoid endless and what he took to be fruitless philosophical controversies. His proposal was to substitute precise concepts, to substitute for our vague and imprecise natural languages various precise, engineered languages in which disputes could always be settled in accord with precise rules. Perhaps not every question could be decided, but in 'undecidable' cases presumably it should at least be clear that they are undecidable, so that disputing 'internally' would be pointless.[18]

We described Carnap's notion of 'explication' in chapter 2. We return to explication at this point to note that similar difficulties attend any Carnapian attempt to remove the possibility of philosophical controversy by appeal to 'explication,' which invariably involves the replacement of 'vague and imprecise' concepts by concepts governed by explicit and (usually) precise rules. The problem that we noted above was that stipulations of precise concepts do not invariably answer questions concerning concepts with which we began, which we took ourselves to understand prior to any linguistic engineering. The fact that a linguistically engineered statement of similar syntactic form can be constructed and definitively answered does not obviously engage the question involving the concepts with which we began.[19]

4.8 Some Recent Connections between 'Conceptual Truths' and Ontology

As we noted in the overview to this chapter, our discussion of some connections between analyticity and ontology does not provide an overview of the entire landscape. That landscape is far too expansive. In the following sections, we will nevertheless mention a few recent developments that fall within the broad purview of Carnapian or Quinean views concerning analyticity and ontology, and compare some of these developments to the theory of analyticity that we present in chapter 6. We will first note some work by Stephen Schiffer on what he calls 'pleonastic concepts' and 'pleonastic propositions.' We will then briefly describe an ongoing controversy concerning the meaning of the existential quantifier, and the bearing this dispute is taken to have concerning controversies about mereology.

At a certain broad level of abstraction, one might label 'Carnapian' any view concerning ontological questions according to which at least some such questions are best thought of as settled by appeal to stipulation, rules of language, conceptual truths, analyticity, or some kindred notion. In this relatively permissive sense of 'Carnapian,' we could consider Stephen Schiffer's approach to questions concerning the existence of propositions, entities purportedly expressed by some sentences, to be a Carnapian one. According to Schiffer, propositions are what he calls 'pleonastic' entities. His account of pleonastic entities is rather complicated and is designed to avoid a number of difficulties that he considers. But the basic idea is that propositions are among a distinctive class of entities:

> Propositions are mere shadows of the sentences yielding them in something-from-nothing transformations; they come softly into existence, without disturbing the preexisting causal order in any way. That is why

claims that they exist may be conservatively added to the truths we had
before those claims were added. (Schiffer 2005, 370)

The details of a 'something-from-nothing transformation' and 'pleonastic
concept' will not be recounted here. But Schiffer's proposal is quite similar
in a number of ways to the position we will develop in chapter 6 (see especially section 6.9).[20]

One puzzling feature of Schiffer's approach is evident in the above quotation. He takes pleonastic entities' avoidance of 'disturbing the pre-existing
causal order' to be a centrally important feature of them. Yet his definitions of the relevant terms ('something-from-nothing,' 'pleonastic concept') do not invoke causation at all, but rather have to do mostly with
logical features, a form of logical 'conservativeness.' Presumably Schiffer
takes the logical conservativeness conditions on adding various 'something-
from-nothing transformations' to entail the causal inertness of the 'pleonastic entities' thereby 'yielded.' Schiffer also uses the term 'pre-existing
causal order,' suggesting that on his view propositions do not exist prior to
some human activities, perhaps. In any case, our own proposals concerning both mathematical entities and what we will call (in chapter 6) 'pure
and impure stipulata' are quite similar in broad outline, in that like Schiffer
we appeal to something akin to stipulations with existential consequences
in our accounts. There are differences between our approaches, however.
One is that our approach appeals to rules governing the uses, in particular
the evidential profiles, of some statements, according to which no possible
empirical evidence is counted against their truth. It may turn out that various 'conservativeness' constraints and causal inertness constraints may be
required by our account in order to ensure the coherence of the background
linguistic practice (which practice permits the introduction of such stipulations). But we do not *define* our notions of stipulata as entities that meet
such logical conservativeness or causal inertness constraints. Our focus will
instead be on what is understood as permitted to count as evidence for or
against various special, stipulative statements (cf. section 6.2f.).

4.9 Quine's Criterion of Ontological Commitment, Causality, and 'Exists'

A number of authors have raised objections to Quine's view that 'to be is to
be the value of a bound variable' (1953a, 15; discussed in section 4.2 above).
According to Quine, we are ontologically committed to all and only entities

that are in the domain of quantification of our best empirical theories (of physics in particular). An interesting contrasting view is given by Jody Azzouni in a lengthy and sophisticated defense of his position concerning mathematical abstracta (Azzouni 1994, 2000, 2004). According to Azzouni, we are effectively forced to accept that mathematical statements that are applied within the empirical sciences are true, or at the very least, his argument is supposed to show that we as a matter of fact ought to be interpreted as taking them to be true, and we are justified in so taking them. Among these true mathematical statements are statements such as 'There are prime numbers between 20 and 30.' If we adopt Quine's criterion of ontological commitment, along with Azzouni's anti-instrumentalism concerning such statements, then in accepting this statement we are thereby committed to the existence of prime numbers between 20 and 30, leaving aside whether we are committed to 20 and 30, or other numbers as well. To make a very interesting story short, Azzouni proposes that there is an existence predicate in natural language that is not characterizable solely by appeal to the existential quantifier, even as 'objectually' understood (that is, understood as ranging over objects in the domain). Azzouni (2004) argues that what we require in order to accept an entity as genuinely existing is that there be some plausible, broadly causal, account of how we could acquire knowledge of its existence and nature.[21]

In contrast to the kind of view presented by Azzouni, Mark Colyvan argues in *The Indispensability of Mathematics* (2003) that it is a mistake to impose causal requirements on what we should adopt among our ontological commitments. Colyvan considers a variety of possible 'Eleatic principles,' or proposals concerning the ways in which causal connections to knowers might be taken to be required for the genuine empirical justification of existence claims. He provides a variety of arguments that none of the 'Eleatic' proposals that he considers are plausible or seem well-motivated. Among his most interesting arguments are those purportedly showing how mathematical entities can play crucial roles in empirical explanation even when these entities cannot plausibly be assigned a causal role within the explanations. Colyvan's arguments provide a further indirect defense of a broadly Quinean position concerning mathematical ontology in particular.

A third, somewhat Carnapian view is that presented in Marc Balaguer's *Platonism and Anti-Platonism in Mathematics* (Balaguer 1998) According to Balaguer, a version of mathematical realism, which he calls 'full-blooded Platonism,' is defensible. Full-blooded Platonism states that any consistent mathematical theory is true of some structure within a realm of mathematical facts.

However, a fictionalist position, according to which no mathematical abstracta exist, is also defensible, Balaguer argues. Finally, the very fact that there is no way of showing whether full-blooded Platonism or fictionalism is true shows (via further elaboration) that there is no fact of the matter as to whether such abstracta exist. It may be somewhat misleading to call Balaguer's position 'Carnapian,' for a number of reasons. One is that Balaguer seems not to be at all attracted to a 'conventionalist' view of logic that Carnap at times expressed (cf. section 1.8, above). But Balaguer's position shares a central feature with Carnap in that both are 'non-factualist' concerning ontological questions.

4.10 Eli Hirsch and Ted Sider on Mereological Principles

Recall from chapter 1 that Carnap was concerned early in his career to avoid 'pseudoquestions' in philosophy (cf. sections 1.8, 2.2.5, 2.6). Pseudoquestions might include 'merely verbal disputes.' What 'merely verbal disputes' are is a nontrivial matter, although clear cases are simple enough to construct. As we noted above, despite what Carnap may have hoped, it is not a straightforward matter to show that various ontological disputes were in effect merely verbal disputes, in the sense that they could be readily resolved by adopting one language or another.

One recent controversy has concerned whether various mereological sums exist as entities over and above their parts. For example, is the Eiffel Tower, together with ('summed' with) a particular ping-pong ball, a further entity? Or is there no such entity as the ping-pong-Eiffel-Tower? A variety of positions claiming to answer this kind of question have been defended. Some 'nihilists' think that there is no such thing, really, as the ping-pong ball or the Eiffel Tower to begin with. According to nihilists, there are really only the metaphysical atoms, and other 'things' that we seem to refer to do not really exist. The nihilists then owe an account of how we are to make sense of our ordinary talk and the apparent contents of thought. A second contrasting approach is 'universalism.' Universalists think that given any two distinct existent concreta, there is a further entity, their mereological sum. They then owe us an account of why ordinary speakers, along with many philosophers, deny that there is such a thing as ping-pong-Eiffel-Tower. Philosophers who find neither nihilism nor universalism attractive options have proposed still further positions with ontological commitments intermediate between nihilism and universalism. Some appeal to ordinary language uses, and attempt to 'read off' what sorts of entities the ordinary speaker is ontologically committed to. Such an 'ordinary language' approach might try to more clearly exhibit the ontological commitments supposed to be implicit in our ordinary linguistic practices. The main difficulty faced by such approaches seems to be the complicated, ad hoc, and apparently unprincipled nature of ordinary talk concerning what exists. A fourth alternative is to adopt a broadly Quinean approach akin to what we canvassed in section 4.2. This approach would construct a 'best overall scientific account' in a regimented language, and from it try to read off the ontological commitments of that best theory.

Finally, a fifth approach, which most closely resembles the Carnapian approach in ESO, is to try to show that there is no fact of the matter concerning which position (universalism, nihilism, etc.) on mereological principles is correct. There are simply different notions of 'part,' 'whole,' 'sum,' and perhaps 'exists' that can be employed by speakers of a language. Because of this, to the extent that anyone is correct, it is the ordinary-language mereologist who seeks to describe the notions of 'part,' 'exist,' and so on that we actually employ. Eli Hirsch is among the best-known defenders of this sort of position (Hirsch 2005). Others, however, seem to find similar positions attractive (see, e.g., Chalmers 2007). A contrasting view is given by Ted Sider (2003), who defends the objectivity of ontological questions. Sider adopts a position concerning ontological disputes that appears to be broadly Quinean in the following respect: he follows Quine and David Lewis in thinking that all questions, including ontological ones, are to be decided, not by something akin to stipulation, but by appeal to the best overall theory, where that 'theory' covers absolutely everything under the metaphysical sun.

4.11 The 'Canberra Project': A Resurrection of Carnap's *Aufbau*?

Recall that Carnap sought in the *Aufbau* to show how our experience could be logically 'constructed' from basic elements, such as sensory experience, plus relations, such as the relation of similarity, defined over those elements (cf. section 1.8). From this collection of basis facts, Carnap showed how to logically construct statements concerning the 'inter-subjective' world described by physics or psychology from 'autopsychological' basis elements and statements. These logical derivations were to proceed via analytic statements that in effect provided rules for deriving the higher-level statements (of physics and so on) from the basis. Recently Frank Jackson, David

Chalmers and others have elaborated a picture that is similar in a number of ways to the original *Aufbau* proposal. The main difference seems to be that the 'bridge principles' used to derive statements involving concepts outside of the basis set (of concepts) are not taken to be 'analytic,' but are rather said to represent 'a priori entailments.'

The Canberra project involves a number of philosophical controversies, and we can here only raise some fairly standard objections to the Canberra project that are connected to the issue of analyticity, along with some responses that defenders of the project make, as we understand them. Our main reason for including this discussion, brief though it is, is that the Canberra project is an interesting contemporary view with conceptual and historical ties to a view that makes essential appeal to a notion bearing at least a family resemblance to analyticity.

A very helpful outline of the picture proposed by advocates of the Canberra project is given by Chalmers (2008). To begin, grant that there is a complete description of the world in some privileged or basic vocabulary. Let us call this vocabulary C(anberra)-basic. The facts as described in this special vocabulary may be jointly termed the C-basis facts. All non-C-basis statements that are true are supposed to follow, 'a priori,' from the C-basis facts.[22] The entailments proceed via something akin to 'Carnap conditionals' linking the C-basis to the non-C-basis.[23] In short, the general picture looks like this:

C-basis statements

$C^* \rightarrow Q$ ('a priori entailments' or 'analytic' statements; C^* is from C-basis, while Q is not)

Q (some non C-basis statement)

Some familiar examples discussed by philosophers are taken to fit this picture. Consider identity statements. Suppose that we imagine a complete description of the world in the language of physics. How can we come to know that water is (in the sense of 'is identical to') H_2O? According to Canberrans, we come to know this by appeal to an a priori knowable entailment via something like our prior concept of water, together with a description in the language of physics of our actual situation. Knowledge of our concept of water is encoded by our a priori capacity to know a conditional that has something like the form, 'If the watery stuff around here is largely composed of H_2O molecules, then water is H_2O.' The precise form of the conditional, and what is to go into the antecedent, is controversial and perhaps somewhat indefinite, for it may be only infinitarily expressible, according to Canberrans, although even if it is, this is not taken by them to preclude a priori knowability. But in any case, as long as we know a priori that if the watery stuff around here is composed largely of H_2O molecules, then water is H_2O, and furthermore the statement 'the watery stuff around here is largely composed of H_2O molecules' (or whatever the antecedent is taken to be) is translatable into, or expressible via, the C-basis vocabulary, then one can infer a priori that water is H_2O from the C-basis facts together with the a priori knowable entailment (via the conditional).

If this is the correct story as to how identity statements such as 'water = H_2O' are knowable, then the Canberrans see it as having implications for the legitimacy or knowability of mind–body identity statements. The view is something like the following (again, glossing over a considerable host of detail). We understand how we have come to know that water is H_2O, that heat is molecular motion, that lightning is electric current flow through the atmosphere causing ionization, and so on. We have come to know these identities by coming to know the basis facts (some collection of physical facts), together with our prior concepts of water, heat, lightning, and what have you. However, the mind–body identity statements do not seem to be knowable in this C-admissible way. There is no a priori conditional (or entailment, if one prefers) of the form, 'If so and so is the case, then pain is C-fiber firing.' That it is difficult, or impossible, to come up with an a priori knowable entailment from purely physical facts to identities involving pain shows that there is a profound disanalogy between supposed mind–brain identity statements and other scientifically accepted identity statements. The latter unproblematically follow from uncontroversial physics via fairly uncontroversial, and a priori knowable, entailment relations. The former do not.

The general Canberra picture is quite similar, structurally, to the one proposed by Carnap's *Aufbau*. The main differences seem to be that Carnap's 'basis' facts were (or could be) phenomenal, ultimately reducible to 'perceived similarity' relations within the realm of phenomenal experience. The Canberra project leaves open what the basis facts are, but they plausibly include something akin to descriptions in some language of physics.[24] Their similarity may suggest, though, that there are reasons to worry that it is destined to face similar difficulties.

Among the best-known objections to Carnap's *Aufbau* is Quine's objection that at a crucial stage, when deriving facts about space-time distributions of events, Carnap appeals to merely 'inductive' principles such as theoretical simplicity and elegance.[25] Once such methods are introduced, however, it becomes difficult to retain the original motivation of the project. The motivation was, very roughly, to show how one could come to know a variety of truths involving complicated theoretical concepts (including concepts of unobservable entities such as atoms), as well as describe an 'objective,' inter-subjectively shared world, such that the story of how we come to know these facts and descriptions involves only epistemically and conceptually unproblematic statements (phenomenal and 'analytic' statements, respectively) and unproblematic inference principles, i.e., logical rules. If one allows merely inductive methods of inference such as inference to the best explanation, such that the best theory may be the most simple or elegant in some intuitive but undefined (arguably, indefinable) sense, then the rest of the project seems superfluous, or at the least, the conceptual reduction part of the picture does. Allowing appeal to theoretical virtues, one can propose any theory whose statements and language are selected so as to provide the best, most theoretically virtuous, explanation of the basic phenomena. Most importantly, the concepts need not be logically definable in terms of the concepts used in describing the basic facts, and the statements involving non-basic concepts need not follow logically or a priori from the basic facts. The only constraint is that the theory predict and explain in relatively virtuous ways, that is, in 'simple' or 'elegant' ways.

We can apply this sort of objection to the simplified argument against mind–body identities as follows. Let us call the advocate of merely inductive inferences the 'inductivist.' The inductivist may respond to the Canberran anti-reductionist about the mind in something like the following way. 'Here is how we come to know identities in general. We consider some "basic" data (which both sides can be taken to agree on), and consider what would best explain that data, so far as we know. If our simplest overall account says that, for example, Hesperus is Phosphorus, or that water is H_2O, then by God, that's what we should believe. Such belief is fallible, to be sure. But there is no reason to think that there is any a priori knowable conditional linking such identities to the basis facts even in the uncontroversial cases just mentioned. The linkage is merely inductive. But even if you convinced us that there are a priori linkages in these particular cases, there remains a problem akin to the one that Quine raised against Carnap's *Aufbau*. It is that one needs to appeal to merely inductive principles even in the construction of the "basis" itself. How the theory of physics comes to be known or justified in the first place is not via deduction from some prior phenomenal realm but inductively, by appeal to something like inference to the best explanation. So the Canberran is already committed to inductive principles of inference anyway. Why should he balk, then, at inductive inferences to identity statements? Picking on identity statements in particular seems ad hoc and unmotivated, then, even by the Canberran's own lights.'

The Canberra project is connected to lively controversies between some of the keenest philosophical minds presently working. So are disputes concerning the nature and existence of propositions, mathematical abstracta, mereological principles, and the meaning of 'exists.' Whether a version of the analytic–synthetic distinction, such as the one we shall propose, can shed some further light on the disputes we have recounted remains to be seen, but we will suggest in chapter 6 some ways in which it might.

4.12 Chapter Summary

In this chapter we first reviewed Quine's approach to ontology with an emphasis on Quine's physicalism and the relation between his physicalism and his rejection of 'intensional' notions and entities. We then summarized Quine's arguments for his famous 'indeterminacy of translation' thesis, according to which there is no fact of the matter concerning what is meant by any given expression of any language. We distinguished it from the related but distinct 'inscrutability of reference' thesis, according to which there is no fact of the matter concerning what expressions of language refer to. Next we considered some objections to Quine's assumptions and his methodology, including some central objections from Chomsky, according to which Quine appears to be making a fairly trivial point concerning underdetermination of theory by data, and then inflating the significance of underdetermination by restricting the data available to linguists by presupposing a realism concerning physics, while at the same time adopting a different attitude toward entities appealed to by other scientists like linguists. We noted that Quine's presupposition of the fundamentality of physics is what leads him to his 'nonfactualisms' about meaning and reference.

Next we discussed Carnap's approach to ontology, with a special emphasis on his proposals in 'Empiricism, Semantics, and Ontology' (ESO). We suggested that Carnap's position, as outlined in ESO, has many features that lead to a Quinean sort of position that we discussed in chapter 3. We argued that Carnap's view suffers from a number of defects, and some of these defects provide avenues for Quineans to reject the 'internal/external' question distinction, the analytic–synthetic distinction, and to then treat all theoretical questions as questions to be settled by appeal to broadly pragmatic criteria of theory choice. In particular, the central question, 'are there numbers?,' is to be settled not 'internally,' by appeal to rules of language associated with number-terms and number-concepts, but by appeal to the same sorts of theoretical virtues that enable us to answer 'are there electrons?,' namely, empirical adequacy and theoretical simplicity, beauty, or what have you. We suggested reasons why Carnap is ill-positioned to argue against the Quinean's rejection of the two sorts of question. We also raised a variety of further objections to Carnap's overall methodology, according to which the way that philosophers should resolve ontological disputes is by positing languages with precise rules. Among the main objections to Carnap's proposal is that when philosophers ask a question such as 'are there numbers?,' it seems beside the point to note that there exist languages such that that string of words has a trivial 'answer.'

In the final sections of the chapter we outlined a few recent developments related to ontological and methodological disputes that separated Quine and Carnap and that surround the analytic–synthetic distinction. One recent work that we discuss is Schiffer's proposals concerning 'pleonastic concepts.' Schiffer is interested in capturing a notion that clarifies the connection between some puzzling 'abstract' entities, propositions in particular, and he does so by appeal to something akin to conceptual truths or definitions from which the existence of the puzzling entities logically follows. Another recent development comes from the work of Azzouni. Among the arguments that Azzouni makes is that Quine is wrong to assimilate genuine ontological commitment to the existential quantifier. Instead, Azzouni thinks that our ordinary notion of existence imposes the requirement that anything said to genuinely exist must be such that there is an intelligible (broadly causal) story as to how we can know that it exists. We next turned to disputes concerning the existence of strange mereological sums, such as the object, if any, that is the 'sum' of a nose and the Eiffel Tower. Eli Hirsch has argued at some length that there is no interesting dispute to be had other than resolving questions concerning what our ordinary concepts of genuine objects entail. Hirsch thinks that disputes relating to such mereological concepts are in an interesting sense 'merely verbal,' harkening back to Carnap's early work debunking what he thought were merely verbal problems and other 'pseudoproblems.' Ted Sider, by contrast, adopts a more Quinean view concerning such disputes, that they are to be resolved by appeal to theoretical virtues of a sort appealed to in order to resolve 'are there electrons?', Finally, we considered a program, the 'Canberra project,' that consciously shares many features with Carnap's early *Aufbau* project. One feature in particular connects to analyticity, in that advocates of the Canberra project invoke what they call 'a priori entailments' in place of what Carnap would have considered 'analytic truths,' where the a priori entailments connect a fundamental or 'privileged' language or realm of facts to the more controversial or less fundamental language or realm.

4.13 Further Reading

The classic works of Quine and Carnap that we mention in this chapter include Carnap's ESO (1956a) and Quine's (1960) book *Word and Object*, as well as various essays of Quine including 'On What There Is' (1953a) and 'Ontological Relativity' (1969b). As we saw, Noam Chomsky's criticism of Quine's indeterminacy of translation thesis, entitled 'Quine's Empirical Assumptions' (1975), remains an important one, and the text in which it has been reproduced includes Quine's response, along with other significant essays on Quine (Davidson and Hintikka, 1975). A related dispute concerning the scientific reputability of analyticity is in Katz 'Where Things now Stand with the Analytic–Synthetic Distinction' (1974) and Harman's response 'Katz' Credo' (1976). For Schiffer's account of pleonastic concepts see Schiffer (2003). Balaguer (1998) argues for a non-factualism concerning the existence of mathematical abstracta. Azzouni's views are propounded in several books, all of which are well worth reading, and his (1994), (2000), and (2004) are especially pertinent to issues discussed in this book. Glock's (2003) contains a chapter on ontology that is very clear and provides a valuable overview of many criticisms of Quine's ontological views. For the Canberra project, a fine example is Frank Jackson's (1998) book *From Metaphysics to Ethics*, as well as many recent works by Jackson and other Canberran sympathizers such as David Chalmers (2008).

5

ANALYTICITY AND EPISTEMOLOGY

5.1 Introduction and Overview

There are good reasons to give Carnap's elaborations of analyticity and Quine's criticisms of Carnap's positions a central place in our book. However, there is a broader class of views which, while different in various details from Carnap's projects, have nevertheless been highly influential within philosophy at large. The class that we have in mind is the view labeled by its adherents 'logical empiricism,' and (at times) by its antagonists 'logical positivism.' One of the main purposes of this chapter is to identify, in section 5.2, a number of core theses that typify logical empiricism, with a special emphasis on the position of one highly influential logical empiricist, A. J. Ayer. Our account will be especially focused on the logical empiricists' treatment of analyticity and its relation to a priori knowledge or justification. In section 5.3 we will critically discuss the core logical empiricist theses we have introduced, with a special focus on Ayer's proposals. In section 5.4, we will supplement our critique with a look at Laurence BonJour's (1998) very detailed criticisms of central logical empiricist claims which he has presented in his recent book *In Defense of Pure Reason*. In our discussion we respond to some of BonJour's arguments purporting to show that an appeal to analyticity neither resolves nor even sheds any light on epistemological problems. In the next section (5.5), we turn to an account of Quine's own 'naturalized epistemology' insofar as it bears on the issue of analytic truth. Our discussion of Quine's naturalized epistemology will then lead us back to the circularity objection to Quine's use of science that we considered in the last chapter (section 4.5), for several philosophers have seen within Quine's epistemology the resources for defending him against charges of circularity, and in section 5.6 we consider in detail one such defense, due to Richard Schuldenfrei (1972). We end the chapter with another important development since Quine's 'Two Dogmas' attack on analyticity. In his seminal book *Naming and Necessity* (1980), Saul Kripke has argued that the logical empiricists wrongly conflated necessity, apriority, and analyticity, regarding these properties as coextensive – even necessarily so. To the contrary, Kripke argues, these three notions are distinct. Among Kripke's best-known arguments are those purporting to show that there are both a priori knowable, yet contingent, statements, and also that there are necessary truths that are knowable only a posteriori. We briefly recount Kripke's central arguments in section 5.7, and note how these arguments can pose a challenge to some standard accounts of analyticity – a challenge we shall return to in chapter 6.

5.2 Analytic Truths and their Role in Epistemology: The 'Classical' Position

Our discussion of the epistemological role of analytic statements, and of the consequences of rejecting them, begins with a summary and critique of what we call a 'classical' position on analyticity. The *locus classicus* of the classical position comes from A. J. Ayer's famous *Language, Truth and Logic* (Ayer 1946, hereafter LTL). We believe that the primary theses that constitute the classical position can all be found in some form in LTL. However, we do not intend the following discussion to be an interpretive exegesis of Ayer's book. Rather, we believe that what Ayer gave expression to is a prima facie plausible account of analytic statements and their relationship to knowledge and justification, an account that was broadly shared, with different emphases and details, by several prominent logical empiricists. Many elements of the account can be found in the Vienna Circle (which Ayer visited as a young man), and some of its theses find earlier expression in Kant, Hume, Wittgenstein, and Frege.

The classical view of analyticity, then, is comprised of the following claims:

> 1. *Factual statements are all and only statements that can be justified by appeal to experience, to empirical evidence. A proposition is synthetic when its truth is determined by the facts of experience.*

This idea was made explicit by Ayer, who spoke of the 'validity' of a statement as determined by experience (LTL, 79), but variants of it can be found in Wittgenstein, Schlick, and Carnap. Recall from chapter 1 that in his *Tractatus*, Wittgenstein argued that the only genuine propositions were those that pictured possible states of affairs – ways that the world may or may not be. Schlick largely followed Kant's characterization of a posteriori synthetic judgments as having their basis in experience, although he and other Vienna Circle members rejected synthetic a priori judgments, as we saw in chapter 1 (cf. Schlick 1985, 77).

> 2. *Some statements express necessary truths. They include equations and theorems of mathematics, statements of geometry, laws of logic, and certain generalizations such as 'no point is both red and green all over' which are not reducible to logic.*

The idea that arithmetic, logic, geometry, and certain statements of science and metaphysics express necessary truths was, we have seen, defended at length by Kant, and by many others since. Kant regarded it as unintelligible to speak of an arithmetical equation being possibly false, for its truth derived from the very conditions that make our experience possible. Frege denied that the laws of logic were conceivably false, declaring that they were partially constitutive of what we call 'thinking,' a point echoed, albeit for different reasons, by Schlick (1985, 337).

> 3. *No statement can be known to be necessarily true on the basis of empirical observation.*

This point was, as we have seen from chapter 1, defended by Kant. Ayer and the Vienna Circle accepted it, again with the qualification that no substantive or 'ampliative' necessities are known a priori (cf. LTL, 75ff.; Schlick 1985, 76f.).

> 4. *No necessary truth would ever, under any conditions, come to be regarded as disconfirmed by empirical evidence.*

Ayer defended this important point at length against the possibility, raised by J. S. Mill, that mathematical truths might be a species of empirical knowledge. We discuss below his defense which, again, has echoes of Kant's defense of the same claim. In both Wittgenstein's *Tractatus* and Carnap's *Aufbau*, this point was taken to be a consequence of the fact that expressions of necessary 'truth' (in the qualified form these authors acknowledged them) were taken to be direct consequences of the logical framework that makes descriptive language possible in the first place (cf. Carnap 1967, 177f.).

5. *Necessary or universally valid statements can be interesting or surprising.*

This is another point emphasized by Ayer, and discussed below. Seemingly necessary truths, such as those of mathematics, seem capable of conveying information that is not trivial, a point which Kant accommodated by distinguishing necessity expressed by analytic statements from that expressed by the synthetic a priori. With the abandonment of the synthetic a priori, the Vienna Circle and its followers like Ayer had to provide an alternative explanation of the apparently 'surprising' character of necessary truth.

6. *A proposition is analytic when its validity depends solely on the definitions of the symbols it contains.*

This idea had several variants. In the *Tractatus*, Wittgenstein thought that the truth of the propositions of logic could be computed 'from the symbol alone' (1986, 6.12f.). In the *Aufbau*, Carnap expanded the idea to the claim that all theorems deducible from the definitions of a language alone are analytic (1967, 176). Ayer proposed an extended version of this idea which we discuss below (LTL, 79).

7. *All and only analytic statements express necessary truths.*

The notion that analytic statements express truths was present in Kant and Frege, each of whom described analytic statements as true (cf. Kant 1965, B11; Frege 1974, 4). Their doing so was connected with each philosopher's account of a priori knowledge, albeit more centrally in Frege's case than in Kant's, given Kant's acceptance of the synthetic a priori. Wittgenstein adopted a somewhat different view; recall from chapter 1 that he denied that the statements of logic are genuine propositions, although they 'show' the logical structure of language and the world (1986, 5.43f.). For the early Wittgenstein, all necessity was *logical* – there was no possibility of necessity that did not reduce to logical necessity (1986, 6.37). The Vienna Circle tended to follow Wittgenstein in this regard, treating all expressions of necessary truth as analytic statements. Recall, however, that the Vienna Circle and its followers such as Ayer were dissatisfied with what they took to be the 'metaphysical' elements of Wittgenstein's notion of *showing* (cf. Carnap 1967, 282–3), and accepted them as propositions with a truth value (cf. ibid., 176; LTL, 83). This left them with the problem of explaining the nature of our alleged knowledge of such truths, this time without Kant's synthetic a priori to appeal to. We consider Ayer's proposed explanation below.

> 8. *The truth of analytic statements is 'trivial' or 'obvious,' or can be determined from the statement alone.*

This idea is, as we have noted, hinted at in Kant, who regarded analytic truths as 'explicative' and hence unable to expand our knowledge. Frege regarded them as serving as guiding principles for attaining truth. And Wittgenstein thought them to be determinable from the symbol alone. As we will see, Ayer combined many of these ideas, saying that they are both trivial and determinable from the statement alone (although this did not prevent them from being interesting and surprising, according to Ayer).

> 9. *Denials of analytic statements lead to self-contradiction, and are therefore 'self-stultifying.'*

Ayer endorsed this broadly Kantian idea as well (LTL, 84). His reasons, however, derived more from Carnap than from Kant, for like other Vienna Circle members Ayer did not regard analytic truths as 'containing' their predicate term in their subject term (although Schlick endorsed this view in his earlier work; cf. 1985, 76). Rather, Vienna Circle members such as Carnap suggested that the denial of analytic truths would involve the denial of a logical truth, given a priori specification of those truths. This preserved, it was thought, the idea that analytic truths were undeniably true, while avoiding the postulation of metaphysically suspect entities such as eternal, Platonic logical objects (such as Russell's theory of logical truths seemed to require) or facts.

> 10. *Analytic statements are true by convention.*

This was the Vienna Circle's most distinctive contribution to a theory of analytic truth. The idea traced its roots both to Wittgenstein's theory that the truths of logic were tautologies, and to the conventionalism of philosophers of science such as Poincaré. As we have noted in chapters 1 and 2, Carnap combined these ideas in his *Aufbau*, asserting without argument that logic and mathematics are conventions governing the use of symbols, and the tautologies formed from them (1967, 178). Schlick too regarded the formal sciences as matters of convention, and suggested more broadly that a descriptive language was a matter of stipulated conventions (1985, 69f.).

> 11. *Analytic truths are senseless, but in a way distinct from the way that metaphysical utterances are senseless. They elucidate or illustrate the way in which we use certain symbols, by indicating or showing the conventions or rules of syntax justifying those uses.*

This last idea derived, once again, from the *Tractatus*, which invoked a distinction between the 'senseless' pseudo-propositions of logic, and the 'nonsensical' statements of metaphysics (Wittgenstein 1986, 4.12f., 4.461). Carnap extended this idea by eliminating Wittgenstein's corresponding saying/showing distinction, as we have noted, and regarded analytic truths as meaningful reflections of syntax. Ayer would attempt to combine both the idea that such truths are strictly senseless with the Carnapian idea that they express rules of syntax, as we discuss below (LTL, 79).

The conjunction of these eleven theses forms an interconnected account of analytic truth and its place in knowledge and justification. This account treated analytic statements as fundamentally framework-constitutive truths, which conventionally lay out the representational and inferential basis of language. Their conventionality explained how analytic truths are knowable a priori (being stipulations we have made), while nonetheless blocking the apparently metaphysical commitments of Kant, Frege, and Wittgenstein.

5.3 Objecting to the Classical Position

Nonetheless, there are a number of difficulties with this position that we wish to explore. Once again, our immediate focus will be on A. J. Ayer's *Language, Truth and Logic*, although we believe that many of the objections we consider are applicable to elements of the other positions mentioned above, particularly the positions of Vienna Circle members such as Carnap and Schlick.

One problem that is likely obvious to contemporary readers is that the classical position appears, in point 5, to conflate universal generality both with what most philosophers would now call 'metaphysical' necessity and with epistemological certainty. If one wants to be sympathetic, one can appreciate how one might reject metaphysical necessity, and think that all modalities are what we would now call 'epistemic' modalities. But this con-cession does not help with the conflation of generality (that a purported law has been conformed to in n observed cases is no guarantee that it will be substantiated in other unobserved cases, no matter how large n becomes) with necessity, even if the latter is interpreted epistemically. For present purposes this will not matter, since we can focus on a class of cases which might be plausibly taken to be 'universally applicable' as well as both meta-physically necessary (not contingent) and epistemically certain, and neither known nor justified on the basis of experience. Let us label 'nonempiri-cal' those statements that express contents that seem to be justified non-empirically. This term could be taken to be question-begging against the Quinean, but our present purpose is merely to summarize the classical position rather than to defend it.

Theses 2, 3, and 4 all segregate the notion of necessary truth from empiri-cal experience, and thesis 7 equates necessary truth with analyticity. This, however, generated the difficulty of accounting for the apparent justification or knowledge of nonempirical, analytic truths. Ayer attempted to give an account which began by rejecting rivals that denied certain of the classical position's claims, such as claims 3 and 4. One such rival is the approach of J. S. Mill (later revived in a slightly different form by Quine). According to Mill's more 'radical' empiricism, contrary to appearances, apparently non-empirical knowledge is really empirically justified after all. For example, a statement like '2 + 5 = 7' is justified by countless observations of oranges or billiard-balls or what have you.[1] Ayer considered (LTL, 75ff.) how some simple arithmetical truth might be disconfirmed by experience. He argued that there is no conceivable case of that sort, contrary to what Mill requires. Ayer argued that no matter what we observed, we would never give up the statement that two times five equals ten. Rather, we would always take it that there was some other explanation for the false prediction resulting from the multiplication claim together with various other hypotheses. For example, we might propose that we had miscounted, or that some new item had spontaneously appeared or disappeared. We would never, under any conditions, come to think that empirical evidence had refuted the statement that two times five equals ten. Likewise for statements of Euclidean geom-etry. Ayer thought that if we measured the angles of what we took to be a Euclidean triangle and the angles did not sum to 180 degrees, then we would try to explain that discrepancy by appeal to some hypothesis such as that the sides were bent, or that the angles were measured incorrectly, or give some other reason for the discrepancy. Ayer's final example is of truths

of logic. Echoing Frege, he thought that we would not under any circumstances reject the law of excluded middle. (It is not clear that he had in mind
only empirical counterevidence here, but we might sympathetically assume
that he is taking this for granted.) After this brief account, Ayer rather boldly
stated that 'There is no need to give further examples. Whatever instance we
care to take, we shall always find that the situations in which a logical or
mathematical principle might appear to be confuted are accounted for in
such a way as to leave the principle unassailed' (LTL, 77). While those sympathetic to the logical empiricist view may be convinced that Ayer is correct,
it is a striking example of Ayer's brashness and directness.

In chapter 6, we will present a view that is in general agreement with
Ayer and the classical position concerning the non-empirical natures of
mathematical statements, but we note here that the example from geometry
in particular is not an initially strong one for either our position or Ayer's.
Examples from geometry are contentious, and we think that they are prima
facie cases that favor the Quinean empiricist rather than any defender of a
distinction akin to an analytic–synthetic distinction who, like Ayer, assimi-
lates geometrical axioms to the class of analytic claims. Quineans can point
out that what had been taken to be an unassailable principle of geometry
knowable a priori, such as Euclid's parallel postulate, turned out to be false,
as a matter of empirical fact. One can attempt to respond to Quine here by
distinguishing between 'physical' geometry and 'mathematical' geometry,
thereby performing what the Quinean philosopher Michael Resnik calls the
'Euclidean rescue' (which 'rescue' the authors are also inclined to perform
with many geometrical examples). Nevertheless, the example on its face
supports the Quinean/Millian rather than the defender of the 'analyticity'
of mathematics, in our view. It is the analyticity advocate rather than the
Quinean who has more work to do to make sense of such cases in a way
that coheres with his view.

Thesis 6 of the classical position states that a proposition is analytic when
its validity depends solely on the definitions of the symbols it contains, a
characterization that comes directly from Ayer (LTL, 78). Ayer added that
a proposition is synthetic when 'its validity is determined by the facts of
experience.' He gave as an example of the latter, 'There are ants which have
established a system of slavery,' and an example of an analytic proposition
'Either some ants are parasitic or none are.' The synthetic statement requires
empirical observation to establish, whereas the analytic one 'provides no
information whatsoever about the behavior of ants, or, indeed, about any
matter of fact' (79).

This idea is subject to a number of objections. One distressing feature of Ayer's discussion is his failure to distinguish notions that should be kept separate. First, it is not clear whether Ayer is distinguishing sentences from what they express. The term 'proposition' is thus often ambiguous in his writings. While this ambiguity can be harmless in many, even most ordinary contexts, it is not harmless in the present context, as we shall see presently. Second, Ayer's use of the term 'validity' is unclear as well. He might have intended 'validity' to be synonymous with 'truth,' or he might have intended it to be synonymous with 'justification.' Next, Ayer's distinction between the analytic and the synthetic is not obviously mutually exclusive or exhaustive. His characterization of analyticity is in terms of the truth or justification of an analytic statement 'depending on' definitions of the terms, whereas his characterization of 'synthetic' involves dependence on experience. Connected with this, it is unclear what 'depending on' means – is it entailment, or some other relation? While one can argue that 'dependence on' experience precludes 'dependence on' definitions and vice versa, it is far from obvious that the two preclude one another. If definitions are factual and based on experience, then being based on or dependent on definitions does not preclude dependence on experience. A related question that arises, not addressed by Ayer, is the status of the 'definitions' on which the truth of analytic statements depends. We might be willing to grant that some statements are such that their truth is entailed by the truth of some 'definitions.' But Ayer's account of analyticity only helps with these non-basic analytic claims, and does not help at all in accounting for the special status of the definitions themselves. This problem looms especially large in the case of logic, as we explain below.

One of the most basic problems with the classical positions thesis that analytic statements are 'non-factual' (an idea implicit in theses 2 and 3) is that it is unclear what the argument for this thesis comes to, assuming it is not a mere stipulation as to how Ayer and others propose that we use the term 'factual.' This problem is apparent in Ayer's own discussion. As we saw in chapters 2 and 3, Quine and others frequently object that no clear sense can be made of the idea that the truth of some claim does not depend on facts. Consider the statement 'Either some ants are parasitic or none are.' Why isn't this sentence made true by the fact that either some ants are parasitic or none are? When one reads Ayer, unfortunately, no satisfactory answer is given to this question. Ayer presumably took it to be obvious that analytic statements are not made true by facts. It is arguable that Ayer's conflation of *being made true by* facts and *being justified by* facts made it harder for him to find room for the question concerning whether facts of experience *make analytic sentences* true as opposed to whether experientially known facts *justify our acceptance of* analytic statements. Another consideration that seemed to drive Ayer to claim that analytic statements are non-factual is that they do not provide information about facts of experience. What this appears to come to is that such statements are necessary, and so they apply to all experiences. But no argument is given for the claim that necessary truths are not factual. It's possible that the claim amounts to simply a stipulation. We do not object to such a stipulation, but if we accept it we should not then be misled into thinking that some intuitive, pre-stipulation notion 'non-factual' applies to these statements, and that this non-factuality *explains* some other important feature of the statements.

An alternative way of justifying the idea behind theses 2 and 3 revolves around the 'language-constitutive' role of analytic statements, an idea we introduced in our discussion of Carnap in chapter 2. Analytic truths express the conventions according to which we infer and justify statements about the world, without themselves being such statements. The problem, however, is that this idea assumes a distinction that many, such as Quine, deny. We have seen many of his objections in chapter 3. As we there attempted to show, there are possible lines of response available to the defender of analyticity here, but they tend to go beyond the guiding theses of the classical position. We will sketch an alternative proposal in chapter 6.

Another class of objections to the classical position concerns thesis 9, and in particular the attempts, notably Ayer's, to explain precisely what is wrong with the denial of analytic statements. Since the problem with denying them is not that the denials do not fit experience (in the way that denial of an obvious empirical truth fails to 'fit' experience), Ayer requires another account. But what he provides is unfortunately very thin.

Consider what Ayer said is the significance of analytic statements. While they are not factual, nevertheless they are not 'senseless in the way that metaphysical utterances are senseless. For, although they give us no information about any empirical situation, they do enlighten us by illustrating the way in which we use certain symbols' (LTL, 79). With respect to a color-exclusion statement, he wrote,

> I am not talking about the properties of any actual thing; but I am not talking nonsense. I am expressing an analytic proposition, which records our determination to call a color expanse which differs in quality from a neighboring color expanse a different part of a given thing. (79)

Ayer considered another example of a purportedly analytic claim and said that 'I am thereby indicating the convention which governs our usage of the words "if" and "all"' (ibid.). Thus analytic statements 'illustrate' uses of symbols, they 'record our determination' to apply expressions in certain ways, and they 'indicate conventions' governing usages.

Various questions can be and have been raised concerning Ayer's proposals. One is what Ayer's argument is for the claim that analytic statements 'give us no information about any empirical situation.' The reason appears to be that they seem necessary, and so hold in any empirical situation. But that is not an argument in support of the claim that necessary truths are all non-factual, but the mere assertion of Ayer's position. One can look long and hard at Ayer's discussion and fail to find any argument that all necessary truths are non-factual, that they do not describe any empirical situation. If someone insisted that the thing about necessary truths is that they describe all actual as well all possible empirical situations, Ayer would appear to not have much to say beyond repeating his own contrary view. There is no good reason given in LTL for denying that necessary statements are factual.

Thesis 7 of the classical position poses further problems. For his part, Ayer seemed to take analytic statements to be true rather than false or truth valueless (a point made explicitly (at LTL, 83), where he says that axioms of geometry are true if they are consistent). Indeed, if they are not true, then it is unclear why they are troublesome for the empiricist to begin with. Ayer adopted a form of emotivism about ethical statements, so he was aware of the sort of view according to which sentences that appear to be truth valued are not genuinely true or false. Yet he did not adopt an emotivist strategy for purportedly analytic statements. If they are not true or false, for example, they are not the sorts of things that can be known at all, so there is no question of our knowledge of them or of their 'necessity' (what could be meant other than necessary truth?) or their 'certainty' or their 'generality' (again, what could be meant besides their general truth, their truth in all cases?). But his three characterizations as 'illustrating,' 'recording,' and 'indicating' are all three features that seem truth valueless. One can indicate, illustrate, or record well or badly, but it seems odd to say that one indicated truly or illustrated truly or recorded truly. To the extent that analytic statements are true, Ayer never told us what their (truth-evaluable) contents are. We will discuss this worry further in the next section of this chapter when we consider BonJour's objections to the 'moderate empiricist's,' which is essentially the logical empiricist's, approach to analyticity and apriority.

A further objection returns to thesis 2, according to which a single, uniform account of analyticity extends from logic and mathematics to color-exclusion. With respect to color-exclusion in particular, we might consider how plausible an account such as Ayer's is on its face. We believe that nothing, nor any part of a thing, can be bright scarlet and emerald green all over. Is our belief best accounted for as akin to a stipulation that governs our use of the word 'part' or of 'thing' or even of 'color'? While color-exclusion has puzzled philosophers for much of the last century, it seems implausible that the best explanation of our thinking that nothing is both scarlet and emerald green all over simultaneously is our acceptance of some stipulation governing color words, or any words for that matter. It certainly seems that we can already know what scarlet looks like, what emerald green looks like, what parts and things and simultaneity are, and come for the first time, on 'reflection,' to think that it is impossible for anything to be 'bicolored.' It seems that we could come to know this without even knowing words for the respective colors.[2]

We do not pretend that these matters are straightforward. We are only pointing out that the classical position's assimilation of our knowledge of color-exclusion examples as akin to knowledge of 'linguistic stipulations,' as is implied by theses 2, 7, and 10, can seem rather implausible on its face, however well the appeal to analyticity-based explanations might work for other cases such as mathematical examples or examples from logic. Among the conclusions of this book will be that one should separate a variety of questions. One is whether some 'analyticity-like' notion can be illuminating for some philosophical purposes. Another is whether *some* interesting 'analyticity-based' explanations of purported knowledge or justification can succeed. A third is whether appeals to analyticity enable us to *dispense altogether with a priori intuition* or provide a defense of logical empiricism.

Thesis 9 states that denials of analytic statements lead to self-contradiction, and are therefore, in Ayer's terminology, 'self-stultifying.' Unfortunately, Ayer did not explain what 'self-stultifying' comes to beyond contradicting oneself. There are a number of confusions that arise in his discussion (cf. LTL, 84). One is that he says that we cannot deny analytic sentences 'without infringing the conventions which are presupposed by our very denial, and so falling into self-contradiction.' It is hard to understand what conventions Ayer is referring to if it is not linguistic conventions. But contravening a linguistic convention is not in itself the same thing as uttering a self-contradictory claim. If I misuse 'bachelor' in the sense that I violate the conventions for its application, and apply it to some women, then I have 'fallen into contradiction' in one sense, in that I have contradicted rules that

I myself adopted (or perhaps thought I had adopted). But it is not obvious at all that I thereby contradict myself in the sense of uttering a contradictory statement.[3] In fact, it is unclear what would count as the intentional simultaneous adoption of two contradictory conventions or rules.

A further objection to the classical position concerns theses 6 and 7. This objection is that the classical position does not provide a satisfactory account of the necessity of logical truths. For even if all analytic statements were reducible to 'tautologies,' truths of logic, their truth and necessity and our knowledge of them would require the truth, necessity, and knowledge of logical truths. Along this front the classical position has remained at best obscure, and appears confused on a number of points. Ayer's failure to clearly distinguish the sentences of a language from the propositions expressed by those sentences may partly explain his confusion. Ayer stated that

> It is perfectly conceivable that we should have employed different conventions from those which we actually do employ. But whatever those conventions might be, the tautologies in which we recorded them would always be necessary. For any denial of them would be self-stultifying. (LTL, 84).

We have already raised the question, what is wrong with 'self-stultification'? Leaving that aside, an obvious objection to Ayer's account (one BonJour points out; see below) is that while our conventions may determine what sentences express, our conventions seem largely independent of the truth of propositions that have nothing to do with human conventions. For example, we may have adopted conventions in virtue of which 'Tigers' refers to tigers, and by which 'Tigers are large mammalian predators with striped fur' expresses the proposition that tigers are large mammalian predators with striped fur, but the fact that tigers have striped fur has nothing to do with human conventions. There may be some evolutionary explanation of why tigers have striped fur, but there is no explanation of the color patterns on tigers' fur that makes essential appeal to human convention. It is only if one confuses the sentence 'tigers have striped fur' with the proposition that the sentence expresses or the fact that makes it true (assuming there are facts) that one might think otherwise. But once the distinction between sentences and what they express is raised, it would appear that Ayer had not progressed at all toward explaining why logical truths are necessary. And recall that other conventionalist accounts of necessary truth, like Carnap's, offered no more than Ayer's (cf. section 1.8). Even appeal to 'self-stultifying beliefs' does not obviously help, since at best that would explain why we should believe the propositions, not what makes them true or necessary (unless one adopted a pragmatist 'success-based' concept of truth, which Ayer does not do).

Finally, we should briefly consider thesis 5, which holds that analytic statements, in spite of their being 'uninformative' and 'non-factual,' are often both interesting and surprising. Ayer's own explanation for this feature appealed to the limitations of our faculties (LTL, 85–6). We do not grasp at once all of the logical consequences of what we know, nor the entirety of logical and mathematical truths. Thus, Ayer argued, we can be surprised and interested to be shown such a truth that had not yet occurred to us.

It is, however, difficult to make good sense of Ayer's explanation. If analytic truths are uninformative, then how can they inform us of anything, even the consequences of our own conventions? Presumably what Ayer would say is that analytic truths can be informative in a degenerate or special sense, namely, they give us insight into consequences of the conventions that we have adopted. But even here, the account might seem to remain haunted by the earlier objections to his account of our knowledge of logical necessities. For recall that logical necessity is reduced to convention by thesis 10. As such, what we are learning when we learn the consequences of a convention is what 'follows,' in accord with our 'logical conventions,' from other conventions. More puzzles lie in the vicinity. Is it a matter of convention what follows from our other conventions? If so, do we require further conventions for unpacking how our second-order conventions apply to our first-order conventions? Leaving regress worries aside (see our discussion of Quine's argument against logical conventionalism in section 3.9), it can seem that the classical position is implicitly assuming a fixed background of logical necessity that applies non-conventionally to our first-order conventions. But as we have seen, and discuss further below, such a non-conventional background logic would leave the classical position without an adequate logical empiricist account of the truth, necessity, and our knowledge of logic.

5.4 BonJour on Moderate Empiricism

Among the chief philosophical virtues of the notion of analyticity according to most logical empiricists was that it provided an initially promising way to preserve their empiricism while granting that not all statements are justified empirically. According to Ayer, for example, all genuine statements ('cognitively meaningful' statements) are either empirical statements whose justification is empirical, or else are analytic. Analytic statements were also taken to be necessarily true. Since it is difficult to see how the necessary truth of any statement could be established, or even justified, empirically, analyticity provided a promising avenue for accounting for the many apparently justified, yet necessary, truths. These included truths of logic, truths of arithmetic, and 'definitional truths' like 'red is a color' and 'whales are mammals.' Analyticity also included apparently necessary yet non-empirically justified statements such as 'nothing is both red and green all over simultaneously' (color-exclusion), mathematical claims like 'there are no square circles,' and statements like 'everything colored is extended' and 'F = ma' (arguably a definition), along with a host of other statements that were difficult to assimilate to the class of empirically justified statements, or at least seemed so prior to the Quinean arguments in 'Two Dogmas.'

Analyticity thus carried a heavy explanatory burden, but it has not been easy to say exactly how analyticity is supposed to accomplish all the tasks assigned to it. Laurence BonJour, in his book In Defense of Pure Reason (1998), presents a lengthy critique of what he calls 'moderate empiricist' attempts to account for the justification of non-empirical statements by appeal to analyticity. Moderate empiricism is, roughly, what has been historically called 'logical empiricism,' and it stands in contrast to Quine's later 'pragmatic empiricism,' which BonJour calls 'radical empiricism.' We will not attempt to cover BonJour's impressively concise yet thorough discussion and all of his objections to the various best-known attempts. Instead, we will focus on those objections that we take to be most important for the purposes of this work, which eventually does attempt to defend a notion akin to analyticity and its relevance to some non-empirically justified statements.

We should note before proceeding that BonJour's purpose is different from ours, and so not all of the theses that are important to his project are essential to ours. With respect to some questions that he addresses, we can simply remain agnostic. In particular, we are not here attempting to defend 'moderate empiricism,' nor to show that all justification is empirical justification, even justification for non-analytic statements. Hence we can agree with BonJour that moderate empiricists did not have a satisfactory account of the justification of logical truths. But granting this does not require that we agree with BonJour that justification of logical truths requires appeal to intuition, or that other, non-logical truths that nevertheless seem paradigmatically 'analytic,' such as many stipulative definitions, require such an appeal, either. We will, in chapter 6, argue that some statements are epistemically distinctive, that their distinctiveness is shared by a variety of statements of a wide range of 'logical forms,' and that this distinctiveness does not require an appeal to a priori intuition.

BonJour notes that there are a number of distinct 'moderate empiricist' accounts of analyticity and of how analytic statements are justified, and it is at best unclear whether they are mutually consistent. He suggests that the continued popularity of something like the moderate empiricist view is the result of a failure to keep track of precisely what version of the view is to be defended, thereby enabling moderate empiricists to switch to another version of the view when any one version is shown to be inadequate. We agree to some degree with BonJour on this front. A contributing factor to the difficulty here may be that some notions in the vicinity, such as that of a stipulative definition for the purposes of abbreviation, are taken to be trivial and not in need of further elucidation, leaving their status open to a variety of objections from both the rationalist such as BonJour and the 'radical empiricist' such as Quine.

Along related lines, BonJour raises a collection of interconnected objections to the strategy of appeal to 'convention' or 'linguistic rules' and related notions. One can read quite a bit of logical empiricist literature and yet fail to find a careful account of precisely the relation between facts concerning what conventions have been adopted by some language users, on the one hand, and facts about, say, numbers or colors.[4] Two obvious or natural first attempts are suggested by Carnap (see sections 1.8 and 2.2.2 above). One attempt, deriving from the *Aufbau*, would be to say that a statement that is 'true by convention' such as, supposedly, '$1 + 1 = 2$,' expresses the fact that some linguistic convention has been adopted (cf. Carnap 1967, 178). A second attempt, deriving from Carnap's *Syntax* and subsequent work, would be to treat a truth by convention as something akin to a proposal or suggestion, or perhaps an imperative (cf. Carnap 1937, 52). A potential problem with the first attempt is that it seems to make the expression of a convention out to be an empirical claim concerning language users, and so not necessary or a priori. On the other hand, the second attempt makes the convention out to be neither true nor false, since neither proposals nor suggestions or imperatives are true. Yet the statement '$1 + 1 = 2$' seems true. Even those who deny its truth are usually inclined to treat it as having a truth value. On their face, then, neither of these options seems to be helpful. Ayer, as we noted, claims that the denial of at least some analytic statements is 'self-stultifying,' but this takes us no further given that it is never made clear in his discussion what 'self-stultifying' comes to.

In an attempt to bring some clarity to these issues, we wish to present a suggestion concerning the relation between linguistic conventions and the distinctive epistemic status of some statements. We will focus on what we take to be the clearest case, that of stipulative definitions of a particular sort, namely those stipulative definitions that are clearly and explicitly introduced as empirically indefeasible. Whether there are any actual examples in natural languages, and how the answer to this question is relevant to the overall dialectic concerning analyticity, are questions that we will return to in chapter 6. But for definiteness, consider the notion of a *frenchelor*. A frenchelor, we stipulate, is a French bachelor. The notion *frenchelor* has no interesting role within any scientific theory, and even if a closely related notion turns out to, we hereby explicitly introduce a norm of use that precludes treating our notion *frenchelor* as a theoretical notion. It is, we might say, intended to be taken as purely classificatory.

Suppose that we ask whether there is some linguistic convention among readers of this text, concerning the linguistic item 'frenchelor.' We are inclined to say that we have adopted a convention of taking the statement 'Frenchelors are French bachelors' as both true (and if desired, as expressing some true proposition or other) and as empirically indefeasible. It is empirically defeasible in the sense that the proposition *that the sentence* 'Frenchelors are *French bachelors*' *is true* is itself empirically indefeasible. That this proposition, *that the sentence expresses something true*, is indefeasible, should not be confused with the *proposition expressed* being indefeasible, although in this case (and in the case of many common stipulations) the proposition is also empirically indefeasible.[5]

What is the relation between the linguistic convention and the apriority of the statement 'Frenchelors are French bachelors'? BonJour is correct to argue in similar cases that it is neither that a sentence like 'Frenchelors are French bachelors' expresses a proposition concerning linguistic conventions that have been adopted, nor is it that subsequent utterances of 'Frenchelors are French bachelors' have as their contents proposals concerning linguistic usage, or linguistic commands (although we can easily imagine some utterances of that sentence having such roles). Rather, we adopt the convention of treating the sentence as true, as expressing a true proposition. We thereafter take ourselves to express a true proposition when we utter tokens of that sentence. We all understand that no empirical evidence counts against its expressing a true proposition, except for the 'indirect' sort of evidence that might show that people no longer accept that convention to govern that sentence. (We will merely note here that there is an interesting question concerning whether, and if so how, a community can come to discover its own collective intentions.)

Sentences like these have some fairly obvious distinctive features that typical descriptive statements fail to have. Consider a statement that bachelors are wealthier than average, or that bachelors tend to die younger than married men. Both statements are of a sort that empirical evidence of a 'straightforward' type, that is, evidence concerning something other than linguistic intentions or practices involving the word 'bachelor,' can disconfirm. In contrast, 'Frenchelors are French' is such that the only sort of evidence apparently relevant to our taking it as expressing a true proposition is evidence concerning linguistic behaviors or concerning meanings, at least for those non-Quineans willing to countenance meanings.[6] Thus in the sort of case envisaged for frenchelor, the stipulation sentence, 'Frenchelors are French bachelors' is understood to be true and that it is true is understood to be indefeasible, and this common understanding constitutes a difference in epistemic profile from typical descriptive statements or hypotheses. Since how we are using a term is normally taken to be implicitly understood and known, it can also seem that given this implicit knowledge, such a stipulation is known to be true in the absence of further (non-linguistic) empirical investigation, and in that sense seems justified a priori. Our beliefs concerning the truth of many explicit stipulations might be given similar explanations, and if we are justified in such beliefs, then our justification for our beliefs in stipulations seems to have a different, distinctive profile or type not shared by non-stipulations. We develop many of these ideas, such as that of common understanding and of the distinctive profile of stipulations, in chapter 6.

BonJour at one point grants (1998, 56) that there may be a philosophical account that helps us to understand our justification for some explicit stipulations, although it is unclear why he concedes this given the rest of his highly critical discussion of the prospects of any account of this sort. In any case, he raises a few other objections that are raised by a number of writers who find suspicious any appeal to linguistic conventions as a source of knowledge of necessary truths. One is that the adoption of linguistic conventions seems optional in a way that various truths, such as truths of logic or mathematics, seem not to be. BonJour cites as one example the convention that is shared by Americans and most other contemporary societies, of driving on the right side of the road, which seems to be 'optional' in the simple sense that we might have driven on the left, as in the UK.

We will suggest a partial response here to this objection that certain truths such as logical truths seem not to be arbitrary in the way that conventional rule adoptions are.[7] One aspect of our response is to note that at least in many cases, once a collection of terms, and the principles understood as indefeasibly 'defining' them, have been in use for some time, it can seem that those very concepts are somehow privileged or uniquely correct in some interesting sense. That these well-known principles are correct for the familiar terms and concepts expressed by the terms can be confused with the impossibility of introducing similar but distinct collections of interdefined concepts, or terms expressing them. For example, we might think that running the bases in baseball in a counterclockwise direction would be incorrect, given what baseball is. In that case it is easy to think of alternatives that are in the vicinity, such as the possibility of a game 'just like' baseball except that the base sequence is inverted. In other cases alternatives 'in the vicinity' can be either hard to think of or hard to see at all. There are some practices such that altering any of their most fundamental or 'defining' features yields a very different, perhaps even an unintelligible 'practice.' For instance, many philosophers find the notion of 'paraconsistent logics,' or logics that attempt in a certain way to tolerate inconsistencies, to be unintelligible. It is hard to see what other rules to add to a practice so that we continue to speak of 'truth' and 'falsehood' along with a 'negation' that obeys different rules from those within 'classical' two-valued logic. Advocates of paraconsistent logics, and of their intelligibility and their characterizations as 'alternative logics' in particular, do their best to convince the rest of us that their 'logic' is indeed enough like 'logic' to count as logic, and a paraconsistent one at that. (See, e.g., Priest, 2006, 2008) Whether or not paraconsistent logics are possible or intelligible, our basic point here is simply that spaces of alternatives can contain relatively 'sparse' regions, where there seem to be few similar alternatives to practices and the conventions accepted within them, and relatively 'lush' regions where many similar alternatives suggest themselves. The fact that some conventionally adopted practice falls within a 'sparse' region of alternatives does not by itself show that the principles of the practice are not conventionally adopted. Even where such practices arise 'naturally,' in the absence of intentional or 'explicit' stipulation or convention, the sparseness or lushness of alternatives does not, it seems to us, show that the principles of the practice must be justified in some way, by appeal either to a priori intuitions or to empirical or pragmatic reasons for their adoption.

Another objection that BonJour raises to moderate empiricism is that appeal to a notion of 'implicit definition' does not help to explain our knowledge of the truth of the propositions expressed by the implicit definitions. The argument proceeds roughly as follows. Someone claims that, say, some axioms of some branch of mathematics 'implicitly define' some operation, in the sense that the truth of the axioms entails a fixed interpretation for various symbols. For example, suppose that someone stipulates that '50 OP 5 = 10,' '6 OP 2 = 3,' along with perhaps other schemata, which jointly entail that 'OP' denotes the ordinary division operator on the domain of integers. One might say that the stipulations 'implicitly define' the meaning of 'OP.' BonJour's objection to this idea is that the notion of implicit definition does not help at all to show how we know, for example, that 50 OP 5 = 10. Rather, it is only our prior knowledge that 50 divided by 5 equals 10 that enabled us to see that the correct interpretation of 'OP' was division. This type of argument can be generalized (see 1998, p. 50), and BonJour takes the generalized version to show that appeal to implicit definition in this, its only legitimate form, is hopeless as a means of understanding our knowledge of the truth of the propositions expressed by such implicit definitions.

The nature of 'implicit definition' is complicated, but we will nevertheless outline a possible response to BonJour's objections in their generalized form. First, we will stipulate that an *explicit definition* of a term is a statement of universally quantified biconditional form, with the defined term on one side of the biconditional and the remainder on the other side. An *implicit definition* of F is any meaning-conferring statement not of this form. In particular, we will say that some statement partly implicitly defines the meaning of a term F just in case it is understood that the statement (which will contain the term F somewhere) must come out true on any acceptable interpretation. So a truth-evaluable statement of any grammatical or logical form (not to say any statement at all) can be used as partly implicitly defining the meaning of term F, as we are using 'implicit definition.' We might take 'explicit definition' as a special case of a more inclusive class 'implicit definition,' or we might take the two classes to be mutually exclusive. It will not much matter for present purposes, as we will be focusing on the non-biconditional forms of 'implicit definitions.'

Part of BonJour's worry is that when asking how we know that some statements are true, or in some cases even necessary, appeal to implicit definition can never be epistemically illuminating. A type of case that seems problematic for BonJour is any case in which some collection of terms are all interdefined, and are only interdefinable. In such cases our only handle on what counts as falling under one of the interdefined concepts is meeting some condition expressible in terms of other concepts within the class. If this is the case for all of the concepts in the class, that is, the concepts are in a broad sense all 'circularly' defined, it can seem as though the extent to which we understand any of the concepts is in terms of their relations, which in some cases are conventionally adopted or stipulated, to other concepts within the interdefined class. For one example of such a 'circularly defined' notion, consider how we understand what a bishop in chess is. Let us imagine that a game like actual chess had been stipulatively defined in the first instance in, say, 1903. The rules might include claims like, 'the bishop is placed next to the queen prior to the first move,' etc. Suppose we are playing chess on a computer. If this is possible, then one collection of pieces must be labeled 'white.' If we ask how we know that those pieces are the white pieces, what can be the answer? It seems as though a plausible answer is something like, 'well, they just are, by stipulation.' BonJour might deny the plausibility of this answer. But why? He might say that what must be going on is that we are intuiting which pieces are the white ones, or that alternatively we are simply unjustified in calling some of the pieces white. Yet in many chess sets, some of the pieces are reddish and the others are greenish. Which ones are really the white ones? This and similar mysteries are likely to remain unanswerable in any justified way unless we are allowed to appeal to some stipulation, and the white pieces and the black pieces are mutually interdefined.

Recall that we are not attempting to show that all cases of purported a priori knowledge can be illuminatingly accounted for by appeal to something like convention or stipulation. We are not attempting to vindicate 'moderate empiricism,' or to refute 'rationalism.' We only want to show that some cases can be dealt with by appeal to implicit or explicit definition. Our point is that something akin to stipulation can be illuminating in some cases that BonJour rejects.

As we will discuss further in chapter 6, we can clarify the epistemic status of some 'stipulative definitions' of certain concepts in a way that can be extended to shed at least some light on principles taken to govern some concepts not initially introduced via stipulation. Consider the notions of truth, reference, and satisfaction. Some basic principles governing these notions and their interconnections seem both non-empirically justified, and also jointly partly constitutive of our grasp of the concepts.[8] We say 'partly' since it is unclear whether we should also take, for example, some basic 'logical truths,' or claims that these logical truths are true, to be partly constitutive of the concept of truth. Arithmetical notions may also be interdefined with other notions in a family (such as 'successor,' and perhaps 'number'), even if the practice of arithmetic arose gradually, not via some initial stipulation of its structure in all its complexity and definiteness. To the extent that these principles are understood as holding, and to be neither empirically justified nor answerable to empirical evidence (other than the usual caveat of granting that there is empirical 'linguistic data' concerning what linguistic intentions and beliefs are had by speakers), then their epistemic status shares much of its profile with that of explicitly stipulatively introduced notions.

5.5 Quine's 'Epistemology Naturalized'

Almost twenty years after publishing 'Two Dogmas,' Quine published another highly influential paper concerning epistemology. Quine's 'Epistemology Naturalized' (1969a, hereafter 'EN') is among his most famous works. Quine's paper had wide-ranging implications for epistemology, many of which are beyond the scope of this book. But we do want to trace a few connections between his proposal to 'naturalize' epistemology and features of his views that we have already discussed in chapters 2 and 3. In this section we will review some of the central themes and arguments of EN, emphasizing the most important connections to analyticity, and in particular, to the status of mathematical truths.

In EN, Quine explained how traditional epistemology has failed in all of its attempts to satisfy a 'Cartesian quest for certainty' (1969a, 74), or to provide a way of 'strictly deriving the science of the external world from sensory evidence' (75). Quine thought that in spite of these failures:

> Two cardinal tenets of empiricism remained unassailable, however, and so remain to this day. One is that whatever evidence there is for science is sensory evidence. The other is that all inculcation of meanings of words must rest ultimately on sensory evidence. (75)

One question to raise here concerns Quine's appeal to the notion of 'evidence,' which in effect would replace what other philosophers have taken to be an 'evidence' relation with another relation that is broadly causal. Whether this is a benign replacement reflecting a proper understanding of what evidence relations really are, or whether Quine's proposals in EN really amount to changing the subject from epistemology to etiology, has been a subject of subsequent debate among epistemologists.

Quine thought that the 'cardinal tenets' that remain 'unassailable' in traditional epistemology are what might be taken to motivate a continued interest in Carnap's *Aufbau* project, or some variant of it, 'in which the sensory content of discourse would stand forth explicitly' (75). As Quine noted, Carnap 'was seeking what he called a *rational reconstruction*. Any [such] construction . . . would have been seen as satisfactory if it made the physicalistic discourse come out right.'(75) The crucial passage in EN accused Carnap's reconstructions of being 'make-believe,' asserting that

> The stimulation of his sensory receptors is all the evidence anybody has had to go on, ultimately, in arriving at his picture of the world. Why not just see how this construction really proceeds? Why not settle for psychology? (Quine 1969a, 75–6)

Quine's objection to Carnap highlighted a circularity problem with the *Aufbau* that we considered above (section 2.2.1). But in the same passage, Quine went further to propose a radical re-orientation of epistemology:

> If the epistemologist's goal is validation of the grounds of empirical science, he defeats his purpose by using psychology or other empirical science in the validation. However, such scruples against circularity have little point once we have stopped dreaming of deducing science from observations. If we are out simply to understand the link between observation and science, we are well advised to use any available information, including that provided by the very science whose link with observation we are seeking to understand. (ibid.)

Consistent with his naturalism in other domains, Quine here freely endorsed the use of empirical results, from psychology and elsewhere, to attempt to resolve epistemological issues in the foundations of science. His naturalized epistemology combined this use of empirical science to explain the nature of knowledge with the rejection of 'first philosophy' as Carnap and the tradition had conceived of it. One difficulty that one encounters in this passage is Quine's movement back and forth between what might be called 'causal' notions and epistemological, justificatory relations. For example, he states that stimulations of sense-receptors are all that one 'has to go on' in constructing one's world-picture. Yet sensory-receptor events are physical events without any clear semantic contents, while one would expect world-pictures to have propositional contents, and the 'has to go on' locution normally is intended to denote an evidential or justificational relation rather than a causal one. Notice also how the sequence of Quine's rhetorical questions passes from raising questions concerning description of actual sequences of causation/justification versus merely possible 'rational reconstructions,' to issues concerning circularity of justification in Carnap. One might be interested in how human beings *in fact* come to think that some theoretical claim is true, as opposed to merely explaining how one *might have* done so or could do so. If so, then mere 'rational reconstruction' will not satisfy a desire for description of the actual processes.[9] But that is a different distinction from whether one is interested in an account of the actual *causal* sequences involving retinal stimulations and sound productions, on the one hand, or interested in the actual *reasoning* performed, and the question of whether the steps within that reasoning are genuinely *justificatory*, on the other.

However, we wish here to explore a different set of concerns by showing how proposals similar to Quine's can be made within logic and mathematics, and then considering Quine's attitudes toward them. Imagine reading a paper with a different title, 'Mathematics Naturalized.' In it the author notes various historical developments within logic and the supposed 'foundations' of mathematics. The logicians present accounts that are intended to bear on how mathematics is derived via 'logical principles' from various 'axioms.' These logicians think that various mathematical beliefs taken as 'justified' are indeed justified, at least conditionally on the justification of some basic premises that they call 'axioms.' They find that some statements, such as the 'continuum hypothesis,' are neither provable nor disprovable from any widely accepted axioms, in the sense that no syntactic structure of a particular accepted kind connects axioms to a statement of the continuum hypothesis. After noting this and other interesting developments, the author of 'Mathematics Naturalized' raises a number of rhetorical questions:

> But why all this creative reconstruction, all this make-believe? The axioms, blotches of ink on various sheets of paper, are all the evidence anybody has had to go on, ultimately, in arriving at his picture of the mathematical world. Why not just see how this construction really proceeds? Why not settle for psychology?

A seemingly obvious response to such questions would be to point out that we are interested in how mathematical statements are *justified* on the basis of axioms. The psychology of mathematical belief is a potentially interesting subject of study, but it is not the concern of the philosopher of mathematics. It seems to many philosophers that judging whether some particular account of the actual or possible justification of mathematical statements is a correct one is different from judging the adequacy of an account of the causal sequences involved in the movements of a mathematician's fingers or larynx.

Before proceeding, we note that Quine's rejection of meanings or propositional contents would seem to force on him a rejection of any relation that intuitively presupposes them, such as the relation of something being 'evidence for' or providing 'justification for' some claim. Quine must find some surrogate notion of 'evidence for' that holds between sentences rather than their meanings. The surrogate, given his notion of a sentence as something like a physical property had by various sounds or ink-blots, should end up being a relation that intelligibly holds between such physical concreta (or physical types, if we are considering relations between what might be called sentence-types). It seems natural, then, to appeal to causal relations as one's surrogates for these notions, given the prior commitments that Quine has adopted.

One question that Quine takes to remain interesting to the epistemologist, even after 'naturalizing' epistemology, is 'how evidence relates to theory, and in what ways one's theory of nature transcends any available evidence' (83). An initial question concerns the word 'transcends.' Is Quine presupposing that some relations, 'logical entailments,' are epistemologically interesting and relevant to justification, and that no other relations are epistemologically interesting or relevant? The notion 'transcends' here has to mean in effect 'does not logically follow from.'[10] Yet here several questions arise. One is, on what basis does Quine think that logical entailment relations are the only epistemologically or justificationally relevant relations? It would seem that there is no argument given for this view. But without such an argument, consideration of whether some theory is logically entailed by some data is of limited epistemological interest. Perhaps there is some other relation that constitutes justification of the theory on the basis of the data, a relation that is not logical entailment. Quine's own view of justification seems to be an unspecified form of hypothetico-deductivism, such that theories that are not logically entailed by data may nevertheless be justified.

Given Quine's views concerning the empirical status of logical principles themselves, further methodological puzzles arise. For example, how do we tell whether our theoretical beliefs 'transcend' observation (in the only respect in which Quine can have in mind here, in that they do not follow logically from observation statements)? It would seem that we must presuppose a capacity for determining whether some statements logically follow from other statements in order to determine whether ones that we actually systematically infer from some empirical data 'transcend' that data. But the notion of logical entailment, according to Quine, is itself theory-dependent, and ultimately justified, if justified at all, empirically.

We certainly do not claim that empirical research is irrelevant to epistemology. For example, various studies have shown that human beings are frequently prone to a number of fallacies, both logical and probabilistic (see Kahneman, Tversky, and Slovic, 1982). In the less-controversial cases, it is clear on reflection that a fallacy has been committed by the subject. But such judgments presuppose a capacity to distinguish good from bad inferences. And this capacity cannot arise in the first instance via empirical psychological research, for reasons broadly similar to those Quine himself gives to show that the capacity cannot be acquired in the first instance by a decision to adopt an explicit convention (see chapter 3). That is, just as application of conventions presupposes a prior understanding of logical notions, psychological research into fallacious reasoning presupposes a capacity for distinguishing at least some fallacies from valid inferences. In the more controversial fallacy cases, one can question whether the semantics of the statements involved in the inferences should be altered in such a way as to convert the inferences into justified ones. Alternatively, one can evaluate inferences as justified or not depending upon typical or intended context or background assumptions. In short, while in clear cases empirical research can show that human beings have tendencies to perform unjustified inferences, in clear cases one must appeal to general capacities for distinguishing justified from unjustified inferences, and furthermore these capacities do not arise in the first instance in any straightforward way from empirical research into linguistic behavior of the sort that Quine proposes that we substitute for epistemology.

As we have tried to show, many potential problems beset Quine's proposal in EN to replace epistemology with empirical psychology. It is undoubtedly a major part of the explanation why a more 'traditional' form of epistemology continues several decades later. While neurological studies are sometimes claimed to be important for epistemology, their epistemological significance is often controversial.

5.6 Quine and Evidence: Responses to Circularity

In the previous chapter, we introduced a potential circularity problem for Quine's indeterminacy of translation arguments that was based upon criticisms raised against Quine by the linguist Noam Chomsky. We argued that

Chomsky's criticisms, and Quine's response to them, revealed that Quine's indeterminacy arguments rested upon an assumption of physicalism. As such, we claimed that these arguments carried no weight against opponents who do not share Quine's physicalist assumptions, and that Quine's attempt to use the indeterminacy arguments as supporting either physicalism or a broader form of naturalism was circular. A number of other authors have noted that Quine assumed a naturalist or physicalist starting point, and that he then proceeded to argue in a circle to the conclusion that we should be naturalists in epistemology and elsewhere. But, it has been argued, Quine's circle is a virtuous one that does not undermine his overall position or the force of his arguments. We will here consider two such lines of response, one developed by Richard Schuldenfrei (1972), and a second suggested by Tim Crane (2003).[11] Both responses, and Schuldenfrei's in particular, propose a defense on Quine's behalf that invokes his epistemological views.

Schuldenfrei sees Quine as arguing for two related theses: first, that there is fundamentally only one kind of entity in the world, namely that studied by natural scientists (physical objects), and second, that there is only one kind of knowledge, namely the kind that natural scientists have (1972, 5–6). Schuldenfrei argues that Quine's indeterminacy of translation argument supports the first thesis by showing that the postulation of 'intentional idioms' that invoke meanings or propositions as mental entities, is eliminable, because such idioms provide 'little gain in scientific insight' (ibid.; cf. Quine 1960, 221). Quine's argument for this claim is that: 'Intentional idioms are ruled out of the domain of science on the basis of the generalization that science ("real science," that is) tends toward objectivity ("real" objectivity)' (Schuldenfrei 1972, 12). By contrast, the notion that translation is *determinate* requires 'subjective' idioms such as 'meanings, propositions, subjunctive conditionals' (10), Schuldenfrei thinks. But a comprehensive world picture does not require these subjective idioms, at least when canonically represented in Quine's preferred notation of first-order logic (cf. chapter 4).

Schuldenfrei grants that this argument is circular, remarking that 'there remains [in Quine's position] a circularity. Its unavoidability should be clear from the fact that in doing the theory of science, part of which requires saying what a science is, Quine admits to having to adopt a position on substantive science' (12). That is, Quine must take a stance on what 'real science' is, one which excludes the sorts of intentional (and intensional, we might add) idioms that Chomsky thought should be included. Without this stance, Quine's indeterminacy of translation argument reduces to a much weaker claim of underdetermination of theory by data, following the argument from Chomsky we saw above, as Schuldenfrei himself acknowledges (9–10). But while granting the circularity, Schuldenfrei claims it is not vicious. His argument for this begins by noting what he calls 'one of the important insights' of Quine's work, which is that Quine's concept of evidence includes

> the acceptance of systematic simplicity as evidence on a par with all other evidence. For the evidence in favor of bodies, the evidence of our senses, is not statistical evidence; it is not a question of cases supporting generalizations. This evidence is the product of systematic simplification and integration. (13)

Schuldenfrei sees these ideas as deriving from Quine's attack on meanings, propositions, and analyticity. He notes that Quine's attack on meaning in 'Two Dogmas' is 'based on an epistemological holism which is clearly based, in turn, on the conception of evidence we just mentioned. It is precisely because simplicity plays such a crucial role in testing scientific hypotheses that no particular claim can be reduced to its "empirical content"' (14). He then argues that these points about simplicity and holism allow Quine to *exclude* certain other claims that we might previously have regarded as claims of 'real science' or as reports of data:

> If a claim helps us organize experience, we have evidence for that claim. Some claims that help us organize experience conflict with the data. Reliable experience tells us which theory is correct, and theories tell us which data are reliable. Circularity, or the potential for it, is built into this conception of evidence . . . Thus, by accusing Quine of determining what his data are, and what science is, on the basis of his theory, and vice versa, we are only accusing him of actually making use of what he regards as the basis, if not the extent, of scientific method – the search for a simple and well integrated theory, even if it requires excluding what were previously regarded as data. (15)

As we understand his argument, Schuldenfrei regards Quine's emphasis on systematic simplification as supported by his attack on the 'second dogma' of empiricism. Since no claim can be reduced to its empirical content, we must consider any claim in the context of the system of sentences constituting the broader theory within which it is embedded. But,

Schuldenfrei continues, this fact allows other factors, such as systematic simplification and 'integration,' evidential weight. Hence, Quine's position is not viciously circular, for the benefits his assumptions provide in organizing our experience can justify his stance on what real science is, even though that stance in turn is used to exclude other conceptions of what real science is, such as Chomsky's.

We wish to make two points in response to Schuldenfrei's defense of Quine, as we understand it. The first is simply that it shows at most only that Quine's position on what counts as 'real science' would be justified if it were further established that the organizational benefits of Quine's assumptions about what real science is outweigh the benefits of other, different sets of assumptions. Schuldenfrei makes no claim to argue for the antecedent here, but only for the whole conditional. The conditional establishes at most that Quine's position is not viciously circular. It does not establish that Quine's position on what real science is is the best one, or even the best among rivals. Showing that Quine's position on science is in fact better than rivals at organizing our experience would, we believe, involve the defender of Quine in a not-inconsiderable difficulty. It would, for example, involve showing that Quine was right to hew to his broadly behaviorist approach to linguistics and psychology, even though the subsequent course of those sciences has moved in a decidedly non-behaviorist direction. This point should not be lightly dismissed, we believe. If it cannot be established that Quine's position on what counts as real science is the best among rivals, then we are not in a position to favor it over seemingly better contenders, even if those contenders include as theoretical posits the intensional and intentional entities of the sort Quine rejects. In other words, if a linguist could plausibly argue that his theory, which includes intentional and intensional entities, is better than Quine's at organizing our experience, we would then be in a position to reject not just Quine's account of real science, but Quine's entire account of language insofar as it rejects such entities.

However, even the weaker claim that Quine's view is not viciously circular, which Schuldenfrei does defend, is problematic, we believe. For Schuldenfrei's account leaves unanswered how we are to determine which theory is correct, and which account of real science is better able to organize, simplify, and integrate our experience. Nor do Quine's own discussions of theoretical virtues like simplicity appear to provide any help to Schuldenfrei's arguments. Of simplicity, for instance, Quine and Ullian wrote that it contains a 'nagging subjectivity' that we could not expect nature to 'submit to' (Quine and Ullian 1978, 72–3). This concession from Quine would seemingly allow for the type of 'subjective idioms' that Schuldenfrei thought Quine's position excluded. More problematically, Quine and Ullian observed that 'Physicists and others are continually finding that they have to complicate their theories to accommodate new data,' and suggesting that in this selection process the simplest hypothesis that accommodates that data might nonetheless be the likeliest (73). The problem with this account is that it presupposes a model of simplicity which takes the data that scientists work with as *given*, whereas Schuldenfrei's defense of Quine requires the much stronger claim that what counts as data is itself decided in part by simplicity considerations, in which case it is unclear why physicists and others should have to 'complicate' their theories at all.

This problem can be put more generally. Schuldenfrei's appeal to simplicity and integration, and to the ability of a claim to help us 'organize experience' as criteria for deciding what to count as real science or genuine data is in a situation similar to the one that we noted (chapter 4) faces Carnap's standpoint in 'Empiricism, Semantics, and Ontology.' The problem in outline is this: either we use empirical data to help us to determine whether a given theory satisfies these criteria, or we do not. If we do use empirical data, then the circularity that Schuldenfrei hoped to defuse by appeal to criteria like simplicity reappears at another level, for we are now faced with the question of how to decide which empirical data ought to be used in determining which theories are simplest, best integrated, and most helpful in organizing experience. For example, what should we count as data for the purposes of linguistic interpretation and translation, what are the experiences we need to 'organize'? Should we include the 'complexities . . . that come of the subjects' concurrent preoccupations and past experience' (Quine 1981, 184), or should we filter these out as 'white noise'? On the other hand, if we do not use empirical data to help us to determine whether a given theory satisfies the criteria of simplicity, integration, and the like, then what guides our application of them? Here it is of little use to appeal again to 'pragmatic' considerations like simplicity, integration, since it is precisely in the context of applying these considerations that the difficulty arises.

There is nonetheless a further way of defending Quine here that is worth mentioning and that involves a kind of radical extension of his views. Tim Crane, for example, has proposed defending Quine from a related kind of circularity charge leveled by BonJour (Crane 2003). BonJour argued that Quine's assumption of behaviorist premises in attacking analyticity is question-begging, for reasons broadly similar to those we canvassed in our discussion of Chomsky in chapter 4 (cf. BonJour 1998, 63f.). Crane responds by suggesting that BonJour had not fully appreciated the way in which

> Quine would simply reject the traditional epistemologist's talk of epistemic justification. From a Quinean perspective, calling the Quinean approach 'question-begging' misses the point. Quine is not trying to present an argument for his radical conclusions from uncontroversial premises; rather, he is using a variety of rhetorical and dialectical methods to persuade philosophers that their old ways of thinking are, in a certain way, empty. (Crane 2003, 503)

Crane does not himself endorse this interpretation. Nonetheless, as a reading of Quine it has some plausibility (a similar reading of Quine is suggested in Ricketts (1982). We have observed in earlier chapters that for Quine, there is no 'fact of the matter' about what we mean. If one takes seriously Quine's rejection of meanings and intentions, and further takes seriously his treatment of our use of language as being simply the 'triggering of our sensory receptors in the light of previous triggering of our sensory receptors,' then why assume that there is a fundamental difference between 'traditional epistemic justification' and rhetorical persuasion? From Quine's perspective, on this interpretation, perhaps all that really matters is that his audience have their sensory receptors stimulated in such a way that they exhibit assent behaviors to statements expressing a 'fully realistic attitude toward electrons and muons and curved space-time,' and exhibit dissent behaviors toward statements asserting the existence of meanings, synonymies, analytic truths, and the like. Why does it matter whether this stimulation takes the form of traditional arguments rather than rhetorical methods? Perhaps question-begging or viciously circular arguments are acceptable if they carry enough rhetorical force to achieve the kinds of changes in our dispositions-to-assent that Quine seeks.

So construed, Quine's philosophy stands at odds with one of the most basic epistemological distinctions in the western tradition, that between reasoned argument and rhetorical persuasion. This by itself would not mean Quine is mistaken, but it does raise a question about what it even means to argue with a Quinean who adopts this radicalized version of his position. Someone who challenges Quine's opening premises would perhaps be interested in knowing that this 'radicalized' Quine intended to change her mind through rhetorical persuasion, rather than through non-question-begging arguments from uncontroversial shared premises. That said, we prefer not to attribute to Quine such a radically a-rational approach to philosophical persuasion, though we must acknowledge that it remains unclear how to best resolve the above-noted circularities in justification that seem to arise for the overall Quinean picture.

5.7 Kripke on Apriority, Analyticity, and Necessity

As we noted in our discussion of Ayer's treatment of analyticity and apriority in *Language, Truth and Logic*, Ayer seemed rather careless and confused with respect to the relations between 'generality,' 'certainty,' 'necessity,' and other notions such as truth, assertibility, and 'validity.' Logical empiricists more broadly adopted the position that the a priori and the analytic coincided, along with the necessary. Saul Kripke provided a novel collection of arguments for distinguishing many of these notions in his wonderful book, *Naming and Necessity* (1980) (hereafter NN). We summarize his main arguments here (see NN 34–9, 54ff.), and focus on his reasons for distinguishing apriority and necessity in particular. Kripke does not say much about analyticity per se, but his examples of purportedly a priori contingent statements might be naturally construed as analytic (although they need not be so taken). Furthermore, given the logical empiricists' assumption that necessity, apriority and analyticity all coincide, his arguments for distinguishing apriority and necessity are relevant to the broader debates concerning analyticity.

Kripke has two main arguments for distinguishing apriority and necessity. The first relies on mathematical statements whose truth values we do not yet know, and may never know (NN 36). Consider Goldbach's Conjecture (GC), according to which all even numbers greater than 2 are the sum of two primes. No one has proved or disproved GC as of this writing. Yet either GC or its negation is true, and if true, necessarily true, and if false, necessarily false. The fact that we at some time, or even for all time, don't know whether GC is true by itself has no bearing on whether GC or its negation is knowable a priori, and Kripke eventually grants this. Even if GC is independent of the axioms of set theory, and remains in some sense 'undecidable' on the basis of accepted fundamental mathematical axioms, if true it is necessary, and if false it is necessarily false. Furthermore, Kripke thinks that it is plausible to take GC to be either true or false, whether we can know its truth value or not. To the extent that Kripke's assumptions are correct, they show at the very least that necessity does not entail a priori knowability, and thus a priori knowability and necessity do not coincide.

The more interesting and influential reasons for distinguishing apriority and necessity stem from the arguments that Kripke introduces to show that there are some 'statements' that are both a priori and contingently true, and other 'statements' that, while necessarily true, are knowable only a posteriori. His most famous argument involves Wittgenstein's 'meter bar' example. We think that this example introduces some irrelevant complexity, and arguably misrepresents Wittgenstein's positions.[12] So instead we will use a slightly simpler example due to Gareth Evans (1985). Evans stipulates the following:

> (J) Julius is the inventor of the zipper (if there is a unique inventor of the zipper).

The parenthetical clause will be ignored for most of the discussion, but we include it to avoid possible complications concerning applicability of the stipulation in all possible situations. We are to think of the stipulation, following Kripke, as a 'reference fixing' stipulation. We should not think of this stipulation as yielding a synonymy between 'Julius' and 'the inventor of the zipper.' The arguments supporting the apriority and contingency of J are partly constituted by the arguments for the notion of a 'reference fixing' as opposed to a 'synonymy generating' stipulation.

Let us consider whether 'the' 'statement' J is necessary or contingent.[13] Suppose, in particular, that there is a unique inventor of the zipper. Then 'Julius' presumably refers to that individual. One might naturally add that it does so 'by stipulation.' Now let us consider whether it is necessarily true that this individual, Julius, invented the zipper if any unique individual did. Well, Julius could have gone into taxidermy instead of textile engineering, and if Julius had gone into taxidermy, then he probably would not have invented the zipper after all. Someone else might have. So it seems that, intuitively, the following is true if there is a unique inventor: It is not necessary that Julius invented the zipper, if there is a unique inventor of the zipper. Thus, Evans or Kripke might argue, the statement J is not necessary.

On the other hand, it seems that we know, without doing any empirical research (beyond, at least, what is required to grasp the stipulation as a stipulation, i.e., empirical research concerning the language itself), that J is true. In this sense it seems that statement J is a priori. Nothing that we could learn empirically, at least nothing that is not about language, to the effect that we had misheard J, say, could undercut our justification for believing that J is true. Or at least it is arguably so. Furthermore, it seems plausible that we do know (and are justified in believing) J. So J seems a priori. But in the previous paragraph, we showed that J is not necessary, but contingent. Thus it seems that the statement J is both a priori and contingent. Among the things that we might take away from this and indefinitely many readily constructible similar examples is that necessity and apriority do not coincide, even in extension.

Kripke also argues that there are necessary yet a posteriori statements as well. Consider a situation in which the following two 'reference-fixing' stipulations are introduced into our language:

(H) Hesperus is (=) the star visible in the evening (if there is a unique star visible in the evening.)

(P) Phosphorus is (=) the star visible in the morning (if there is a unique star visible in the morning)

Now suppose that Hesperus is identical to Phosphorus as a matter of fact. Then the statement that Hesperus is Phosphorus is true just in case Phosphorus is Phosphorus. Consider the statement, HP: 'If Hesperus and Phosphorus exist, then Hesperus = Phosphorus.' If Hesperus is in fact identical to Phosphorus, then given the 'reference-fixing' that has already taken place via the acceptance of H and P, it would seem that the statement HP is necessary. For how could some existent entity fail to be self-identical? And yet it also seems that we could only have come to know that HP is true by doing some astronomical observation. Thus HP is also a posteriori rather than a priori.

A full evaluation of the HP example is beyond our book; however, Soames (2002) has a particularly lucid discussion of this and other purported examples of a posteriori necessities. Soames thinks that Kripke is mistaken about this particular sort of identity example of a posteriori necessity, but that there are nevertheless plausible examples of a posteriori necessities. We will focus on the contingent a priori instead, since it is the most pertinent to our discussion of analyticity. There is a large body of literature on this topic, but we will here attempt to concisely present one sort of reservation about Kripke's arguments.[14]

Our main reservation with Kripke's argument is this: it seems false that there is a single entity that is both known a priori and that is contingent. Different philosophers provide different accounts of this reservation and ways of drawing a distinction. But that there is some distinction to draw seems right to many philosophers. The worry is easiest to see if we construct a different example that brings out a motivation for distinguishing at least two relevant things.

Suppose that we introduce the statement QFT, via the following stipulation OM:

> (OM) Let 'QFT' express the conjunction of all true statements in Stephen Weinberg's books and papers concerning quantum field theory, if there are any (otherwise 'QFT' expresses a logical truth).

We might think of 'QFT' as abbreviating some as yet intuitively unknown collection of other statements. In any case, we seem to be able to construct arguments for the apriority of QFT analogous to those that Kripke provides for the meter bar, and the ones that we proposed concerning Evans' Julius example. It seems, for example, that once we know that OM has been stipulated, we know that QFT is true, and we know this in pretty much the same way that we know that it is true that Julius invented the zipper. We reflect on the stipulations given, and see that they entail something, in this case the truth of QFT. Now, it seems wrong to say that we know the proposition expressed by QFT (most of the readers of this book likely do not, for example). It seems natural to think that hardly anyone who accepts the stipulation OM knows any quantum field theory. Similar examples can be readily constructed, whether the stipulations are reference-fixers for names of individuals, or for predicative terms, or for proposition-expressing terms. Thus the puzzle is this. On one hand, it seems that the sort of argument that Kripke gives for our a priori knowledge of various 'statements' leads to absurd results for similar-looking cases that are easily constructed. On the other hand, the Kripkean sort of argument does seem to entail that in some sense or other, such 'statements' might naturally be described as known.

Philosophers have differed about how to resolve this puzzle. Some have tended to argue that, contrary to what Kripke claims, the real or genuine semantic content to be attributed to the sentences in question is not contingent. Others have argued that there are two semantic contents, one which is known a priori, and another which is contingent. The latter are known as 'two-dimensionalists.'

Two dimensionalism comes in various stripes.[15] One type distinguishes between our knowledge that a sentence expresses a true proposition on the one hand, and knowledge of the proposition expressed on the other. Precisely when we ought to describe someone as knowing a proposition p, as opposed to knowing that *p* is true, is not a trivial matter, however. It is as difficult as, and similar to, characterizing a *de re* versus *de dicto* distinction with respect to propositional attitudes. That is, in some cases it would seem correct to characterize someone as *knowing of* or *believing of* some individual IND that IND has some property, whereas in others we might instead describe a person as knowing that IND has some property, but not *knowing of* or *believing of* IND that he/she/it has the property. These matters are not central to the analyticity disputes, and so we will not pursue them further.

To anticipate our own view in the next chapter, we distinguish between what we call a 'statement,' which is a sentence-as-understood or a sentence as it is taken to be governed by distinct various norms or conventions, from something like a 'proposition expressed' by a sentence on an occasion. Statements can be governed by distinct evidential norms (such as, for example, the norm that no empirical evidence is counted for or against the truth of a particular statement, or that a statement express a true proposition), even when they might be said to 'express the same proposition' in some specifiable sense. Roughly speaking, something like the 'logical form' of two sentences can be the same, and yet the two sentences can be understood differently, such that one is understood as empirically indefeasible (as a type of stipulative definition, for example), and the other is understood as an empirically defeasible empirical hypothesis. We pursue this thought in the next chapter.

5.8 Chapter Summary

In this chapter we first summarized what we called the 'classical position' concerning analyticity, which is a collection of interrelated theses more or less broadly accepted by a wide range of logical empiricists. We raised some objections to the resulting picture, particularly the highly influential version presented by A. J. Ayer in his *Language, Truth and Logic*. We found that if one carefully disentangles some central issues, it appears that the classical picture as presented by Ayer does not satisfactorily resolve questions concerning our apparent a priori knowledge of various necessary propositions, including logical and mathematical statements. Among the key difficulties are that propositions are not distinguished from sentences, that modal necessity, apriority, and generality are conflated, that necessity seems merely stipulatively correlated with 'triviality' or 'containing no information' rather than the latter features *explaining* necessity or our a priori knowledge of necessity, that it is not made clear what the relation is between linguistic conventions and the truth of analytic statements, and that is not made clear what is wrong with denying analytic statements beyond labeling such denials 'self-stultifying.'

We then discussed some objections to the classical position by Laurence BonJour, with an emphasis on BonJour's objection that appeal to analyticity, and to stipulative 'implicit definition' in particular, does not help at all in accounting for any cases of purported non-empirical knowledge. We briefly recount BonJour's line of objections to 'implicit definitions' and their bearing on purportedly non-empirical or a priori knowledge, arguing that while BonJour is correct in some of his criticisms of the classical position or 'moderate empiricist' view concerning analyticity, he does not show that appeal to implicit definition is never illuminating or helpful, even for statements involving stipulatively defined terms.

Next we summarized Quine's arguments in his paper 'Epistemology Naturalized,' and raised some objections to the line of argument that Quine provides in that paper. We noted a possible circularity involved in Quine's overall position concerning empirical support for physicalism itself, along with some possible lines of defense suggested by Schuldenfrei and Crane.

Finally we briefly recounted Kripke's arguments for disentangling the notions of analyticity, apriority, and necessity, including his arguments for the existence of statements that are known a priori and yet contingent, and other statements that are knowable only a posteriori, and yet necessarily true. We raise an objection to the idea that some of his examples of contingent a priori statements genuinely involve a single entity that is both known a priori and yet contingently true.

5.9 Further Reading

A. J. Ayer's *Language, Truth and Logic* (1946) is a perennial classic. In spite of its flaws, it is easy to understand how the position elucidated there captured the imaginations of a generation of scientifically minded philosophers. BonJour's book *In Defense of Pure Reason* (1998), particularly the chapters on Quine's 'radical empiricism' and on 'moderate empiricism,' is very highly recommended. Peter Hylton's *Quine* (2007) is a recent and very detailed survey of Quine's entire philosophy, including a fine discussion of his naturalized epistemology. Philip Kitcher's essay 'The Naturalists Return' (1992) gives a sympathetic overview of what many philosophers have taken to be the philosophical consequences of Quine's naturalized epistemology. Among the more accessible of Quine's work is a book he co-authored with J. Ullian, entitled *The Web of Belief* (Quine and Ullian 1978). This book develops many of Quine's epistemological and methodological ideas in an approachable way. Anil Gupta's *Empiricism and Experience* (2006) defends a sophisticated and novel version of empiricism that is designed to improve on the version defended by logical empiricists. Kripke's *Naming and Necessity* (1980) is a must-read for all philosophers who want to engage contemporary metaphysics and epistemology. Frank Jackson's *From Metaphysics to Ethics* (1998) provides a helpful introduction to both two-dimensionalism and to the framework of the currently ongoing 'Canberra project.'

6

ANALYTICITY
REPOSITIONED

6.1 Introduction and Overview

As we have seen from earlier chapters, particularly chapter 3, the dialectic between the defender of and objector to the analytic–synthetic distinction is complicated and concerns fundamental issues connected to epistemology, semantics, and ontology. A goal of the present chapter is to provide an overview of a response to the attacks on analyticity by Quine and later by Harman. We give Harman such a prominent place in the discussion because we think that he has the clearest, most pointed, and most complete collection of objections to the notion of analyticity. Although Harman and Quine may not agree on all matters of detail, Harman has produced what we think is a fairly natural and forceful extension of the Quinean position to issues in epistemology and particularly semantics. Moreover, many other philosophers who oppose an analytic–synthetic distinction redeploy essentially the same arguments given by Quine and Harman. So we think that it is a worthwhile endeavor to both clarify the structure of, and provide a response to, these arguments.

We will begin in sections 6.2–6.5 with a particular approach to a distinction that is akin to the analytic–synthetic distinction. We say 'akin to' the distinction rather than 'the analytic–synthetic distinction' in order to avoid begging questions against an objector who accepts our distinction but wishes to deny that it 'really is' the analytic–synthetic distinction. We will give our reasons for thinking that our proposed distinction is a distinction worth drawing, and a distinction that many of the arguments of Harman and Quine are taken to undermine. Part of the purpose of this book is to help to unravel different issues that might otherwise be illicitly conflated. So we will grant some of the points made by Quine and Harman, but in section 6.6 we will show why we deny that their arguments undercut all interesting distinctions that are closely related to an analytic–synthetic distinction. While we will often follow common practice and refer to 'the' analytic–synthetic distinction, we actually think that there is a family of distinctions with different motivations, and only some members of the family are defended here. One unsatisfying aspect of many discussions of analyticity is that the responses to the attacks on the notion tend to focus on rebutting arguments against the distinction without supplying a positive account. Since many of these arguments lead to something like a stand-off, the absence of a positive account of analyticity is taken to be a win by default by the Quinean. We have a somewhat more ambitious aim here. We wish to respond to the objections by supplying an account of a few subvarieties of what might be called 'analytic' statements, give examples of them, and show how our account can grant many of the main points made by analyticity-skeptics while showing how other objections are at best question-begging and at worst grossly implausible. A disadvantage of our approach is that we must defend a potentially controversial positive account. But we think that this disadvantage is outweighed by providing a means of seeing more clearly what distinctions Quinean objections genuinely undermine and what distinctions might be preserved.

One of the most important and serious lines of objection from Quine and his defenders is their argument that, even if the notion of analyticity is coherent, it is of no philosophical importance (cf. sections 3.6, 3.10). A part of our response to this line of objection will be, in sections 6.8–6.9, to sketch how we think our proposed notion of analyticity can be used to provide an alternative to the broadly empiricist justification of basic mathematical principles defended by Quineans. Finally, we will provide an analogy in section 6.10 that we hope might tie together many of the various lines of thought that we have considered. Part of our intent in presenting the analogy will be to suggest that each of the main protagonists presented in our book has adopted a perspective that is in a certain important sense 'optional.'

6.2 The Best Cases: Stipulations and Mathematics

Our focus will be on what we take to be the best cases for the advocate of analyticity. The best case, we think, is that of explicit stipulations of a particular sort. Even fairly recently, Lycan has attempted to explain away the nagging case of explicit stipulation on behalf of the Quinean (Lycan 1991). Quine himself makes what appears to be a mistake in allowing explicit stipulation as a 'really transparent case of analyticity' (Quine 1953, 26). Most later advocates of the Quinean position, including Quine himself, seem to grant that this is an error, and some of their main arguments, such as the argument that 'there is no distinction between postulates and definitions' which we considered in section 3.9, explicitly renounce the existence of any principled, scientifically or philosophically illuminating distinction between explicit stipulations and other 'postulates' or 'hypotheses.'[1] We show how to draw such a principled distinction that illuminates some philosophical issues, and how the arguments against analyticity in general fail as objections to our distinction. We then apply a similar distinction to what we think is the next best case for the analyticity advocate, namely, mathematical stipulations. It has long been taken for granted that once philosophers dispense with analyticity, then if one does not wish to appeal to 'mathematical intuition,' one is forced to adopt an empirical account of mathematical knowledge and justification. We argue that when we are clear as to how an interesting distinction between types of statement can be drawn, we can explore applications of similar distinctions to illuminate various apparently non-empirically justified statements, such as mathematical statements and others.

6.3 One Type of Statement that Might Be Reasonably Called 'Analytic'

The paradigm case that our account begins with is that of explicit stipulative definitions. Consider again the notion of a *frenchelor* that we introduced in section 3.2. Suppose that we say, in the presence of a number of other English speakers, 'Frenchelors are French bachelors.' Suppose in addition that those present understand the statement as stipulative. Suppose further that no one has used the term 'frenchelor' before this occasion, and everyone agrees to use it to apply to all and only French bachelors. Finally, suppose that everyone takes it for granted that no empirical evidence counts against the statement 'Frenchelors are French bachelors.' The exact reason why people might take this for granted is, we think, beside the point for present purposes. Perhaps on other similar occasions they were explicitly instructed to take certain statements to be true and empirically indefeasible, and after a while a practice arose such that in many cases the explicit notification was superfluous. Perhaps a subtle difference of intonation was employed, a difference that has always been used in the past in similar situations.

When people take something as understood, as something implicitly given in a situation, we might also say that they 'share a common belief' to that effect. What we have in mind here for 'sharing a common belief that p' is not merely that they all believe that p, but that everyone believes that everyone or almost everyone else believes that p, and so on. It is a belief-analog of 'common knowledge.' We sometimes say that it is 'understood that p' when there is a shared common belief that p.

Supposing all of this, what has occurred when it is common understanding that a statement is to be taken to be true and indefeasible? To answer this, let us first consider the notions 'statement,' 'sentence,' and 'proposition,' as we will employ them in our discussion.[2] A *sentence*, for present purposes, is a structured item used on an occasion as a linguistic expression of a sort typically used to perform a truth-evaluable speech-act. We do not supply a technical definition of the concept here.[3] Our main purpose for introducing it is in order to draw a contrast between, on the one hand, an item with a syntactical structure, disregarding how that item is typically used or even what the words within it are taken to refer to, if anything, and on the other hand, the *rules* or norms that actually govern the employment or use of that syntactically structured entity within a language community. We take a sentence to have a definite 'syntactic form.' This syntactic form may be taken to determine, at least partially, what interpretations are admissible, given this syntactic form. We do think that typically, when stipulations are introduced into a language, there is a background of standard rules of grammar and interpretation that imposes constraints on admissible interpretations, which interpretations supply referents for individual words.

However, for present purposes we wish to draw attention to a kind of rule governing the uses of some expressions that is not determined by what might be called its logical or syntactic form. The kind of rule that we have in mind governs what sort of evidence is permitted to count for or against the truth of the sentence, and/or what the sentence expresses. While the logical form of a sentence typically constrains what further rules concerning evidential relations may be coherently imposed given the rest of the rules already in place, it does not completely determine these further evidential rules. For that reason we introduce a special use of 'statement.' A statement is a sentence together with some interpretation or some understood rules for using the sentence, where those rules may include rules governing what sort of *evidence* may be relevant to the truth of the sentence. These rules or norms will include norms for appropriate assertion of the sentence, for defending assertions of it, for supposing it, for asking whether it is true, and others. Looking at a sentence that is recognizably English, but containing a novel term, we may not be able to figure out simply from the syntactic form of the sentence what rules are understood as governing its assertion or its truth. As we shall see below, we think that a distinctive type of use for some sentences is a stipulative use. Stipulative uses of sentences involve treating those sentences as used in accord with rules or conventions of a particular type, which we explain further below.

Finally, we follow fairly standard usage and use the term 'proposition' to refer to an abstract object that is in some way correlated to a sentence. We do not commit ourselves to any particular set theoretic or other representation of a proposition, however. It might be taken to be a function from possible worlds to truth values, or it might be a set of possible worlds, or it might be a location within some possible inference relations, themselves taken to hold between other abstracta. The proposition is supposed to be an abstract object whose features represent in some interesting way the norms governing some canonical statement that 'expresses' that proposition.

6.4 Aside on 'Two-Dimensionalism'

A variety of proposals have been made for distinguishing two sorts of 'semantic contents' that some sentences of natural languages can have, and that can be represented by some abstract function involving possible worlds and their constituents. For example, if we consider an utterance of the type 'I am here now,' we can ask whether the semantic content of that utterance is necessary or contingent. A 'two-dimensionalist' is liable to distinguish two different semantic contents that can be associated with this utterance. One content, C_1, is roughly constructed from the actual referents of the sub-expressions of the utterance. C_1 may be taken to be something like the proposition that is true just in case a particular individual, the actual referent of 'I,' is at a particular location, the location that is the actual referent of 'here,' at the time referred to by 'now.' That the actual referent of 'I' (the utterer) is at a particular location at a particular time is typically a contingent matter, and so this content C_1 may be taken to be a contingently true proposition. How the second content, C_2, is to be understood varies across different theories, and we will not provide an overview of all of these theories here.[4] One such account of C_2 is in terms of a 'character.' The character of an utterance type is a function from 'contexts' to propositions or contents of the C_1 sort. So, in the case of the utterance 'I am here now,' since the character always maps the utterance in any context to a proposition that is true at the world of that context, there is a sense in which its C_2 content is 'necessary.' (See our discussion of G. Russell in section 6.7.) The situation is similar for other contemporary accounts, although the details are complicated and lead to somewhat different pictures.

Our main purpose in noting these discussions of semantic contents is to distinguish our own way of characterizing analyticity* from an account that appeals to semantic contents constructed from possible worlds. We do not object to all such constructions. In fact there is much to be learned from studying them, we believe. Our main reservation is that we think that the best way to capture the difference between analytic-like statements and others is in terms of the norms or conventions that are understood to govern their uses; in particular, we focus on norms governing what sort of evidence is permitted to count for or against these statements. Given some understood norms, one can sometimes construct a formal 'semantic content' that in some respects expresses or captures those conventions. But we resist the thought that what genuinely *explains* the special or distinctive status of analytic statements is facts about 'reference determiners,' or the fact that there exist various abstract functions mapping expressions to entities across possible worlds. We think that any order of explanation runs the opposite way; to the extent that one explains the other, it is the linguistic conventions that explain why possible-worlds models are to be constructed in such-and-such a way, rather than the other way around. (See our discussion of G. Russell on analyticity, section 6.7. See also our discussion of Kripkean contingent a priori 'statements' in section 5.7.) So we are in agreement with many two-dimensionalists that to the extent that one counts a content akin to the C_1 content above for various philosophically interesting statements, there is nevertheless some other type of 'content' in the vicinity that is different from this C_1 content. However, we do not think that the most illuminating way to capture what is distinctive about analytic statements is to provide a possible-worlds representation of a semantic content for them. Again, our fundamental worry is that while such possible-worlds frameworks can *represent* at least some aspects of the distinctive status of analytic statements, such frameworks can also misleadingly be thought to *explain* the distinctive status. Instead, we think that their distinctiveness is best captured by appeal to the rules or conventions understood to govern their uses. There is a difference here between our broader metaphilosophical perspective and that informing the work of Carnap, Quine, and many other philosophers, and we will look at this difference in the final sections of this chapter.

6.5 Analyticity* and T-Analyticity

A statement (sentence-as-used/understood-on-some-occasion), then, is a candidate for being 'analytic' in our present sense. Instead of 'analytic,' we shall call such statements 'analytic*,' to emphasize the special, explicitly stipulated technical sense that we are using. We will discuss what we take to be the relation between this notion and 'analyticity' as historically discussed later in the chapter.[5]

Treating statements, as opposed to sentences, propositions, or something else as analytic* has some advantages. For one thing, it makes definite the sort of thing that should be in the extension of the term 'analytic*.' As we have seen in earlier chapters, one of the factors in the controversy over analyticity was that it was not altogether clear what sorts of things were properly called 'analytic,' sentences or propositions. What analyticity* does is specify the sort of item that is properly taken to be analytic*, namely sentences as understood on an occasion, such that various norms of use for that sentence-as-used are understood. Another advantage is that it clarifies some confusing cases such as some of the Kripke 'contingent a priori' examples. In such cases, the stipulative sentence can be said to 'express the proposition' that is empirically defeasible (and contingent, as Kripke contends), while also on that occasion being such that the utterance of that sentence, taken as a statement, is such that the sentence cannot be false, cannot actually express a false proposition on that occasion.

So let us now state precisely what kind of statement is analytic*, and draw an important distinction among analytic* statements that will prove relevant to our proposed application of analyticity* to mathematics. When we introduce a stipulation of our particular indefeasible sort into our language, we introduce a coordinative rule concerning some stipulation sentence s, which states:

(Stip) Sentence s expresses some true proposition p (in our language L). Furthermore, the proposition q, *that s expresses a true proposition* (in L), is empirically indefeasible. No empirical evidence counts in favor of or against the truth of q.

When speakers of L accept Stip as a coordinative rule for speaking their language, we say that *s* is analytic* in L, or for speakers of L.

An important further distinction may be drawn within the class of analytic* statements. Note that analyticity* in general merely requires the indefeasibility of the proposition *q*, that *s* expresses some actually true proposition *p*, rather than indefeasibility of *p* itself. In mathematical examples, whatever proposition *p* that stipulation *s* expresses is itself taken to be empirically indefeasible. It is not just that '2 + 2 = 4,' for example, is taken to express some true proposition. The proposition *itself* is taken to be immune to empirical counterevidence. This leads to a further notion of 'transcendental stipulation':

> (TStip) Sentence *s* expresses some true proposition *p*. Furthermore, the proposition *q*, *that s expresses some true proposition p*, is empirically indefeasible. Finally, proposition *p* is empirically indefeasible (no empirical evidence counts for or against the truth of *p*).

Let us call analytic* statements that are also transcendental stipulations 't-analytic.' It may well be that the majority of actual analytic* statements are also t-analytic. But some examples that philosophers have considered at length are analytic* but not t-analytic. In particular, Kripke's 'meter bar' case, and related examples such as Evans' 'Julius' case (see section 5.7) are not. Consider Evans' example J: Julius is the inventor of the zipper (if someone is the inventor of the zipper). To the extent that J is understood as an indefeasible stipulation, sentence J is understood to express some true proposition or other. That requirement is what 'does the work' with respect to 'reference fixing.' However, whatever proposition is actually expressed, on a Kripkean account, is an empirically defeasible proposition. A proposition that states of some individual that he or she invented something is the sort of proposition that empirical evidence counts for or against. Such cases are rare, and this is among the factors that may make them appear surprising. Insofar as stipulations are 'normally' transcendental, we may find it surprising and puzzling how the proposition expressed can be contingent and empirical, even though the sentence expressing it is known to be true, and in some sense known a priori to be true. Our distinction between the two sorts of indefeasible stipulation helps to make such examples less puzzling, we think. Furthermore, as we will argue below, mathematical existence claims can be treated as stipulative as long as we require them to be transcendental stipulations rather than merely analytic*. Some might have thought on the basis of Kripke-style 'contingent a priori' cases that indefeasible stipulation cannot be relevant to mathematics, because indefeasible stipulation does not guarantee the indefeasibility of the proposition expressed by the sentence stipulated. But if we draw the distinction between merely analytic* stipulations and t-analytic ones, we leave room for an account of mathematical stipulations that also requires the propositions expressed to be empirically indefeasible.

Before we turn to defend our notion of analyticity* from some of the main objections to analyticity, we note some possible sources of misunderstanding. First, consider the assertion that analytic* statements are empirically indefeasible. It may be thought that some empirical evidence can count against the truth of absolutely any sentence, or against the claim that a given sentence expresses some true proposition. In particular, any empirical evidence that shows that a sentence is not governed by the rule or convention that we thought it was, within our own community for example, would arguably count as empirical evidence against the truth of the sentence, or that the sentence expresses a true proposition. For example, we might have thought that, according to what we believed was a widely accepted stipulation or analytic* statement, 'elm' just means 'a tree that looks like the one in this picture [pointing to photo],' only to later discover that biologists have another criterion and some trees that look like that are not elms. Haven't we thereby empirically discovered the falsehood of 'Elm trees are trees that look like that [pointing to photo]'? Our response is to acknowledge that such cases can naturally be counted as empirically discovering the falsehood of a sentence that we as a matter of fact take to make a stipulative, analytic* statement. However, the fact that there can be empirical evidence concerning what language we or others actually speak, or what norms we or some other community actually take as governing an expression, does not show that there is not a distinctive sense of 'empirically indefeasible' that nevertheless applies to analytic* statements. To make a longer (and we think interesting) story short, what we mean by 'empirically indefeasible' is intended to include only empirical data that does not concern language and uses of linguistic expressions of the language in which the stipulation is expressed. We could label such empirical evidence 'non-linguistic' empirical evidence. We realize that this is vague and not altogether satisfactory as it stands. Nevertheless, we do think that there is a distinction between, on the one hand, empirical evidence concerning language use itself, such as empirical evidence concerning how a given community actually uses a given expression, what rules govern it, and so on, and, on the other hand, more ordinary or standard empirical evidence that is not directly evidence for or against a particular form of language use. For example, empirical evidence concerning what percentage of a given adult population are bachelors would fall into this latter, standard kind of evidence. Evidence about how a given language community uses 'bachelor,' whether, e.g., they regard it as correctly applied to trees or to people, would be an example of the former kind. We think that is a clear enough distinction to motivate a distinction between analytic* and other statements that are not empirically indefeasible in the same distinctive way.

We have repeatedly used 'rule or convention' and 'norm or convention' to refer to what is understood to govern the use of an expression. The reason is that we prefer to avoid taking a definite stand on the question whether there are genuine linguistic norms, linguistic 'oughts' governing how language users ought to speak or use expressions. However, unlike Quine we do think that there is an intelligible difference between whether an expression is used as an empirical hypothesis or description, and whether it is used as a rule, and that this difference extends 'behind the lines' of the initial use of statements to ordinary use. We gave our reasons for this in section 3.9. We are inclined to think that there are rules and norms. But we nevertheless do not need to defend this claim in order to provide a way of characterizing analyticity*. What is crucial for our account is that there be a way of marking out a distinctive 'use profile' for some sentences as used within some communities, and that this profile can illuminate differences that might otherwise remain philosophically puzzling. Our account is thus compatible with the possibility that the presence of a convention within a language community might be somehow reducible to behavioral dispositions, for example. Yet it is also compatible with a view, which we happen to hold, that denies conventions are reducible in this way. But our account of the distinctive status of analytic* statements can remain neutral about what rules, norms, or conventions ultimately are.

6.6 How Analyticity* Avoids Many Common Objections to Analyticity

The Circularity objection: analyticity cannot be given an account of in terms independent of a family of intensional notions such as synonymy, necessity, meaning, or intension.

Despite being perhaps the best-known objection to analyticity, we think that the circularity objection that we considered in chapter 3 is among the least powerful and the least philosophically interesting. We mention it first simply to get it out of the way and to get to more interesting objections. We have already explained in sections 3.3 and 3.6 why many philosophers have not found the charge of circularity compelling, at least outside of Quine's disputes with Carnap, and we will not repeat those points here. Our positive proposal of the concept *analytic** has the advantage that it does not require explanation in terms of an appeal to the 'technical' intensional notions that Quine objected to in 'Two Dogmas' and that Harman continues to object to. Rather, we appeal to the more ordinary notion of a rule or a convention concerning a linguistic expression. As we have seen, Harman has tried to preserve circularity worries by arguing that 'analytic' is a technical notion, so that unlike commonsense or ordinary concepts which may only be 'circularly' characterizable, the defender of analyticity owes us an account of the notion that does not make circular appeal to other technical notions. Whatever virtues this argument might have, it seems to us that the notion of a rule is a non-technical notion, an ordinary notion that we apply in many other uncontroversial contexts. That a community has adopted a convention or considers something to be a rule is even behavioristically ascertainable. Hence, even a hard-core behaviorist need not demur from allowing such notions into the picture. In fact, we noted in chapter 3 that Quine himself endorses the notion of an explicit convention, arguing that it allows us to make sense of the notion of a convention (cf. Quine 1966, 112, quoted above). So in this respect, analyticity* provides an additional response to Quine's 'circularity' worries about analyticity, beyond the many responses we noted in chapter 3.

> *The indeterminacy of synonymy objection: Whether, for arbitrary sentences A and B, they mean the same thing or not is indeterminate. Since analyticity is essentially the same concept (readily interdefinable with) synonymy, analyticity is similarly ill-defined and indeterminate.*

Harman (1973, 109–10) seems to think that the basic mistake made by the analyticity advocate is thinking that 'means the same as' is an equivalence relation rather than a similarity relation. However, our notion of analyticity* does not require that there are meanings, or that there is some true theory of synonymy, or even that there be facts of the matter as to what is synonymous with what in the general case. All that the advocate of analyticity* needs to be committed to is the existence of principles of good translation, such that clearly analytic* statements are translated into clearly analytic* statements. Although many will think that principles of good translation are intended to or required to answer to facts of the matter about meanings, objecting to Quine/Harman by appeal to facts about meanings may be taken to beg the question against them in this context. Our account has a significant advantage here. For there is no need to think that there are meanings or even an equivalence relation 'means the same as' in order to defend the claim that good translation preserves clear analyticity*. For if all that one wants to do is show that there are some kinds of statements that are importantly different from others, there is no obvious need to appeal to meanings or synonymy, as opposed to something that Quineans themselves accept, namely, principles governing good translation, or better and worse translation. This fact can be easily missed. The existence of principles of good (or better and worse) translation is something that Quine and his defenders generally do and indeed *must* accept. We saw that such principles appear on any standard reading of Tarski's Convention T, which Quine accepts (cf. section 2.8), and saw how the Quinean is likely to appeal to them in our reconstruction of the debate between Quine and Grice and Strawson (section 3.6). We do not deny that there are meanings or that there are equivalence relations that can be either discovered or stipulated concerning what should count as 'means the same as.' But the acceptability of introducing a notion like analyticity* can be motivated without settling controversial questions about the existence or nature of such things, because it can be defended by appeal to the very same kinds of principles that Quine and Harman accept, namely, principles governing good (or better and worse) translation.

We cannot overemphasize the importance of this point. For it provides a way to jettison some of the core arguments against 'analyticity' and kindred notions. In the Quinean's preferred accounts, it is taken for granted that synonymy or sameness of meaning must be vindicated in order to vindicate analyticity. Then some brief arguments are introduced (typically following the broad outline of Quine's 'Two Dogmas') to show that synonymy is suspect for a variety of reasons. Much later, after the ensuing debate has become unwieldy and difficult to keep track of, any attempted distinction between 'change of meaning' and 'change of theory' is given a Quinean treatment, by appeal to the notion of a 'good translation.' But what typically goes unnoticed in all of this is that the Quinean has no non-question-begging, or even plausible account justifying precisely the principles of good translation that he suggests (unless one is a special variety of Quinean behaviorist, that is). Here the Quineans gain a rhetorical advantage, in that

when concerns are raised about the excessive permissiveness of Quine's proposed principles of good translation, the concerns are typically motivated
by appeal to meanings or synonymy. This enables the Quinean to move
to a position of relative strength, attacking meaning and synonymy, while
avoiding having to defend his own principles of translation directly. When
more plausible principles of good translation are considered, we get back
a distinction that looks quite a bit like the analytic–synthetic distinction, a
distinction that does not appeal to synonymy at all.

A related issue here concerns exactly how to justify principles of good
translation. This question is very rarely raised without appeal to meanings and meaning preservation, and this fact has shielded Quineans from a
serious difficulty, we think. Harman claims that the fundamental error of
the advocate of analyticity is treating synonymy as an equivalence relation
rather than a similarity relation. We can summarize our central response to
this as follows: the fundamental error of the Quinean is the failure to notice
that the question of what counts as a good translation lurks in the background of their own position, and that a very plausible criterion of good
translation, namely, preservation of clear analyticity*, preserves a notion of
analyticity and bypasses most of the Quinean's central objections to it. Further, what counts as a good translation seems to be a matter that cannot be
settled by appeal to empirical evidence, beyond at best what, as an empirical
fact of the matter, linguists actually employ.[6] And even here, the presence
of such empirical data concerning linguists' translational practice does not
necessarily work to the Quineans' advantage, as long as we have no assur-
ance that it does not conflict with the Quinean view. To be sure, if linguists'
translational practice does conflict with the Quinean view, Quineans like
Harman can claim that the linguists must have learned a 'bad philosophical
theory' (see the 'witch/nonwitch' discussion, below). But note that here
Quine and his defenders are not in a position to reply that the fact that what
counts as a good translation goes beyond what can be empirically settled
shows that there is no such thing as a good translation, or no 'fact of the
matter' about what such a translation might be.[7]

Precisely what should count as principles of good translation will likely
remain indefinitely contestable. Nonetheless, it seems a fairly obvious and
plausible constraint on good translation that analyticity* ought to be preserved across good translations, at least for some philosophical purposes.
(We need neither assert nor deny that we must adopt the same principles
for all translational purposes.) For instance, principles of translation that
permit translation of a stipulative definition in one language to an empirical

hypothesis in another are, we believe, implausibly permissive on their face. And to claim that basically all that we should strive for is preservation of 'assent/dissent' to sentences seems far less plausible, for it is far too generous to constrain what should count as correct translation. Worse yet for Quine and Harman, the analyticity* advocate can simply grant that for some purposes, looser translations governed by less demanding principles of a sort acceptable to Quineans need not be ruled out. To reject analyticity*, what the Quinean requires is something much stronger, namely a compelling reason to think that the only acceptable constraints on good translation will fail to include any requirement that analyticity* be preserved. There may very well be no way of definitively settling the matter of what should count as good translation. But we think that it is the analyticity* advocate who has the more plausible and defensible position along this front.

One reason that people have thought that analyticity is closely associated with synonymy, is that in many paradigmatic cases of stipulative definition, the stipulated definition has had the form of a universally quantified biconditional, such as:

For any x, x is a bachelor iff x is unmarried and x is a man.

In the context of an explicitly stipulated biconditional, it is easy to think that the expression defined 'means the same as' some expression that defines it. While we agree that in such cases there are often synonymies present, we do not think that analyticity* in general requires appeal to meanings or to the single equivalence relation 'means the same as.' We do appeal to the notion of a rule or to a convention, but as we noted in our response to the circularity objection, such an appeal seems to be acceptable even within a Quinean framework.

> The witch/nonwitch objection: Some defenders of analyticity (e.g., Grice and Strawson) argue that philosophers often agree as to which statements in an open-ended collection of example statements are analytic and which are not, and that this fact shows that there is some notion akin to 'analytic' that such philosophers grasp, whether or not they can provide an illuminating account of the distinction. However, this simply shows that people (philosophers in particular) can be taught a bad theory of language, and can use it to draw distinctions where none really exist. The agreement (even in open-ended classes of cases) does not show that there is a real analytic–synthetic distinction any more than the fact that people in Salem, Massachusetts might have agreed as to who is a witch and who is not shows that there is really a witch/nonwitch distinction.

This analogy extends a line of objection we introduced in section 3.6. To begin, a clarification of this analogy is in order. Harman himself grants that there is a witch/nonwitch distinction. Witches are women with supernatural powers, non-witches are either non-women or have no supernatural powers. What he means, as he explains (Harman 1967, 127), is that there is no witch/nonwitch distinction that both conforms to what speakers meant by 'witch' and is such that the class of witches has a nonempty extension. We mention this in case it might have been thought that the witch/nonwitch analogy helps to show what some Quinean arguments were intended to show, namely, that there is no intelligible distinction to be drawn between the analytic and the synthetic, rather than merely that there are in fact no analytic statements. Harman's point might be restated as follows: there is no real distinction between people called 'witches' by believers in witches and those not called 'witches' by them, or at least no distinction of the type that was believed to hold.

With this qualification in mind, we think that Harman's analogy fails when directed at a notion like analyticity*. One respect in which it does so is that there are different types of distinctions in play in the witch case and the analytic* case. What it is to be a witch is to have a special causal profile. By contrast, what it is for a statement to be analytic* is for it to be used in a particular way, and to be understood in a particular way. That is, analyticity* is what might be termed 'response-dependent.' In using this term, we do not mean to say that our responses in the case of explicit stipulation are unintentional (as they may be with concepts such as 'beautiful,' and according to some philosophers, with color concepts). So we might call the notion of analyticity* an 'intention-dependent' concept or the distinction between analytic* and other statements an intention-dependent distinction. Many other examples of such concepts can be given. Being a chess-bishop is intention-dependent in much the same way. What makes something a chess-bishop, most of us likely think, is in large part that we take it to be a chess-bishop, that we take it to be governed by particular rules or conventions. It might more properly be called a 'belief and intention-dependent' concept, or an 'attitude dependent' notion. It is not that we think that the mini-sculpture that we have designated a chess-bishop on some occasion has special causal powers that explain why we are unable to move it in certain ways. If anything, one might say that we assign it a role within a practice, and we form intentions of the sort required to be counted as engaging in that practice. Likewise, what it is to be a linguistic item in the first place derives from the beliefs and intentions concerning it. And the notions 'belief-dependent' and 'intention-dependent' do not seem to us to require appeal to any notion of belief or intention that Quine and Harman do not themselves accept. Thus, despite what Harman repeatedly asserts concerning our intentions relating to sentences, in some cases, our intentions relating to sentences are determinative. For precisely what it is for a statement to be analytic* is for people to have the right sorts of intentions with respect to it.

Does being a chess-bishop cause anything? There is a permissive and fairly natural way of speaking that allows us to respond to a question like, 'Why don't you move that piece over here?' with something like, 'Because it's a bishop, and bishops only move diagonally in chess.' The 'because' in this answer can make it look as though the piece's being a bishop is part of a causal explanation of my moving it in the way I do. Again, there is sense to be made of such a picture. It is a fact about my psychology that I have adopted a convention of treating a certain mini-sculpture in accord with particular rules or conventions, and my having adopted those conventions, which is constitutive of the piece's being a chess-bishop, is partly causally explanatory of my moving the piece in the way that I do. But none of this assigns the chess-bishop an occult power. Consider a more complicated case, such as being a prime minister. In some cases it might be said that the fact that someone is a prime minister is constituted by some complicated convention that has been adopted, facts about the intentions and actions of many people. Being a prime minister can, however, also invest someone with causal powers that non-prime ministers do not have. Perhaps only the prime minister can declare war, for example. A speed-limit sign has causal powers in the sense that its presence is likely to cause some people to slow down below some value. But this causal power is not 'occult' like that of witches, but instead results from a complicated and intertwined panoply of shared conventions and beliefs.[8] The main point that we want to emphasize here is that there is a large and open-ended class of similar distinctions between things where the distinction is what we might call 'intention-dependent' or 'convention-dependent.' The witch analogy, in our view, does not engage the sort of intention-dependent feature that distinguishes concepts like analyticity*.

A further strand of the response to the witch analogy is connected to another of the central worries that are raised concerning analyticity, namely, that it does not do any interesting explanatory work within empirical science (including linguistics and psychology). The connection is roughly the following. The real (or at least a central) problem with the notion of analyticity, according to Harman, is that it doesn't genuinely explain any real phenomenon, just as witchhood does not genuinely explain any real phenomenon. Just as we no longer believe that there are women with supernatural powers, nor that supernatural powers are required to explain their odd behavior, and so on, so too we ought now to no longer believe that there are statements that are true in virtue of meaning. Meanings are occult (in a pejorative sense) entities or relations, like those features purportedly had by witches. Nothing genuinely requiring explanation is explained by appeal to meaning or its even more illegitimate sibling, analyticity. There are no meaning entities, nor is there such a thing as meaning the same as something else.

This is a part of a more general line of objection, which we consider next.

> The 'Non-explanatoriness' objection: Analyticity does not explain any empirical phenomenon. Thus it is an illegitimate concept to introduce into scientific philosophy. In particular, appeal to analyticity does not explain why some statements are true. There is no sense to be made of 'truth in virtue of meaning.' Furthermore, there is no good sense to be made of our knowledge of some truths by appeal to knowledge of meanings. Aside from other difficulties, there are no meanings, and there is no such thing as synonymy, at least in any technical sense required to carry out any acceptable explanation of the sort considered.

The non-explanatoriness family of objections, which we addressed in section 3.10, is taken by Harman to be among the central objections to analyticity. We can grant many of Harman's claims that analyticity has not proven explanatory, but we deny that this provides a reason for rejecting the notion as illegitimate or as 'unscientific' in a pejorative sense.

Recall that our notion of analyticity* does not depend on an appeal to meanings or to sameness of meaning. For this reason, we are inclined to think that all of the strands of the non-explanatoriness argument that appeal to the non-explanatoriness, unintelligibility, or non-existence of meanings or sameness of meaning are irrelevant to whether analyticity* is legitimate or acceptable. We do not find all of the arguments against meanings or sameness of meaning convincing. On one hand, we are inclined to agree with Harman that it is at best unclear whether either meanings or synonymy are explanatory of empirical phenomena in the way some linguistically inclined philosophers (e.g., Chomsky 1975 or Katz 1974) seem to think. On the other hand, we are inclined not to worry about accepting some abstracta commonly associated with meanings, such as propositions.

We discuss such abstracta later on in this chapter, when we discuss the notions of 'pure stipulata' and 'impure stipulata.' However, we do not want our primary response to the non-explanatoriness objection to rest on that discussion. Instead we will try to explain how an appeal to analyticity* and kindred notions can illuminate epistemologically puzzling phenomena such as our apparent non-empirical justification for believing some statements, among other things. That the notion of analyticity* can be illuminating does not entail that analyticity must be a causal/explanatory notion if, for example, it can clarify something that is otherwise puzzling, such as apparently non-empirical justification.

Let us first consider the common locution 'analytic claims are true in virtue of meaning.' A variety of attempts to spell out what this locution means have proven problematic. Quine and Harman, as we saw in chapters 2 and 3, have a number of serious objections to at least some of the most prominent attempts. The fact that it is hard to see how meanings can 'make true' sentences, or how knowledge of meanings can explain knowledge of truth, is one of the reasons that have led Quineans to reject the idea of analyticity. Does analyticity* fare any better in accounting for 'truth in virtue of meaning,' or even 'knowledge of truth in virtue of knowledge of meaning'?

We would grant to Harman and Quine that the truth of analytic* statements, if indeed they are true (this is considered further below), is not explained by their meaning, or the meanings of their constituent words, except in an attenuated or loose sense that we'll talk about shortly. Rather, our view is that a statement's being taken to be true and indefeasible is *constitutive* of the meaning of the statements (or sentences-as-understood). It is not that their meaning *explains* their truth, or explains their being taken to be true. Rather, what it is to be analytic* *just is*, in part, to be understood to be taken to be true and empirically indefeasible. It may be worth noting that appeal to 'meaning' is unnecessary for present purposes. If one prefers, one can adopt the Quinean attitude toward synonymy and meanings and instead explain things in terms of that which is preserved in good translation, rather than meaning. Thus our view can be roughly rephrased as follows: what it is for a statement to be analytic* is to have the linguistic community take it as true and take it as indefeasible. Furthermore, this feature is to be preserved across good translation.[9]

We are thus suggesting a kind of 'explanatory reversal' here that constitutes another crucial feature of our defense of analyticity*. We will say below why we think that our position remains relevant to the analyticity debate even with this reversal. Other philosophers, such as Wittgenstein and Schlick, have suggested a similar reversal of direction of explanation in other cases.[10] And the fact that Harman argues that our intentions concerning sentences (that they turn out true, in particular) do not ensure that they are true, suggests that he takes himself to need to refute this sort of 'reverse explanation' view of analyticity.

Despite the fact that talk of meanings 'explaining' truth or of knowledge of meanings explaining knowledge of truth is misleading at best, we think that such locutions can be harmless in ordinary cases. For example, if our child asks us how we know that all bachelors are unmarried, it seems natural to respond, 'That's just the definition of "bachelor," it means unmarried man.' There is a loose sense in which the meaning 'explains' the truth of explicit stipulations of the sort we're considering (analytic* statements). The fact that 'bachelor' means 'unmarried man' within the relevant linguistic community can naturally be taken to entail that all bachelors are unmarried, and in that sense our knowledge of the meaning of 'bachelor' can 'explain' our knowledge that all bachelors are unmarried.[11] Correctly classifying 'bachelors are unmarried men' used in a particular way as being akin to a stipulation clarifies the relevant aspects of its justificatory status.

Even this loose sense of explanation seems to require that analytic* statements are in fact true and in fact known, for otherwise there would be nothing to explain. So are they in fact true, known, or justified? Our short answer is that it is not clear that our position requires taking a stand on this matter. One can decide, perhaps arbitrarily, to include them in the extensions of truth, knowledge, or justification. Things will proceed most fluidly in ordinary usage if we do take them to be true, justified, and known, but for careful philosophical purposes, it remains to be shown whether there is a clearly best convention to adopt concerning whether to take analytic* statements to 'really' be true, known, or justified, or whether there are good non-conventional theoretical justifications for claiming one or the other. A slightly longer answer is provided below, in reply to the next objection:

> 'Saying it doesn't make it true': Stipulating something does not make it true, nor does it justify us in believing it.

In response, note that we do not assert that stipulations are epistemically justified. Nor do we deny it. We assert that they have a distinctive normative profile, which more specifically is a distinctive epistemic/evidential profile. Whether we are really, for ultimate philosophical purposes, justified in adopting a stipulation is a matter for further reflection, and the acceptance of certain sentences as analytic* does not require taking a definite stance on the matter, as far as we can see. What we do resist is the thought that stipulations *require* some epistemic or pragmatic justification in order to be a part of a coherent practice. We find somewhat bizarre, for example, Kitcher's expression of sympathy with this aspect of the Quinean view. Kitcher thinks that concepts introduced stipulatively are such that the stipulations require 'warrant,' in the form of empirical evidence supporting their applicability within useful empirical theories. This warrant is required for us to know the truth of the stipulations by which the concepts are introduced, he thinks.[12] We think to the contrary that a stipulatively introduced concept such as *frenchelor*, regarded as an example of analyticity*, can be perfectly coherent, usable, and comprehensible, quite independently of whether there are any interesting applications for it, and so independently of whether the stipulations involving it are empirically 'warranted.' Similarly, novel branches of mathematics generated by novel mathematical axiom systems or mathematical stipulations may have no known or even expected non-mathematical uses. We think one must preserve a distinction between the *intelligibility* of a concept, and the truth of stipulations concerning it, on the one hand and its empirical *applicability* or *fruitfulness* on the other.

The observation that analytic* statements, including mathematical examples, are not obviously 'genuinely justified' may seem to be a difficulty for applications of such statements, for example within empirical theories. If for all we know (qua philosophers), analytic* statements may not be true or even justified, how can we legitimately employ them within science, or even in everyday life for that matter? The answer is that a coherent practice that allows the introduction of analytic* statements will need to have rules concerning permissible indefeasible stipulation introduction. Not just any old sentence in English can be employed as analytic*, while still cohering with the rest of the accepted practice. For example, we cannot simply assert that the average rainfall in a certain Nepalese village is 32 inches per year, and defend the statement by claiming that it is stipulative, or analytic*. The reason is that this sentence (and the terms within it) already has norms or conventions governing its normal or standard employment, and thus its introduction as stipulative would not cohere with these pre-existing conventions. Furthermore, analytic* statements collectively must not entail any statement on which empirical evidence bears, on pain of an incoherent practice.[13] In short, a practice that permits the introduction of analytic* statements, if it is to be a coherent (intelligible) practice, will have rules for their introduction that prevent any difficulty that will not arise in what we might call a Quinean practice, in which analytic* statement introductions are ruled out. A false empirical prediction resulting from a mathematical stipulation together with some empirical claims can lead to either a rejection of the empirical claims or to a shift to a different mathematical theory. Quineans might describe such a shift as an empirically justified shift in one's mathematical theory, but on our view that misdescription results from excessively permissive standards of translation. Our point here is not that permitting analytic* statements within one's practice is preferable in some pragmatic way to disallowing them. We are merely showing here why there is no obvious pragmatic *deficit* brought about by allowing analytic* statements, instead of treating all sentences as akin to 'empirical hypotheses' as Quineans are wont to do.

> *Objection: All claims are hypotheses or 'postulates.' There is no distinction between postulates, or empirical hypotheses, and stipulations.*

This statement is a consequence of a line of reasoning that we considered in chapter 3 (section 3.9). It has an odd status, in that how best to understand it is a matter of controversy between the Quinean and ourselves. As we saw in chapter 3, Quine acknowledged cases of 'legislative postulation' or definition, but such referred only to the 'act' and not to its 'enduring consequence' for subsequent language use (1966, 112). A Quinean like Harman takes this to be a true description of actual languages, and contemporary 'reformed Quineans' who accept alethic modalities might even claim that it truly describes all possible languages. In contrast, from our point of view it seems to be an expression of the Quinean stance rather than a true description of all possible or comprehensible practices. We see this claim as akin to the statements, 'We don't point at people' or 'Wearing a hat at the dinner table just is not done' in their common uses. We next consider a number of possible interpretations of the objection that there is no difference between postulates and definitions.

First, the Quinean might intend such a claim as an empirical description of actual natural languages, as seems to be suggested by Quine's talk of legislative definitions not having an 'enduring consequence' for language use. Yet so construed, we think that this is false, and fairly obviously so, given that we do on occasion make explicit stipulations and we do mathematics, which nearly everyone, besides certain defenders of Quine, takes to be non-empirical. The treatment of mathematics as a kind of empirical hypothesis, which as we saw (section 3.7) was an outgrowth of Quine's holism, poses a continuing, nagging difficulty for the Quinean position, we think, despite a number of thoughtful defenses of a broadly Quinean account of mathematics (e.g., Colyvan 2003; Kitcher 1983; Resnik 1997). Quineans can attempt to do what they think empirical scientists often do, which is to introduce some story as to why, appearances notwithstanding, the data (concerning mathematicians' behavior, say) is actually to be interpreted in the way Quineans suggest that it should be. They might then provide stories whose purpose is to show how some mathematical statement that is now taken to be true might possibly (epistemically) be 'given up' and no longer taken to be true. How convincing one finds these stories seems to be highly correlated with how sympathetic one is to the Quinean viewpoint on independent grounds. It seems very unlikely that anyone was first led to an empiricist view of mathematics by an examination of mathematical practice, independently of prior philosophical commitments to a strong form of empiricism. Our second response to this first interpretation is to say that from a non-Quinean perspective, the question of whether actual language users would do this or that with a given expression is irrelevant to whether some possible language community could be best interpreted as employing some statements as analytic*. What 'best interpreted as' comes to will likely remain controversial between the Quinean and the non-Quinean, since the Quinean will always take a 'best interpretation' to be merely a 'translation' with fairly minimal (even behavioristically insufficient) imposed constraints of goodness, rather than the more plausible and illuminating ones that preserve analyticity*.

A second interpretation of the claim that there is no difference between 'postulates' or 'hypotheses' and explicit stipulative definitions would be to treat this claim as a normative proposal, one which is justified on pragmatic grounds. That is, a Quinean might claim that adoption of a Quinean 'radical empiricist' stance toward linguistic practices, including our own, is pragmatically the best approach (perhaps with the caveat 'for the purposes of doing empirical science'). Our response to this is to request a demonstration or even an argument for this claim. It seems to us that there is at best nothing to choose between the two sorts of practices. Whether one is taking what one decides to call 'mathematics' as analytic* or as a highly theoretical empirical hypothesis, as long as one understands what one is doing, it is hard to see why the former approach will lead to a less well-developed empirical scientific practice than the latter. If anything, we worry that many confusions can arise (such as fruitless searches for empirical justifications of mathematical principles) if one is not careful to distinguish empirical hypotheses from mathematical statements. It may turn out that a consistent Quinean may be able to do science about as well as the non-Quinean. But what reason is there to think that science would be improved if scientists adopted a Quinean account of mathematics? We are unaware of any. Moreover, there are philosophical benefits to seeing how alternative, non-Quinean practices are possible, whether or not they describe actual practice.

> F = ma was thought to be a definition, but was empirically falsified, and similarly for a host of other examples from science: Within science, what had been thought to be stipulative turned out to be empirically defeasible. Consider 'F = ma.' This was taken to be a law by Newton, but many later physicists and philosophers took it to be a definition of 'force.' But later on, Einstein showed that mass obeyed a different equation . . . etc. (Many other examples can be enumerated.)

As we saw in chapter 3 (section 3.7), Quine radically extended the confirmational holism suggested by Poincaré, Duhem, and Carnap to produce this powerful line of attack against analyticity. Here, we agree with Quineans that practically all nonmathematical statements employed within empirical sciences are of an empirically defeasible sort, in the sense that if we examine actual or counterfactual practices with such sentences, it is usually plausible to think that their truth would be taken to be disconfirmed by empirical evidence. Granting that practically all nonmathematical statements used in the empirical sciences are empirically defeasible is, on the one hand, a significant concession, for it constitutes a retreat from accepting many examples that the logical empiricists, and Carnap at every stage of his philosophy, would have included as examples of analytic statements within empirical science. But on the other hand, this concession also frees us from having to respond to a wealth of examples cited by Quineans against the logical empiricists. We think that analyticity* is more narrowly applied in actual practice than the logical empiricists and Carnap claimed. But we also think that many explicit stipulations and mathematical statements are clear examples of non-empirical statements, and that they are employed in accord with conventional norms that are quite distinct from those governing empirical hypotheses, even highly 'theoretical' hypotheses. We discuss the case of mathematics at some length later in this chapter.

It may be possible to practice science in a very regimented way, such as Carnap proposed, and in which it is absolutely clear which are the analytic* statements and which are theoretical hypotheses. However, in most real, nonmathematical cases that we can think of, there seems to be a strong inclination to identify entities and concepts across theories even when the theories employ stipulatively defined notions, and the stipulations within the two theories are incompatible. For instance, in section 3.9 we noted an example Putnam gives of the scientific definition of the momentum of an object as its rest mass times its velocity. Given this definition, it may appear to be an analytic truth that an object's momentum is its rest mass times its velocity. In the context of Newtonian physics, it might further be true that momentum is conserved in a perfectly elastic collision. But as Putnam pointed out, within special relativity, the constraint that momentum be conserved requires that it not be exactly equal to rest mass times velocity. This in turn seems to require that we abandon the claim that M is analytic. Here it appears that our earlier belief that M is analytic turned out to be fallible – as fallible as Newtonian physics itself proved to be – and this in turn seems to support Quine's position that the analytic–synthetic distinction isn't useful (cf. Putnam 1983; Quine 1966a). Our position with respect to such cases is that to the extent that such a 'translational' practice of using what seems to be the same concept in different theories is taken to be acceptable within the empirical sciences, then such examples show that this practice should grant that there are very few or in some domains no nonmathematical examples of analytic* statements within empirical sciences. Unlike mathematical concepts such as 'prime number' or 'Hilbert space,' even defined concepts that are properly nonmathematical, like 'momentum,' tend to be associated with causal laws. To the extent that what these causal laws are is an empirical matter, concepts defined via connections to these laws are going to be answerable to empirical data as well, even if originally introduced in a way that seemed stipulative. That is why we suspect that it is most common to see clear cases of analytic* statements (other than mathematical ones) outside of empirical science, in which something like classification is the main purpose rather than causal explanation or prediction, and where there is no tacitly understood background of empirical laws to which the concepts in the analytic* 'definitions' are tied. There are a number of other objections that are either explicit or implicit in Harman's full repertoire. We will end with an assortment of them.

> *Analyticity* doesn't explain knowledge of logic.* [Therefore, it is unhelpful for one of the primary cases for which analyticity was introduced.]

When we introduced the notion of analyticity*, we implicitly assumed a fixed background of logic and grammar (in the ordinary sense of 'grammar'). So our appeal to analyticity* does not seem suited to provide an account of that background logic itself. Recall here that Quine posed a similar objection to the notion that logic might be the conventional stipulation of (analytic) truths that we discussed in chapter 3. Quine pointed out that drawing inferences from such alleged conventions presupposed the very logic they were supposed to stipulate. What prevents a similar objection from being leveled against our account?

Two points of clarification are in order before saying anything further about logic. First, we do not pretend to have provided a complete account of all non-empirical knowledge and justification, and logic is a particularly difficult case that we do not present an account of. (Logic is discussed further in chapter 5, 'Analyticity and Epistemology.') More importantly for present purposes, though, we deny that one needs to solve the problem of a priori justification in *all* cases in order to illuminate *one important type of case*, namely, the case of analytic* statements which are explicit stipulations understood as such by a linguistic community. Among our purposes in this work is disentangling a variety of issues. We do not think that one must resolve the status of logical principles, and our justification for adopting them, in order to clearly show how some statements are importantly different from others with respect to how empirical evidence bears on them.

One issue that might worry some readers is the following. Suppose that a Quine-inspired account of the justification of logical principles is adopted, according to which such principles are also answerable to empirical data, in that our best overall theory of the data might in some sense include principles of logic other than classical logic. Then if we think that all of our 'best overall theory' employs the same nonclassical logic, mathematics is included in that 'best overall theory,' and so we will be forced to alter our mathematics. The issues here are complicated, but here is one simple opening response on behalf of analyticity*. A community that recognizes some analytic* statements might simply continue to do 'classical mathematics' but also consider the novel developments of 'nonclassical mathematics.' This is in fact what has happened in the face of 'intuitionistic logic,' although by far most mathematics employs classical logic rather than intuitionistic logic. There is no non-question-begging argument that we are aware of that our current mathematics would have to be given up if the logic of the language of our best fundamental empirical theories is nonclassical, and in this restricted sense we can agree with the attitude that Carnap took toward such matters (cf. section 2.2.2).

It is far from clear whether revisions of logic on the basis of empirical data are genuinely intelligible in any case. The example cited repeatedly by Quine, Putnam, and many others is the supposed alternative 'logic' of quantum mechanics (cf. Quine 1953, 43; Putnam 1979, 174–97). After over fifty years of research along many avenues, 'quantum logic' has (argu-ably) gone precisely nowhere, other than in popularizations of physics. And the problems associated with the development of a quantum logic are not empirical, so far as we can tell. Rather, they are primarily conceptual. What would it be to change the background logic of a theory, exactly? What does the causal or even mathematical structure of a state space have to do with 'logic,' exactly? What is logic, exactly? In the absence of a compelling account along these fronts, the at times wildly speculative and often obscure claims to the effect that quantum systems 'obey a nonclassical logic' does not currently aid the cause of the Quinean radical empiricist view concern-ing logic. Perhaps in the future it will, but not at present.

A final worry that we should raise concerning our view is that we pre-suppose the existence of a background logic, even for mathematical prac-tice, and yet we have not supplied any clear distinction between logic and mathematics. Is set theory a part of logic, or a part of mathematics? What about mereology, is it a part of logic? We admit uncertainty on this front. To the extent that it remains highly doubtful that one can distinguish logic from mathematics in a philosophically illuminating way, and to the extent one is thereby forced into an account of our knowledge or justification of logic that does not cohere with taking mathematical statements to be con-sequences of t-analytic statements, to just that extent we will be forced to give up the account of mathematics developed below. But it very much remains to be seen whether such an outcome is forced upon us, in part for some of the reasons that we have just discussed, as well as many other dif-ficult issues pertaining to logic and its relation to mathematics.

> *Analyticity* is not analyticity: 'Your notion analyticity* is acceptable, but it's not the historical notion of analyticity. Also, even if we grant explicit stipulations, what does that have to do with the bulk of the supposed examples?'*

It is true that our notion of analyticity* does not solve all of the epistemic problems that beset the logical empiricists who thought that a single notion of analyticity could be deployed for mathematics, logic, many theoretical principles such as F = ma, and various seemingly a priori bits of know-ledge such as color exclusion principles. We remain agnostic as to whether some accounts that generalize the notion of analyticity* can be adapted to illuminate a wider range of apparently a priori knowledge. We are hopeful on this front, but we are not in a position to provide accounts of logic, and some difficult examples of a priori knowledge such as color exclusion, in particular. Thus our defense of analyticity* might be thought of as a defense of one variety of analyticity, rather than of analyticity in general. To the extent that mathematical statements are an interesting distinctive subvariety of analytic* statements, and we argue below that they are, we could say that we have defended two varieties of analyticity.

If one insists that the statement that analytic claims are true in virtue of meanings is itself analytic*, where the relation 'in virtue of' is supposed to be explanatory, we are willing to grant that we are not defending any notion of analyticity.[14] In that case our defense of a distinction between an important type of statement and ordinary empirical 'theoretical hypotheses' should be viewed as part of a project of distinguishing different strands of the dispute between the analyticity advocate and the Quinean radical empiricist. We also do not intend or attempt to vindicate the 'moderate empiricism' of the logical empiricists. Nor do we try to show that one can dispense with any appeal to a priori intuitions in a fundamental account of all knowledge and justification, as the Vienna Circle hoped to do. To the extent that one thinks of the meaning of 'analytic' as essentially (analytically*?) tied to the success of the moderate empiricist project as a whole, we are willing to stop calling our notion analyticity* a type of analyticity.

Nevertheless, we think that there are good reasons for claiming that analyticity* is a notion akin to analyticity, and that its deployment illuminates some philosophical questions that have continued to remain obscure in the ongoing dialectic between Quinean radical empiricists, apriorists, and small pockets of closet moderate empiricists, as well as the large and growing cadre of classical metaphysicians interested in the metaphysics of parts, modality, and semantics. To the extent that we have disentangled one notion, analyticity*, from others in the conceptual vicinity and shown how it can be defended against the Quinean onslaught against analyticity in general, and how the notion of analyticity* might be applied to at least some examples of apparently non-empirical knowledge and justification, we have succeeded in our central aim.

6.7 Some Brief Comments on
Two Other Approaches to Analyticity

Our introduction of analyticity* as a way of illuminating analyticity differs from other approaches, and we will briefly explain our attitude toward two important contemporary approaches. Before discussing them, we should note why we do not endorse what is sometimes called 'Frege-analyticity,' according to which analytic truths are those truths that yield logical truths by substitution of synonyms for synonyms (see section 1.5). One reason is that we prefer to avoid defending synonymy, as we noted in the previous section. Another is that we think that Frege's account may be insufficiently general, in that it does not obviously permit assimilation of arbitrary mathematical stipulative axioms to the class of analytic truths. A third is that we think that the notion of Frege-analyticity does not by itself fully illuminate the distinctive epistemic profile of stipulative definition, and in that respect does not provide for responses to many Quinean objections. However, while we do not here defend Frege-analyticity, as far as we know our approach is compatible with its way of treating at least some examples of statements that seem naturally assimilable to the class of analytic truths.

> *Approach 1: Analytic claims are those claims such that their denials manifest some failure of understanding, a lack of linguistic competence, or reveal that the speaker denying them is intentionally adopting an alternative use of an expression.*

We are sympathetic to the general view of approach 1 that someone who denies an analytic truth, such as 'All squares have four sides,' reveals a failure to understand some of its component expressions (such as 'square'), or is using them in a different way.[15] But while this view has some attractive features, we think it has some potentially significant drawbacks. One difficulty is that there is no clear connection between adopting this approach and granting an epistemic distinctiveness or special epistemic status to analytic truths. For example, it may be that someone who denies that Santa Claus lives at the North Pole typically manifests a failure to understand how 'Santa Claus' is normally used. But this observation has no obvious connection to how or whether the statement that Santa lives at the North Pole is known. It does not even seem to require the truth of the statement used in this 'criterial' fashion. Similarly for mathematical examples: it may be that denials of basic arithmetical claims manifest failure to understand their standard uses, but this does not by itself show how or whether we know such claims, or are even justified in believing them, or that they are true.

A second worry that we have concerns appeals to 'linguistic competence.'[16] How linguistic competence is appealed to in various versions of approach 1 can vary, but as a broad generalization we are concerned that what counts as having linguistic competence with a term from a natural language is difficult to characterize. It is less clear, we think, that we ought to count as linguistically incompetent someone who denies a meaning-giving statement involving a term, than it is that a good translation scheme ought to preserve some rules governing statements. Suppose, for example, that someone employs the sentence 'there are prime numbers' as an empirical hypothesis, and provides a coherent interpretation of the hypothesis, including what counts for or against its truth. They explain why the rest of us fell prey to a common illusion, according to which the sentence is not empirical. The thought experiment might be filled out in such a way that we are not inclined to call the person linguistically incompetent. They may, nevertheless, be using the sentence or expression differently than we take ourselves to use it, and for that reason decide not to translate their sentence 'there are prime numbers' into ours, as we use it or take ourselves to use it. On the other hand, we are liable to agree with much of what advocates of approach 1 claim concerning constraints on linguistic competence, and do not take a stand here as to whether it is correct. Nevertheless, we think that our appeal to rules of language, including what is permitted to count as evidence for or against some special statements, provides a fairly direct route to understanding analyticity, particularly with respect to the special epistemic status of analytic statements.

> Approach 2: Analytic statements are statements whose truth is guaranteed by facts concerning reference determiners of the component expressions.

Gillian Russell's recent book *Truth in Virtue of Meaning* (2008) adopts this second approach to analyticity. While it is impossible to provide a complete overview of her position and our relationship to it here, we think that it is worthwhile to briefly describe and explain some of the main differences between our approach and hers, because her book pursues a version of approach 2 in greater detail and clarity than any other. Naturally, there may be other ways of filling out approach 2 that do not fall prey to the kinds of concerns that we discuss below. But we think that her work deserves special 'canonical' status as an exemplar of approach 2, since she pursues it at length and in detail and ends up with a generally plausible and defensible position.

Russell is primarily concerned with capturing some interesting notion of 'truth in virtue of meaning,' where meanings are things associated with individual words, and meanings and truth values of whole sentences are explained by appeal to the meanings of the words constituting those sentences. She is engaged with what might be termed a 'formal semantic' project. There are some sentences whose truth can be determined via something like a calculation or proof from various premises about word meanings, she thinks. Russell's approach is also based within the framework of possible-world semantics. She appeals to what are called 'reference determiners' for words, which provide referents of words as a function of 'context of utterance,' as well as in some cases 'contexts of introduction.' 'Contexts of introduction' are, roughly, contexts in which a term was first introduced via something like a stipulation, whether by an 'ostensive' definition or by some description. Very roughly, Russell's view is that there are some sentences that are distinctive in a way that is worth capturing for some philosophical purposes, and these are sentences which are such that any token or utterance of the sentence is true in its context of utterance. Although her distinction is not straightforwardly concerned with epistemic issues, it is frequently the case that in addition to the sentence's truth in fact being determined by facts concerning reference determiners of its component words, competent speakers are often able to come to know that these sentences are true by appeal to facts solely concerned with 'reference determiners' of the component words, and without appeal to other empirical facts besides those necessary to justify the premises about reference determiners.[17]

A second component of Russell's view involves adopting an account of reference determiners, contexts, and 'characters' that is derived from the work of Kripke and David Kaplan. She works out the details of a distinction between sentences that could be naturally characterized as 'true in virtue of the meanings' (where meanings are facts concerning reference determiners), and the majority of sentences which are not true in all contexts of their utterance.

Although we are not defending an empiricist view, our own approach is partly motivated by the sorts of epistemological concerns that motivated the logical empiricists, and which frequently seem to be at the center of disputes concerning analyticity and apriority. While Russell is somewhat interested in how her semantic approach to analyticity might turn out to bear on some epistemic concerns that philosophers have had, her primary concern seems to be with semantics rather than epistemology. If it turned out that analyticity had no interesting connection to apriority, for example, she would probably not find that troubling. In fact, in the final chapter she explicitly agrees with Quineans with respect to their doubts concerning a priori justification or knowledge. A related difference between our approaches is that we would like to provide an account of analyticity that connects in interesting ways with knowledge that has been taken to be paradigmatically a priori, such as mathematical knowledge or justification. Her approach has essentially nothing to say concerning the justification of mathematical stipulations, beyond perhaps noting that analyticity in her sense does not yield any apparent way to treat mathematical claims as interestingly different from empirical ones with respect to their justification. We take mathematical stipulations to share important features with nonmathematical stipulations, and we think that this provides a potentially illuminating way to see something distinctive about mathematical epistemology. By contrast, for all that Russell says, her notion of analyticity appears compatible with the possibility that Quine is correct, and mathematics is justified in the same broadly empirical way that other theoretical claims and entities are justified.

Unlike Russell, we are also somewhat less inclined to take on board the entirety of contemporary philosophical semantic theory of possible worlds and 'reference determiners.' While we do not in this work dispute the significance of this dominant approach, we prefer not to make our response to Quine and Harman and others of their sympathizers depend too heavily on the adoption of this framework. We have seen that Quineans are skeptical of many 'intensional' entities and theoretical posits, such as explanatory frameworks involving possible worlds, and we are concerned that responding in a way that presupposes this framework might appear to be question-begging in the debate over analyticity.[18]

Perhaps the main difference between Russell's approach and ours is that she takes various claims for granted that we think need to be argued for in the dialectical context. Among these claims, the most central one concerns stipulations. Russell says very little in her book about what stipulations are. What little she does say suggests that she takes it for granted that various stipulations concerning 'reference determiners,' for example, are 'up to us' or even 'up to me' in some cases. So, for example, if the word 'bachelor' had first been introduced via stipulation, such as 'Let the word "bachelor" refer to all and only unmarried men,' then in her view the 'reference determiner' profile for 'bachelor' would at that stage have been fixed (2008, 208, footnote 6). Elsewhere (211) she says that even if she is wrong about what facts determine the referent of 'bachelor' in English, that would not change the fact that in her own idiolect, the word 'bachelor' refers to all and only unmarried bachelors. We do not wish to dispute her assertions that such reference-determining facts are 'up to us,' or even 'up to me' in some cases. But we do not think that one can simply take this for granted in a serious discussion and defense of analyticity with a Quinean. We have engaged these Quinean objections throughout this book, and we would expect that a Quinean would likely respond to Russell something as follows: 'Look, Ms. Russell, simply asserting, or "postulating," that bachelors are unmarried men in a vain attempt to "fix reference" so that the sentence comes out true does not guarantee that the assertion or postulate is true, even in your own idiolect (even if there were such things as idiolects). It may turn out that our best overall theory of the world includes the claim that bachelors are all and only unmarried men, but it may not. If it does not, then if the best translation scheme from our current language into that later language (that includes the best overall theory) translates homophonically, then in that case it will turn out that the statement that bachelors are all and only adult males will have been shown empirically to have been false, however insistently you or your community asserts it at present . . .' And so on. Russell simply does not address this entire aspect of a dialectic that we take to be central to the dispute concerning analyticity.

Another, related difference between Russell's approach and our own is that her account makes an essential appeal to facts concerning 'reference determiners,' whereas our approach focuses on what we would take to be the more basic phenomenon of the nature of stipulations (along with other statements that are not engaged with empirical evidence in the standard way) which statements, in at least many cases countenanced by Russell, determine or explain the facts about reference determiners. A way of bringing out why we prefer our own approach on this front, aside from our concerns about her minimal account of stipulations, is to pose a dilemma for Russell. Either stipulations that are meaning-determining are acceptable, and in some sense guarantee the truth of the stipulation in the absence of empirical evidence or other pragmatic support, or they do not. If they do not, then Quine is correct, and Russell's approach fares no better than our own on this front. That is, contrary to both Russell's view and our own, Quine would be right that whether 'A bachelor is a married man' is not 'in some sense up to us,' but is instead a matter for further empirical research into the 'best overall theory' of reality. Further, whatever facts do ultimately 'determine references,' it is not essential to a language or a sentence-qua-sentence-of-L that the terms refer to what they do, and so such sentences are not fundamentally different, semantically (referentially), from any other sentences. On the other hand, if stipulations *are* in some important sense 'guaranteed' to be true, as we believe, then it seems possible to explain how the truth of 'A bachelor is an unmarried man' is guaranteed by the correct account of stipulations, without appeal to 'reference determination.' Russell would presumably disagree with this. She seems to think that the correct explanation of how we know that various sentences are true in any relevant 'contexts' must appeal to facts about reference determination, meta-linguistic claims about the references of words, which are then used, along with 'linking principles,' to justify object-language statements. But it is unclear to us why appeal to empirically justified statements concerning reference determination is essential to justifying stipulations. Furthermore, the justification of these meta-linguistic statements concerning reference determination, if there is any, seems to us to require appeal to stipulations, themselves taken to be either justified or to justify the further meta-linguistic claims and then the object-language statements.

For example, consider Russell's treatment of 'Bachelors are unmarried men.' It will look something like:

Premise: 'Bachelor' refers to all and only unmarried men.

(Justification (?): empirical facts concerning conventions or stipulations concerning the term 'bachelor')

Conclusion: Bachelors are unmarried men.

Russell presumably would take the conclusion to be demonstrated by this argument. But how is premise 1 justified? What justifies its introduction? Russell does not say much about this, but what she does say (2008, 208–11) suggests that she thinks that its justification involves facts concerning what stipulations have been adopted by some relevant linguistic community. That some statement is stipulated, she seems to think, justifies premise 1 and other similar premises, and that premise 1 is essential to justifying the statement that bachelors are unmarried men.

In contrast, it seems to us that we can give an equally good account without appealing to empirical facts concerning language users and their decisions. If we are asked to justify 'Frenchelors are French bachelors,' we might just say, 'that's a stipulation.' A more formal representation might include a rule, 'Stip,' that allows for the introduction of a stipulation at any stage of an argument. The justification of the conclusion that bachelors are unmarried men in such an argument will not be empirical, contrary to what Russell seems to have in mind, any more than the appearance of 'Let a = F(b),' considered as a reference stipulation concerning constant 'a,' turns a mathematical proof containing it into a (partially) empirical justification. The conclusion of such a mathematical argument is not justified by appeal to facts about the community of mathematicians and what conventions they have adopted. Similarly for the conclusion that bachelors are unmarried men, in our view.

This is not intended as a refutation of Gillian Russell's views. To repeat, we can agree with the majority of what she writes in her excellent book on the topic. Our differences are more of emphasis, differences of what we take to be philosophically central and illuminating. We think that appeals to empirical linguistic facts concerning reference determiners are not as illuminating of the distinctive status of stipulations or mathematical statements as we would want in an account of analyticity. While we countenance appeals to reference-determination, we think of such facts as playing a role in representing distinctive roles rather than in explaining these roles. The idea that appeals to facts about reference-determination are explanatory may partially explain why Russell does not take on many of the Quinean and Harmanian arguments in the way we have. And we think that a more illuminating account of the special epistemic status of stipulations and other philosophically (epistemically) puzzling statements requires careful elaboration of stipulation itself, whereas Russell's account, like most others that we are aware of, takes the notion of stipulation for granted rather than explaining how stipulations are epistemically or semantically distinctive.

6.8 Mathematical Claims as T-Analytic

One consequence of the rejection of analyticity has been the need to provide an alternative 'empiricist' account of justification of basic mathematical principles. According to Quineans, mathematical truths are justified by successful applications within scientific theories. In particular, whatever mathematical principles are appealed to essentially, or 'indispensably,' within empirical explanations are empirically supported to the extent that the empirical theory as a whole (including its 'mathematical parts') is empirically supported.[19] Often it is applications within physics that are stressed as the most important by Quineans, and for our present purposes it is these applications that we will have in mind.

The main problem for this empiricist account of mathematics is that it seems false, and fairly obviously so. Even after considerable reflection on Quinean arguments, it remains unbelievable to many. Mathematicians as a matter of fact typically ignore empirical data in their normal activity, at least the sort of empirical data that Quineans claim support various mathematical principles.

Quineans have provided a variety of ways of dealing with this prima facie devastating objection to their view. As we saw in section 3.7, Quine's approach was to deploy his 'web of belief' metaphor in a way that placed some sentences that scientists believe 'away from the periphery,' 'near the center' of the web. Arithmetical statements, for example, are unlikely to be revised on the basis of empirical data, Quine granted. But their empirical indefeasibility for practical purposes is a result, he thought, of the fact that arithmetical sentences play important theoretical roles in a variety of applications within science. They are thus connected to other parts of the web of belief in very complicated ways. Hence any revision of our arithmetical beliefs (changes in the set of sentences to which we 'assent') would require very complicated revisions to a host of other beliefs. The overall pragmatic costs of such revision are overwhelming, and Quine thought this explains why such revision is so rare or even nonexistent.

Putnam raised some important objections to the Quinean picture in his paper 'The Analytic and the Synthetic' (Putnam 1975, 33ff.). In section 3.8, we noted that Putnam challenged Quine's idea that analytic truths such as mathematical theorems are not (usually) revised due to their centrality to the web of belief. Putnam further contends that Quine has things precisely backwards when he portrays arithmetic as empirically unrevisable due to the many connections it has to the rest of the web of belief. One basic worry is easy to see: while many connections yields a high pragmatic cost of revision, many connections can also yield many ways of generating false empirical consequences in applications, and thereby generate many potential avenues of counterevidence, in which case mathematical statements should appear to be *more* open to revision than most others, not less. Against Quine, Putnam suggests that the analytic statements, if any, tend to be 'one-criterion' terms, terms that are distinctive precisely in virtue of their paucity of connections to other statements or beliefs, other than the one stipulative connection. For example, consider 'For any x, x is a bachelor iff x is an unmarried man.' Because of its logical form, if the only way of determining whether something is a bachelor is to determine whether it is an unmarried man, no possible data could refute or provide counterevidence (of a straightforward sort) to the truth of the sentence. It is precisely their minimal connection with the rest of the web that permits us to continue to accept these sentences as true no matter what empirical evidence requires of the remainder of the web of belief.[20]

We are inclined to think Putnam's objection points to a serious problem in the Quinean account. Nevertheless, we do not agree that the only statements that may be acceptably treated as empirically indefeasible are 'one-criterion' terms. We think that the situation is more complicated than that. Our view is that linguistic rules or conventions should collectively allow for a coherent, intelligible practice. As we discussed above, there are coherence constraints to which an intelligible stipulation practice must answer. But it is not the logical form of a sentence, or merely how many logical entailments to other statements are accepted, that determines the coherence of stipulation practice. As we explain further below, we think that mathematical statements are distinctive, in particular they are 't-analytic,' and that an understanding of this fact enables mathematicians and scientists to avoid incoherent practices even though mathematicians can stipulate mathematical axioms of arbitrary (consistent) logical form and largely ignore empirical data in their research, and even though mathematics is interwoven in a panoply of empirical applications.

There are a number of other ways of defending a broadly Quinean picture from worries about the prima facie empirical indefeasibility of mathematics. A particularly noteworthy one is given by Michael Resnik (1997), who distinguishes between 'global' and merely 'local' applicability of theoretical principles. It is beyond the scope of this discussion to show that no Quinean defense of this sort can possibly succeed. We will merely note one more problem for the view: much of mathematics has no known empirical applications, and yet there seems to be no distinction drawn internal to mathematics between the 'empirically supported' branches and the empirically unsupported branches. If the Quinean account that we are describing is correct, then mathematicians have long proceeded in apparently blissful ignorance of what should be an important distinction. Appeals have been made by Quine and others (e.g., Colyvan 2003, 110) to a distinction between 'recreational mathematics' and non-recreational mathematics. Yet this seems to us an ad hoc distinction with no independent motivation beyond an attempt to defend the Quinean picture against an apparently devastating objection.[21]

One alternative to the Quinean conception of mathematics returns to the notion of intuition that we saw developed in Kant and Frege. Recall from chapter 1 that both of these philosophers considered mathematical knowledge to be fundamentally distinct from other types of knowledge, and knowable a priori. It is currently an interesting controversy whether a priori knowledge or justification should be rejected out of hand, or rejected for empirical reasons, or for reasons that it is unintelligible, or non-explanatory. There is a substantial, and perhaps growing, minority of philosophers who argue on behalf of a priori intuition.[22] We, however, would prefer to do without it, at least for much of mathematics. Instead, we focus on the question whether some notion of analyticity, such as analyticity*, can provide a 'third path' between the Scylla of radical empiricism and the Charybdis of a priori intuition.

This is not a monograph on mathematics, so our discussion will be briefer than would be necessary for our account to be fully convincing or satisfying. Nevertheless, we will pursue the topic at some length, since we believe that mathematical statements provide among the best, perhaps the best, candidates for an interesting application of a notion like analyticity* or t-analyticity.

> Objection 1: Mathematics is not arbitrary. Analytic* statements, arbitrary explicit stipulations, are. Therefore mathematics is not analytic*.

We have considered a version of this objection in our previous discussion of BonJour's objections to 'moderate empiricism' and appeals to 'implicit definitions' (see section 5.4). We will provide a similar response here. As it stands, the objection requires some refinement. Not all analytic* stipulations need to be 'arbitrary,' in the sense that no important concept is introduced via such stipulations. It is true that analyticity* allows one to introduce a wide range of concepts with an open-ended set of possibilities, and with varying degrees of arbitrariness. Yet at the same time, it certainly seems correct to say that $2 + 2 = 4$, and that this arithmetical statement is true, certain, necessary, and not an arbitrary stipulation. Our knowledge of this truth may be difficult to give an account of, but its truth, and the corresponding falsehood of $2 + 2 = 5$, seems beyond serious dispute.

A response that our analytic* approach can give to the apparent non-arbitrariness of this kind of truth is the following. Some statements are not explicitly stipulated, as a historical matter, when they are first introduced into our language. Instead, a language community often begins to employ an expression in a more or less well-defined way, in accord with more or less well defined rules. Now, in the twenty-first century, we might reflect on the actual rules that we take for granted with respect to some statement, in particular a mathematical statement. We might come to realize on reflection that none of us would take any empirical evidence for or against the truth of $2 + 2 = 4$ (see our response to the next objection for a more precise account of indefeasibility in mathematics). We might then come to think that the epistemic status of the statement that $2 + 2 = 4$ is essentially the same as it would be if it had first been introduced via an explicit indefeasible stipulation. In fact, as we saw in our discussion of TD, this suggested account of the development of the explicit stipulation seems to be one Quine was willing to countenance (cf. Quine 1966a, 97, quoted in section 3.9 above).

Next, once a concept has already been introduced, and its rules are already well-defined and understood by a community, it can seem that there is no disputing that $2 + 2 = 4$. 'That's just part of what we mean by "2," etc.,' we might say if someone were to ask us for a justification, although what someone would say in response to a request for justification might be complicated, and depend on one's background philosophical views, if any. In any case, our knowledge of, or justification for, our belief that $2 + 2 = 4$ might be similar to our knowledge of, or justification for, our belief that bachelors are unmarried. Whether or not anyone ever first introduced the term 'bachelor' via an explicit indefeasible stipulation, it seems very odd and counterintuitive to deny that bachelors are unmarried. That is, once a term is familiar and understood to be associated with a particular concept (or use-profile for the term), then it is no longer an arbitrary matter to employ that understood term differently from its customary use. The analyticity*-based account is that mathematical statements involving well-known concepts already widely used (with terms conventionally associated with those concepts) are non-arbitrary in precisely the sense that statements, even indefeasible ones, involving other concepts are non-arbitrary. It is not that 'bachelors are unmarried' could not possibly be used in some other way (i.e., that 'bachelor' could be used to express another concept), but rather that, given the way that we in fact use 'bachelor,' we adhere to the rule that the sentence 'bachelors are unmarried' is true and indefeasible. Similarly, according to the analyticity* account, it's not that '$2 + 2 = 4$' could not be used differently, or that the numeral '2' couldn't be. Of course they could be. But the rules that we actually use and take for granted with respect to it require us to treat such sentences as true. That we learn the rules so early in life may partly explain why we find it unintelligible to deny such statements. It can come to seem that the concepts themselves are metaphysically attached to the numerals in such a way that it's just impossible to deny the truth of basic arithmetical statements like $2 + 2 = 4$. Here too, there is no reason to think this broad account would be unacceptable to the Quinean, for Quine endorsed a broadly similar suggestion, saying that conventions, including those of logic and mathematics become conventional:

> through behavior, without first announcing them in words; and that we can return and formulate our conventions verbally afterward, if we choose . . . It must be conceded that this account accords well with what we actually do. (1966a, 98)

A further complication, however, is that mathematical notation is typically 'language transcendent' in the sense that nowadays, whatever 'language' one speaks in the ordinary sense, English, Chinese, or what have you, we all write mathematics in a common notation. This may add to the sense that mathematical notation is somehow privileged, and that numerals in standard Arabic decimal notation are attached to their referents in a nonarbitrary way. But this kind of metaphysical attachment between expressions and their referents is an illusion.

> Objection 2: Mathematical statements are not empirically indefeasible as required by the analyticity* account. For example, if we read a statement following the word 'theorem' in a book, that provides empirical evidence for the truth of the statement. Similarly, if a famous mathematics professor says 'I think that p is true,' particularly for some mathematical statement p in her area of specialty, this provides defeasible, empirical evidence for the truth of p. In addition, computer calculations and proofs result in ink patterns on paper or on computer screens. The presence of those patterns at those locations provides empirical evidence for or against the truth of various mathematical statements. Thus it is just false, and obviously so, that mathematical statements are empirically indefeasible.

It is certainly true that mathematical statements are empirically defeasible in some sense, as these examples show. But let us consider carefully what that sense is. The analyticity* account should say that mathematical claims are distinctive with respect to their relation to empirical evidence, that they are related to it in a distinctive way, one different from the way 'standard' empirical descriptions are. They should not say that the statements are such that no empirical data is relevant to any justifications for any epistemic agents in any situation.

The examples used in objection 2, in which empirical evidence bears on mathematical statements, are not accommodated by our earlier caveat (section 6.5) that we exclude consideration of evidence concerning meanings or language use when we say that the truth of analytic* statements is empirically indefeasible. The fact that a brilliant mathematician, such as Andrew Wiles, finds it plausible that p *can* be evidence for the truth of p, even when everyone is already fully in agreement concerning the common understanding of the expressions involved. Allowing for such empirical evidence requires the specification of a distinctive way that empirical evidence is understood to bear on the mathematical.

In order to see this distinctive way in which empirical evidence bears on the truth of mathematical statements, let us introduce the notion of a first-order or 'canonical' justification for mathematical statements. A *first-order/ canonical justification* for a mathematical statement requires a logical derivation from either justified mathematical statements or axioms.[23] Such a derivation or 'proof,' which includes an acceptable calculation as a special case, is what we will call a 'canonical justification' of a mathematical statement. Importantly, a first-order justification of a mathematical statement is not allowed to contain any premises justified by empirical statements.[24] A *second-order justification* of a mathematical statement is a justification for the claim that there is a (possible) first-order justification for that claim.

We are now in a position to express more precisely the distinctive sense in which mathematical statements are empirically indefeasible. The only cases in which empirical evidence can support or undercut a mathematical statement (aside from empirical evidence concerning linguistic usage, as noted in section 6.5) is in a second-order way. That is, any justification of a mathematical statement that appeals to empirical evidence is a second-order justification, a justification of the assertion that there exists a first-order justification of that claim. Likewise for apparent empirical counterevidence to a mathematical claim; it is part of a second-order justification for the assertion that there exists a first-order proof of the falsity of that claim. This view captures what we the authors mean when we claim that mathematics is empirically indefeasible.[25]

> Objection 3: Existence claims cannot be stipulated. One cannot define things into existence.
> Consider unicorns. One may indeed stipulate, for example, that all unicorns are horsey-
> looking creatures with a single horn protruding from their foreheads. But that does not
> entail that there are unicorns. It would be bad practice to allow ourselves to stipulate that
> there exist unicorns, since in fact there are none. Similarly, we can stipulate that if anyone

is Santa Claus, that individual lives at the North Pole, gives presents to good kids and coal to bad kids, and so on. But again, we cannot, whatever kids might hope for, stipulate that Santa exists. Finally, God has been thought to be knowable by appeal to something like a definition. But this Anselmian line of reasoning was long ago seen to be fallacious. In short, it is just obvious that we can't permit existential stipulations. But within mathematics, basic principles of set theory, arithmetic, and other theories posit the existence of a variety of abstracta, such as the empty set, the number 0, and the successor function. So it cannot be that such entities are introduced by stipulation, for the sorts of reasons just given.

This objection is arguably the most difficult to answer. For besides the sorts of arguments just given, there are deeply seated intuitions that seem to make the appeal to analyticity* a non-starter as an account of our justification of existential mathematical statements, even if we grant its plausibility for statements without existential entailments.

Recall that the fundamental feature that makes a statement analytic* is that it is taken to be true, and to be empirically indefeasible, as a matter of common understanding. One form of objection 3 is the worry that things cannot be created or put into existence by acts of stipulation, apart from special cases such as the stipulation that exists as the result of an act of stipulation. The thought that we cause a statement to be true by treating it as an indefeasible stipulation, or by treating it as analytic*, needs to be distinguished from the view defended here. For this talk of causation is misleading and unnecessary. Consider in the first instance the stipulation 'Frenchelors are French bachelors.' Suppose that it is granted that the statement is analytic, in an imagined situation in which it is understood as explicitly stipulated (as true and indefeasible). Must we say that the proposition expressed by the statement was not true until we performed the act of stipulation? It is difficult to see why. It seems right to say it was always the case that frenchelors are all and only French bachelors. It turns out that frenchelors did not always exist; they only existed when there were some French bachelors. But their existence depends on the existence of French bachelors, not on any act of stipulation. The thought that acts of stipulation (or as it is often put, the adoption of 'conventions') *cause* the truth of the propositions expressed is at best an unnecessary addendum to some possible view, and more likely the result of a confusion. We deny that acts of stipulation generally either create entities or cause the propositions expressed to be true, although there are some special cases in which this might be said to occur, cases of 'impure stipulata' that we discuss below.

Now let us turn to mathematical stipulations. Let us suppose that some mathematician writes down an 'axiom,' a stipulation concerning some mathematical entities which are novel in the sense that they are studied for the first time (not in the sense that they are existing for the first time). Suppose that the stipulation entails that some mathematical entities exist, that is, it entails some statement with the logical form of an existence claim. For reasons similar to the ones given above, there is no need to think that an act of mathematical stipulation created any entities, or caused the existential claim to be true.

Even if this problem is avoidable by the analyticity* account of mathematics, we still face the objection that existential statements are, intuitively, true or false independently of acts of stipulation, in which case it seems illicit to stipulate existence claims. We can try to stipulate that Santa exists, or that unicorns exist, for example, but we will fail, at least in the sense that we will not produce a true assertion. Before considering our response, a potential confusion must be removed. Recall the example of frenchelors. Whether all frenchelors are French is a factual matter independent of whether anyone stipulates anything. Failure to see this may be a result of conflating two things:

1   Our seeing to it that some particular sentence in our language expresses the fact that frenchelors are French, and that some term in our language expresses the concept frenchelorhood, on the one hand, versus,
2   Our seeing to it that frenchelors are French bachelors.

The latter is something we never 'saw to'. That frenchelors are French bachelors was always the case, at least according to the view espoused here. What the stipulation brings about is facts concerning *what proposition a sentence expresses*, rather than *the truth of what is expressed*.

With this distinction in hand, let us return to the objection that some existential statements are false (whether we know them to be false at some time of interest or not). Whether some entity exists or not is a matter of fact, the objector says, and hence, in stipulating existence claims there is a risk of making a statement that is understood to be governed by two conflicting constraints: the rule that *s is to be taken as true*, and the constraint that *s is to be taken as false* given the empirical facts (as in the case of Santa and unicorns). Thus the objection is that allowing existential stipulations risks a sort of incoherence in our overall linguistic practice permitting stipulation.

Our response is that mathematical statements (stipulations, axioms) are understood in such a way that they simply do not lead to the sort of incoherence in our overall practice as attempts to stipulate that Santa exists or that unicorns exist. That is why mathematical statements are understood as expressing 'immune' propositions, propositions that no empirical proposition counts for or against. Numbers, sets, and all other mathematical entities are not like Santa. Evidence can exist showing that Santa does not in fact live at the North Pole, but numbers, sets, and the like are understood as precisely the sorts of concepts such that no possible empirical evidence counts for or against their having instances. The practice of introducing empirically indefeasible stipulations, particularly the 'transcendental' variety that express mathematical claims, is designed precisely to allow for the introduction of statements for which there is no risk of empirical or experiential disconfirmation, either of the truth of the statement or of the proposition expressed.

Some potentially troublesome cases, more troublesome than Santa at least, are God and causally isolated 'universes.' We can only provide suggestive remarks in our reply here.[26] God is understood to be potentially causally active in the empirical world, and thus is the sort of entity that some possible empirical evidence could count for or against. This fact prevents God (so conceived) from being an entity whose existence can coherently be stipulated. We cannot coherently accept a rule that entails that no empirical evidence counts against the truth of some statement, while accepting other rules that commit us to accepting that some empirical evidence counts against the truth of that statement. Another feature that God is commonly taken to have is conscious states. To the extent that the existence of God's experiential states are evidence (for Him, the experiencer) for God's existence, this fact provides another way of distinguishing God from the sort of entity that can be coherently stipulated as existing, and thus preventing a practice that allows an analytic* statement to entail God's existence.

Causally isolated universes, and/or parts of such universes, provide one of the most difficult cases for the treatment of mathematical statements in terms of the notion of analyticity*. We do not yet think that these sorts of entities undermine the project, but they do raise some questions that are not easily answered.[27] First we will state some disanalogies between causally isolated 'concreta,' such as chunks of matter, and mathematical 'abstracta.' (We write 'concreta' and 'abstracta' in scare-quotes because we are inclined to propose a refinement or a new distinction with which to replace this standard one. See the discussion of 'stipulata,' section 6.9.) One is the following: for any chunk of matter, call it 'Chunk,' there is possible empirical evidence that could count for or against its existence. Such chunks are precisely the sorts of things that empirical evidence could count for or against, we think. Numbers and other mathematical objects are different in precisely this respect. We can put the claim more precisely in the following way:

> (CH) for any chunk of matter Chunk, there is a possible world w in which some possible experience (had in w) could count against Chunk's existence at that world.

CH can be re-expressed as follows: given any such chunk, even if we are considering it as in fact (actually) in a causally isolated universe from us, there is another possible world in which that very chunk could have, or perhaps would have, made a difference to some experience at that world. We might even think that the truth of such a subjunctive is partly constitutive of the concept of a chunk of matter. To the extent that a principle like CH seems plausible, a slightly stronger claim might also seem plausible:

> (CH*) for any chunk of matter Chunk, there is a possible world, call it 'EI,' which is empirically indistinguishable from the actual world up to the present, and is such that at some future time there is empirical evidence for or against the existence of Chunk in EI.

A way to think of a model for CH* is to consider two physical space-time manifolds, M1 and M2, where M1's past and present is empirically indistinguishable from that of the actual world, and that they are initially spatiotemporally (in particular, causally) disconnected. At some time t a 'wormhole' begins to causally connect the two universes, and this opens up the possibility of empirical data supporting the existence of Chunk. To the extent that for any chunk of matter, such a scenario is possible, then for any chunk of matter, we might, for all we know, eventually have evidence for or against its existence.

If a principle like CH* is plausible, then this might help to make sense of our reluctance to allow stipulations that entail the existence of chunks of matter. The reason is that we might worry that a practice that allows this is incoherent, in the following respect. On one hand, for any chunk of matter Chunk, CH* suggests that for all we know we will or might have empirical evidence for or against the existence of Chunk. On the other hand, stipulations of the sort we are concerned with, analytic* statements, are rules that preclude precisely this possibility, empirical evidence counting for or against their truth. So allowing Chunk to be known to exist via stipulation commits us to the statement that no evidence will count for or against Chunk's existence, and yet given the truth of CH*, it also commits us to the statement that some empirical evidence might, for all we know, count for or against Chunk's existence.

Things seem different with respect to the merely possible, including merely possible chunks of matter. For merely possible (non-actual) chunks of matter, on some views, are such that any such chunk is by metaphysical necessity causally disconnected from the actual. To the extent that such a view of the merely possible is coherent, it leaves open the possibility of stipulative practices that allow stipulations to entail the existence of merely possible, non-actual chunks of matter. Most readers will have heard of David Lewis' view concerning possible worlds, according to which these are 'concrete,' spatiotemporal manifolds (in a sense that includes the matter within them), but these manifolds are merely possible rather than actual. Many philosophers have found Lewis' postulation of such worlds troubling, but have difficulty saying why. The difficulty in explaining why David Lewis is wrong in positing a large number of merely possible concrete worlds may be illuminated if it turns out that a coherent stipulation practice is compatible with a wide range of acceptable stipulations concerning the merely possible. Unfortunately, at present we do not have an account of how modal notions are best understood as connected to stipulation practice. We must leave these interesting issues unresolved for now.

Are there other stipulations that can be used to raise problems for the notion of analyticity*? We have not yet seen any for which some answer cannot be given. One general sort of question that arises for stipulation practices as we conceive them is precisely what types of stipulations should be permitted, or can be permitted while preserving the coherence of the practice. This is a large and difficult question that we cannot answer at present. We hope that we have said enough to at least motivate further work to answer the question. Our main purpose at present is to show how some objections that have been taken to show that an analyticity* approach to mathematics is a non-starter are answerable, and that the project ought to be pursued further. We think that appeal to stipulation and a version of analyticity in order to illuminate mathematics is worthy of further philosophical reflection, after decades of relative neglect.

6.9 A Further Potential Application: Pure and Impure Stipulata

Finally, we have a somewhat speculative application of our notions of analyticity* and t-analyticity. Certain ontological disputes are notoriously difficult, and certain entities are notoriously difficult to categorize, and analyticity* may help illuminate some of these puzzling issues. Consider the example of impure sets, sets whose members are 'concreta.' In particular, let us suppose that the elements of the set **Imp** = {**a**, **b**} are both known to exist via empirical observation. Now, is **Imp** concrete or abstract? This question is not easy to answer. One natural answer is that sets are abstract, so **Imp** is abstract. If this is correct, we are left with a further puzzle: it seems that our knowledge of the actual existence of **Imp** is a result (in part) of empirical evidence supporting the existence of **a** and of **b**. How can we come to know that an abstractum exists by appeal to empirical evidence? There are similar puzzles in other settings. Consider fictional characters. It seems natural in some contexts to say things like, 'The fictional character Sherlock Holmes was created by Sir Arthur Conan Doyle.' What such a claim means, whether it is true, whether its truth commits us to the existence of fictional characters, and other questions have been given a variety of interesting answers. At present we will simply suggest that perhaps the existence of a fictional character can follow from empirical facts concerning the activities of an author, via a stipulation of a conditional statement form whose antecedent is an empirical statement and whose consequent is of the form of an existence claim that does not logically follow from the antecedent. That is, we can coherently adopt as a stipulation some claim of the form: 'Whenever blah blah, then the fictional character so and so exists.' The form of such a stipulation will look similar to the conditional that we use to infer from the existence of **a** and of **b** to the existence of the set **Imp** containing **a** and **b**.

To the extent that existential stipulations are coherent, it seems to us that we should also accept such conditional or 'impure' stipulations whose antecedents are knowable empirically, but whose consequents entail existence claims concerning objects that seem not to be empirical objects in a difficult-to-specify sense. Such a proposal might also shed light on a number of related disputes, such as for example those concerning the existence of propositions, or those concerning the existence of various 'weird' mereological sums, although it remains to be seen whether it would in fact do so. We are optimistic that once we have a clearer picture of the coherence of possible or actual stipulation practices, a number of related problems may be clarified. A further elaboration of our picture may also provide a clearer picture of how to distinguish 'theoretical entities' such as electrons from mathematical abstracta such as Hilbert space vectors, even though appeal to both may be in some sense 'logically indispensable' to applications of empirical theories, although such further elaboration is beyond the scope of the present work.

6.10 Some Methodological Remarks

The debate concerning analyticity is considered to be settled in many circles. In those circles, Quine fairly definitively showed that analyticity is either unintelligible, uninstantiated, unexplained, or otherwise problematic. But the influence of this demonstration remains limited, for many philosophers continue to talk about 'conceptual truths,' and at least some of the applications of the notion of 'conceptual truth' are indistinguishable from earlier applications of the notion of analyticity. Carnap seemed not to understand Quine's objections along some fronts. And as we saw in chapter 3, there are reasons for this, not the least of which is that Carnap's position can be rather difficult to distinguish from Quine's supposed alternative. What we will do in these final sections of our discussion is briefly make a case that both Quine and Carnap, and even some of their 'ordinary language philosopher' critics, had overall views concerning philosophical methodology that to us seem at best optional, and at worst misleading or even counterproductive to philosophical progress.

Recall that Carnap was interested in resolving, or dissolving, philosophical disputes. He thought that the best way to do this was to insist that questions are framed within some precisely specified language, which language had definite and precise rules for saying what counts as evidence for what, what is entailed by what, when a sentence is assertable, and so on. Once the rules of a language are precisely specified, he thought, there should be no room for significant philosophical dispute concerning the answer to the sorts of questions that philosophers are interested in. So, for example, before we ask, 'are there numbers?,' we are urged to adopt a precise artificial language and then ask either the 'internal' question or the 'external,' pragmatic question. The latter question may be difficult to resolve definitively, but this merely 'pragmatic' indefiniteness seemed acceptable to Carnap. In chapter 4, we provided a number of reasons for thinking that Carnap's suggestions along these fronts are unsatisfactory. One of the basic respects in which it is philosophically unsatisfactory is that even if one grants that precise artificial languages can be adopted which definitively settle whether some sentence is true in that language, it is very difficult to see why the truth or falsehood of such a sentence has any bearing on the question of interest, namely, whether there really are numbers.

One way to think about Quine's view is as adopting the Carnapian framework, but insisting that the background language for all descriptions, including that of language frameworks themselves, uses only predicates of physics, or other predicates that can be appropriately 'vindicated' empirically as playing explanatory roles within our best overall empirical theory, which Quine took to be physics. The selection of physics per se is not structurally crucial to Quine's position.[28] His main move, it seems to us, was to treat philosophers and language themselves as items within the realm of the empirical, as the sorts of things that one should attempt to explain empirically, or subsume into an overall theory all of whose predicates and ontology had an empirical justification. This is the view of Quine we advanced in chapter 2. Justification is then subsumed to an empirical notion, a causal notion, and eventually assimilated to 'pragmatic justification.' In addition, Quine insisted on a particular account of empirical justification, roughly hypothetico-deductivism. Thus we might say that he adopted Carnap's language-engineering project and selected a particular feature to optimize in one's engineering (empirical hypothetico-deductive optimality), along with a constraint that all acceptable predicates should be paraphrasable in terms of physical ones. This constraint is to be strictly enforced in accounts of all phenomena, even linguistic phenomena. But the constraint is not independent of the selection of the feature to be optimized, namely, causal, explanatory, and/or predictive virtues. To the extent that physics is whatever theory best exhibits these empirical virtues, it is fairly natural to assign its predicates a special role in constraining further engineering.

These issues are very complicated and we do not pretend to definitively settle them here (even Carnapian stipulation does not seem to help, as we argued in chapters 4 and 5). What we would like to suggest is how both the Carnapian picture and the Quinean empirically radicalized version of it seem optional, and how adoption of the Quinean perspective that regards all interesting questions as fundamentally empirical ones can lead to a misguided appeal to empirical data to illuminate philosophical problems.

Consider the following analogy to illustrate what we mean in calling the adoption of these perspectives 'optional.' Suppose that a community finds itself with a collection of legal and political rules, a 'common law' tradition that extends back as far as any historical records show. Imagine that no one knows how the collection arose, but everyone employs the common law as a guide to legitimate political activities, including what activities count as legal or politically 'legitimate.' Much but not all of this common law is written down in a document, the Tablet. Among the rules are rules concerning what sorts of new attributions of legitimacy may be added to the current store of rules in the Tablet. There are even rules as to who gets to decide what new rules may be added to the Tablet. Many of the laws and rules within the tradition seem to have fairly obvious economic motivation. But some just seem correct, for some acts seem legitimate politically even though their legitimacy has no apparent connection to economic benefits. For example, suppose that it just seems that police officers are to wear blue uniforms. Practically everybody throughout recorded history appears to agree that blue uniforms are the unique legitimate color for a police uniform. And yet no one knows about any economic impact, positive or negative, that the adoption of such a rule might provide. Even more mysterious are some of the special legitimation ceremonies that seem to contain a number of features with no discernible economic impact, either positive or negative. Such seemingly economically unjustified rules in the Tablet have led to various puzzles concerning knowledge of their legitimacy. Some more reflective members of the community are puzzled as to how it first came to be known that blue is the uniquely correct or legitimate color for police uniforms. Some of the radical, troublesome elements within the community begin to raise questions concerning whether blue really is the uniquely legitimate color for police uniforms. A few even deny that blue is a legitimate color for police uniforms at all. Similar disputes arise concerning other issues, such as what side of the road is the correct or legitimate one to drive on, the color of road signs, judges' robes, times of day at which various proceedings occur, why water from a barrel must be used in a legitimate marriage ceremony, and so on.

A Carnapian in the ranks grows weary of these disputes. He notes that if one merely added some further rules, or employed a new Tablet – Tablet* – that explicitly deals with the disputed circumstances, there would be no more room for rational dispute, at least concerning what the verdict of Tablet* is. He proposes that all future disputes should be handled in the same way, by the construction of a novel Tablet* that explicitly deals with any new and controversial case that arises. Whether any action is legitimate 'in reality' is a pseudoquestion, the Carnapian insists. All that we can intelligibly do is select one of many possible artificially precise Tablet*s that supplies an obvious verdict, and perhaps then consider what pragmatic consequences follow from adoption of that Tablet* as the constitution. Unfortunately, the Carnapian remains unclear as to precisely what the pragmatic virtues are that should lead us to prefer one artificial Tablet* over another. But economic impact, maximizing gross communal product or output (GCP) is explicitly enumerated as a virtue of adoption of a Tablet*. Yet the Carnapian insists that there are some statements in such constructible Tablet*s, which one can know to be correct rules governing legitimacy of an action independently of knowing that action's economic impact. How one can tell which rules have this special economics-transcendent status is that they are written in red ink rather than black ink on Tablet*s, or distinguished by some other syntactic markers.

Now a Quinean comes along and questions the distinction between the red laws and the black laws. He agrees with the Carnapian that pragmatic benefits accrue from the adoption of some economically characterizable patterns of behavior. But the Quinean insists that all that is required for something to be justifiably or legitimately written on the Tablet is for it to lead to economic benefits, that is, maximizing GCP. There is no distinction between 'legitimate but merely stipulated laws' or 'laws adopted by convention' and the laws of behavior that maximize GCP. At a certain time, one can add to the current Tablet some hypothesis concerning a behavior that will be promoted or discouraged, leading to an increase in GCP. Initially, there may be no basis for writing some such proposal on the Tablet, and in that sense it is initially adopted by convention. But this is a mere 'passing trait,' and over the longer term it, like any other economic hypothesis, is to be placed on the Tablet if and only if it is a result of our best attempt at maximizing GCP. If a rule is indispensable, given the other rules, to the overall economic success, then it should remain on the tablet, and otherwise it should be erased.

There are also a few 'ordinary Tablet interpreters' who insist that the only way to discover whether any controversial case is indeed legitimate is by carefully analyzing how the Tablet has actually been applied in the past. Some of the more ambitious ordinary Tablet interpreters even claim that all controversies can be shown to be results of confusions over actual applications of the Tablet.

Finally, a small but vocal group of 'optionalists' within the community suggest another way. They agree with the ordinary Tablet interpreters that much can be gleaned from examination of how the Tablet is applied in ordinary, noncontroversial situations. But they demur from the philosophical utopianism according to which all problems will dissolve and controversies will be avoided if one simply analyzes actual practices of application. They agree with the Carnapians that there are a number of Tablets that could be constructed, with different pragmatic virtues and vices, and that we should be tolerant of various proposals or other tablet practices, as long as they are coherent. But they disagree with the Carnapians along several fronts as well. For one, optionalists do not pretend to settle or avoid all legitimacy disputes, nor do they aspire to this goal. They think that there are genuinely perplexing problems that do not vanish simply by adopting a more precisely defined practice. They also reject the idea that all proposed Tablets are to be introduced solely for some pragmatic economic purpose. For instance, there can be theoretical insights to be gleaned from considering the space of the possible or the intelligible, independently of pragmatic questions whether to adopt one or another proposal. Comparison of our actual practices to other possible or intelligible practices can yield illumination of our actual practices, the optionalists believe. In addition there is a pragmatic benefit to understanding the space of possible practices, some of which are more similar, others of which are quite different from our own. But the philosophical benefits of self-understanding are valuable in themselves, these philosophers think, independently of any economic benefits that might accrue from the adoption of one Tablet or another.

The optionalists also agree with Quineans against the Carnapians that when one considers actual practice, one finds that far more of the current contents of the Tablet than previously supposed are taken to have an economically revisable status, that is, be revisable in the face of economic data, just as the Quineans claim. In this sense the Carnapian view of any or all of the contents of the Tablet as akin to economically indefeasible stipulation is descriptively false as a matter of fact. Yet they disagree with the Quineans on a number of points as well. First, they think that we can make sense of a practice in which some of the laws written on some possible or actual Tablet can be economically unrevisable. And they point to some rules concerning legitimacy that are economically indefeasible in that they deal with matters that have no bearing on economic success. For example, rules concerning hand signaling procedures to start various affairs, or what color uniforms various officials are to wear, or the colors and images on what is counted as legitimate money, can be shielded from revision in the face of economic data partly in virtue of the fact that they can be designed to have no economic impact. And perhaps more importantly, the optionalists think that evaluation of all laws by a single criterion, a sort of economic optimization, is optional at best. While they grant for purposes of argument that one could adopt such a practice, they deny that one must do so, and insist that even if one chooses to engage in such a practice, it can be helpful to understand that their choice is optional.

A further element can be introduced into the analogy. Suppose that the Quinean says either that the Tablet does (implicitly) or should include the following statement: 'What is legitimately on the Tablet is legitimized solely by appeal to economic virtues, GCP optimization and the like.' The optionalists could concede that this is an option, or rather, is at least a prima facie one, since they note that there may be incoherencies in the overall practice that are not yet noticed. The Quineans might claim that this very principle is itself optimal for purposes of maximizing GCP, and so is to be included (by appeal to that very principle), and is not optional. The optionalists' obvious response is to note the circularity in the Quinean appeal to their own principle to justify itself, as well as reminding the Quinean that optionalists continue to resist the thought that the ultimate goal of the philosophical analysis of issues pertaining to the Tablet must be that of producing an economically optimal collection of legitimization practices.

We hope that the various analogies between the language case and the Tablet thought experiment are apparent, and that further reflection on them is illuminating. Economic impact is the analog of empirical predictive virtue. Legitimacy is an analog of justification. Noting differences between statements whose governing rules are designed to avoid incoherence in a global economic practice is analogous to our proposals concerning practices permitting explicit stipulations, and perhaps mathematical and even some metaphysical statements. As with the rules to avoid incoherent economic practice, our rules for the introduction of these special statements can be designed to preclude their bearing on empirical matters. Producing economically virtuous political–legal schemes is a valuable goal, as is producing empirically virtuous theories. But the process of engineering schemes for meeting these goals should not be conflated with the process of better understanding our own actual scheme, which understanding is partly constituted by placement of that scheme within a space of other merely possible, but intelligible schemes. Even keeping engineering as our goal can motivate investigation of other engineering goals and other intelligible ways of meeting whatever goals one might imagine. But we think that there are theoretical virtues that are largely independent of linguistic engineering. Seeing novel possibilities and unforeseen patterns that could intelligibly guide us is desirable in itself.

6.11 Chapter Summary

In this chapter we introduce a notion, analyticity*. Analytic* statements are akin to chess-pieces in that they are sentences-as-understood or sentences-as-used. The main distinctive feature of analytic* statements is that these sentences are understood to be taken to be true and empirically indefeasible, in a sense that we try to clarify by ruling out empirical data concerning language use itself, and later, in mathematical cases, ruling out 'second-order' empirical evidence for the existence of non-empirical justifications. Treating a sentence as true and empirically indefeasible imposes some constraints on other features of the sentences that are understood as analytic*. In particular, they must not entail or even provide evidence for any empirical propositions concerning the character of any experiences.

Our purpose in introducing the notion of analyticity* is to illuminate disputes concerning the kindred notion of analyticity, with a particular emphasis on the epistemological distinctiveness that analytic statements were (and in some circles still are) taken to have. We argue that a coherent or intelligible linguistic practice can permit the introduction of analytic* statements into the language. We then argue that all of the main objections to analyticity raised by Quine and Harman, which are the most powerful that we are aware of, can be answered by appeal to a distinction between analytic* statements and others, and showing how one can deploy this distinction in ways similar to the way logical empiricists deployed analyticity. In the process of answering the objections to analyticity, we disentangle some issues. For example, we argue that appeal to synonymy is unnecessary in order to defend analyticity*, and thereby deflect the complicated arguments against meanings and synonymy as inessential for drawing a principled, epistemically relevant distinction between statements. Instead we appeal to a notion that Quineans themselves must appeal to, the notion of a good translation scheme. Another crucial move from our point of view is an 'explanatory reversal' of sorts. We do not think that the meanings of the words defined via an analytic* statement explain the truth of the statement. Rather, we think that the fact that we take a particular statement to be true and empirically indefeasible is what gives the defined words their meaning (or, as we explain without appeal to meaning, what constrains acceptable translations of the statements).

Many philosophers take the notion of a linguistic stipulation or stipulative definition as given, while most Quineans continue to deny that such stipulations are anything more than 'hypotheses' that can be empirically disconfirmed. We look more carefully at what a linguistic stipulation is, and connect it to the notion of a rule of language of a particular kind. This enables us to better understand both why one can coherently permit empirically indefeasible stipulations, and how they are different from theoretical hypotheses. It also helps to clarify another matter that is not often clear, the relation between the truth of an analytic* stipulation and our actions of adopting a convention or rule. The relation is simple in outline: we add a rule to our language according to which a sentence (usually containing some novel term) is to be taken to be true and empirically indefeasible. The content of the statement does not thereby become some description of a social act, nor must it become a theoretical hypothesis. Analytic* statements have their own, epistemically distinctive profile.

We introduce a subcategory of analyticity* called 't-analyticity.' T-analytic statements are analytic* statements that are governed by a further rule, namely, that the proposition expressed by the statement is itself empirically indefeasible. We introduce this notion in order to provide a sketch of an approach to mathematical statements and their distinctive epistemic profile that seems to many non-Quineans to be non-empirical. Kripke has made famous the existence of at least some apparently indefeasible stipulations, such as 'Julius is the inventor of the zipper, if there is one,' which nevertheless one could describe as expressing a proposition concerning an individual and empirically accessible features of that individual. T-analyticity distinguishes mathematical stipulations from this sort of 'contingent a priori' statement. In our sketch of our approach to mathematics we respond to some initial objections that are sometimes thought to be devastating to the project of taking mathematics to be analytic. The three objections that we consider are: (1) that mathematical statements, unlike arbitrary linguistic stipulations, do not seem arbitrary; (2) that mathematical propositions are not empirically indefeasible (testimonial evidence, ink patterns in textbooks or on computer outputs can provide empirical evidence for or against their truth); and (3) that existence claims cannot be stipulated (God, Santa Claus, and causally isolated Lewisian possible worlds are discussed). Our response to objection 1 is that a term introduced stipulatively can eventually become so familiar that various truths pertaining to it (including stipulative ones) seem obvious, and that this accounts for our taking '2 + 2 = 4' to be obviously true. To answer objection 2 we refine our notion of 'empirically indefeasible' to exclude what we call 'second-order' empirical evidence for the existence of a non-empirical 'first-order' justification or evidence. The final objection is the most fundamental, and we explain how some entities, such as Santa, are such that we do not in fact disallow empirical evidence from counting against his existence, and similarly for God and (actually) causally isolated chunks of matter. We think that mathematical entities are understood differently, such that empirical evidence simply does not count against the truth of mathematical statements, whether existence claims or others.

We then briefly recount a further potential application of analyticity* to other ontological disputes concerning mereological principles, fictional entities, and impure sets. Our tentative account is that 'conditional' analytic* statements can permit inferences from empirical facts to claims concerning the existence of 'impure stipulata.' For example, it might be stipulative or analytic* that when an author writes a novel, some fictional characters come into existence. These entities, if they exist, are not related to activities of authors in the way that some physical processes cause others to exist, since the latter, unlike the former, are empirically defeasible. Fictional characters seem to be akin to stipulated entities, but they are distinct from 'pure' stipulata such as pure sets in that their existence is understood to 'depend' (in the stipulative sense described) on empirical facts.

We next explain the differences between our approach in this work and other approaches that have attracted attention from philosophers. One approach to analyticity says that analytic statements are exactly those whose denial manifests a failure to understand the terms involved. While we are sympathetic to much in the vicinity of this approach, we stop short of endorsing it, for reasons that include the vagueness of what is required to count as 'competent' with a term or a concept expressed by a term, and the concern that it does not obviously have resources to explain why such statements are supposed to be a priori or empirically indefeasible. The other approach we consider is that of Gillian Russell (2008), for whom the paradigm case of analyticity is 'I am here now.' Our main difference with her approach is that she focuses on making sense of a notion of 'true in virtue of meaning' that she supposes to be explanatory. Roughly, she takes analytic statements to be those such that facts concerning 'reference determination' of the terms within the sentence entail the truth of the sentence in all possible contexts of utterance. While we agree with most of what she says, we are interested in capturing a notion that preserves an epistemic distinctiveness, a type of empirical indefeasibility in particular. Russell's notion does not seem to help to explain the apparent epistemic distinctiveness or 'non-empiricality' of some stipulations and of mathematical statements. In our view, the non-empirical nature of analytic statements is among the most important and distinctive features that they are taken to have, and central to the historical disputes between Quine and the logical empiricists, including Carnap. Also, Russell takes the notion of a meaning-conferring stipulation for granted, and does not take seriously Quinean objections to either meaning or to the special status of stipulative definitions, whereas we try to illuminate stipulative definitions further and thereby directly engage with the Quineans along this front.

In our final section we draw an analogy to an imagined community with a 'Tablet' whose contents are taken to govern what political and other actions are legitimate. We consider Carnapian, Quinean, and other attitudes toward the contents of the Tablet as a means toward obtaining a perspicuous view of the overall dialectic concerning contents of the Tablet, including disputes as to whether some statements on the Tablet are distinctive. We hope that further reflection on this analogy might yield some insights into the disputes concerning analyticity, including their seeming immunity to non-question-begging resolution, and into philosophical activity pertaining to disputes concerning statements within our own language.

6.12 Further Reading

A recent work on metaphilosophy pertaining to mainstream 'analytic' philosophy is Timothy Williamson's *The Philosophy of Philosophy* (2007). With respect to analyticity, see his chapters 3 and 4 in particular. Gillian Russell's book *Truth in Virtue of Meaning* (2008) is an extended treatment of analyticity conceived in a way different from ours. We discuss our differences in section 6.7, but we highly recommend her work to those interested in analyticity. Two of Hans-Johann Glock's works are highly pertinent to analyticity and Quine and connections of these questions to broader issues in philosophy. One is his *Quine and Davidson on Thought, Language and Reality* (2003) the other *What is Analytic Philosophy?* (2008). P. M. S. Hacker's *Wittgenstein's Place in Twentieth-Century Analytic Philosophy* (1996), particularly his chapter on Quine, gives his take on the relationship between Quine and analytic philosophy. Other fine works by Hacker, too many to enumerate here, elaborate a broadly Wittgensteinian view concerning the missteps of contemporary inheritors of analytic philosophy. Oswald Hanfling's *Philosophy and Ordinary Language: The Bent and Genius of Our Tongue* (2000) is a recent overview of ordinary language philosophy as it relates to Quine and other more recent developments. For Quinean approaches to the philosophy of mathematics, we recommend *Mathematics as a Science of Patterns* (Resnik 1997) and *The*

Indispensability of Mathematics (Colyvan 2003). The references on meta-ontology cited in chapter 4 are also connected to the broader methodological disputes between Carnapians, Quineans, and others that continue to be hotly debated on the contemporary scene.

GLOSSARY OF PHILOSOPHICAL TERMS

abstract/abstractum/abstracta: while there is no universally accepted definition of 'abstract,' abstracta are abstract objects. The least controversial examples of abstracta are numbers and other mathematical objects such as pure sets. Other possible examples are properties. The central feature that abstract objects are typically taken to share is a lack of spatial location. For example, neither the number 17 nor the property of being one meter long seem to have spatial locations. Other accounts define abstract objects as those which do not stand in causal relations. Sometimes lack of temporal features is taken as essential to being abstract, but this is more controversial, since, for example, numbers might be thought to exist at all times.

analytic/analyticity: analyticity has been taken to be a property of sentences, propositions, judgments, or statements. In contemporary use, a sentence or statement is analytic if and only if it is true solely in virtue of the meanings of its constituent terms (but note various alternative definitions considered throughout the text). Analytic statements have been claimed to have one or more of various properties, including: being necessarily true, being knowable a priori, being knowable with certainty, being vacuous, being empty of cognitive content, being tautologous, being true under any interpretation, being verified 'come what may,' and being empirically untestable. Other properties asserted of analytic truths include being such that their subject concept is contained in their predicate concept, being such that their denial involves a violation of the law of non-contradiction, and being such that to deny them is to exhibit a lack of linguistic competence with respect to the constituent terms.

analytic*: an analytic* statement is a sentence-as-used. An analytic* statement is a sentence understood by the linguistic community as follows: the sentence *s* expresses a true proposition *p*, and that proposition (that *s* expresses a true proposition *p*, not the proposition *p* expressed) is empirically indefeasible. Analyticity* is introduced in this text as a way of capturing what is essential to a common form of stipulation, and as a way of representing a distinctive class of statements that share many of the features associated with analytic truths, in particular, the fact that they are taken to be empirically indefeasible.

a posteriori judgment/proposition: a proposition that is knowable or justifiable by appeal to sense experience, but not knowable solely by appeal to reflection, reason, or intuition.

a priori judgment/proposition: a proposition the truth or falsity of which is knowable without appeal to sense experience, such as by reflection, reason, or intuition.

Aristotle's (categorical) logic: the earliest western logical theory which formed the core of western logic for over two thousand years. Aristotle's logic was assumed by philosophers such as Kant and Bolzano, and it largely confined itself to categorical propositions of a few relatively simple forms (such as 'All F are G' or 'Some F are not G'). Aristotle's logic was largely displaced by Frege's *logic*.

atoms, mereological: entities that are not decomposable into, or do not have, proper parts.

bivalence, principle of: a view that all propositions have two possible truth values, truth or falsehood.

color-exclusion principle: the principle that nothing can be two different colors all over at the same time. This principle is an example of something that seems a priori knowable, and yet it is not obviously reducible to a law of logic, and it resists subsumption into the class of arbitrary stipulations concerning color-words or the concepts expressed by these terms.

concept vs. linguistic term: a linguistic term is a word or expression from a language. A concept can be expressed by a word. For example, the linguistic term or word 'red' expresses the concept *red*. That same concept can be expressed using other words. For example, the German word 'rot' also expresses the concept *red*.

concrete/concretum/concreta: concrete objects or concreta have spatial locations, causal effects, or both. 'Concrete' is often contrasted with 'abstract.'

confirmation/disconfirmation: evidence for a hypothesis h confirms h, whereas evidence against h disconfirms h. 'Infirmation' is synonymous with 'disconfirmation.'

confirmational/Quinean holism: the view that individual statements or sentences are not confirmed individually by evidence. Rather, theories or even entire 'webs of belief' are confirmed or disconfirmed as wholes. The view was adopted in various forms by Poincaré, Duhem, Carnap, and Quine, among others.

constitutional system: in Carnap's work, a constitutional system is a system of basic concepts for a given domain (such as geometry, or economics) along with an explicit definition of other concepts on the basis of the basic concepts.

contingent proposition/entity: a proposition that is true, but not necessarily true, is contingent. An entity that exists but does not exist necessarily is a contingent entity.

conventionalism: to be a conventionalist about some realm of truths (whether sentences, propositions, or facts) is to think that their truth or falsehood is in some interesting sense a matter of linguistic choice, or choice of representation scheme. Poincaré famously argued that whether our space is curved is merely a matter of our conventional choice for representing it. Einstein thought that whether light travels the same speed in all directions is a matter of conventional choice of description. Some philosophers think that ethical truths are a result of somewhat arbitrary social conventions.

Convention T: Tarski's famous 'adequacy condition' on any acceptable definition of truth for a language. According to this adequacy condition, any reasonable definition of truth for a language L must entail all biconditionals of the form 'sentence s is true iff p,' where p is the sentence in the meta-language of L that correctly translates sentence s from L.

definiendum: a term to be defined.

definiens: the terms by which a definienum is defined.

definite description: an expression of the form 'the so and so,' such as 'The baker who lives around the corner' or 'the seventh largest planet.'

definition, explicit: a definition of the form S = the so and so, if S is an individual, or of the form Fx iff $\varphi(x)$, where φ specifies the defining conditions for being F. This is the most common and uncontroversial understanding of 'definition.' Contrasted with implicit definition.

definition, implicit: a definition of a term solely in terms of a specification of statements, which could be axioms or laws, which are true of it. For example, it is sometimes said that the axioms of geometry implicitly define the notions *point*, *plane*, and *line* by stating basic truths relating them to each other. Contrasted with *explicit definition*.

domain of quantification: the set or collection of objects that are understood as being talked about when someone utters a statement with either a universal quantifier ('For all . . .') or an existential quantifier ('There is/are . . .'). For example, if we're with a dozen friends at a party, and someone at the party says 'Someone brought wine,' there would be an understood domain of quantification that included people at the party. Similarly, if at an orchestra practice the conductor says, 'Everybody should pick up their instruments,' the implicitly understood domain of quantification would include only people in the orchestra. In arithmetic, the implicitly understood domain of quantification is the natural numbers.

doxastic conservatism: a view according to which one should change one's beliefs in the face of new evidence in such a way as to 'minimize belief changes' in some interesting sense. Different philosophers who accept such a principle might defend different versions of it, and define 'minimal belief change' differently.

emotivism: a view that interprets some class of statements that seem to be expressing truth valued statements to instead be expressions of emotion. For example, emotivism about ethical statements might say that to utter the sentence 'Helping that woman was the right thing to do' is to express a positive emotion toward the action of helping the woman, rather than to assert a true or false statement.

empiricism, moderate: the form of empiricism defended by logical empiricists, according to which all genuine, substantive knowledge is justified by appeal to sense experience, but which explains our knowledge of non-empirical statements such as logical truths and mathematical truths by appeal to some notion akin to analyticity. Moderate empiricists thus grant that there is a priori knowledge in some sense, but claim that such knowledge is not substantive or factual, but is instead trivial in some way, or tautologous.

empiricism, radical: the form of empiricism according to which all knowledge and justification must involve an appeal to sense experience. Alternatively one could define radical empiricism as the view that nothing is knowable or justifiable purely a priori, but that we may know a great deal a posteriori.

epistemology: the philosophical study of knowledge. Epistemology includes the analysis of the concept of knowledge, conditions under which knowledge is attained or attainable, and analysis of closely related concepts such as *justification* and *evidence*.

evidence profile: a term introduced in this book to refer to a feature of statements. Evidence profiles characterize what sorts of evidence or data can or do confirm or disconfirm the statement. We claim that analytic* statements have distinctive evidence profiles, in that sense experiences and their contents neither confirm nor disconfirm them. In contrast, empirical hypotheses are confirmed or disconfirmed more or less directly by sense experiences.

explicandum: the word or concept to be explicated.

explicans: the account given when explicating a concept; the terms in which the concept or word is explicated.

explication: a form of conceptual clarification that consists of replacing an unclear or inexact concept with a clearer or more exact surrogate concept. In some forms of explication, such as Carnap's, the surrogate concept is often introduced within the context of a *formal system*. Unlike explanations, explications involve the replacement of the inexact concept with a different, though related, concept.

extension: the extension of a concept or linguistic expression is the set of things to which the concept or linguistic expression truly applies. For example, the extension of the predicate 'is red' is the set of red things. The extension of 'is a prime number less than 10' is the set $\{2,3,5,7\}$.

extensional notion: an extensional notion is a notion or concept whose meaning is fully captured in terms of the extensions of sets of actual objects.

fallibilism: a fallibilist about a realm of facts or propositions believes that whether or not the facts obtain or the propositions are true is not something that we can know with certainty. For example, a fallibilist about ethical judgments thinks that we can never be certain that we are correct concerning the correctness of these judgments. A fallibilist about knowledge thinks that one can know a statement without having reasons or justification which logically entail the truth of that statement. Someone can be a fallibilist about one realm, such as the realm of empirical science, while being infallibilist concerning another realm, such as the realm of mathematics or revealed theology.

fictionalism: a view that treats the statements of some realm as analogous to statements from fictional stories. Thus a fictionalist about arithmetic will say that there is a standard, well-known story about what are called 'numbers,' and when we say that one plus one is two, we really mean something like 'according to the standard number-fiction, one plus one equals two.' There are fictionalists about ethical statements, modal statements, statements about the contents of minds, and other domains.

first-order logic: the logic that allows quantifier domains to range only over individuals. In contrast, second-order logic permits quantification over arbitrary sets of objects, or quantification over properties. Some logics permit quantification over propositions.

formalism: a view of mathematics which regards mathematical statements as strings of uninterpreted symbols or words, arranged in accord with 'formal' rules for transforming them. According to a straightforward form of formalism, to say that one plus one equals two is to say that in a standard formal system of arithmetic, the string '$1 + 1 = 2$' is the last step in a sequence of strings that conform to rules as to what counts as a 'proof.'

formal system: a formal system is a system of symbols together with well-defined rules of transformation. The rules typically govern what sequences of symbols are to count as 'grammatical' or 'well-formed,' as well as what sequences of well-formed expressions count as 'proofs' within the formal system.

Frege-analyticity: a Frege-analytic statement is one that can be transformed into a logical truth by the substitution of synonyms for synonyms. For example, if 'bachelors' is synonymous with 'unmarried men,' then the statement 'All bachelors are unmarried' is Frege-analytic, since we can transform it into 'All unmarried men are unmarried' by the substitution of synonyms for synonyms.

Gödel sentence: a 'Gödel sentence' for a formal system for arithmetic is a sentence that can be shown to be neither provable nor disprovable in that system. In fact, it can be shown that a Gödel sentence is true just in case it is not provable in the system, and in that sense 'says of itself' that it is not provable. Thus it is true just in case it is not provable. If the system is consistent, it is not provable, and so true, yet unprovable.

Gödel's incompleteness theorem: Proven by Kurt Gödel, this result says roughly that in any consistent formal system in which arithmetic can be expressed or represented, there are statements of arithmetic that are neither provable nor disprovable within that system. This theorem is also sometimes known as Gödel's first incompleteness theorem, to contrast it with a second, related incompleteness result.

holism, confirmational/Quinean: *see confirmational/Quinean holism.*

homophonic translation: the translation of one expression into a syntactically identical expression. Typically, an English-speaker will translate other English-speakers' sentences homophonically. However, if a seeming English-speaker utters strange-enough things when understood 'homophonically,' then following the *maxim of minimum mutilation*, one might decide to translate what they say non-homophonically.

Hume's Fork: David Hume's division of all objects of human knowledge into either relations of ideas or matters of fact. The division has some similarities with the later distinction between analytic and synthetic statements.

hypostasize: to posit or speculatively infer an entity or type of entity. Hypostatized entities are often reified or wrongly regarded as real or concrete instead of posits or conjectures.

hypothetico-deductivism: a view of confirmational methodology, according to which a hypothesis H is confirmed by observed data E just in case E can be logically inferred from H together with other confirmed theoretical or empirical statements.

identity conditions: apply to classes or objects of some type, and are conditions or characteristics sufficient to individuate members of that class of objects. For example, sets are individuated by their extensions, in the sense that sets x and y are identical just in case they have the same extension. Quine objected to possibilia (possible but not actual objects) and other entities such as meanings or propositions partly in virtue of the fact that it seemed to him unclear the conditions under which two arbitrary possible entities, two propositions, or two meanings, were the same or different.

indeterminacy of reference: see *inscrutability of reference.*

indeterminacy of translation: a thesis defended by Quine according to which given any two languages L_1 and L_2, *there is no fact of the matter* in general as to which sentences of L_1 correctly translate any given sentence of L_2. Indeterminacy is to be distinguished from mere *underdetermination* of a translation, or the claim that the data never permits us to know which translation is correct. Surprisingly, Quine included among the cases of indeterminacy the case in which L_1 and L_2 are the same languages, in the sense of the same sets of sentences.

individuation, criteria of: criteria which specify what counts as the same object or type of object. For example, individuation criteria for an individual horse might include its spatiotemporal location, and individuation criteria for the type (kind) *horse* might include distinctive physiological features of horses. See also *identity conditions*.

inferential relations: relations having to do with what can be logically inferred from what. For example, in standard logic, a sentence A is correctly inferable from the set {A, A→B}; this is an inference relation that holds between A and the set.

infinitarily expressible: a notion is infinitarily expressible if it is expressible using an expression that is infinitely long. If a notion or statement is only infinitarily expressible, then no finitely long expression expresses that notion or statement. For example, some real numbers would be specifiable only infinitarily, in terms of an infinitely long decimal expansion.

infirmation: a synonym used by Quine for 'disconfirmation'; see *confirmation/ disconfirmation*.

inscrutability of reference: Quine's thesis that no referential term has a determinate referent.

instrumentalism: a view concerning scientific theories according to which theories are not best thought of as true or false, but rather are instruments for inferring correct predictions about observable facts or data. Instrumentalists sometimes go beyond mere agnosticism and deny scientific realism, or the view that scientific theories truly or falsely describe reality.

intension: a somewhat loose concept that in the broadest sense refers to those features of meaning that cannot be characterized in extensional terms. Thus for instance, if the extension of 'red' is the set of all red things, the intension of 'red' is whatever else is required to generate, identify, or individuate that set. One common attempt to make this idea more precise treats the extension of a predicate such as 'is red' to be the actual set of red things, and further assigns the predicate 'is red' a function from possible worlds to extensions at those worlds. According to this account, 'is red' has an extension at each possible world w, and this function from worlds w to extensions is its intension. Relatedly, a truth-evaluable sentence has as its extension its actual truth value, and as its intension either a function from worlds to truth values or a set of possible worlds (corresponding to the worlds at which the sentence is true).

intentional notions/concepts/entities: some authors use 'intensional' rather than 'intentional.' Entities or notions/concepts associated with a theory of intensions. Such entities and notions/concepts include propositions, meanings, and other entities or notions/concepts whose nature seems not to be captured or explained solely extensionally, that is, solely by appeal to sets of objects.

internal vs. external questions: Carnap's distinction between questions that can be raised and answered by appeal to rules governing correct application of some system of language (the internal questions), versus those that cannot be answered by appeal to such 'language internal' rules, but if coherent at all, concern whether to adopt the system of language as a whole.

intuition: in philosophical contexts, intuition is a mode of apprehending certain phenomena, such as objects, propositions, or facts, that does not rely on sensory experience or inference. Intuition is often, as in Kant, regarded as a direct mode of apprehension, in the sense that it does not rely upon signs or concepts. Rationalists typically assert that intuitions can be a source of knowledge of some propositions, such as mathematical or logical truths, while empiricists typically deny this.

intuitionism: in philosophy of mathematics, a view according to which mathematical objects are mental constructions. Intuitionists historically have argued that this conception leads to different (nonclassical or 'intuitionistic') rules of logic and mathematical proof.

liar paradox: the paradox surrounding a family of statements similar to the following: 'This sentence is false.' If true, the sentence is false, and if false, then it is true. Yet this is a paradox if it is assumed that no sentence is both true and false. Tarski proposed disallowing statements within a language that express their own truth or falsehood as a way of dealing with such paradoxical statements.

logic: while there is no uncontroversial characterization of logic, in general terms logic is the study of inferences and formal systems. Logic can be broadly divided into the study of deductive and inductive inferences. Contemporary logic often proceeds through the specification of formal systems, which includes the specification of a 'logical vocabulary,' together with rules for correctly inferring sentences of various forms (containing terms from the logical vocabulary), such as the words 'and' and 'or,' along with quantifiers such as 'for all' and 'there are.'

logical positivism: sometimes called 'logical empiricism,' or more recently 'moderate empiricism.' A view associated with members of the *Vienna Circle*, the main element of which (for the purposes of this book) is that there is a distinction between analytic and synthetic statements. Further logical positivist theses include the claims that all substantive or synthetic knowledge is empirical, based on experience, whereas analytic statements are knowable without appeal to experience, but are non-substantive.

logicism: a theory of arithmetic initially proposed by Frege, according to which all arithmetical statements, such as 'there are prime numbers greater than one million', can be translated into, or shown to derive from, some logical truths, given certain definitions. Modified versions of logicism were proposed by Russell and Whitehead, among others.

maxim of minimum mutilation: Quine's label for a principle of *doxastic conservatism*.

mereology: the theory of the 'part of' relation and of kindred notions. A mereological theory might contain among its principles the principle that 'for any two distinct objects a and b, there is a mereological sum a*b, distinct from both a and b.'

meta-language: the language ML used to talk about some language L of interest, where L is the *object-language* being talked about.

meta-ontology: a term that has recently become popular, referring to the philosophical theory concerning the nature and proper methodology for ontology, including the nature of existence claims. For example, a meta-ontological question might be whether there is a fact of the matter concerning various ontological claims such as whether there are numbers or arbitrary mereological sums.

modality: in contemporary usage, having to do with possibility and necessity. A modal feature of a statement, for example, is that it is contingently true or necessarily false. Sometimes 'alethic modality' is used for this notion when other 'modalities' are being discussed.

naturalism: naturalism is the philosophical view that all phenomena can be explained or known using the entities, laws, theories, and/or methodologies of empirical science. Naturalism comes in a variety of forms. Thus, a naturalist about ontology might claim that all and only those phenomena that are recognized by some or all the empirical sciences are real. A naturalist about epistemology will likely hold that only those forms of inquiry and justification used in the empirical sciences are possible sources of knowledge. A methodological naturalist will maintain that science alone provides proper standards for inquiry. Each of these forms of naturalism has further subvarieties.

necessary truth: a proposition that is true and could not have been false.

Neurath's boat: Otto Neurath's metaphor, according to which scientists and philosophers are in a situation that is analogous to that of sailors struggling to remain afloat at sea. Scientists and philosophers must begin by using their existing, inherited theories and beliefs to explain and predict the world, just as sailors use their boat to remain afloat at sea. Modifications or improvements to theories must begin from this intellectual inheritance, just as the sailors can only modify or improve the boat they are on. The metaphor of Neurath's boat is intended to contrast with a more 'foundationalist' view of knowledge, according to which we can build knowledge from first principles accessible to all.

nihilism, universalism (mereological): a mereological 'nihilist' thinks that the only objects that really or ultimately exist are 'atoms' which are indivisible into proper parts. A mereological universalist thinks that for any collection of distinct objects (atoms or otherwise) there is a further genuine object, their mereological sum. Intermediate views are possible, according to which some but not all such 'sums' of objects exist.

noncontradiction, principle of: the principle according to which it is false (in most versions, necessarily false) that both p and not-p, for any arbitrary proposition p. The principle is sometimes held to apply to sentences of a language rather than to propositions.

object-language: any language being described or talked about. The *metalanguage* is the language used to talk about the object-language.

objectual interpretation: an objectual interpretation of a quantifier such as 'for all' is normally contrasted with a 'substitutional' interpretation. Consider for example the statement 'For any number n, 2n is even.' An objectual interpretation says that the statement means that for any number, two times that number results in an even number. A *substitutional interpretation* would assign it the meaning that for any numeral (number-word) that you substitute into the schema '2n is even,' a true sentence results. The distinction is thought to be relevant to some debates concerning the existence of abstract objects, because if one can show that quantified arithmetical statements are best interpreted substitutionally, then committing oneself to the truth of such statements does not commit one to the existence of numbers, but only to sentences or substitution-instances.

observation sentence: a sentence whose verification or full justification results immediately from experience or observation. In Quine's theory, observation sentences are associated with dispositions to assent under certain patterns of sensory stimulation and dissent under other patterns, and a speaker has acquired the observation sentence if he or she has acquired these dispositions to assent and dissent.

ontological commitments: entities that one must take to exist to the extent that one accepts some theory or believes some statements. For example, if someone believes that two plus two equals four, then on some views they are ontologically committed to the existence of the numbers two and four, as well as perhaps the plus function and perhaps even the relation of identity (equality).

paraconsistent logic: a system of rules akin to logical rules that includes among its logical vocabulary a term governed by rules similar to the rules governing our negation sign, but that permits some 'contradictions' of the form 'Both p and not-p' to be true, or both true and false. Paraconsistent logical systems thus might be said to 'permit contradictions.'

paradigm case argument: an argument form that appeals to a 'paradigm case' of a concept or notion in order to show that the notion has a nonempty extension. Some concepts, such as 'is vermillion (in color)' might be thought to mean 'is similar in color to this patch (pointing at a "paradigm" of vermillion).' Any concept that is correctly defined by appeal to a paradigm case arguably must have a nonempty extension, the paradigm case itself. On the other hand, Harman argued that pointing to a paradigm case of the concept 'witch,' for example, does not establish that there are really witches.

Peano axioms: basic principles or 'axioms' from which the truths of ordinary arithmetic are logically derivable, first discovered/invented by the Italian mathematician Guiseppe Peano.

phenomenalism (sense-data theory): a view according to which talk of ordinary objects such as chairs or tables or planets is 'really' or correctly translated into complicated statements concerning sense-experiences that are liable to occur if other sense-experiences occur. In other words, phenomenalists reduce or translate ordinary object talk into talk about actual or possible sense experiences.

physicalism: a form of naturalism which includes the further claim that physics is the most basic or fundamental science, and that all truths are reducible to truths expressible in the language of physics, or that all phenomena are in principle explainable using only the language, methods, and theories of physics.

Picture Theory of the Proposition: Ludwig Wittgenstein's theory of propositions in his book *Tractatus Logico-Philosophicus*. According to it, propositions are a species of picture. Like pictures, propositions depict or fail to depict the way things are (are true or false) in virtue of consisting of elements that share a form with the facts that they depict. The picture theory of the proposition influenced the *Vienna Circle*'s treatment of language and logic.

possibility, epistemic vs. metaphysical: the truth of a proposition is epistemically possible just in case for all we know, it might be true. Thus epistemic possibility has some connection to what we know. Metaphysical possibility, in contrast, is supposed to be capturable without appeal to what knowledge we have. For example, if mathematical truths are metaphysically necessary, then if Goldbach's conjecture GC (thus far neither proved nor disproved by mathematicians) is true, it is metaphysically necessary, and if false, it is metaphysically impossible. On the other hand, since we don't know whether it is true or false at present, it is epistemically possible (relative to our current state of knowledge) that GC is true, and also epistemically possible that GC is false.

predicate: as this term is used in contemporary philosophy and logic, the predicate of a sentence is that component which includes the copula plus a property or relation expression.

predicate logic: see *first-order logic*.

primality testing, quasi-empirical: in some cases, quasi-empirical methods are used to check whether some extremely large natural number N is prime. Such methods proceed by checking whether randomly selected numbers less than N have a particular property, a property that over half of the numbers less than N share if N is composite. If many randomly selected numbers less than N fail to have the property, then with a high probability N is prime.

Principle of Bivalence: the principle that for any statement, there are exactly two truth values, true or false. The principle of bivalence is denied by *intuitionism*.

Principle of the Excluded Middle: the logical principle that the formula 'p or not-p' is always true.

Principle of Tolerance: Carnap's claim that 'in logic there are no morals.' Carnap took the principle of tolerance to express his position that there is no fact of the matter as to whether a given system of logic is 'correct,' but only pragmatic questions as to whether adopting one system of logic over another achieves certain purposes.

proposition: a proposition is taken to be what is expressed by a meaningful sentence. On this intuitive picture, the English sentence 'Snow is white' expresses the same proposition as the German sentence 'Der Schnee ist weiss.'

proxy function: a function that maps one set of objects onto another set of objects.

quantifier: an expression of amount, broadly construed to include non-specific terms like 'some' and 'all.' The main 'quantifiers' used in standard first-order logic are the universal quantifier, expressed by the English 'for all' or 'for any,' and the existential quantifier expressed by the English 'for some' or 'there exist/are.' Mathematical logicians have introduced more general notions applicable to other operators such as 'most' or 'many' and others, but these do not play a role in this book.

Quine–Duhem Thesis: see *confirmational/Quinean holism*.

radical translation: Quine's term for the translation of a completely unfamiliar language into one's own.

rationalism: a view according to which rational intuition is a source of justification or knowledge.

reductionism (Quinean): As used by Quine, reductionism is the view that each statement within the language of empirical science has a collection of observations (or observation statements) that would verify or confirm it, and another set of observations that falsify or disconfirm it. According to Quine's *confirmational holism*, reductionism is a mistake, since statements are only confirmed or disconfirmed by evidence in the context of an overall background theory of which they are a part.

Russell's paradox: a paradox constructed from a principle of Frege's logical theory, according to which for any concept expressible in Frege's language, there is a set of things to which the concept applies. Russell's paradox is generated by the concept 'set of sets that are not members of themselves,' which is expressible in Frege's language. Suppose that there is a set corresponding to this concept. Is it a member of itself? If it is, then it is not, and if it is not then it is. Since either possibility leads to a contradiction, Frege's logical system was shown to be inconsistent.

salva veritate, substitutable: two terms are substitutable *salva veritate* in some sentences just in case when they are substituted for each other, the truth value of the sentence remains the same.

satisfaction: a notion introduced by Tarski in his development of a 'theory of truth' for some formal languages. The main point for the purposes of this book is that 'true' is defined using the term 'satisfies,' i.e., truth is defined by Tarski by appeal to the notion of satisfaction.

semantics: the theory of meanings of expressions of language.

sentence: a sequence of words, or of letters and spaces, that conforms to certain syntactical or grammatical formation rules. The main contrast for the purposes of this text is that between sentences on one hand, and the rules governing their standard employment or use, on the other. Sentences are thus here contrasted with how they are typically understood or used or what they mean.

statement: as used in this text, a statement is a sentence-as-understood. A sentence is to a statement as a mini-sculpture is to a chess-bishop. The latter is a piece-as-understood or as-used. The mini-sculpture, like a sentence, could be used in many ways depending on intentions of users, but nevertheless often it is understood or presupposed on any given occasion of use that they are being used as chess-pieces or as vehicles of linguistic acts.

stimulus-analytic: Quine's term for a sentence that is assented to given an arbitrary prompting stimulation. 'There are cats' is stimulus-analytic, on Quine's account.

stipulation: as used in this book, there are two uses of 'stipulation,' one an act of stipulating, the other the statement stipulated. In the second sense a stipulation is a sentence used in a particular way, often to at least partially fix the meaning of a term. In an act of stipulation connected to our notion *analytic**, a rule is introduced into the language such that a particular sentence-type is to be taken as true (expressing a true proposition) and its truth is to be taken as empirically indefeasible.

stipulatum: as used in this book, a stipulatum is an object whose existence is entailed by some analytic* statement. Stipulata are contrasted with theoretical entities like electrons, whose existence is not entailed by stipulations or analytic* statements, but rather follows (perhaps only inductively, not logically) from empirical evidence together with various non-stipulative hypotheses.

substitutional interpretation: an interpretation of quantifiers in logic according to which bound variables in quantified formulas have terms or expressions as substitution instances, instead of objects. See *objectual interpretation*.

synthetic: a proposition or judgment is synthetic if it is not a logical consequence solely of analytic statements. Synthetic statements have been asserted to have additional properties. These properties have included, but are not limited to, the ability of synthetic statements to possess 'cognitive content,' to be 'expansive' or 'ampliative' (expand knowledge when known), not to be knowable with complete certainty, to be contingent, to be knowable only a posteriori, and to have their truth or falsity partially determined by matters of language-independent fact.

syntax: in contemporary usage, syntax concerns those features of language having to do with shapes and orderings of linguistic characters and symbols, and not with meanings (although syntactic features may be correlated with semantic ones).

synthetic a priori: according to Kant, synthetic a priori judgments are such that their predicate concept is not contained in their subject concept (hence they are not analytic, by his definition) and yet they are knowable a priori and are such that knowledge of them is 'ampliative,' that is, it expands what we know. *Analytic* judgments, by contrast, are not expansive. Kant regarded true judgments of arithmetic and geometry, as well as certain metaphysical judgments, to be synthetic a priori. Kant thought that synthetic a priori truths exist and that their existence required philosophical explanation, for it meant that substantive knowledge could be had independently of experience.

tautology: a statement that is trivially or 'vacuously' true. A more technical and contemporary notion of 'tautology' defines tautologies as compound statements that remain true no matter what the truth values of the component statements are.

Theory of Descriptions: Russell's theory of expressions of the form 'The so and so . . .' Among other things, the Theory of Descriptions provided a model for showing how a type of statement that appeared to have a problematic logical and epistemological status could be given a tractable logical analysis.

underdetermination (of theory by data): the phenomenon that in general, any finite quantity of empirical data, no matter how large and detailed, is logically compatible with more than one theory (in general, with infinitely many theories).

universal: an abstract object that is held to explain how it is that two numerically distinct individuals can be of a single type. For instance, that Black Beauty and Silver are both of the type *horse* (or that 'horse' is truly predicated of both) is held to be explained by their both being somehow connected with or 'participating in' the universal of horse.

verificationism/verifiability criterion of meaning: a view shared by many logical empiricists, and by Quine, according to which a statement or sentence is meaningful only if there are well-defined conditions under which the statement would be verified or falsified (or, for later versions, confirmed or disconfirmed) by experience or observation.

Vienna Circle: A group of philosophers, mathematicians, and scientists that met in Vienna from 1928 to 1936. Among other theses, the Vienna Circle defended, and became identified with, a version of *logical positivism*.

web of belief: Quine's metaphor for our entire collection of beliefs at a given time. Our beliefs are thought of as interconnected like a spider's web, so that changing one belief is analogous to severing or altering parts of the spider's web, which causes changes in other parts of the web.

NOTES

1 Conceptions of Analytic Truth

1 For a further discussion of these ideas in Hume, see Dicker (1998, 35–60), and Meeker (2007).

2 Like his contemporaries, Kant used the term 'judgment' where philosophers today would more likely use a term like 'proposition.' 'Judgment' and 'proposition' are not, of course, synonyms. We could say that a proposition is the content of a judgment. And judgments, but not propositions, can be regarded as the product of an act, for instance. Such differences won't play a significant role in our discussion here, however, and we will regard 'judgment' and 'proposition' as loosely synonymous for the purposes of our historical exposition.

3 Gillian Russell (2008) resurrects and generalizes Kant's 'containment criterion,' by in effect providing a recipe for transforming all statements into logically equivalent subject–predicate form.

4 Kant also seemed to think that number required spatial intuitions. For a development of these ideas see Friedman (1992a) and Shabel (2003).

5 Frege did not use variables or speak of 'propositional functions' in the way common to contemporary logic, but instead used 'content strokes' and an alternative notation. His notation appears in Frege (1972, 128f.).

6 This can be done so that the definition is not circular, as it may appear to be stated in this natural way.

7 Frege did not take the same approach to geometry, which he regarded as consisting entirely of *synthetic* statements. The axioms of geometry were not analytic because unlike analytic truths they cannot be proved without appealing to axioms belonging to 'the sphere of some special science' (1964, 2). The axioms and theorems of geometry are restricted to the particular area of spatial objects. Those of logic, on the other hand, are perfectly general, and insofar as mathematics is derivable from

them, the propositions of mathematics, but not of geometry, can be regarded as analytic.

8 Quantifier notation makes this rather clearer: $(\exists x)$ ((x begat Charles II and x was executed) and ((y) if y begat Charles II then y = x)).

9 We discuss the views of the Vienna Circle concerning analyticity at greater length in chapter 5. As we there note, not all of these theses were held by all Vienna Circle members.

10 In his 'Intellectual Autobiography' Carnap wrote that that he felt as if Russell's appeal for 'a school of men with scientific training and philosophical interests, unhampered by the traditions of the past' had been directed to him personally (1963b, 13).

11 For a discussion of Carnap's early use of intuition, and his later rejection of it, see Richardson (1998, 153–8, 179–80).

12 See for instance Russell (1959, 111ff.), and the preface to his (1937), for such uses of intuition (described as 'direct acquaintance').

13 Besides Quine (Quine 1969, 74f.), this interpretation is suggested by Nagel (1961, 123) and Putnam (1981, 181).

14 See for example Haack (1977), Coffa (1991), Friedman (1987, 1992), and Richardson (1996, 1998).

15 See for example Richardson (1996, 311), Coffa (1991, 225f.).

16 This 'neutral attitude toward the various philosophical forms of language' was later described by Carnap as something that 'remained the same throughout my life' (1963b, 18).

2 Carnap and Quine

1 See Gödel (1967) for a translation of the original paper. In our discussion of Gödel's and related results, we are going to avoid complicated locutions that would express the results more precisely. Our focus is on some important connections between results in mathematical logic such as Gödel's and the development of Carnap's thinking rather than on details of the results themselves. There are many sources of formulations of these results, from the intuitive and informal to the highly formal. See Nagel and Newman (2001), or for a more sophisticated yet non-technical overview, see Franzen (2005).

2 Adding the negation of G to consistent S also yields a consistent theory, although the resulting theory is not true in standard arithmetic. Beth (1963) raises interesting difficulties for Carnap related to this.

3 Carnap regarded Gestalt psychology as a promising candidate for providing these basic elements, cf. pp. 62, 108 of Carnap (1937). The role of empirical results in the formulation of the system of the *Aufbau* was reaffirmed by Carnap decades later in his (1963b), pp. 16–17.

4 In chapter 1 we noted an alternative interpretation of Carnap's *Aufbau*, according to which it is not attempting to found knowledge in the 'autopsychological' realm, but rather 'intersubjectivizing,' or showing how the objective divides from the subjective. However, even on this alternative interpretation, a variant of the circularity problem remains. For a discussion of this, see Richardson (1998, 189f.).

5 We can see the possible effects of Carnap's debate with Neurath in Carnap (1987, 1995). In these papers, written in the 1930s, Carnap avoids empirical psychology. He replaces such 'material mode' characterizations of subjective experience in favor of using the 'formal mode' of speech for what he now called 'protocol sentences.'

6 Russell did not share Frege's attitude toward logicism here, however. For Russell, logicism seemed to allow him to show that both logic and mathematics were synthetic a priori. See Russell (1937, 457).

7 Carnap proposed another way of bypassing Gödel's results for his Language I. If there are no 'morals' in logic, that is, nothing that constrains logic from 'outside' it, why not allow proofs with infinitely many premises or steps? For Language I, he proposed a rule of inference (today often called an 'omega-rule'), which allows the derivation of statements from infinite sets of other statements (1937, 37–8). However, the price of adopting an infinitary omega-rule is a high one. What, after all, would an infinitely long or infinite-premise proof be like? Formalists like Hilbert would almost certainly have rejected any omega-rule: as we have noted, the cornerstone of Hilbert's project was to restrict us to those mathematical objects which are 'intuitively present as immediate experience prior to all thought.' And intuitionists like Brouwer would have rejected it too: no finite human mind can 'construct' the infinite series of premises or steps that the omega-rule requires. If Carnap intended his Language I to help philosophers sort-out their philosophical disagreements using a common formal language, as he did, it seemed to be a bad way to start.

8 There are difficulties in carrying out Carnap's suggestion. Unless there is a recursively enumerable sequence of languages that in the limit generate all arithmetical truths, which there is not, Carnap's appeal to meta-languages does not clearly circumvent incompleteness and yield a complete account of analytic truth. But we merely note this difficulty. In much of our discussion we will simply assume that Carnap takes himself to have a way around this 'incompleteness problem' in providing a complete theory of analytic truth, by appeal to some indefinite sequence of meta-languages.

9 As commentators have subsequently emphasized, Carnap's *Syntax* method of characterizing the relation of consequence in Language II was semantical in all but name (*cf.* Coffa 1987, 1991; Ricketts 1996; Creath 1991).

10 For example, in characterizing the analyticity of the sentence '$(x)(\exists y)(x{+}1 = y)$,' Carnap had to appeal to a meta-language proof that any valuation of 'x' will, given the definition of '+,' yield a valuation of 'y' such that the sentence will turn out analytic (*cf.* 1937, 107). This point is emphasized by Coffa (1987, 554–7).

11 In languages without 'descriptive predicates,' the converse is true as well. We are here simplifying the exposition. In *Syntax*, Carnap defines '(L-) determinate' in terms of 'analytic' (115), further defines 'analytic' in terms of 'consequence,' then concedes that the notion of consequence goes beyond what is demonstrable (133). Note also that Carnap did not identify 'analytic' with 'determinate' for all languages, since the introduction of 'P-rules' might allow an extension of the notion of analyticity beyond determinacy (173). We discuss this presently.

12 It's worth remarking that in *Syntax*, Carnap did not regard P-rules or P-consequences as analytic. Analytic statements were confined to L-valid sentences, that is, sentences which either contain only logical expressions (as these are characterized in

section 50 of *Syntax*), or which are such that every sentence obtained by substituting descriptive signs for primitive descriptive signs is valid (1937, 181).

13 This is a simplification; Carnap's full definition treats the logical vocabulary as the
intersection of all those maximal classes of vocabulary such that everything say-
able in them is determinate (1937, 177–8). See Creath (1996) for a discussion of
this idea. As Creath shows, Carnap's proposal faces severe technical problems. For
our purposes here, what matters is the role that this characterization of the logical
vocabulary plays in a language-general characterization of 'analytic,' and the consequences of Carnap's later abandonment of these ideas.

14 Carnap (1937, 181–2). Again, the actual definition of 'L-valid' (which Carnap makes
synonymous with 'analytic' on p. 182) is more complicated.

15 Thus for example, if '&' and '~' are logical expressions, the sentence '~(p & ~p)'
is analytic. And if 'temperature' is a descriptive expression, the sentence 'The
volume of a gas increases proportionately to its temperature' is synthetic, because
it is *not* the case that the result of substituting 'temperature' in this sentence for
another descriptive expression ('red,' perhaps) is determinate. Note that there are
some analytic statements that do contain 'temperature' or any other descriptive
vocabulary, such as 'If this gas has a temperature, then this gas has a temperature.'
However, not *all* statements containing 'temperature' are analytic, which is why it
belongs to the descriptive vocabulary (*cf.* 1937, 180). Moreover, whether a particular
vocabulary item is logical or descriptive may change with changes to the rules of a
language (*cf.* ibid., 178–9).

16 It is not clear that Carnap would have found room for a distinction between there
being such facts and there being a way of finding out or establishing such facts.

17 See Ricketts (1996) and Friedman (1999) for a more detailed discussion of these
ideas.

18 The exact procedure here is again (very) complicated. Roughly, quasi-syntactical
sentences must be equipollent with certain L-truths, where two sentences are equipollent if they have the same sets of consequences, *cf.* (1937, 233–7), especially
Carnap's two examples, pp. 234–5.

19 Thus the formal correctness condition would allow us to say that, for any x, $C(x)$ iff
$\psi(x)$, where 'C' does not occur in 'ψ.' In his 'Semantic Conception of Truth,' Tarski
expressed this idea using a distinction between the object-language in terms for
which 'true' was defined, and the meta-language in which that definition was given.
The reason for his doing so will be discussed below, but the correctness condition
was thus expressed as the constraint that 'the meta-language [should] not contain
any undefined terms except . . . terms of the object-language; terms referring to the
form of the expressions of the object-language, and used in building names for these
expressions; and terms of logic. In particular, we desire *semantic terms* (referring to
the object-language) *to be introduced into the meta-language only by definition*' (351).

20 This point is easier to see if the object-language is a foreign language like German.
The sentence '"Dieser Tisch ist schwartz" is true iff this table is black' makes clear
that the sentence named on the left-hand side of the biconditional is not the same
as that used on the right-hand side to give its truth-condition.

21 Philosophers have subsequently proposed ways of representing the notion of truth
within a language. See, e.g., Martin and Woodruff (1975).

22 The resulting adequacy condition requires that a meta-language predicate is adequate for designation in an object-language if the meta-language's name for an object-language expression is a translation of that expression into the meta-language (ibid., 53–4). So for example, in a simple object-language in which the sign 'c' denotes what, in the meta-language, we would denote by the word 'Chicago,' then the adequacy condition for designation requires that it be true that any meta-language expression for the sign 'c' (such as: 'the constant sign "c"') designate what 'Chicago,' the meta-language's translation of the constant sign 'c', designates.

23 It is worth observing a distinction between Carnap's and Tarski's formal methods here. Carnap used the adequacy condition for truth to specify his object-languages; they are a component of the rules in terms of which sentences and their constituent expressions have a meaning. Tarski did not; for him the object-language was specified by means of 'translations' of object-language terms into the meta-language, without using the definition of truth, *cf.* Tarski (1944, 433 note 24).

24 The adequacy condition was simply the above-stated condition that, for any purported L-truth S_i in S, 'The sentence (in M) "S_i is true in S" is an L-implicate in M of the rules of S.'

25 Carnap's intent behind these examples has sometimes been understood as an attempt to give behavioral criteria for 'analytic' of the sort that Quine requested (as we discuss below). However, this is a misunderstanding. Carnap's seeming behavioral 'criteria' for 'analytic' are simply attempts to provide a 'pre-systematic' counterpart to the formally explicated notion. This explicated notion was not intended by Carnap to be a concept with empirical content. We discuss this point further in chapter 3.

26 There was also a second limitation in the notion of 'holding in every state-description in S_1.' Carnap explained 'holding' as follows:

> That a sentence holds in a state-description means, in non-technical terms, that it would be true if the state-description (that is, all sentences belonging to it) were true. A few examples will suffice to show the nature of these rules: (1) an atomic sentence holds in a given state-description if and only if it belongs to it; (2) ~S_i holds in a given state-description if and only if S_i does not hold in it . . . (9).

Now, to specify what it is for all the sentences of a state-description to be *true*, Carnap must define what it is for a sentence of a language to be true. At this point, Carnap's account reverts to the earlier account of truth given in *Introduction to Semantics*, and which we outlined above. By these methods, however, the notion of a sentence's being true in all state-descriptions in a given language S_1 rests on the rules defining truth in S_1. The notion of a sentence 'holding in every state-description' is not specifiable independently of the meta-language used to formulate the truth-conditions according to which state-descriptions 'hold.' As in *Introduction to Semantics*, Carnap still had to identify L-truths by enumerating the truth-rules that generate them, in the meta-language, on a language-by-language basis, and in a way that on further reflection does not seem to escape the circularity problem.

27 The idea of quasi-syntactical replacements for pseudo-object sentences also faced

a second problem in semantics, which is that there was no clear semantic notion correlate to that of a quasi-syntactical property. What semantical property of, say, designating *expressions* could be correlated with the things those expressions designate, such that sentences about that semantic property could replace sentences about the objects (purportedly) designated? The very idea scarcely makes sense. Moreover, designation becomes an acceptable semantic property for Carnap, as we have seen. So the idea that there could be 'quasi-semantical properties' akin to the 'quasi-syntactical properties' of the *Syntax* is not only implausible, it is unmotivated after Carnap accepts semantical notions like designation.

28 Carnap continued to maintain that statements like '"Five" designates a number' would prove within frameworks to be analytic on the grounds that linguistic rules would make 'Five is a number' and '"Five" designates five' analytic (ibid., 217). Note that following Carnap's earlier reasoning, this analyticity is only expressible in a meta-language.

29 We discuss the role and nature of these pragmatic benefits further in sections 4.5–4.6.

30 Much of the correspondence between Carnap and Quine, including their correspondence about analyticity, has been published in Carnap and Quine (1990), *cf.* also Quine (1991).

31 '[L]anguage, in its mathematical form, can be constructed according to the preferences of any one of the points of view represented; so that no question of justification arises at all, but only the question of the syntactical consequences to which one or other of the choices leads, including the question of non-contradiction.' (Carnap 1937, xv).

32 Indeed, by the time of 'Empiricism, Semantics, and Ontology,' Carnap had radicalized this idea to the point that he regarded questions about the adoption of linguistic frameworks to be entirely 'non-cognitive' in character (*cf.* Carnap 1956b, 214).

33 For a very thorough discussion and criticism of Quine's 'disquotational' theory of truth, see Marian David (1994).

3 Analyticity and Its Discontents

1 Philip Kitcher considers an example of a stipulated definition of 'acid,' and explicitly denies the warrant of the stipulation that one might have naturally thought is trivially true and warranted. By parity of reasoning, to the extent that 'frenchelor' does not play a useful explanatory role within empirical science, an assertion that frenchelors are French would be 'unwarranted' according to Kitcher, and Kitcher seems to think that there is no good reason to believe that it is true. See Kitcher (1983, 82ff.).

2 We noted in chapter 2, section 2.2.4, how a very similar view is first espoused by Carnap.

3 Some of Quine's defenders have claimed that Quine is justified in assuming his own naturalistic perspective in arguing against other philosophers. We will consider some of these arguments in chapter 4 section 4.5, and chapter 5 section 5.6.

4 See Glock (2003, 75) for a development of this objection to Quine.

5 That he had such a language-general definition requires that he had a way of avoiding incompleteness by appeal to a hierarchy of meta-languages.

6   See for instance Creath (2004), Friedman (1987, 1992), George (2000), Loomis (2006), O'Grady (1999), Richardson (1996, 1998), and Ricketts (1994). For a recent defense of Quine's criticism of Carnap, see Gregory (2003).

7   Elsewhere, Carnap proposed a similar test for the synonymy of two expressions, thereby apparently supporting the empirical acceptability of the notion of synonymy (Carnap 1956b, 237–40).

8   There is a third notion that might be called 'empirical content$_3$' or 'empirical virtue,' worth distinguishing from the other two. A concept is *empirically virtuous* in this sense just in case it is essential to successful applications of our best empirical theories. It seems to us that this third notion is what later disputes concerned. The fundamental argument against analyticity, on this construal, is that it is not 'empirically virtuous.'

9   This is a point is emphasized by Creath on Quine's behalf (Creath 2004, 50).

10   A paradigm case argument argues for the nonempty extension of a concept by appeal to a 'paradigm case' in which the concept purportedly applies. It is taken to be unintelligible to deny of a paradigm case of concept c that c applies to it.

11   Although this claim has been challenged; *cf.* De Rosa and Lepore (2004).

12   See Glock (2003, 90) for an attempted response to Putnam's example.

13   Richard Creath has made this point on Carnap's behalf (Creath 2004).

4 Analyticity and Ontology

1   Whether his view is best understood as a form of 'global instrumentalism' or instead as a form of 'realism' is an issue that we do not take a stand on here.

2   The Neurath boat analogy is misleading in some respects. For example, a boat, even one that we start with, floats on a given background, with an ocean and bits of flotsam in the vicinity. Quine and Carnap would both have taken the background itself to be variable, although for different reasons. Quine would have taken the entire ship+ocean+flotsam to be discovered via empirical research. Carnap would have taken some features of the ship+ocean+flotsam structure to be conventional, a result of optional choices of language. The Quinean perspective leads to questions concerning what the goal of scientific theory construction is. If there is no background against which to evaluate the goodness of ships, then it is unclear what makes one ship+ocean+flotsam proposal better than another.

3   For more thorough discussions of Quine's theory, see Orenstein (2002) and Hylton (2007).

4   We use 'theory' rather than 'theory/language,' but recall that Quine denies that there is a genuine distinction between theory and language.

5   There are other objections to the elimination of names in this way. One is that the notion 'Pegasizing' is only intelligible by appeal to the name from which is introduced. See, e.g., Glock (2003).

6   For more detailed discussions of this issue, see Kirk (1986), Glock (2003, chapter 6), and Hylton (2007, chapter 8).

7   Ken Gemes has raised an interesting objection to Quine's claim that there can be *incompatible* translation manuals that fit all linguistic behavior. Gemes argues that Quine's view concerning the equivalence of theories that agree on all observations

entails that any two translation manuals ('theories of translation') that make the same predictions concerning linguistic behavior should be taken to be equivalent rather than 'incompatible.' See Gemes (1991).

8 That there is an independent argument here has been highlighted by Hylton (2007, 220).

9 Quine's point here is different from the coherence problem that we noted is raised by Gemes (1991).

10 See Gemes (1991).

11 We argue in chapter 6 that analyticity does not require appeal to strict synonymy.

12 We return to the status of Quine's proposals concerning translation in chapter 6.

13 See Gemes (1991) for further discussion.

14 Glock (2003) argues at length for a similar conclusion that Quine presupposes rather than establishes many of his physicalistic and anti-intensionalist theses.

15 There is a very complicated and ongoing dispute concerning the reality of intensional entities or notions. For one notable exchange, see Katz (1974) and Harman's response (1976).

16 See, e.g., Atchinstein (2007).

17 The roots of this Quinean line of criticism may well lie in Carnap's treatment of physical languages in the *Syntax*, *cf.* our discussion at the end of section 2.2.4.

18 How Carnap thinks that mathematically undecidable mathematical statements were to be adjudicated is an interesting matter that we cannot go into here. For a discussion, see Beth (1963).

19 For further discussion, see Strawson (1963).

20 A careful comparison of our views is out of place in the present work, in which such ontological concerns are not the central ones, although they provide among the most potentially fruitful applications of the concept *analytic** that we introduce in chapter 6.

21 For another view that tries to distinguish different uses of quantifiers that are not ontologically committing, see Hofweber (2005).

22 We use 'C-basis facts' and 'non-C-basis facts' as an abbreviation here, even though advocates of the view may be reluctant to countenance facts, and furthermore the C-basis facts may be all the facts there are, and these C-basis facts are what 'make true' the true non-C-basis statements.

23 If we replace 'a priori entailments' with 'analytic* statements,' the view could be expressed as, all entities not logically entailed by the C-facts are pure or impure stipulata. See chapter 6 for further discussion.

24 As we noted in chapter 1, there is an alternative interpretation of Carnap's *Aufbau* according to which he is also agnostic about what the basis elements are. See Richardson (1998) for a defense of this interpretation.

25 Roughly speaking, the problem here was that Carnap supplied no explicit definition for the relation between a sensory quality and a space-time quadruple. As Quine put it, Carnap had provided

> no indication, not even the sketchiest, of how a statement of the form 'Quality *q* is at *x;y;z;t*' could ever be translated into Carnap's initial language of sense-data and logic. The connective 'is at' remains an added undefined connective; the canons [guiding the ascription of sensory qualities to space-time points] counsel us in its use but not in its elimination. (Quine 1953, 40)

In other words, at this basic level of his program Carnap had implicitly used a concept ('is at') that was introduced using 'canons' (such as maximizing accord with other experiences and minimizing change through time), which canons were different from the official criteria of explicit definition.

5 Analyticity and Epistemology

1 We will not digress here to go into the details of how such a Millian account would go. We mention it only to note that Ayer is aware of the view but rejects it as implausible, although not definitively refuted. For a more detailed criticism of Mill's position, *cf.* Frege (1974, 30ff.). On p. 38 Frege derisively refers to 'Mill's piles of pebbles and gingersnaps.'

2 BonJour raises this problem in his argument for rejecting Ayer's 'moderate empiricism.'

3 As we saw in chapter 1, Kant's containment criterion of analyticity provided a possible way of unifying the idea of misusing an expression with that of uttering a contradictory statement. Ayer, however, rejected Kant's account and insisted that the containment criterion ought to be distinguished from the contradictoriness criterion (LTL, 77f.). Hence, Ayer could not appeal to Kant to help his position here.

4 We provide a survey of conventionalism in the logical positivist movement in Juhl and Loomis (2006). For more detailed analyses of conventionalism in logical positivism, see Friedman (1999), Creath (1992), and Baker (1988). As Friedman points out (1999, 67), much of the 'conventionalism' in early positivists like Schlick and Poincaré was more akin to Duhemian, or even Quinean, holism than it was a developed theory of a priori knowledge by stipulation.

5 This qualification is introduced because in certain 'Kripke style' cases of 'a priori contingent' statements, the apriority or empirical indefeasibility of the two propositions comes apart. We introduce such cases in section 5.7 below, and discuss them further in chapter 6.

6 We note that even this evidence might be taken as irrelevant in some situations, such as one in which I choose to employ some convention independently of whether others have adopted it. But things can get complicated enough on these fronts, and there are many possible different imaginable cases, that we will grant that some empirical evidence concerning linguistic usage might count for or against the truth of the stipulation that is in fact taken to govern *frenchelor*.

7 We discuss this issue as it pertains to mathematics in chapter 6.

8 Actually, it is arguable that 'satisfaction' was indeed introduced stipulatively by Tarski via a simple recursive definition, connected to truth in accord with his stipulations (*cf.* Tarski 1944, 353). What other source do we have for our grasp of the technical semantic notion *satisfaction*?

9 There is a substantial literature surrounding Quine's naturalized epistemology. Somewhat sympathetic reconstructions or extensions of his view include Kitcher (1992), Hookway (1988, 1994), Bishop and Trout (2004), Kornblith (2005). Orenstein (2002), and Hylton (2007). For more critical discussions, see Sosa (1983), Fogelin (2004), Kim (1998), and Glock (2003).

10 If we instead interpret Quine as eliminating the notion of justification from

epistemology, it is unclear how to make sense of the question of whether theory 'transcends' evidence. Quine has not provided any causal substitute for justification relations or logical entailment relations that would give sense to the question.

11 Another recent attempt to defend Quine against the charge of circularity here is provided by Hylton (*cf.* 2007, chapter 4). Hylton's argument, we think, is similar to Schuldenfrei's in that Hylton regards the increased explanatory power of Quine's position as justifying Quine's adoption of a particular conception of science (83).

12 See Loomis (1999).

13 We add scare-quotes to 'the' because we will presently recount a possible objection to the Kripkean presupposition that there is a single thing that is both a priori and contingent in this sort of case.

14 For very detailed discussions see, e.g., Soames (2002) and Salmon (2005).

15 See, e.g. Chalmers (2006) for an illuminating overview of varieties of two-dimensionalism. For harsh criticisms of at least some forms of two-dimensionalism see Soames (2004). For sympathizers see Jackson (1998) and Chalmers (2006).

6 Analyticity Repositioned

1 Harman nowhere notes this Quinean acceptance of abbreviative stipulation in 'Quine on Meaning and Existence I,' for example. His arguments do not provide for such an exception. Lycan, in his 'Definition in a Quinean World' (1991), considers the possibility of providing a Quinean way of accommodating such abbreviative stipulation, and his discussion ends in pessimism.

2 Although we have our own local employments intended for present purposes, we think that our uses of the terms will correspond reasonably well with what many philosophers have meant by the terms.

3 We have not seen any satisfying account of the notion *sentence*. Most frequently, the set of sentences of some artificial language are 'defined' by rules of syntactic construction. For present purposes we take the notion to be understood, and understood in such a way that characterizing something as a sentence does not fix the norms governing its conventional uses.

4 For a helpful overview, see Chalmers (2006).

5 We are not distinguishing between 'speaker meaning' and 'conventional meaning' for present general purposes. We are considering the 'best' or 'ideal' case in which everyone shares a common understanding of the proceedings.

6 This is as opposed to empirical questions of the form, 'is S a good English translation of R?', which might appeal to such principles, taken as already given in the background, together with empirical data for answers.

7 Interestingly, Harman seems to agree with us that some 'semantic' questions seem to be answerable only 'arbitrarily.' See his discussion of the twin-Earth cases in which an Earthling travels to twin-Earth and the question when her word 'water' begins to refer to XYZ (Harman 1999, 221).

8 For a description of such conventions and beliefs in the context of simple examples of conventions, see David Lewis (1969).

9 We think that many of the claims concerning meanings or synonymies can be paraphrased in similar ways by appeal to principles of good translation, and will

frequently take this for granted in other discussions to avoid excessive repetition and to facilitate brevity.

10 Thus for instance, Schlick claimed that 'The principles of identity, contradiction and excluded middle say nothing at all about the behavior of reality. They simply regulate how we designate the real' (1985, 337). Similar ideas appear in Wittgenstein's later writings (see e.g. Wittgenstein 1994, part I sections 117ff.). We think that our treatment of analyticity* statements as true in virtue of the way they are treated by a linguistic community is broadly similar.

11 It can entail this via standard moves from claims stated in a meta-language to claims within the shared language (see e.g. G. Russell 2008, 198) and 'tacit disquotational principles.'

12 See Kitcher's (1983) chapter on 'conceptualism,' pp. 82ff. Kitcher is not alone in his sympathy for this Quinean perspective, but he provides a paradigm case.

13 See Juhl (forthcoming).

14 For reasons given above, we agree with Quine that meanings do not explain truth or justification in any but a very attenuated and somewhat misleading sense. See also our discussion of G. Russell's approach in section 6.7.

15 For one example of a proponent of this approach, see Glock (2003).

16 G. Russell (2008, 203–7) is a discussion of problems pertaining to appeals to linguistic competence. Williamson (2007, 73–133 (chapter 4)) is a sophisticated and detailed argument against appeals to linguistic competence in accounts of analyticity.

17 We refer readers to Russell's nicely written and very clear book for details of her view (Russell 2008).

18 We are broadly sympathetic with the view that G. Russell seems to have that Quinean arguments against meanings are not persuasive, and so they should largely be ignored in constructing a notion of 'analytic.' Nevertheless, we fear that many Quineans would be liable to take much of what she says as question-begging. We say more about this below, when we consider some examples.

19 Resnik (1997) develops a sophisticated version of Quinean empiricism concerning mathematics. Colyvan (2003) argues for a Quinean view by appeal to various indispensability arguments and by undermining a 'causal' requirement on theoretical posits. Kitcher (1983) is a sophisticated defense of a view that is not straightforwardly Quinean, but is sympathetic to much of Quine's empiricism and 'naturalism.'

20 We also discuss Putnam's 'one-criterion' view in section 3.8.

21 We don't deny that there is such a thing as 'recreational mathematics,' but we deny that what mathematicians would call 'recreational' has anything to do with what Quineans need to treat as 'recreational,' namely, the as yet unapplied and thus (purportedly) 'unjustified' branches.

22 See e.g. BonJour (1998), Pust (2000), and many works by George Bealer, including 'A Priori Knowledge and the Scope of Philosophy,' in Casullo (1999).

23 We here leave aside the further question whether stipulations, and hence axioms, are justified or not, for recall that our account is neutral about whether or not analytic* (and by extension t-analytic) statements have some justification that supports their adoption.

24 The absence of empirical premises is the essential feature of 'canonical' justifications of mathematical statements. So even, for example, Gödel's theorems do not show that there are non-canonical justifications of mathematical statements in our sense of 'canonical.'

25 The interesting case of 'empirical' primality testing is a prima facie counterexample, but a closer look shows that even in such cases we think that the empirical evidence is evidence of the existence of a first-order proof of primality or non-primality. This holds even if as a matter of empirical fact, the only human access to the primality of some number K is via some 'empirical' data of this sort. See the glossary for a brief description of primality testing using random processes, and how empirical premises are involved.

26 See Juhl (forthcoming) for further discussion.

27 See Lewis (2001) for a classic discussion of possible worlds as causally isolated universes.

28 Although Quine's use of physics in defending the indeterminacy of translation thesis *is* arguably central; see section 4.5.

BIBLIOGRAPHY

Atchinstein, Peter. 2007. 'Atom's Empirical Eve: Methodological Disputes and How to Evaluate Them,' *Perspectives on Science* 15, 3, pp. 359–90.

Awody, S. and Carus, A. W. 2001. 'Carnap, Completeness, and Categoricity,' *Erkenntnis* 54, pp. 145–72.

Ayer, Alfred J., ed. 1959. *Logical Positivism*. New York: Free Press.

———. 1946. *Language, Truth and Logic*. New York: Dover Publications.

Azzouni, Jody. 2004. *Deflating Existential Consequence: A Case for Nominalism*. Oxford: Oxford University Press.

———. 2000. *Knowledge and Reference in Empirical Science*. New York: Routledge.

———. 1994. *Metaphysical Myths, Mathematical Practice: The Ontology and Epistemology of the Exact Sciences*. Cambridge: Cambridge University Press.

Baker, Gordon P. 1988. *Wittgenstein, Frege and the Vienna Circle*. Oxford: Basil Blackwell.

Baker, G. P. and Hacker, P. M. S. 1985. *Wittgenstein: Rules, Grammar and Necessity. Volume 2 of an Analytical Commentary on the Philosophical Investigations*. Oxford: Basil Blackwell.

Balaguer, Mark. 1998. *Platonism and Anti-Platonism in Mathematics*. New York: Oxford University Press.

Bealer, George. 1999. 'A Priori Knowledge and the Scope of Philosophy,' in Albert Casullo, ed., *A Priori Knowledge*, Aldershot: Ashgate, pp. 123–45.

Berström, Lars. 1993. 'Quine on Underdetermination,' in R. Bartlett and R. Gibson, eds., *Perspectives on Quine*. Oxford: Blackwell, pp. 38–52.

Berström, Lars and Føllesdall, Dagfinn. 1994. 'Interview with Willard Van Orman Quine in November 1993,' *Theoria* 60, pp. 226–31.

Beth, E. W. 1963. 'Carnap's Views on the Advantages of Constructed Systems over Natural Languages in the Philosophy of Science,' in P. A. Schilpp, ed., *The Philosophy of Rudolph Carnap*. La Salle, IL: Open Court, pp. 469–502.

Bishop, Michael A. and Trout, J. D. 2004. *Epistemology and the Psychology of Human Judgment*. New York: Oxford.

Boghossian, Paul. 1996. 'Analyticity Reconsidered,' *Nous* 30, 3, pp. 360–91.

Bohnert, H. G. 1986. 'Quine on Analyticity,' in L. E. Hahn and P. A. Schilpp, eds., *The Philosophy of W. V. Quine*. La Salle, IL: Open Court, pp. 77–95.

BonJour, Laurence. 1998. *In Defense of Pure Reason*. Cambridge: Cambridge University Press.

Bolzano, Bernard. 1973. *Theory of Science*, translated from the German by B. Terrell. Dordrecht: D. Reidel.

Burge, Tyler. 1992. 'Philosophy of Language and Mind 1950–90,' *Philosophical Review* 101, 1, pp. 3–51.

Carnap, Rudolf. 1995. *The Unity of Science*, translated by Max Black. London: Thoemmes Press.

———. 1987. 'On Protocol Sentences,' translated by Richard Creath, *Nous* 21, 4, pp. 457–70.

———. 1967. *The Logical Structure of the World and Pseudoproblems in Philosophy*. Second edition, translated by Rolf A. George. Berkeley: University of California Press.

———. 1964. 'The Logicist Foundations of Mathematics,' in *Philosophy of Mathematics: Selected Readings*, edited by P. Benacerraf and H. Putnam. Englewood Cliffs, NJ: Prentice Hall, pp. 31–41.

———. 1963. *The Philosophy of Rudolph Carnap*, edited by Paul Arthur Schilpp. La Salle, IL: Open Court.

———. 1963a. 'E. W. Beth on Constructed Language Systems,' in P. A. Schilpp, ed., *The Philosophy of Rudolph Carnap*. La Salle, IL: Open Court, pp. 927–33.

———. 1963b. 'Intellectual Autobiography,' in P. A. Schilpp, ed., *The Philosophy of Rudolph Carnap*. La Salle, IL: Open Court, pp. 3–84.

———. 1963c. 'Quine on Logical Truth,' in P. A. Schilpp, ed., *The Philosophy of Rudolph Carnap*. La Salle, IL: Open Court, pp. 915–22.

———. 1959. 'The Elimination of Metaphysics through the Logical Analysis of Language,' in *Logical Positivism*, edited by A. J. Ayer, translated by A. Pap. New York: Free Press, pp. 60–81.

———. 1956. *Meaning and Necessity, A Study in Semantics and Modal Logic*. Enlarged edition, Chicago: University of Chicago Press.

———. 1956a 'Empiricism, Semantics, and Ontology,' in *Meaning and Necessity, A Study in Semantics and Modal Logic*. Enlarged edition, pp. 205–21.

———. 1956b. 'Meaning and Synonymy in Natural Languages,' in *Meaning and Necessity, A Study in Semantics and Modal Logic*. Enlarged edition, pp. 233–47.

———. 1950. *Logical Foundations of Probability*. Chicago: University of Chicago Press.

———. 1949. 'Truth and Confirmation,' in H. Feigl and W. Sellars, eds., *Readings in Philosophical Analysis*. New York: Appleton-Century-Crofts, pp. 119–27.

———. 1942. *Introduction to Semantics and Formalization of Logic*. Cambridge, MA: Harvard University Press.

———. 1938. 'Foundations of Logic and Mathematics,' in *International Encyclopedia of Unified Science*, edited by Otto Neurath, Rudolf Carnap, and Charles Morris. Chicago, IL: University of Chicago Press, pp. 42–61

———. 1937. *The Logical Syntax of Language*. London: Routledge and Kegan Paul.

———. 1930. 'Die Mathematik als Zweig der Logik,' *Blätter für deutsche Philosophie: Zeitschrift der Deutschen Philosophischen Gesellschaft* 4, pp. 298–310.

———. 1927. 'Eigentliche und Uneigentliche Begriffe,' *Symposion* 1, pp. 355–74.

Carnap, R. and Quine, W. V. 1990. *Dear Carnap, Dear Van: The Quine–Carnap Correspondence and Related Work*, edited by Richard Creath. Berkeley: University of California Press.

Carus, A. W. 1999. 'Carnap, Syntax, and Truth,' in J. Peregrin, ed., *Truth and Its Nature (If Any)*. Dordrecht: Kluwer Academic Publishers, pp. 15–35.

Casullo, Albert. 2003. *A Priori Justification*. Oxford: Oxford University Press.

———. ed. 1999. *A Priori Knowledge*. Aldershot: Ashgate.

Chalmers, David. 2008. 'From the *Aufbau* to the Canberra Plan,' available at <consc.net/papers/aufbau.ppt>.

———. 2007. 'Ontological Anti-Realism,' in David Chalmers, David Manley, and Ryan Wasserman, eds., *Metametaphysics: New Essays on the Foundations of Ontology*. Oxford: Oxford University Press, 77–129.

———. 2006. 'Two-Dimensional Semantics,' in Ernie Lepore and Barry Smith, eds., *The Oxford Handbook of Philosophy of Language*. New York: Oxford University Press, 574–606.

Chomsky, Noam. 1975. 'Quine's Empirical Assumptions,' in D. Davidson and J. Hintikka, eds., *Words and Objections: Essays on the Work of W. V. Quine*. Boston, MA: D. Reidel.

Coffa, Alberto. 1991. *The Semantic Tradition from Kant to Carnap: To the Vienna Station*, edited by L. Wessels. Cambridge: Cambridge University Press.

———. 1987. 'Carnap, Tarski and the Search for Truth,' *Nous* 21, pp. 547–72.

Colyvan, Mark. 2003. *The Indispensability of Mathematics*. Oxford: Oxford University Press.

Crane, Tim. 2003. 'Review of *In Defense of Pure Reason: A Rationalist Account of A Priori Justification*,' *Mind* 112, 447.

Creath, Richard. 2004. 'Quine on the Intelligibility and Relevance of Analyticity,' in Roger Gibson, ed., *The Cambridge Companion to Quine*. Cambridge: Cambridge University Press, pp. 4–199.

———. 1996. 'Languages without Logic,' in R. N. Giere and A. W. Richardson, eds., *Origins of Logical Empiricism*. Minneapolis: University of Minnesota Press, pp. 251–65.

———. 1992. 'Carnap's Conventionalism,' *Synthese* 93, pp. 141–65.

———. 1991. 'Every Dogma Has Its Day,' *Erkenntnis* 35, pp. 347–89.

———. 1990. 'The Unimportance of Semantics,' in *PSA 1990*, volume 2, edited by A. Fine, M. Forbes, and L. Wessels. East Lansing, MI: Philosophy of Science Association, pp. 405–15.

David, Marian. 1994. *Correspondence and Disquotation: An Essay on the Nature of Truth*. Oxford: Oxford University Press.

Davidson, Donald. 1984. *Inquiries into Truth and Interpretation*. Oxford: Clarendon Press.

Davidson, Donald and Hintikka, Jaakko, eds. 1975. *Words and Objections: Essays on the Work of W. V. Quine*. Boston, MA: D. Reidel.

DeJong, Willem R. 1995. 'Kant's Analytic Judgments and the Traditional Theory of Concepts,' *Journal of History of Philosophy* 33, 4, pp. 613–41.

De Rosa, Raffaella and Lepore, Ernest. 2004. 'Quine's Meaning Holisms,' in Roger Gibson, ed., *The Cambridge Companion to Quine*. Cambridge: Cambridge University Press, pp. 181–99.

Dicker, Georges. 1998. *Hume's Epistemology and Metaphysics*. London: Routledge.

Duhem, Pierre. 1954. *The Aim and Structure of Physical Theory*, translated by Philip P. Wiener. Princeton, NJ: Princeton University Press.

Dummett, Michael. 1991. *The Logical Basis of Metaphysics*. Cambridge, MA: Harvard University Press.

———. 1981. *Frege: Philosophy of Language*. Second edition. Cambridge, MA: Harvard University Press.

Ebbs, Gary. 1997. *Rule-Following and Realism*. Cambridge, MA: Harvard University Press.

Evans, Gareth. 1985. *Collected Papers*. Oxford: Oxford University Press.

Fogelin, Robert J. 2004. 'Aspects of Quine's Naturalized Epistemology,' in Roger Gibson, ed., *The Cambridge Companion to Quine*, Cambridge: Cambridge University Press, pp. 19–46.

Foley, R. 1994. 'Quine and Naturalized Epistemology,' in *Midwest Studies in Philosophy Vol. XIX*. Notre Dame, IN: University of Notre Dame Press, pp. 243–60.

Follesdal, D. 1986. 'Essentialism and Reference,' in L. E. Hahn and P. A. Schilpp, eds., *The Philosophy of W. V. Quine*. La Salle, IL: Open Court, pp. 93–5.

Franzen, Torkel. 2005. *Gödel's Theorem: An Incomplete Guide to Its Use and Abuse*. Wellesley, MA: A. K. Peters.

Frege, Gottlob. 1974. *The Foundations of Arithmetic: A Logico-Mathematical Inquiry into the Concept of Number*, translated from the German by J. L. Austin. Oxford: Blackwell.

——. 1972. *On Conceptual Notation and Related Articles*, translated by T. W. Bynum. Oxford: Clarendon Press.

——. 1971. *On the Foundations of Geometry and Formal Theories of Arithmetic*, translated from the German by E. H. W. Kluge. London: Yale University Press.

——. 1964. *The Basic Laws of Arithmetic*, translated by M. Furth. Berkeley: University of California Press.

Friedman, Michael, ed. 1999. *Reconsidering Logical Positivism*. Cambridge: Cambridge University Press.

——. 1992. 'Epistemology in the *Aufbau*,' *Synthese* 93, pp. 15–57.

——. 1992a. *Kant and the Exact Sciences*. Cambridge, MA: Harvard University Press.

——. 1987. 'Carnap's *Aufbau* Reconsidered,' *Nous* 21, pp. 521–45.

Geach, Peter. 1951. 'Symposium: On What There Is, Part I,' *Proceedings of the Aristotelian Society* 25, pp. 125–36.

Gemes, Kenneth. 1991. 'The Indeterminacy Thesis Reformulated,' *Journal of Philosophy* 91, pp. 91–108.

Gentzen, Gerhard. 1969. *The Collected Papers of Gerhard Gentzen*. Amsterdam: North-Holland.

George, Alexander. 2000. 'On Washing the Fur without Wetting It: Quine, Carnap, and Analyticity,' *Mind* 109, 433, pp. 1–24.

Gibson, Roger F., ed. 2004. *The Cambridge Companion to Quine*. Cambridge: Cambridge University Press.

——. 2004a. 'Quine's Behaviorism cum Empiricism,' in Gibson, ed., *The Cambridge Companion to Quine*, pp. 181–99.

——. 1988. *Enlightened Empiricism: An Examination of W. V. Quine's Theory of Knowledge*. Gainesville: University Press of Florida.

Glock, H. J. 2008. *What is Analytic Philosophy?* Cambridge: Cambridge University Press.

——. 2003. *Quine and Davidson on Thought, Language and Reality*. Cambridge: Cambridge University Press.

——. 1992. 'Wittgenstein vs. Quine on Logical Necessity,' in S. Teghrarian, ed., *Wittgenstein and Contemporary Philosophy*. Bristol, Thoemmes Press, pp. 154–86.

Gödel, Kurt. 1967. 'On Formally Undecidable Propositions of *Principia Mathematica* and Related Systems,' in Jean van Heijenoort, ed., *From Frege to Gödel: A Source Book in Mathematical Logic, 1897–1931*, Cambridge, MA: Harvard University Press, pp. 592–619.

Goldfarb, Warren. 1996. 'The Philosophy of Mathematics in Early Postivism,' in R. N. Giere and A. W. Richardson, eds., *Origins of Logical Empiricism*. Minneapolis: University of Minnesota Press, pp. 213–30.

——. 1995. 'Introductory Note to *1953/9,' in *Kurt Gödel: Collected Works, volume III*, edited by Solomon Feferman. Oxford: Oxford University Press, pp. 324–34.

——. 1979. 'Logic in the Twenties: The Nature of the Quantifier,' *Journal of Symbolic Logic* 44, 3, pp. 351–68.

Goldman, A. 1994. 'Naturalistic Epistemology and Reliabilism,' in *Midwest Studies in Philosophy XIX*, edited by Peter A. French et al. Notre Dame, IN: University of Notre Dame Press, pp. 301–20.

Gregory, Paul A. 2003. '"Two Dogmas" – All Bark and No Bite? Carnap and Quine on Analyticity,' *Philosophy and Phenomenological Research* 68, 3, pp. 633–48.

Grice, H. Paul and Strawson, Peter F. 1956. 'In Defense of a Dogma,' *The Philosophical Review* 65, pp. 141–58.

Gupta, Anil. 2006. *Empiricism and Experience*. Oxford: Oxford University Press.

Guyer, Paul, ed. 1992. *The Cambridge Companion to Kant*. Cambridge: Cambridge University Press.

Haack, Susan. 1977. 'Carnap's *Aufbau*: Some Kantian Reflections,' *Ratio* 19, pp. 170–5.

Hacker, P. M. S. 1996. *Wittgenstein's Place in Twentieth-Century Analytic Philosophy*. Oxford: Blackwell.

Hahn, L. E. and Schilpp, P. A., eds. 1986. *The Philosophy of W. V. Quine*. La Salle, IL: Open Court.

Hale, Bob. 1987. *Abstract Objects*. Oxford: Blackwell.

Hanfling, Oswald. 2000. *Philosophy and Ordinary Language: The Bent and Genius of Our Tongue*. London: Routledge.

Harman, Gilbert. 1999. '(Nonsolipsistic) Conceptual Role Semantics,' in *Reasoning, Meaning, and Mind*. New York: Oxford, pp. 206–34.

——. 1996. 'Analyticity Regained?' *Nous* 30, 3, pp. 392–400.

——. 1976. 'Katz' Credo,' *Synthese* 32, pp. 387–94.

——. 1973. *Thought*. Princeton, NJ: Princeton University Press.

——. 1972. *Semantics of Natural Language*. Dordrecht: D. Reidel.

——. 1967. 'Quine on Meaning and Existence I,' *Review of Metaphysics* 21, pp. 124–51.

——. 1967a. 'Quine on Meaning and Existence II,' *Review of Metaphysics* 21, pp. 343–67.

Hilbert, David. 1971. 'Hilbert's Reply to Frege,' in *On the Foundations of Geometry and Formal Theories of Arithmetic*, edited by E. H. W. Kluge. New Haven, CT: Yale University Press, pp. 10–14.

——. 1927. 'The Foundations of Mathematics,' in Jean van Heijenoort, ed., *From Frege to Gödel: A Source Book in Mathematical Logic, 1897–1931*, Cambridge, MA: Harvard University Press, pp. 464–79.

Hintikka, Jaakko. 1974. *Knowledge and the Known: Historical Perspectives in Epistemology*. Dordrecht: D. Reidel.

Hirsch, Eli. 2005. 'Physical-Object Ontology, Verbal Disputes, and Common Sense,' *Philosophy and Phenomenological Research*, 70, 1, pp. 67–97.

Hofweber, Thomas. 2005. 'A Puzzle about Ontology,' *Nous* 39, pp. 256–83.

Hookway, Christopher. 1994. 'Naturalized Epistemology and Epistemic Evaluation,' *Inquiry* 37, pp. 465–85.

——. 1988. *Quine: Language, Experience and Reality*. Stanford, CA: Stanford University Press.

Hudson, Robert G. 1994. 'Empirical Constraints in the *Aufbau*,' *History of Philosophy Quarterly* 11, pp. 237–51.

Hume, David. 1988. *An Inquiry Concerning Human Understanding and Concerning the Principles of Morals*. Oxford: Clarendon Press.

Hylton, Peter. 2007. *Quine*. New York: Routledge.

———. 1993. 'Quine's Naturalism,' in *Midwest Studies in Philosophy XIX*. Notre Dame, IN: Notre Dame University Press, pp. 261–82.

———. 1990. *Russell, Idealism and the Emergence of Analytic Philosophy*. Oxford: Clarendon Press.

Jackson, Frank. 1998. *From Metaphysics to Ethics*. Oxford: Oxford University Press.

Juhl, Cory F. Forthcoming. 'Pure and Impure Stipulata,' *Philosophy and Phenomenological Research*. Vol. 79, no. 3.

Juhl, Cory F. and Loomis, Eric J. 2006. 'Conventionalism,' in S. Sarkar and J. Pfeifer, eds., *The Routledge Encyclopedia of the Philosophy of Science*. New York: Routledge, 168–77.

Kahneman, D., Tversky, A., and Slovic, Paul, eds. 1982. *Judgment under Uncertainty: Heuristics and Biases*. Cambridge: Cambridge University Press.

Kant, Immanuel. 1974. *Logic*, translated from the German by R. S. Harriman and W. Schwartz. Indianapolis: Bobbs-Merrill.

———. 1965. *Critique of Pure Reason*, translated from the German by N. K. Smith. New York: St. Martin's Press.

Katz, Jerrold. 1974. 'Where Things now Stand with the Analytic–Synthetic Distinction,' *Synthese* 28, 3/4, p. 283.

Kim, J. 1988. 'What is "Naturalized Epistemology"?' in J. E. Tomberlin, ed., *Philosophical Perspectives*, vol. 2. Atascadero, CA: Ridgeview, pp. 381–405.

Kirk, Robert. 1986. *Translation Determined*. Oxford: Oxford University Press.

Kitcher, Philip. 1992. 'The Naturalists Return,' *The Philosophical Review* 101, 1, pp. 53–115.

———. 1983. *The Nature of Mathematical Knowledge*. Oxford: Oxford University Press.

Kneale, Stephen. 2000. 'On a Milestone of Empiricism,' in *Knowledge, Language and Logic*, edited by A. Orenstine and P. Kotatke, London: Academic Publishers, pp. 237–344.

Kornblith, Hilary. 2005. *Knowledge and Its Place in Nature*, Oxford.

———. 1994. *Naturalizing Epistemology*. Second edition. Cambridge, MA: MIT Press.

Kripke, Saul. 1980. *Naming and Necessity*. Cambridge, MA: Harvard University Press.

Lavers, Gregory. 2004. 'Carnap, Semantics and Ontology,' *Erkenntnis* 60, pp. 295–316.

Leibniz, Gottfried W. F. 1981. *New Essays Concerning Human Understanding*, translated from the German by P. Remnant and J. Bennett. New York: Cambridge University Press.

Lewis, David. 2006. 'Empirical Equivalence in the Quine–Carnap Debate,' *Pacific Philosophical Quarterly* 87, pp. 499–508.

———. 2001. *On the Plurality of Worlds*. Oxford: Blackwell.

———. 1969. *Convention: A Philosophical Study*. Oxford: Blackwell.

Loomis, Eric J. 2006. 'Empirical Equivalence in the Quine–Carnap Debate,' *Pacific Philosophical Quarterly* 87, pp. 499–508.

———. 1999. 'Necessity, the *A Priori* and the Standard Meter,' *Synthese* 121, 3, pp. 291–307.

Lycan, William. 1991. 'Definition in a Quinean World,' in J. Fetzer, D. Shatz, and G. Schlesinger, eds., *Definitions and Definability: Philosophical Perspectives*. Dordrecht: Kluwer Academic Publishers, pp. 111–31.

Martin, R. M. 1963. 'On Carnap's Conception of Semantics,' in P. A. Schilpp, ed., *The Philosophy of Rudolf Carnap*. La Salle, IL: Open Court, pp. 351–84.

———. 1952. 'On "Analytic".' *Philosophical Studies* 3, pp. 65–73.

Martin, R. M. and Woodruff, P. 1975. 'On Representing "True-in-L" in L,' *Philosophia* 5, pp. 217–21.

Mates, Benson. 1951. 'Analytic Sentences,' *Philosophical Review* 60, pp. 525–34.

Meeker, Kevin. 2007. 'Hume on Knowledge, Certainty, and Probability: Anticipating the Disintegration of the Analytic–Synthetic Divide?' *Pacific Philosophical Quarterly* 88, pp. 226–42.

Mellor, D. H. 1995. *The Facts of Causation.* London: Routledge.

Millikan, Ruth. G. 1984. *Language, Thought, and Other Biological Categories.* Cambridge, MA: MIT Press.

Nagel, Ernest. 1961. *The Structure of Science: Problems in the Logic of Scientific Explanation.* New York: Harcourt, Brace and World.

Nagel, Ernest and Newman, James R. 2001. *Gödel's Proof.* Revised edition. New York: NYU Press.

Neurath, Otto. 1983. *Philosophical Papers 1913–1946*, edited by R. S. Cohen and M. Neurath. Dordrecht: D. Reidel.

O'Grady, Paul. 1999. 'Carnap and Two Dogmas of Empiricism,' *Philosophy and Phenomenological Research* 59, 4, pp. 1015–27.

Oberdan, Thomas. 1992. 'The Concept of Truth in Carnap's *Logical Syntax of Language*,' *Synthese* 93, pp. 239–60.

Orenstein, Alex. 2002. *W. V. Quine.* Princeton, NJ: Princeton University Press.

Pap, Arthur. 1958. *Semantics and Necessary Truth: An Inquiry into the Foundations of Analytic Philosophy.* New Haven, CT: Yale University Press.

Perry, J. 1979. 'The Problem of the Essential Indexical,' *Nous* 13, pp. 3–21.

Priest, Graham. 2008. *Doubt Truth to be a Liar.* Oxford: Oxford University Press.

———. 2006. *In Contradiction: A Study of the Transconsistent.* Oxford: Oxford University Press.

Proops, Ian. 2005. 'Kant's Conception of Analytic Judgment,' *Philosophy and Phenomenological Research* 70, 3, pp. 588–612.

Proust, Joelle. 1989. *Questions of Form: Logic and the Analytic Proposition from Kant to Carnap*, translated by Anastasios A. Brenner. Minneapolis: University of Minnesota Press.

Psillos, S. 2000. 'Rudolf Carnap's "Theoretical Concepts in Science",' *Studies in the History and Philosophy of Science* 31, 1, pp. 151–72.

Pust, Joel. 2000. *Intuitions as Evidence.* London: Routledge.

Putnam, Hilary. 1988. *Representation and Reality.* Cambridge, MA: MIT Press.

———. 1983. '"Two Dogmas" Revisited,' in *Philosophical Papers III: Realism and Reason.* Cambridge: Cambridge University Press, pp. 87–97.

———. 1981. *Reason, Truth and History.* Cambridge: Cambridge University Press.

———. 1979. *Philosophical Papers I: Mathematics, Matter and Method.* Cambridge University Press.

———. 1975. *Philosophical Papers II: Mind, Language, and Reality.* Cambridge: Cambridge University Press.

Quine, Willard Van Orman. 1998. *From Stimulus to Science.* Cambridge, MA: Harvard University Press.

———. 1994. 'Response to Dreben,' *Inquiry* 37, pp. 500–1.

———. 1993. 'In Praise of Observation Sentences,' *Journal of Philosophy* 90, pp. 107–16.

———. 1991. '"Two Dogmas" in Retrospect,' *Canadian Journal of Philosophy* 21, 3, pp. 265–74.

———. 1990. *Pursuit of Truth.* Cambridge, MA: Harvard University Press.

———. 1986. 'Autobiography of W. V. Quine' in L. E. Hahn and P. A. Schilpp, eds., *The Philosophy of W. V. Quine.* La Salle, IL: Open Court, pp. 3–46.

———. 1986a. 'Reply to Herbert G. Bohnhert,' in L. E. Hahn and P. A. Schilpp, eds., *The Philosophy of W. V. Quine.* La Salle, IL: Open Court, pp. 93–5.

——. 1986b. *Philosophy of Logic*. Second edition. Cambridge, MA: Harvard University Press.

——. 1986c. 'Reply to Geoffrey Hellman' in L. E. Hahn and P. A. Schilpp, eds., *The Philosophy of W. V. Quine*. La Salle, IL: Open Court, pp. 206–8.

——. 1981. *Theories and Things*. Cambridge, MA: Belknap Press of Harvard University Press.

——. 1980. *From a Logical Point of View*. Second edition, revised with a new Foreword by the author. Cambridge, MA: Harvard University Press.

——. 1975. 'To Chomsky,' in D. Davidson and J. Hintikka, eds., *Words and Objections: Essays on the Work of W. V. Quine*. Boston, MA: D. Reidel, pp. 302–11.

——. 1973. *The Roots of Reference*. La Salle, IL: Open Court.

——. 1970. 'On the Reasons for the Indeterminacy of Translation,' *Journal of Philosophy* 67, 6, pp. 178–83.

——. 1970a. 'Philosophical Progress in Language Theory,' *Metaphilosophy* 1, 1, pp. 2–19.

——. 1969. *Ontological Relativity and Other Essays*. New York: Columbia University Press.

——. 1969a. 'Epistemology Naturalized,' in *Ontological Relativity and Other Essays*. New York: Columbia University Press, pp. 69–90.

——. 1969b. 'Ontological Relativity' in *Ontological Relativity and Other Essays*. New York: Columbia University Press, pp. 26–68.

——. 1966. *Ways of Paradox and Other Essays*. New York: Random House.

——. 1966a. 'Truth by Convention,' in *Ways of Paradox and Other Essays*, pp. 70–99.

——. 1963. 'Carnap and Logical Truth,' in P. A. Schilpp, ed., *The Philosophy of Rudolph Carnap*. La Salle, IL: Open Court, pp. 385–406.

——. 1960. *Word and Object*. Cambridge, MA: MIT Press.

——. 1953. *From a Logical Point of View*. Cambridge, MA: Harvard University Press.

——. 1953. 'Two Dogmas of Empiricism,' in *From a Logical Point of View*. Cambridge, MA: Harvard University Press, pp. 21–46.

——. 1953a. 'On What There Is,' in *From a Logical Point of View*. Cambridge, MA: Harvard University Press, pp. 1–19.

——. 1953b 'Reference and Modality,' in *From a Logical Point of View*. Cambridge, MA: Harvard University Press, pp. 139–59.

Quine, W. V. and Ullian, J. S. 1978. *The Web of Belief*. New York: Random House.

Resnik, M. 1997. *Mathematics as a Science of Patterns*. New York: Oxford University Press.

Richardson, Alan. 1998. *Carnap's Construction of the World: The Aufbau and the Emergence of Logical Empiricism*. Cambridge: Cambridge University Press.

——. 1996. 'From Epistemology to the Logic of Science: Carnap's Philosophy of Empirical Knowledge in the 1930s,' in Ronald N. Giere and Alan W. Richardson, eds., *Origins of Logical Empiricism*. Minneapolis: University of Minnesota Press, pp. 309–32.

Ricketts, Thomas. 1996. 'Carnap: From Logical Syntax to Semantics,' in Ronald N. Giere and Alan W. Richardson, eds., *Origins of Logical Empiricism*. Minneapolis: University of Minnesota Press, pp. 231–50.

——. 1996a. 'Pictures, Logic, and the Limits of Sense in Wittgenstein's *Tractatus*,' in H. Sluga and D. Stern, eds., *The Cambridge Companion to Wittgenstein*. Cambridge: Cambridge University Press, pp. 59–99.

——. 1994. 'Carnap's Principle of Tolerance, Empiricism, and Conventionalism,' in P. Clark and B. Hale, eds., *Reading Putnam*. Cambridge, MA: Basil Blackwell, pp. 176–200.

——. 1982. 'Rationality, Translation, and Epistemology Naturalized,' *Journal of Philosophy* 79, pp. 117–36.

Rosenberg, A. 1999. 'Naturalistic Epistemology for Eliminative Materialists,' *Philosophy and Phenomenological Research* 59, 2, pp. 335–58.

Russell, Bertrand. 1959. *The Problems of Philosophy*. Oxford: Oxford University Press.

——. 1956. 'On Denoting.' Reprinted in *Logic and Knowledge*, edited by R. Marsh. London: Allen and Unwin, pp. 39–55.

——. 1956a. 'On the Nature of Acquaintance.' Reprinted in *Logic and Knowledge*, edited by R. Marsh. London: Allen and Unwin, pp. 125–74.

——. 1937. *Principles of Mathematics*. Second edition. New York: Norton and Co.

——. 1937a. *The Philosophy of Leibniz*. Second edition. London: Routledge.

——. 1932. 'The Relation of Sense-Data to Physics.' Reprinted in *Mysticism and Logic*. New York: Norton, pp. 145–79.

——. 1932a. 'Knowledge by Acquaintance and Knowledge by Description.' Reprinted in *Mysticism and Logic*. New York: Norton, pp. 209–32.

——. 1932b. 'On Scientific Method in Philosophy.' Reprinted in *Mysticism and Logic*. New York: Norton, pp. 97–124.

——. 1919. *Introduction to Mathematical Philosophy*. New York: Macmillan.

Russell, B. and Whitehead, A. N. 1997. *Principia Mathematica to *56*. Cambridge: Cambridge University Press.

Russell, Gillian. 2008. *Truth in Virtue of Meaning*. Oxford: Oxford University Press.

Salmon, Nathan. 2005. *Reference and Essence*. Second edition. Amherst, NY: Prometheus Books.

——. 1993. 'Analyticity and Apriority,' *Philosophical Perspectives* 7, Language and Logic, pp. 125–33.

Sarkar, Sahotra. 1996. *The Legacy of The Vienna Circle: Modern Reappraisals*. New York: Garland.

——. 1992. '"The Boundless Ocean of Unlimited Possibilities": Logic in Carnap's *Logical Syntax of Language*,' *Synthese* 93, pp. 191–237.

Schiffer, Stephen. 2005. 'Pleonastic Propositions,' in Bradley Armour-Garb et al., eds., *Deflationary Truth*. La Salle, IL: Open Court, 353–81.

——. 2003. *The Things We Mean*. Oxford: Oxford University Press.

Schilpp, Paul A., ed. 1963. *The Philosophy of Rudolph Carnap*. La Salle, IL: Open Court.

Schlick, Moritz 1985. *General Theory of Knowledge*, translated by A. E. Blumberg. La Salle, IL: Open Court.

Schuldenfrei, Richard. 1972. 'Quine in Perspective,' *Journal of Philosophy* 69, 1, pp. 5–16.

Searle, John. 1987. 'Indeterminacy, Empiricism, and the First-Person,' *Journal of Philosophy* 84, pp. 123–46.

Shabel, Lisa. 2003. *Mathematics in Kant's Critical Philosophy: Reflections on Mathematical Practice*. New York: Routledge.

Sider, Ted. 2003. *Four-Dimensionalism: An Ontology of Persistence and Time*. Oxford: Oxford University Press.

Soames, Scott. 2005. *Philosophical Analysis in the Twentieth Century, Volume 1: The Dawn of Analysis*. Princeton, NJ: Princeton University Press.

——. 2005a. *Philosophical Analysis in the Twentieth Century, Volume 2: The Age of Meaning*. Princeton, NJ: Princeton University Press.

——. 2004. *Reference and Description: The Case against Two-Dimensionalism*. Princeton, NJ: Princeton University Press.

——. 2002. *Beyond Rigidity*, Oxford: Oxford University Press.

Sosa, Ernest. 1983 'Nature Unmirrored, Epistemology Naturalized,' *Synthese* 55, pp. 49–72.

Stein, Howard. 1992. 'Was Carnap Entirely Wrong, After All?' *Synthese* 93, pp. 275–95.

Strawson, Peter F. 1997. *Entity and Identity*. Oxford: Clarendon Press.

———. 1963. 'Carnap's Views on Constructed Systems versus Natural Languages in Analytic Philosophy,' in P. A. Schilpp, ed., *The Philosophy of Rudolph Carnap*. La Salle, IL: Open Court, pp. 503–18.

Stroll, Avrum. 2001. *Twentieth-Century Analytic Philosophy*. New York: Columbia University Press.

Tait, William, ed. 1997. *Early Analytic Philosophy: Frege, Russell, Wittgenstein*. La Salle: Open Court.

Tarski, Alfred. 1944. 'The Semantic Conception of Truth,' *Philosophy and Phenomenological Research* 4, 6, pp. 341–76.

Uebel, Thomas E. 1996. 'Anti-Foundationalism and the Vienna Circle's Revolution in Philosophy,' *British Journal for the Philosophy of Science* 47, pp. 415–40.

———. 1996a. 'Conventions in the *Aufbau*,' *British Journal for the History of Philosophy* 4, 2, pp. 381–97.

———. 1992. 'Rational Reconstruction as Elucidation? Carnap in the Early Protocol Sentence Debate,' *Synthese* 93, pp. 107–40.

van Heijenoort, Jean, ed. 1967. *From Frege to Gödel: A Source Book in Mathematical Logic, 1897–1931*. Cambridge, MA: Harvard University Press.

Vuillemin, Jules. 1986. 'On Duhem's and Quine's Theses,' in L. E. Hahn and P. A. Schilpp, eds., *The Philosophy of W. V. Quine*. La Salle, IL: Open Court, pp. 595–618.

Wang, Hao. 1987. *Reflections on Kurt Gödel*. Cambridge, MA: MIT Press.

White, Morton. 1951. 'The Analytic and the Synthetic: An Untenable Dualism,' in Sidney Hook, ed., *John Dewey: Philosopher of Science and Freedom*. New York: Dial, pp. 316–30.

Williamson, Timothy. 2007. *The Philosophy of Philosophy*. Oxford: Blackwell.

Winnie, John. 1975. 'Theoretical Analyticity,' in Jaakko Hintikka, ed., *Rudolph Carnap, Logical Empiricist*. Dordrecht: D. Reidel, pp. 149–59.

Wittgenstein, Ludwig. 1994. *Remarks on the Foundations of Mathematics*. Revised edition, edited by G. H. von Wright, R. Rhees, and G. E. M. Anscombe. Cambridge, MA: MIT Press.

———. 1986. *Tractatus Logico-Philosophicus*, translated by C. K. Ogden. London: Routledge and Kegan Paul.

Wright, Crispin. 1980. *Wittgenstein on the Foundations of Mathematics*. London: Duckworth.

Yablo, Stephen. 1998. 'Does Ontology Rest on a Mistake?' *Proceedings of the Aristotelian Society Supplementary Volume* 72, pp. 229–61.

INDEX